The Allure of Empire

The Allure of Empire

American Encounters with Asians in the Age of Transpacific Expansion and Exclusion

CHRIS SUH

OXFORD
UNIVERSITY PRESS

OXFORD
UNIVERSITY PRESS

Oxford University Press is a department of the University of Oxford. It furthers
the University's objective of excellence in research, scholarship, and education
by publishing worldwide. Oxford is a registered trade mark of Oxford University
Press in the UK and certain other countries.

Published in the United States of America by Oxford University Press
198 Madison Avenue, New York, NY 10016, United States of America.

Library of Congress Cataloging-in-Publication Data
Names: Suh, Chris, author.
Title: The allure of empire : American encounters with Asians in the age of
transpacific expansion and exclusion / Chris Suh.
Description: New York, NY : Oxford University Press, [2023] |
Includes bibliographical references and index.
Identifiers: LCCN 2022060622 (print) | LCCN 2022060623 (ebook) |
ISBN 9780197631621 (paperback) | ISBN 9780197631614 (hardback) |
ISBN 9780197631645 (epub) | ISBN 9780197631652
Subjects: LCSH: United States—Foreign relations—Japan. | Japan—Foreign
relations—United States. | United States—Foreign relations—20th century. |
Japan—Foreign relations—1912–1945.
Classification: LCC E183.8.J3 S845 2023 (print) | LCC E183.8.J3 (ebook) |
DDC 327.73052—dc23/eng/20230105
LC record available at https://lccn.loc.gov/2022060622
LC ebook record available at https://lccn.loc.gov/2022060623

DOI: 10.1093/oso/9780197631614.001.0001

Paperback printed by Marquis, Canada
Hardback printed by Bridgeport National Bindery, Inc., United States of America

For my mother and my father

CONTENTS

NOTE ON ROMANIZATION

In Romanizing Korean and Japanese words, I have used the McCune-Reischauer and Hepburn systems, except in the case of well-known geographical names such as Seoul and Tokyo. Korean and Japanese names are provided with family names preceding given names, except for historical figures who were better known by their Anglicized names during their lifetimes (such as Syngman Rhee and Kiyoshi Karl Kawakami). All English translations of Korean sources are my own, and for research I relied on Korean translations of Japanese government sources in edited volumes published by Kuksa P'yŏnch'an Wiwŏnhoe (the National Institute of Korean History).

ACKNOWLEDGMENTS

This book exists because a large number of people supported me through what has been a long and, at times, difficult journey. I wrote the final version of this book during the COVID-19 pandemic, and the rise of anti-Asian hate inevitably influenced how I thought about my research and taught my courses in Asian American history and US-Asia relations. Before the pandemic, my view of the past was framed by various events and experiences that, for better or worse, prevented me from having a straightforward academic trajectory. Because I have lost touch with many people along the way, some of them on this list might wonder how I ended up writing a book titled *The Allure of Empire*. But this is a product of conversations I had with them in different chapters of my life, and I hope it will serve as a basis for new conversations about some of the enduring problems in our world that I have attempted to address with this book.

I conducted most of the research for this book as a doctoral student at Stanford University. My adviser, Gordon H. Chang, patiently guided my intellectual development throughout my time in graduate school, and years after I finished my dissertation, he graciously read the penultimate version of this book. His influence is apparent on every page, but I am most grateful that he always encouraged me to take ownership of my work. Likewise, Shelley Fisher Fishkin has been a source of steadfast support in all the years I have known her. Even as I filled my dissertation with the exact kind of people that Mark Twain abhorred, she never once doubted that I had something important to say and, in moments of crisis, she went above and beyond to keep me out of harm's way. I began grappling with the central questions of this book in career-changing seminars taught by Yumi Moon and Allyson Hobbs. Now that I am familiar with the life of a junior scholar, I am all the more grateful to them both for taking many hours away from their research and writing to help me with mine. Several professors beyond my dissertation committee deserve gratitude. Estelle Freedman, Jack Rakove, and Richard White kindly saw me through coursework, orals, dissertation chapter workshops, and a practice job talk. Vaughn Rasberry's evenhanded treatment of W. E. B. Du Bois's controversial writings served as my guide as I grappled with the ideas of various historical figures who appear in this book, especially Yun Ch'i-ho's. Cindy Ng, the director Asian American Activities Center, hired me as the center's inaugural graduate student in residence and showed me by example how to best support students. Bina Patel, the director of Counseling and Psychological Services, taught me how to overcome numerous obstacles and celebrate all victories as they came my way.

Many friends provided me with lessons I could not learn in the classroom. Tina Hang, Healy Ko, Vince Moua, and Victoria Yee welcomed me into Stanford's Asian American student community. Claire Rydell Arcenas, Russell Burge, Jeehyun Choi, Julie Huang, Lise Gaston, Hajin Jun, Kevin Kim, Allistair Mallillin, Hannah Marcus, Ana Minian, Ronaldo Noche, George Qiao, Andy Robichaud, Muey Sateurn, Colleen Tripp, Alex Van Gils, Gene Zubovich, and Karen and O'Neil Williams-Provost offered me much-needed support and laughter as I went through many trials and tribulations in the Bay Area. My college roommates Sam Tarakajian and Stephan Meylan let me stay at their San Francisco apartment for weekends away from academia, while other friends from college, including Jesse Bateman, Sara Brown, Masumi Hayashi-Smith, and Olivia Chi, kept up my spirits from near and far. My heartful thanks to Alex Linkin, Zach Marcus, Carmichael Ong, Elias Rodriques, Max Suechting, and Calvin Cheung-Miaw for showing me what true friendship can be.

Another group of friends deserve a paragraph of their own. I had to take two years off in the middle of graduate school because I got drafted by the South Korean army. While I couldn't make any progress on this project during my period of service, this book was inevitably shaped by my military experience. I will forever be grateful to the friends who, in the face of unrelenting cruelty and unspeakable violence, demonstrated the human capacity for kindness, empathy, and humor: Kang Hee Jun, Kim Seung Jun, Nam Ok Hyun, Nam Han Gu, Shin Kyung Min, Yoon Yong Keun, Lee Dong Yeon, Lee Kang, Lee Sun Ho, and Chung In Kyu. Special thanks to Kim Hyun Sung, Seomoon Ji Hyun, Lee Gun Hee, and Chung Tae Won for our lasting friendship.

I was able to get back on track with this project after my military service thanks to the financial support of two units at Stanford: the Vice Provost for Graduate Education's Diversifying Academia and Recruiting Excellence (DARE) program and the Research Institute at the Center for Comparative Studies in Race and Ethnicity (CCSRE). They enabled me to finish my degree at my own pace and, because I remained ineligible to apply for external fellowships until I was putting the finishing touches on this book, they ended up being the only sources of funding that provided me with the essential time away from teaching to focus on research and writing. Thank you, Bridget Algee-Hewitt, Jennifer Brody, Chris

Golde, Anika Green, Patti Gumport, Heidi Marisol López, and Paula Moya, for your support.

For making my research possible, I thank the archivists at the following institutions: the Bancroft Library at the University of California, Berkeley; the Hoover Institution Library & Archives at Stanford; the Charles E. Young Research Library at the University of California, Los Angeles; the Library of Congress; the US National Archives; Yale University Archives, Beinecke Rare Book & Manuscript Library, and Divinity Library; the New York Public Library; the Rare Book & Manuscript Library at Columbia University; the Houghton Library at Harvard University; the Presbyterian Historical Society, Special Collections and University Archives at the University of Massachusetts Amherst; the National Institute of Korean History; and the National Library of South Korea. Four individuals deserve special thanks. K. W. Lee, who attended Yun Ch'i-ho's school as a young man and later worked with Yun's youngest son to transcribe Yun's diary entries in the aftermath of the Korean War, spent many hours sharing his stories with me and helped me convince myself that I had a story worth telling. Ben Stone at Stanford's Green Library helped me access numerous sources, and I remain grateful for all the conversations we had during our long commutes to and from Berkeley. Erica Bruchko at the Woodruff Library and Gabrielle Dudley at the Stuart A. Rose Manuscript, Archives, and Rare Book Library at Emory provided extraordinary support for both this project and my classes.

For the last three years, I've had the great fortune of working in the history department at Emory University, where numerous colleagues have considered my success as their own. I thank my chairs Joe Crespino and Sharon Strocchia, department mentors Jeff Lesser and Jason Morgan Ward, and neighborhood mentors Astrid Eckert and Brian Vick for their expert guidance as I worked to overcome the steep learning curve presented to new junior faculty members, as well as the following colleagues for their unwavering support: Patrick Allitt, Tonio Andrade, Michelle Armstrong-Partida, Mariana Candido, Adriana Chira, Clifton Crais, Teresa Davis, Eric Goldstein, Danny LaChance, Malinda Maynor Lowery, Jamie Melton, Judith Miller, Maria Montalvo, Laura Nenzi, Gyan Pandey, Matt Payne, Jonathan Prude, Tom Rogers, Walter Rucker, Tehila Sasson, Ellie Schainker, Carl Suddler, Allen Tullos, Brian Vick, and Yanna Yannakakis. Department staff members Jazyln Jones, Allison Rollins, and Katie Wilson have helped me in numerous ways, and LaKesia Hayes frequently got me through difficult days on campus by sharing laughs in Bowden Hall. Becky Herring deserves a sentence by herself for the countless ways she has helped me, including the three-days-a-week teaching schedule that enabled me to transform my dissertation into this book without a postdoc or a semester off from teaching.

Several members of the history department are thanked twice for their direct contribution to this project. Jeff and Patrick read and commented on the entire manuscript at its roughest stage; Allen, Astrid, Brian, Carl, Jason, Jonathan, Joe, Maria, Tehila, and Tonio provided valuable feedback on different chapters and the book title; and Teresa labored through the final manuscript to save me from embarrassing errors and prepare the index. This is a much better book because of their collective labor, and I look forward to reciprocating their kindness.

I have many people to thank at Emory beyond the history department. Ever since we met at my job talk, Mary Dudziak has continuously provided me with warm encouragement and wise counsel. I am grateful to Walter Melion and the Bill & Carol Fox Center for Humanistic Inquiry for inviting me to workshop the book's introduction at a critical juncture, as well as to Mary, Tehila, Hwisang Cho, Craig Perry, and Dan Sinykin for their generative comments. Other people who provided generous comments on this work and advice on professional matters include Cynthia Blakely, Julia Bullock, Debbie Dinner, Wendy Fu, Alison Collis Greene, Jonathan Master, Jenny Wang Medina, Kate Nickerson, Tracy Scott, Maria Franca Sibau, Elizabeth Wilson, and Kelley Richmond Yates. The friendship of Frank Gaertner, Susan Elizabeth Gagliardi, Helen Jin Kim, Linny Linh Trinh, and Jane Yang maintained my sanity during a particularly stressful stretch of two and a half years when our community was reeling from the pandemic and anti-Asian violence. As difficult as it has been to work on community events that addressed racial violence, it was a pleasure to work with LaNita Gregory Campbell at the Office for Racial and Cultural Engagement, Andra Gillespie at the James Weldon Johnson Institute for the Study of Race and Difference, and Vice Provost for Diversity and Inclusion Carol Henderson. I am grateful to Deans Michael Elliott, Carl Freeman, and Deboleena Roy for their steadfast support during this crucial period as well.

The biggest source of my intellectual influence at Emory has been my students. I am particularly grateful to the following young people for spending countless hours with me to discuss various problems of the past and the present during office hours and after class: Ulia Ahn, Chloe Atkins, Mikko Biana, Chloe Chen, Sean Chen, Matthew Croswhite, Gray Gorman, Aileen Gopez, Cole Kawanami, Donna Kim, Gabi Kim, Ninad Kulkarni, Chris Lee, Karen Lee, Liz Lee, Ben Levitt, Annie Li, Alyson Lo, Danielle Mangabat, Sid Muntaha, Sun Woo Park, Anika Patel, Kheyal Roy-Meighoo, Yaza Sarieh, Bethany Scheel, Raanya Siddiqui, Bryan Shan, Will Tang, Angelina Tran, Ian Wang, Jane Wang, Jesse Weiner, Alex Western, Stephanie Zhang, Tyson Zhang, Alice Zheng, and Julia Zhong. Double thanks to Yaza and Bethany for photographing many documents at the Rose Library that I consulted for this book.

There is another long list that goes beyond Emory. A career in academia was inconceivable until I met Susan Smulyan in college. I was inspired to enter this profession after working with her on *Major Problems in American Popular Culture* (2011), and I hope she'll be pleased to see the long list of students to whom I have passed down her generosity. I benefited from presenting various portions of this project at academic conferences, and the following scholars helped me improve my thinking with valuable feedback and generative questions: Eiichiro Azuma, Rick Baldoz, Rhae Lynn Barnes, Cindy I-Feng Cheng, John Eng-Wong, Andrea Geiger, Glenda Goodman, Madeline Hsu, Evelyn Hu-Dehart, Moon-Ho Jung, Daniel Y. Kim, Paul Kramer, Selina Lai-Henderson, Bob Lee, Heather Lee, Julian Lim, Karen Miller, Wayne Patterson, Anna Pegler-Gordon, Emily Rosenberg, Penny Von Eschen, Alice Yang, David Yoo, Henry Yu, and Sandy Zipp. Andy Urban generously shared sources and steered me toward a key passage that I had overlooked in a source I already had. Lon Kurashige, who is most familiar with the California archives I examined for this book, kindly read and commented on conference papers that ended up as chapters 4 and 5. John Cheng, Calvin Cheung-Miaw, Shelley Lee, Beth Lew-Williams, K. Ian Shin, Cecilia Tsu, and Judy Wu also gave generous feedback on different parts of this project and, just as important, taught me by example how to navigate the profession with integrity. Likewise, Richard S. Kim read my entire dissertation and provided me with much-needed encouragement and suggestions for improvement when I was on the job market and when I was working on this book. Greg Robinson is a mensch, and I am grateful for our numerous opportunities to collaborate on projects and panels over the past decade. Many years ago, I tested my ideas for chapters 1 and 3 in an article published in the *Journal of American History*. Gratitude is due to the editorial staff and the two sets of peer reviewers (the second of whom had to read it twice) for their insightful comments that have continued to influence my thinking. I am also grateful to the *Journal of American History* for granting me permission to reproduce some passages here. Although Pearl S. Buck only makes a cameo appearance in this book, I would like to thank Brenda Frink and the peer reviewers for my *Pacific Historical Review* article who similarly helped me improve as a writer and a thinker.

Several people worked directly on this book during the pandemic and helped it see the light of day. Before the manuscript went out for peer review, Laura Daly smoothed out the rough edges and reined in my tendency to quote everything I found interesting. Two anonymous readers for Oxford University Press gifted me with generous and exacting comments that enabled this book to reach its full potential. Their encouraging feedback helped me improve the manuscript's shortcomings and build confidence in its strengths. I would like to also thank the OUP delegates who provided kind words about my project. During the final stages, Megan Slemons at Emory University's Center for Digital created the beautiful map that appears in the introduction. Jeremy Toynbee at Newgen patiently guided me through the production process, and Timothy DeWerff meticulously copyedited the manuscript.

My editor, Susan Ferber, expertly shepherded this project from the beginning to the end. It has been a privilege to work with one of the major shapers of the field of US history, of course, and her comments on every page immensely improved this book. Most important, her interest and faith in nurturing this project, and this first-time author, made the daunting process of book writing as enjoyable as possible.

English is my second language, but because of two exceptional mentors it became my primary language, and I was eventually able to write this book. In high school, Betsy Boyd helped me become fluent in English and taught me that writing in my second language need not be a source of weakness. She introduced me to various non-native writers who made their mark in Anglophone literature and encouraged me to cultivate my own voice. I first walked into Lawrence K. Stanley's office during my first-year orientation in college, and over the next four years, he patiently guided my development as a writer and a person. He taught me to approach writing as a mode of discovery, and it is because of him that I gained the confidence to continue writing, even as I struggled with language and remained unsure of where it all might lead.

For close to a decade now, I have been blessed to have Melissa Paa Redwood as my partner. During some of the most difficult periods, she tolerated the worst of me and brought out the best of me. It is no coincidence that, ever since she came into my life, all the things that had once seemed impossible became reality. Although she refuses to take credit, I know it's true. Our cat, Hoshi, will take credit for all that I have achieved during the past six years. All the book's shortcomings, of course, are her father's own. I thank James and Rosedelia Redwood for raising an exceptional human being and for taking care of Hoshi when we were traveling abroad.

I saved the last paragraph for my parents. When we first arrived in the United States two decades ago, no one could have foreseen that I would be making a living by teaching American history to Americans. So much has happened since then, and it would take a whole book, if not more, to recount all that we had to endure to get to where we are today. I thank my father, Suh Kyung Shik, for introducing me to his favorite bands when I was young and taking me on numerous road trips that allowed me to see many parts of the United States that few of my peers did. Those trips undoubtedly planted the seeds of my interest in American culture, and our accidental visit to the Manassas National Battlefield Park in Virginia (on our way to see AC/DC perform at a nearby venue) remains one of my most cherished memories. My mother, Choi Sung Yoon, gave up her professional career to raise me, and it was because of her tremendous sacrifices that I was able to remain and study in the United States as a teenager after my father had to return to South Korea. Whatever good qualities I have as a person is because of her unconditional love, and I will always be grateful for the countless ways she has supported me from near and far. So I dedicate this book to them, with love.

The Allure of Empire

Introduction:
Seeing Race beyond the Color Line

In the summer of 1905, two years after he published *The Souls of Black Folk* (1903), W. E. B. Du Bois returned to his pronouncement that "the problem of the twentieth century is the problem of the color line." In his book, the pre-eminent African American scholar had defined the problem in broad terms, describing it as "the relation of the darker to the lighter races of men in Asia and Africa, in America and the islands of the sea."[1] When he encountered the news of the Russo-Japanese War (1904–1905), a distant conflict he closely followed from Atlanta, he felt compelled to rearticulate the problem. When the American Unitarian Association asked him to contribute an essay on the education of African Americans in the South, Du Bois used it as an occasion to name what he called "the problem of the yellow peril and of the color line."[2]

By identifying the "yellow peril" and the "color line" as two parts of the same "problem," Du Bois invited his readers to connect the Russo-Japanese War to Black-white struggles in the United States. The "Negro problem in America," he argued, was "but a local phase of a world problem," and the war across the Pacific was another conflict between the two sides of the color line. The "white" powers supporting Russia, he insinuated, perceived Japan as a "yellow peril." Like Emperor Wilhelm II of Germany, who popularized the term by warning that Japan's leadership of Asia would force the West to relive the horrors of Genghis Khan and the Mongolian invasions of medieval Europe, many saw Japan's recent victories as the beginnings of a coming apocalypse. But Du Bois interpreted Japanese successes in a different light. They were "epoch-making" events that signaled a bright future for the "yellow" as well as the "brown and black races." By exposing a "white nation" as "distinctly inferior in civilization and ability," he explained, Japan broke the "magic of the word 'white.'"[3] Having witnessed the rise of Jim Crow racism in the United States and the expansion of Western colonial empires in the late nineteenth century, Du Bois believed that Japan's

The Allure of Empire. Chris Suh, Oxford University Press. © Oxford University Press 2023.
DOI: 10.1093/oso/9780197631614.003.0001

victory in the war would inspire a revolution of the "darker races" against white supremacy around the world.

But not all members of the "darker races" shared Du Bois's optimism, especially among those who saw the war up close. According to Korea's vice minister of foreign affairs, Yun Ch'i-ho, every one of Japan's military victories over Russia was a "nail in the coffin" of Korea's independence. In the summer of 1905, Yun grappled with the predicament of Koreans in his diary, which he began keeping in English as a college student in the United States. He admitted that as "a member of the Yellow Race, Korea—or rather I—feel proud of the glorious successes of Japan." It "has vindicated the honor of our race," he wrote, "No braggart American, no arrogant Briton, no vainglorious Frenchman" could now say that "the Yellow man is incapable of great things."[4] Yet his excitement was tempered by his fear that his country, which had been a battleground between Japan and Russia, would fall under Japan's rule upon the war's end.

Yun's fear was grounded in Korea's experience of the war, during which Japan had taken numerous steps to undermine Korea's sovereignty. Days after the first shots were fired, Japan signed a protocol with Korea to station its army in strategic areas across the Korean peninsula. It then forced the Korean Ministry of Foreign Affairs and Ministry of Finance to hire foreign advisers of Japan's choosing. Just a month before Yun unleashed his frustration into his diary, Japan had taken control of Korea's postal, telegraph, and telephone services. Having witnessed the rise of Japanese influence over his home country, Yun worried that Japan's victory in the war would lead to Koreans' subjugation at the hands of a nonwhite empire, a member of "our race."[5]

The difference between Du Bois's and Yun's reactions was not solely a matter of the Korean diplomat's proximity to war. More important, it signaled a difference between the two men's understandings of global inequality. Both of their worldviews stemmed from their personal experiences. Du Bois, born and raised in Massachusetts, spent most of his life on the East Coast of the United States. He expanded his horizons by studying abroad at the Friedrich Wilhelm University in Berlin (1892–1894) and attending the First Pan-African Conference held in London (1900), but what he learned on the opposite side of the Atlantic largely confirmed his existing view, that European and American imperialists created and maintained human inequality based on the hierarchy of white over nonwhite. Yun, three years older than Du Bois, became familiar with the color line when he studied at Vanderbilt University and Emory College (1888–1893). This was why he used the term "yellow race" years before other Koreans did.[6] But what he experienced and witnessed in Asia prevented him from seeing human inequality solely as the problem of the color line. Before Yun went to the United States, Japan had already colonized Hokkaido (1869) and Okinawa (1879). Afterward, it fought a war against China (1894–1895), annexed Taiwan (1895), and competed with European empires for utility and mining concessions from the Korean government in the years leading up to the Russo-Japanese War. For Yun, the conjoined problems of imperial expansion and human inequality in Asia could not be fully understood within a vision limited to the racial hierarchy of white over nonwhite.

To Yun, the idea of the color line was inadequate to capture what was taking place in the broader Pacific world. In the final months of the Russo-Japanese War, he was dispatched by the Korean emperor to Hawai'i, where he investigated the conditions of Korean laborers recruited to work the sugarcane fields. As a Christian convert, he was devastated to learn that the largely male Korean population spent its leisure time drinking liquor and visiting prostitutes. But he was just as disturbed by his observation that the native Hawai'ians, the Kānaka Maoli, were facing extinction. Yun eventually learned that generations of intermarriage between the Indigenous people and white and Asian settlers made it difficult for him to visually identify many native Hawai'ians. Nevertheless, he concluded that they were "dying out rapidly," "unable to survive the struggle for life which the white & other races have imported" to their land.[7]

The struggle for life occupied Yun's mind because he feared that what he saw in Hawai'i was a preview of Korea's future. Even in Hawai'i, where white settlers overthrew the native monarchy prior to US annexation, the Japanese constituted the largest population.[8] What would happen to Korea if Japan were to take over his country after the Russo-Japanese War?

When Yun read the text of the peace treaty upon his return from Hawai'i, he predicted that Japan would do to Korea what the United States and Britain had done to "Hawaii, Cuba & the Transv[a]al Republic." Although Japan did not receive its much-desired indemnity from Russia, the treaty—which was signed at the Portsmouth Naval Shipyard in the United States after President Theodore Roosevelt personally helped negotiate the terms of the peace—set the Asian empire up for postwar expansion. To Japan, Russia ceded the southern half of Sakhalin and transferred its lease of Kwangtung in China's Liaodong peninsula. As for Korea, Russia promised not to interfere with Japan's measures for "direction, protection, and supervision."[9]

Two months after the Treaty of Portsmouth, Japan turned Korea into its "protectorate," a nominally independent state stripped of the right to conduct diplomacy. The United States became the first to recognize Korea's "protected" status and withdraw its minister from Seoul.[10] If Yun had felt a glimmer of admiration for Japan during the war, by its end he was filled with nothing but resentment. While Japan joined the circle of the world's great powers as the sole nonwhite member, Korea was relegated to the status of an imperial possession.

The end of the Russo-Japanese War changed some Americans' view of Japan as well, but for different reasons. A year after the peace treaty, *Collier's* magazine

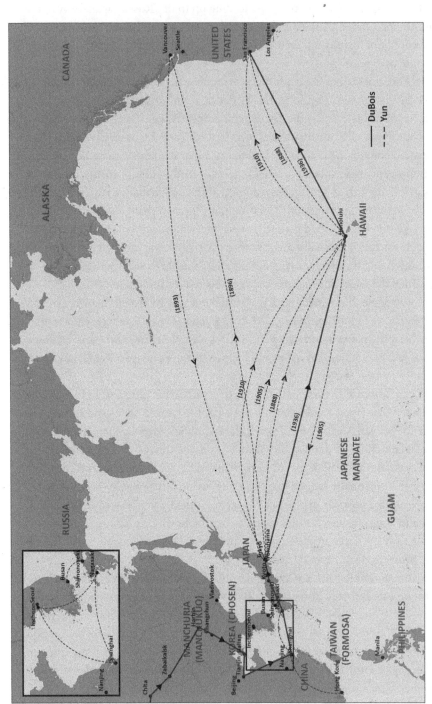

Fig. I.1 Yun Ch'i-ho and W. E. B. Du Bois's transpacific journeys, 1888–1936. Inset: Yun's travels across the Yellow Sea. Map created by Megan Slemons, Emory Center for Digital Scholarship.

republished Du Bois's wartime comments about Japan for a wider audience, under the title "The Color Line Belts the World." In the fall of 1906, the proposition that African Americans and the Japanese were engaged in related struggles was not so easy to accept. Recently, a mob of white supremacists had murdered dozens of African Americans and destroyed numerous Black-owned businesses in Atlanta.[11] Meanwhile, Japan's relationship with the United States remained cordial. After an earthquake and a fire destroyed large sections of San Francisco, Japan emerged as the top international donor to the relief fund established to aid the survivors. When Japanese immigrants in San Francisco faced racial violence and segregation at the hands of white nativists who claimed to be defending their community against the coming "Yellow Peril," the United States government intervened. After Secretary of War William Howard Taft, in his capacity as president of the American National Red Cross, received Japan's donations and publicly expressed America's gratitude, Roosevelt dispatched Secretary of Commerce Victor Metcalf to San Francisco to investigate incidents of anti-Japanese racism.[12] The Roosevelt administration did nothing to address what happened to African Americans in Atlanta.

Perhaps because of this difference, the 1906 version of Du Bois's essay no longer mentioned "the problem of the yellow peril." Only the "problem of the color line" remained after the US government worked to counter the white fear of Japanese invasion.[13] It is unclear whether Du Bois or his editor made this revision, but it was not difficult to see that the global revolution against white supremacy he anticipated was nowhere in sight. Instead of war across the color line, the world witnessed a partnership between Japan and the United States that reinvented racial subjugation outside of the white-over-nonwhite hierarchy. The world came to see what Yun had observed in Korea at the end of the Russo-Japanese War.

Rethinking Race and Empire

Japan's victory over Russia brought lasting changes to the Pacific world, including the United States. It prompted American imperialists to formulate a new strategy of transpacific expansion that relied on collaboration with Japanese imperialists, and the resulting relationship between the two empires frustrated both anticolonial activists in Asia and white nativists in the American West. Just as the "colored races" disagreed over the meaning of Japan's rise as a world power, the "white races" remained divided on the question of Japanese immigration.

By tracking the evolving worldviews and policy decisions that shaped the geopolitical landscape across the Pacific and restricted Asian immigration to the United States, this book reveals how the US government worked to maintain a collaborative relationship across the color line with Japan over the first four decades of the twentieth century. Maintaining this relationship took a great deal of effort. The two powers continuously competed for influence in Asia and frequently conflicted over Japanese immigration to the United States. Anti-colonial nationalisms also posed serious challenges to this relationship. Many Koreans appealed to the US empire for assistance with their anti-colonial struggles against Japan and, in a surprising turn of events, American nativists used the news of Japan's colonial violence in Korea as a pretext to justify the prohibition of Japanese immigration to the United States.

The subject of this study has implications far beyond the relationship between the two empires. Resting at the heart of their relationship was the powerful idea that an "imperial race," like the Japanese, should be treated differently from the rest of the "yellow races," most of whom were colonized and semi-colonized at this time. Americans' separation of the Japanese from other Asian groups mirrored how they arranged the racial hierarchy among the "white races." As historian Thomas Guglielmo has demonstrated, there were two ways of racially categorizing people during this period, one based on color (black, red, yellow, and white), and another based on "scientific" definitions of race that associated cultural and physical traits with geographic locations of origin (such as Anglo-Saxon, Nordic, German, and Italian). Because the two forms of racism coexisted, South Italians, for example, enjoyed racial advantages over nonwhite people in housing, jobs, and schools due to laws that enforced the color line. But they also faced extensive prejudice and persecution from journalists, police officers, and government officials who perceived South Italians as an undesirable "race" responsible for organized crime and other social problems plaguing America.[14]

At a time when the concept of ethnicity had not yet gained currency, this dual definition of race shaped Asians' experiences as well. US naturalization law, which limited citizenship to "free white persons," "aliens of African nativity," and "persons of African descent," categorized the Japanese as one of the races "ineligible to citizenship." But Japan's victory over Russia punctured a hole in the logic of white supremacy. To be sure, there were American missionaries and eugenicists who could not believe a nonwhite people to be capable of achieving what the Japanese did, insisting that the Japanese must be "white."[15] Yet far more commonly held was the belief that the Japanese, as a "yellow" race, surpassed many of the "white" races in their development. From this perspective, the Japanese exemplified how nonwhite people could climb up the human hierarchy by adapting themselves to a Western standard of "civilization," which held colonial empire-building to be the highest stage of human development.

Coming to terms with this form of racial thinking is essential to reinterpreting how the United States emerged as a Pacific power. While the specter of the "Yellow Peril" loomed large in American culture, American policymakers implemented various strategies to avoid confrontation with Japan, even as the United States aggressively expanded across the Pacific in pursuit of power and profit. These strategies were complementary to the infamous "Open Door policy," with which the United States sought to gain a foothold in the coveted China market, as well as the well-documented subjugation of nonwhite peoples in Hawaiʻi, the Philippines, Guam, and American Samoa, where the United States established military bases to secure transpacific passages to China and create a defense system to deter other empires that might attempt to attack the North American continent.[16] But as Yun Ch'i-ho observed during the Russo-Japanese War, the United States treated the Japanese as a partner even though they were part of the "yellow" races. This book explains that, in the four decades following the Spanish-American War (1898), one of the central features of the US imperial enterprise was working with Japan to build and maintain a multipolar order across the Pacific, where a handful of imperial powers collaborated in international governance by dividing the vast oceanic region into smaller, interlocking spheres of colonial rule and hegemonic influence. This order lasted until World War II.

American policymakers built the multipolar order because they recognized the limits of their own power. The United States did not have the military or economic resources to govern the entire Pacific on its own. In fact, no one did. Empires, as historians Jane Burbank and Frederick Cooper have explained, tended to function by incorporating nonhomogeneous peoples, spread across vast regions, into a single polity.[17] The Pacific was simply too big for homogeneous and unipolar rule. Thus, during the Russo-Japanese War, Roosevelt proposed a collaborative framework to keep the Pacific in order. He recommended that Japan establish a sphere of hegemony in the region surrounding the Yellow Sea, just as the United States did in the Caribbean. This did not mean that the United States would keep its hands off East Asia. Roosevelt helped negotiate the Treaty of Portsmouth in large part to help shape an imperial order that would be beneficial to US commercial and military interests.

But a full story of how the United States rose as a Pacific power cannot focus solely on the empire's overseas activities. It must also take account of political conflicts within North America over Asian immigration, which profoundly complicated the United States' efforts to secure its economic and geopolitical interests across the Pacific.[18] For most Americans, immigration was the primary area where they felt the effect of their empire's amicable relationship with Japan. Anti-Japanese movements began to emerge in California, Oregon, and Washington a few years before the Russo-Japanese War. Nativists demanded that the federal government expand the scope of the existing Chinese Exclusion Act (instituted for ten-year periods in 1882, 1892, and 1902, before it was extended indefinitely in 1904) to unilaterally prohibit the entry of Japanese immigrants. But the federal government refused to heed their demand. Instead, in 1908, the State Department committed to a bilateral "Gentlemen's Agreement" with

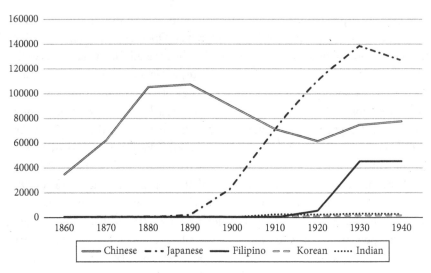

Fig. I.2 Asian American populations in the continental United States, 1860–1940. Includes both foreign-born and US-born populations. Source: US Census, 1910, 1920, 1930, and 1940.

the Japanese Foreign Ministry and entrusted the Asian empire with the task of limiting passports to those it deemed respectable representatives of Japan. This way, the United States avoided instituting an immigration law offensive to Japan, all the while putting an end to the immigration of the Japanese working class, who constituted the vast majority of Japanese Americans. But nativists remained irate. In contrast to their Chinese counterparts, Japanese working-class men already in the United States were allowed, by the terms of the agreement, to sponsor the immigration of "picture brides" from Japan, who in turn put down roots by parenting US-born children. By the time of the 1910 census, the Japanese eclipsed the Chinese as the largest group of Asians in the continental United States, and they continued to grow not only in numbers but also in economic power.[19]

After the Gentlemen's Agreement went into effect, anti-Japanese arguments shifted away from claiming that Asian immigrants' low standard of living created unfair competition for the white working class. With lawyers, journalists, and other white-collar professionals at its helm, a new nativist movement contended instead that the federal policy enabled Japanese Americans to achieve a level of socioeconomic success that should be reserved for the "white" races. Rage against the federal government came to a head in 1913, when California's legislature, over the Woodrow Wilson administration's pleas, instituted the Alien Land Act that prohibited all non-US-born Asians, including the Japanese, from owning agricultural property. While the Act symbolized their ability to fend off federal interference in state's rights, nativists aimed to go further, hoping to shape immigration policy at the national level. For the next decade, California's nativists worked to influence the federal government, which, even as it expanded the scope of Asian exclusion in 1917 by creating the "Asiatic Barred Zone" (primarily to prohibit the migration of British colonial subjects from India), prominently left Japan out of this zone.

By considering overseas empire-building and domestic struggles over immigration as two parts of a single story, this book brings together two areas of scholarship that remain largely separate.[20] But what follows is more than a synthesis of existing literature on empire and exclusion. This study must tread new ground, for the majority of the existing works in both areas approach the subject as Du Bois did, as a series of conflicts between the two sides of the color line.[21] Studies of US overseas empire are often synonymous with narratives of white colonization of nonwhite peoples and nonwhite resistance against white colonizers.[22] Likewise, studies of immigration restriction usually focus on how the US state preserved white supremacy by excluding Asian people at the border and depriving them of their rights within. Alternately, scholars have described how Asian immigrants persevered by circumventing immigration laws to enter the country and asserting their right to belong in the United States through the courts.[23] Even comparative and transnational studies of empire and exclusion tend to characterize this period as one defined by conflicts between the two sides of the color line. According to these works, the United States, Britain, Canada, Australia, and New Zealand created and maintained a global color line not only by colonizing the Pacific but also by instituting Asian exclusion.[24] Meanwhile, colonized people in the Philippines, India, Hong Kong, Hawai'i and elsewhere were inspired by the Japanese, as well as each other, to resist white powers, often with the support and solidarity of African Americans.[25]

But this is not the whole picture. The archives of various imperialists, anticolonial activists, nativists, immigrants, politicians, academics, journalists, missionaries, and converts consulted in the United States and South Korea for this study hold many stories that defy the logic of the color line. They complement the findings of historians who have emphasized that solidarities, among the nonwhite as well as white peoples, largely remained imagined and aspirational during this period. As Eiichiro Azuma has shown, Japanese immigrant elites in the American West engaged in public campaigns to distinguish themselves from the Chinese in the eyes of white Americans. They also denounced intermarriage with Filipinos in their own communities and aligned themselves with white landowners against labor unions. Richard Kim has demonstrated that Korean Americans' diasporic politics prioritized ending Japan's rule over Korea to the point that they often condoned US imperialism and, in some extreme cases, played into white fears of the "Yellow Peril" to campaign against Japanese Americans.[26]

White imperialists and nativists had just as much difficulty forging a harmonious white world. Europe was constantly mired in imperial rivalry before,
during, and after World War I. Throughout this period, the United States was
preoccupied with the possibility of clashing with European powers, especially
in the Western Hemisphere. To be sure, there were American and British elites
who shared utopian visions of unifying the "Anglo-Saxon race" and "English-
speaking peoples" around the world. But as Duncan Bell has argued, their visions
only existed in "dreamworlds." Although nativist campaigns and restrictive immigration laws emerged contemporaneously in the United States and the British
dominions, David Atkinson has shown that each nation's campaigns to prohibit
Asian immigration operated independently of one another, and that each federal
government deployed its own strategy of immigration restriction.[27]

One of the central concerns of this book is how Japan's entrance into the
circle of imperial powers disrupted the color line and prevented the formation
of solidarities among white imperialists and nativists on one side, and among
nonwhite peoples on the other. Japan's victory over Russia inaugurated a new
era in which a nonwhite race could climb up the racial hierarchy to stand among
the strongest of the white powers, signaling that embracing empire provided a
pathway out of racial subjugation. A full understanding of this era, then, requires
a careful investigation of the allure of empire as exemplified by Japan.

The Allure of Progressive Empire

To most Americans, the allure of Japanese empire was the allure of the US empire. The more Japanese imperialism resembled the American, the closer the
kinship between the two countries became.[28] Americans' high opinion of their
own empire, which provided the basis for US foreign and immigration policies
toward Japan, rested on a skewed view of their own relationship with the people
they subjugated. Nevertheless, it became easier for many Americans to condone, and even support, their government's expansionist policies, as overseas
imperialism became modified by the emerging Progressive movement in continental America. In fact, the rapprochement between the United States and Japan
was representative of the larger changes in racial thinking and social relations
wrought by Progressive reform.

In the early twentieth-century United States, as in Western Europe, a wide
range of reformers dedicated themselves to reshaping and expanding the role
of the state, so that it could better protect the most vulnerable populations from
the increasing social and economic inequality that resulted from unfettered industrial capitalism. This is why this period came to be called the Progressive Era.
Their accomplishments included increased government regulation of businesses,

passage of protective laws for women and children, expansion of public educa-tion, improvements in public sanitation, and the introduction of direct primaries in elections.[29] But "progress" was not to be contained to the continental United States. In their colonies, protectorates, and territories, American soldiers and colonial administrators carried out various reform projects by working with economists, teachers, missionaries, doctors, nurses, engineers, and public health officials, many of whom hoped, like domestic reformers, to rein in the human cost of unbridled capitalism and imperialism.[30] In doing so, Americans joined British, French, and German imperialists in "civilizing missions," which justified colonization as a necessary measure to "uplift" and "develop" various "uncivi-lized," "backwards" people.[31]

These imperial reform projects were devised in the interests of the colonizers, but to many Americans, these features made their empire "progressive" in con-trast to that of some of their contemporaries. Americans often defined their own imperial rule against the ferocious violence committed by the Belgian King Leopold II's forces against the Congolese and by the Ottomans against Armenians. Before the Russo-Japanese War, the American perception of the Russian empire took a negative turn as a result of the Kishinev pogrom of 1903, a violent, anti-Semitic riot that took place in the Bessarabia Governorate.[32]

That American imperialists condemned the violence of their European counterparts seems ironic, if not hypocritical. In fact, contemporaries noted this contradiction. After Roosevelt forwarded a Jewish American organization's de-nunciation of the anti-Semitic pogroms to Nicholas II, various African American leaders sent petitions to the Russian embassy in Washington, asking the Russian government to pressure the United States into recognizing its own racial vio-lence.[33] The Atlanta riot of 1906 was not an isolated incident. African Americans endured racial violence every day in the South, both in the legal form of Jim Crow and in the extralegal form of lynching.[34] Mexican Americans and Chinese Americans also faced lynching in smaller numbers in the West, while those living in New York and San Francisco's Chinatowns were subject to surveil-lance and harassment from journalists, social reformers, and police officers who believed that Chinese men posed a unique threat to the nation's moral fiber.[35] In order to implement Chinese exclusion, the US Bureau of Immigration increased border patrols and conducted raids near Canada and Mexico, detained and interrogated new arrivals on Angel Island, and arrested and deported those who had been found guilty of "illegal" entry.[36] In the case of Native Americans, the US state enacted violence in the name of inclusion. After dispossessing Native American lands and committing brutal massacres during the "Indian Wars," the US state forced them into assimilation projects, which included everything from the destruction of religious practices to the separation of native children from their parents and their subsequent placement in boarding schools. The violence

Fig. I.3 A political cartoon published in the United States during the Russo-Japanese War depicts Japan, the "Yellow Peril," as a harbinger of "Justice, Progressiveness, Humaneness, Enlightenment, Tolerance [and] Religious Liberty." It represents Russia as the man holding a whip with the lashes labeled "Absolutism, Persecution, [and] Tyranny." In the man's shadows are Jewish victims of the Kishinev pogrom (1903), and in the background are other groups of people persecuted by the Russian empire including the Finns and the Poles. Udo Keppler, "The Yellow Peril," *Puck* 55, no. 1412 (March 23, 1904). Keppler & Schwarzmann. Library of Congress Prints and Photographs Division, LC-DIG-ppmsca-25833.

perpetrated in North America had direct ties to atrocities committed in the US overseas colonies. Some of the same military officers who murdered Native Americans in the "Indian Wars" were responsible for the torture and killing of Filipinos in the Philippine-American War (1899–1902). [37] The war proved so unpopular in the United States that Roosevelt was forced to declare it over well before the fighting ended. [38]

Yet anti-imperialist sentiments quickly waned as many Americans became convinced of their own success in "developing" Cuba. Although the United States began to rule over Cubans around the same time it began fighting Filipinos, the situation was different in the Caribbean. Cuba was a protectorate, not a colony. Above all, Americans implemented various reform measures to reshape Cuba's administrative, educational, financial, and public health systems to fit their own vision of progress. [39] Imperial reform of Cuba was so well received in the continental United States that even Roosevelt's political adversaries supported it. In the election of 1904, the Democratic candidate Alton B. Parker challenged

Roosevelt with a promise to modify the US Philippines policy to be more like its Cuba policy. Among Parker's key endorsers was William Jennings Bryan, the Democrat who had run for president in 1900 on an anti-imperialist platform against the Republican administration's plans to colonize the Philippines.[40]

The convergence of imperialism and Progressive reform facilitated many Americans' support of the administration's decision to collaborate with Japan. In the fall of 1905, Bryan traveled to the Asian empire, coincidentally on the same transoceanic ship that took Yun Ch'i-ho home from Hawai'i. Japan was Bryan's first international stop on his world speaking tour. After briefly visiting Korea, the Democrat wrote in the *Washington Post* that the Japanese might be able to overcome Koreans' "prejudice" if they focused on the "upbuilding" of its protectorate and the "advancement" of the Korean people. Over the next several months, Bryan visited China, the Philippines, the Dutch East Indies, British India, and British Egypt. When he arrived in England, he declared that Japan's influence on the world was a "beneficent one." Japan set the example for other Asian countries, and if China were to follow its path, he was "confident" that the United States would find across the Pacific "not a yellow peril," but another "powerful co-laborer in the international vineyard."[41]

In the following decades, many Americans similarly perceived the Japanese empire as an agent of progress. This was the result of Japanese colonial elites' strategy to subjugate people according to international norms—norms constructed by European empires in the nineteenth century and adopted by the United States in the twentieth—as well as their efforts to make their work legible to American and British imperialists.[42] In addition to providing guided tours to foreign academics, diplomats, and politicians who visited Japan's colonies, Japanese colonial administrators published, in English, conspicuously titled books such as *Japanese Rule of Formosa* (1907) and *Report on Reforms and Progress in Korea* (1907–1908), the latter of which was published annually until 1939.[43] US government officials and Asia experts often referred to these reports as proof that the Japanese were close to the most advanced "white" races on the scale of human hierarchy. Meanwhile, Japanese immigrant elites in the United States were able to secure white American allies in their struggle against nativists by pointing to the "success" of Japan's colonial projects in Asia.

A decade after the Russo-Japanese War, a revolution led by Japan against the white imperial powers seemed increasingly unlikely, so much so that even Du Bois publicly admitted that his prediction had been premature. In "The African Roots of War" (1915), an essay that is best known for tracing the origin of World War I to the division of Africa among European powers at the Berlin Conference (1884–1885), Du Bois continued to hope that Japan would align itself with other "colored races" against "white" empires. But he could not ignore the possibility that the Asian power, which had "apparently escaped the cordon of this color bar," might "join heart and soul with the whites" against the "rest of the yellows, browns, and blacks."[44]

But this had already happened. In 1910, Japan annexed Korea as a colony. In 1915, just months before the publication of "The African Roots of War," Japan entered the world war at Britain's behest and seized German concessions in Shandong, China, as its own. It then handed the Republic of China the infamous Twenty-One Demands, which, among other things, intended to make China a de facto protectorate.[45]

Korea and China eventually revolted against Japan, but ironically, both turned to the United States for assistance. This was not a result of naiveté. During World War I, the American propaganda machine projected an image of the United States as an anti-colonial power, and it did so by disseminating Wilson's speeches that promised a postwar world order based on the principle of each nation's right to self-determination. In 1919, when Wilson was at the Paris Peace Conference to help shape the world order, Korean and Chinese nationalists sought to make him live up to his promise. This was why the March First Movement, which demanded an immediate decolonization of Korea, and the May Fourth Movement, which demanded an immediate return of Shandong to China, took place in Asia during the conference.[46]

Both Koreans and the Chinese failed to attain their goals as Wilson never intended to provide assistance to Asian independence struggles. Nevertheless, the March First and May Fourth Movements had a long-lasting impact on anti-colonial nationalisms in both countries, as well as on Japanese imperialism. For the next two decades, Japan, like other empires, warded off various anti-colonial movements by adapting to the changing world order. The Japanese army invaded Manchuria in 1931 to secure the Asian empire's economic interests in the three eastern provinces of China, but to appear as a champion of self-determination, it created the puppet state of Manchukuo and insisted that it was assisting the Manchus who sought to claim independence from the Republic of China. As for Korea, Japan implemented a new policy in the 1920s that incorporated Korean elites into colonial governance. This policy of limited self-rule was accompanied by military suppression of Korean guerrilla warfare, which was pushed out to Manchuria and Russia.[47] But as Americans remained captivated by the allure of Japanese empire, the United States did little to challenge Japan's rule in Asia for many years after World War I aside from refusing to recognize Manchukuo as a legitimate state. The bilateral relationship did not begin to collapse until Japan's massacre of Chinese civilians in the Sino-Japanese War (1937–1945) made it all but impossible for people to argue that Japan was a progressive empire.

Excluding Japan's Imperial Subjects

But if the US government remained committed to this relationship with Japan until the late 1930s, why did it abrogate the Gentlemen's Agreement in 1924? And how did the two empires maintain their partnership even after US immigration law relegated Japan to the level of China, India, and other colonized and semi-colonized countries in Asia? Answering these questions requires examining the changing power dynamics within the US government as well as the rising importance of international non-governmental organizations after World War I.[48]

Unlike during the first two decades of the twentieth century, the White House did not have the power to keep the Japanese immigration issue out of Congress's hands. In 1923, when Warren Harding died in office, Calvin Coolidge inherited an executive branch short on allies after several members of its administration had been caught red-handed in a corruption scandal.[49] When the comprehensive immigration bill of 1924 reached his desk, Coolidge had only two choices: sign it into law or have his presidential veto overruled by Congress. Worried that he might lose his party's support for his presidential run later that year, he chose to sign it and publicly express his disapproval of the immigration act's Japanese exclusion provision.

But it was not a foregone conclusion that Congress would be united against Japanese immigration. In fact, the California nativist lobby failed to bring many politicians on Capitol Hill onboard until the Paris Peace Conference, when a wealthy landowner and newspaper publisher named V. S. McClatchy emerged as its new leader and changed its strategy to pursue a line of argumentation that was ironically similar to what Du Bois had said during the Russo-Japanese War. The white-Japanese conflict in the American West, the nativists claimed, was but a local phase of a global problem, which was Japan's expansion. Expediently weaponizing the news of Japan's violent suppression of the March First Movement against Japanese Americans, nativists advocated for Japanese exclusion by warning that, without a stronger federal immigration policy, the Japanese would "colonize" the American West just as they had Korea.

Nativists' new strategy brought profound changes to Korean and Japanese immigrant communities after World War I. Although nativists had little interest in the lives of Koreans, many Korean American elites supported the exclusionists in the hope that they would compel the United States to intervene against Japan in Korea. Some Japanese Americans continued to defend Japan's activities in Asia even as many people began to look suspiciously on their relationship with Japan. But others engaged in public campaigns to actively disassociate themselves from Japan in the eyes of the American government. They recognized it was no longer favorable to cast themselves as members of the imperial race that ruled over other Asians.

Another key issue that shaped the lives of Asian immigrants and the political debates leading up to the abrogation of the Gentlemen's Agreement was Japan's own policy of curbing migration from other parts of Asia. Since the Japanese government unilaterally restricted the entry of laborers from Korea and China, the California nativist lobby argued in newspapers and congressional hearings, it was hypocritical of Japan to criticize the American desire to unilaterally stop Japanese immigration. Although Japan never prohibited the entry of Asian immigrants based on their race, nationality, and geographical origin as the United States did, the knowledge that Japan did have a policy to restrict immigration from Asia served as a convenient excuse for the architects of the Johnson-Reed Act in 1924 to add a provision to the comprehensive immigration bill that would end Japanese immigration as the nativists wished.

The immediate aftermath of Japanese exclusion witnessed anti-American protests erupting throughout Japan, but the two governments maintained a cordial relationship for more than a decade after. They were able to do so in part because Japan found other places to send its "surplus" population. In Asia, Japan had Korea and Manchuria.[50] In Latin America, Japanese immigrants settled in Brazil, Peru, and Mexico.[51] Just as important, the relationship between the two empires remained amicable because elites on both sides worked hard to make it so. Symbolizing their efforts was the Institute of Pacific Relations (IPR), a nongovernmental organization founded in Hawai'i in 1925 with the technocratic vision of ensuring international peace by sharing social scientific research that could help transform American and Japanese policies. Meanwhile, American missionaries and business lobbyists, some of whom were IPR members, campaigned to make an exception for the Asian empire among the races "ineligible to citizenship" in US immigration law by giving Japan, and Japan only, an annual immigration quota. Because of their efforts, the debates over resuming Japanese immigration continued until the Sino-Japanese War. But it was not just the news of Japan's imperial violence that put an end to this debate. During the Great Depression, the United States was even opposed to the mainland-bound migration of Filipino laborers who were US nationals due to colonization. In 1934, it reduced the migration of Filipinos with an annual quota of fifty people in exchange for setting a timetable for Philippine independence.[52]

The decline of US-Japan relations was not simply the result of the growing American awareness of Japan's imperial violence and immigration policy. The Japan that Franklin D. Roosevelt encountered during his presidency was not the same empire that Theodore Roosevelt welcomed into the circle of great powers. The long period during which the United States considered Japan its partner largely coincided with the era of "imperial democracy," which lasted from the

Russo-Japanese War to the Manchurian invasion. During this era, Japan's leaders embraced a form of parliamentary rule that simultaneously supported overseas imperial expansion and democratic reform at home.[53] But during the Great Depression these leaders were eclipsed by fascists who, after entering Japan into alliance with Hitler's Germany in 1936 and with Mussolini's Italy in 1937, put their empire on a path to clash with the United States.

Achieving "Progress" through Empire

One of the most ironic twists of this story is that, as Japan allied itself with the fascist states of Europe and waged war against China, the nonwhite empire announced that it was fighting to free Asia from the clutches of white empires. Japan's Pan-Asianism, which promised an "Asia for Asians," was primarily self-serving propaganda. Nevertheless, it successfully attracted various Korean, Chinese, Filipino, Burmese, Indian, and other Asian elites to Japan's mission to fight against "white" empires.[54] In fact, one of the Koreans who came to embrace Japan in the 1930s was Yun Ch'i-ho, the same man who had feared Japan's rise during the Russo-Japanese War.

Until the Great Depression, Yun showed only sporadic signs of interest in Pan-Asianism. When US-Japan relations were amicable, he remained unconvinced that an Asian empire would better serve the interests of Koreans than a white one. This became especially clear after the Japanese incarcerated him from 1912 to 1915, allegedly for plotting to assassinate the colonial governor but in reality for running a Christian school that the colonists accused of being a training ground for anti-colonial activists. Though he chose not to participate in the March First Movement, and even attempted to dissuade Korean protestors from what he believed to be futile attempts to gain Wilson's attention, Yun remained distrustful of the colonial government. During the 1920s, he denounced the new policy of limited self-rule as a "farce," and rejected favorable comparisons of Korea with the Philippines by pointing out that the United States promised independence to Filipinos "as soon as practicable." When he accepted the IPR's invitation to attend its 1929 conference held in Kyoto, Yun remained alert to what he described as his Japanese hosts' "courteous" but "distrustful" attitude toward their colonial subjects.[55]

But after the Manchurian invasion, Yun began to subordinate his resentment toward the Japanese in the interest of what he now came to believe as the future of the "yellow" races. He was enraged by the white opposition to Japan's establishment of Manchukuo, and he was particularly angry at the United States and Britain whose demand for "open door and equal opportunity" in Manchuria was, in his view, hypocritical, since "the exclusion bills [sic] of America & Canada against the Far-Eastern peoples" prevented Asians from pursuing opportunities in the "white" countries. To him, Japan's actions were a logical response to such racist policies. "Japan has as much right to monopolize the natural resources & opportunities of & in Manchuria as the Americans are monopolizing those of North America & the English, those of Australasia & of Canada," he wrote in his diary.[56] After three decades under Japanese rule, he chose to fight against white supremacy at the cost of acquiescing to the colonial rule in Korea and supporting Japan's invasion of China.

Yun's words did not age well. Since the end of World War II, which brought the collapse of both Japanese and European empires, he has been consistently vilified and depicted as a national traitor by numerous historians and politicians in his home country.[57] Yet during Yun's lifetime many people shared his views, and not just among Asians who believed in Japan's promise of an "Asia for Asians." Various African American leaders from Booker T. Washington to James Weldon Johnson to Marcus Garvey held Japan as a champion of the "darker races" while being fully cognizant of the fact that Japan was a colonizing empire.[58] This was not the case for most African Americans on the left. Like various Asians and Asian Americans who embraced the radical anti-imperialism of the Communist International (Comintern)—established in Moscow during the Paris Peace Conference—they denounced empires regardless of color. The fact that Japan signed a pact with Germany and Italy to combat the Comintern made it easier for many people to see through Japan's propaganda.[59]

Yet Du Bois, the most prominent African American radical of his generation, remained committed to Japan. After intermittently following Japan's activities from a distance for three decades, Du Bois finally visited Japan, China, and Manchukuo when he was returning home from a trip to Germany and Russia in 1936. His public defense of Japan became more effusive than ever before. He argued that there was "clear evidence" that Japan had established services for "health, education, city-planning, housing, consumers' co-operation and other social ends" in Manchukuo. He also applauded the Japanese imperialists for incorporating "the natives into the administration of government and social re-adjustment."[60] His list of Japan's accomplishments bore a striking resemblance to what white imperialists had praised about the benefits of American and Japanese colonial rules across the Pacific over the previous three decades.

Du Bois's rosy view of Japan was not simply a product of his commitment to seeing the world through the color line paradigm. It was also a reflection of his willingness to tolerate, and at times even celebrate, an empire of progressive reform. Even as he excoriated white empires, Du Bois was taken with the imperialist ideas about "civilization" that captivated many of his nonwhite elite contemporaries.[61] In fact, when his view overlapped with Yun's during the 1930s, it was not just because the Korean had come to see the world's problems primarily as battles across the color line. It was also because the American had reconciled with empire as a means to end white supremacy, just as many Pan-Asianists did.

This book thus probes into the problem of empire's allure not only from the perspective of American and Japanese empire builders but also from those of Koreans, African Americans, and other subjugated groups who adapted to, and sometimes even adopted, "progressive" imperialism for their own goals. The contradictory nature of these nonwhite figures' embrace of empire was evident to many of their contemporaries. Revolutionary nationalists and anarchists in Asia, as well as the radical internationalists associated with the Comintern, condemned the nonwhite elites who collaborated with American and European imperialists.[62] In fact, in many cases, their anger was exacerbated by the fact that some of these Asian elites collaborated with imperialists precisely to suppress radicalism.[63] The case of Yun Ch'i-ho is instructive. When he embraced the Japanese empire after the Manchurian Crisis, it was not simply because he bought into the idea of "Asia for Asians." After witnessing younger generations of Koreans gravitate toward communism during the Great Depression, Yun also turned to the Japanese empire as a bulwark against what he believed to be the greatest threat to Christianity in Korea. Anti-radicalism, however, was far from the only feature of empire that made it enticing to numerous nonwhite elites. Until World War II, many radicals including W. E. B. Du Bois genuinely believed that a strong nonwhite empire like Japan would eventually lead a global revolution of the colored peoples against white supremacy. Still, for others, adapting themselves to empires' expectations of nonwhite peoples' "proper" behavior was a matter of survival. In the United States, various Asian immigrants and exiles reshaped their own lives to prove to imperial powers that they were worthy of sovereignty, citizenship, and property rights.

Following such stories, this book shows that the imperial world order that collapsed with the end of World War II was a world that white and nonwhite elites created together, against the aspirations of the radical activists who sought to rid the world of empires. Approaching the imperial world order as a product of complex collaborations across the color line is admittedly a provocative task. But doing so does not reduce white culpability in the creation and maintenance of empires. Nor does it suggest that interracial collaborations operated on equal terms. Even Japan had to consistently struggle for international parity with the white imperial powers, and inter-imperial competition for influence in Asia and conflicts over the immigration issue constantly kept both sides of the color line on alert. But focusing on elites reveals that, before the United States could emerge as a global superpower through its experience in World War II, it relied on these collaborations to secure its interests in the Pacific. In a way, this shouldn't be surprising. European empires had been able to expand in the first place not necessarily because of their military supremacy, but because of their ability to secure African, Asian, and Latin American elites as translators, informants, trade partners, and political allies.[64]

To illustrate how American and Asian elites built and maintained this transpacific imperial order over the first four decades of the twentieth century, the chapters of this book are organized in a roughly chronological order and around several key episodes that crisscross the Pacific. Chapter 1 explores US-Japan-Korea triangular relations during the Russo-Japanese War. It explains that, before the Philippines became an example of "progressive" imperialism, Cuba was the model that both US imperialists and Asian elites expected Japan to follow in Korea. Chapter 2 examines anti-Japanese movements in California and explains how the Gentlemen's Agreement, the 1913 California Alien Land Law, and the beginning of World War I changed the inter-imperial relationship. Chapter 3 returns to Korea by way of the American South and the Philippines to explain why American missionary leaders, as well as the US government headed by Wilson, refused to support the Asian anti-colonial struggles during the Paris Peace Conference. Chapter 4 travels back to California and reinterprets the road to Japanese exclusion in Washington, DC, by explaining how nativists deployed internationally framed arguments for curtailing Asian property rights in California and prohibiting Japanese immigration to the United States. Chapter 5 returns once more to Asia by way of Hawai'i, following a group of white, Asian, and Black elites associated with the IPR who financially and emotionally invested in various social science projects that they believed would lead to mutual understanding. It also tracks how their efforts unintentionally contributed to the League of Nations' decision to condemn Japan's invasion of Manchuria, a decision that led to Japan's departure from the international body in 1933. Chapter 6 traces the transformation of US foreign and immigration policies during the Great Depression. It examines how the changing ideas about race and empire enabled the US government to set the timetable for Philippine independence, consider Hawai'i's statehood, and align itself with China against Japan when the two Asian countries went to war. Above all, it explains that, on the eve of World War II, the Franklin D. Roosevelt administration abandoned the strategy of collaborative transpacific governance with Japan that the United States had pursued since Theodore Roosevelt's presidency.

This long history of inter-imperial relationship came to be forgotten during World War II, when both the United States and Japan redefined themselves against each other as racially incompatible enemies. This racial division justified the brutal war crimes both powers committed against each another in the Pacific Theater. It also led to the mass incarceration of Japanese Americans in the United States, as well as the removal and deportation of the Japanese in Canada, Mexico, and Peru.[65] Wartime amnesia about the earlier years was not unique to

US-Japan relations. Although the United States also defined itself against Nazi Germany, US-German relations had been far closer than either side wanted to admit, especially before World War I.[66]

By the time the United States emerged victorious from World War II, most people around the world found empire an unacceptable form of governance. Decolonization defined the postwar period. Yet even in the age of decolonization, the United States maintained its hierarchical relationship with Asia established during the Progressive Era, and it did so by combining violent counterinsurgency campaigns to suppress radical dissidents with various measures to draw in anti-communist Asian elites.[67] By contributing to the economic development of America's allies in Asia, and by repealing exclusionary immigration laws that had prohibited Asian immigration to the United States, American policymakers continued to persuade a large number of Asian elites that they could secure their self-interests through collaboration with the United States. The willingness of these Asian elites to work within a world led by the United States—even in the face of the United States' undeniable record of violence, subjugation, and impoverishment through colonization and militarization in Asia—evidenced the enduring power of the limited vision of "progress" born out of the Progressive Era. Rather than fighting for universal human equality, many historical figures celebrated the selective inclusion of nonwhite peoples in international governance and their selective incorporation into the American body politic as markers of racial progress. Coming to terms with this history might help explain why the imperial world order led by a few powerful states took so long to dismantle even after World War II, and why the particular form of human inequality created by this order still remains to be completely undone.

1

Empires of Reform

The United States, Japan, and the End of Korean Sovereignty, 1904–1905

In June 1904, President Theodore Roosevelt hosted two Japanese diplomats at the White House. Japan had recently begun a war against Russia, and it had already scored numerous victories on the shores of Korea and Manchuria. Confident that the war would end in the foreseeable future, the president wished to personally discuss with Takahira Kogorō, the Japanese minister in Washington, and Kaneko Kentarō, a special envoy from Tokyo, what Japan could do in the postwar world. Roosevelt disclosed that some Americans and Europeans feared Japan would get a "big head" and enter into a "general career of insolence and aggression." As for himself, he hoped and believed that Japan would take its place among the "great civilized nations," with "a paramount interest in what surrounds the Yellow Sea," just like the United States in "what surrounds the Caribbean."[1]

The Japanese diplomats might have interpreted these words as an encouragement to establish Japan's hegemony in East Asia, but the president made clear that the Caribbean comparison was intended to convey that Japan's entry into the family of "great civilized nations" was conditional. Or at least that is what Roosevelt, prolific letter writer that he was, explained in detail to his confidants after the meeting. He elaborated that Japan should claim a paramount interest in the Yellow Sea, but with "no more desire for conquest of the weak" than the United States had shown "in the case of Cuba." It should also display "no more desire for a truculent attitude toward the strong" than what the United States had shown with respect to Britain and France in the "West Indies." Self-restraint of both desires was a requirement for Japan's full membership in the family.[2]

According to Roosevelt, the Japanese officials well understood the message. Contrary to the fear of a coming "Yellow Terror," they explained, Japan simply

The Allure of Empire. Chris Suh, Oxford University Press. © Oxford University Press 2023.
DOI: 10.1093/oso/9780197631614.003.0002

wished to join the "circle of civilized mankind." Rumors of Japan's plan to attack the US colony in the Philippines, they assured, were "nonsense." As for the
area surrounding the Yellow Sea, Roosevelt and the Japanese officials agreed on
a range of possible arrangements. In Manchuria, Japan would drive out Russia
and hand it over to China. As for China, Japan should respect its territorial integrity, but Roosevelt would also "gladly welcome" any effort by the Japanese to
bring China "along the road which Japan trod." Such a project to "bring China
forward," Roosevelt argued, would ensure the region would be "prosperous and
well policed." The Japanese officials, in turn, explained the limits of their own
imperial ambitions. Japan was aware of the challenges it was going to face "even
in Korea," and it was "satisfied with that job." The president was satisfied with
this answer as well, for it meant, as he had personally recommended to another
Japanese official at the White House three months earlier, that Japan would establish a semicolonial relationship with Korea, "just like we [have done] with
Cuba."[3]

The formation of US policy toward the Pacific during the Russo-Japanese
War would have a lasting impact for the next three decades. The Roosevelt administration built on its recent experience in the Western Hemisphere to formulate a plan to transform the United States into a Pacific power, but at this
time, it had no plans to add new territories to its transpacific empire. The US
colonial project in the Philippines was unpopular among the American people,
and Roosevelt's political opponents sought to exploit it in the election of 1904.
Rather than disengaging from Asia, however, various Americans from the president to diplomats to journalists came to embrace the idea that Japan, along with
Britain, could serve as a key partner of the United States on the opposite side of
the Pacific Ocean. By entering into this inter-imperial partnership, the United
States could secure its interests across the Pacific without expanding its territorial empire and rise as a key player in the emerging multipolar imperial order.

As Roosevelt communicated to the Japanese diplomats, Americans' acceptance of the Japanese as an imperial partner depended heavily on their ability
to restrain their "desire for conquest of the weak." Japanese imperialists were
well aware of this fact. It was no coincidence that Japan, upon the war's end,
decided to preserve the nominal independence of Korea by making the country
its protectorate, rather than annexing the country as the United States did with
the Philippines. While the Philippines continued to be the favorite target of
American anti-imperialists, Cuba—which Roosevelt described as "a kind of a
protectorate"—stood in the United States as proof that the aim of US imperialism was "reform" of its subjugated people.[4]

Of course, this was not how US imperialism looked from its receiving end.
Cubans well understood how US hegemony and its threat of military intervention worked.[5] Likewise, Korean diplomats, immigrants, and students who

traveled to Honolulu, Washington, DC, and Roosevelt's summer home, in Oyster Bay refused to be used as proof of Japan's capacity for imperial reform. They documented Japan's imperial exploitation during the war and presented the evidence to American diplomats, missionaries, and politicians. One such observer was Korea's vice minister of foreign affairs Yun Ch'i-ho, who closely followed Japan's expansion into Korea, as well as the development of a close relationship between Japan and the United States, from his vantage points in Korea, Japan, and Hawai'i.

By the end of the Russo-Japanese War, it was well known among US policymakers, including Roosevelt, that Japanese expansion into Korea was fraught with violence and exploitation. To address these issues, Roosevelt even held a meeting with the Japanese ambassador in Washington to talk about Japanese settler colonialists in Korea. But Roosevelt, US diplomats, and journalists believed that violence and exploitation were simply minor parts of humanity's larger movement toward "progress," an unfortunate but unavoidable phase in the larger enterprise to "regenerate" the races unable to govern or defend themselves. Americans, after all, had an undeniable record of violent conflicts in the history of their own "progressive" empire, and they decided to admit Japan into the family of "civilized nations" in spite of its well-documented instances of an inability to exercise self-restraint toward the "weak." They were confident that all "civilized" powers would eventually make violence and exploitation worth enduring for the world's subjugated peoples.

Turning the Yellow Sea into Japan's Caribbean

Roosevelt played a singularly important role in establishing the United States as a Pacific power, and it was because of him that so many US policymakers came to see Japan as an imperial partner. More than any of his predecessors, he was enamored with Japanese culture. During his first term, he began learning *jūjutsu*, received private lessons in judo, and exercised three times a week with "Japanese wrestlers."[6] When he read Nitobe Inazō's *Bushido: The Soul of Japan* (1899), he was so impressed that he recommended it to his friends and family. In fact, Roosevelt's fascination with *bushido*, which Nitobe translated as the *"noblesse oblige* of the warrior class," was partially responsible for his confident outlook for the Japanese.[7]

Roosevelt's respect for the Japanese was reflective of his commitment to the martial ideal of nationhood, which was inseparable from his ideas about manhood. In his youth, Roosevelt suffered from poor health, but ever since he took up boxing as a fourteen-year-old, he believed that a man's worth should be measured by his willingness to confront adversity in moments of crisis. After his first wife died, Roosevelt moved out to the American West, where the "strenuous life" allowed him to discover his own virility. Upon returning to the East Coast, he used this newfound virility to quickly rise through the ranks of American politics. Within the span of ten years, he served as president of the US Civil Service Commission, president of New York City's Police Commission, and assistant secretary of the navy. When the United States declared war against Spain in 1898 following the mysterious explosion of the USS *Maine* in Cuba, Roosevelt chose to personally participate in combat. He resigned from his post and helped form the First US Volunteer Cavalry, known as the Rough Riders, which was composed of not only cowboys and hunters from the American West but also Ivy League athletes, New York City police officers, and Native American fighters. By defeating the Spanish troops in the Battle of San Juan Hill outside Santiago, Cuba, Roosevelt rose to national prominence, and he eventually rode his war fame to the governorship of New York in 1899 and the vice presidency of the United States in 1900. Although he became president as a result of William McKinley's assassination in September 1901, there was no mistake in Roosevelt's mind that his rise to the top was a result of his manly character, which had been hardened through years of enduring physical challenges and fighting in a war.[8]

By the turn of the twentieth century, Roosevelt believed that the Japanese deserved to be welcomed to the family of "civilized" nations because they had proven, on the world stage, that they could fight just as well as Europeans and Americans. As assistant secretary of the navy, Roosevelt expressed concerns over Japan's designs to take over Hawai'i.[9] But as vice president–elect, he expressed his enthusiasm for Japan's military, which had joined the United States, Britain, France, Germany, Russia, Italy, and Austria-Hungary in the Eight-Nation Alliance to suppress the "Boxer Uprising" in China, a nationwide anti-imperialist movement that aimed to drive out Western influence. "What extraordinary soldiers those little Japs are!" he commented to British diplomat Cecil Spring Rice, who had served as his best man at his second wedding in 1886 and remained a confidant on world affairs for most of his adult life. "Our own troops out in China write grudgingly that they think the Japs did better than any of the allied forces." Roosevelt explained to a German diplomat that Japan's good performance starkly contrasted with the Russians, who were "the worst" among the Allied forces "for plundering and murdering."[10]

By the time he became president, however, few Americans shared his enthusiasm for overseas military activities. The declining enthusiasm had much to do with the Philippines. The Spanish-American War, fought against a European empire, had been enormously popular and reached a swift conclusion in 1898. But the ensuing Philippine-American War, fought against Filipinos demanding independence, was deeply unpopular in the United States. Reports of American soldiers' atrocities, intemperance, and frequenting of brothels in the Philippines prompted a wide range of Americans to mobilize against imperialism, arguing that the soldiers' experience abroad caused male "degeneration." In addition to William Jennings Bryan, the Populist Democrat who had run for the presidency in 1900 against McKinley and Roosevelt, the list of prominent dissenters included Senator George Frisbie Hoar of Massachusetts, who represented an older generation of Republicans continuously fighting against Southern white repression of African Americans after Reconstruction. He argued that the American colonization of the Philippines represented another form of racial oppression. Meanwhile, white supremacist Democrats such as Representative John S. Williams of Mississippi and Senator Benjamin Tillman of South Carolina opposed the Philippines' colonization out of their fear that it would bring in additional nonwhite people to the US body politic. Outside Congress, popular writers such as Mark Twain and various civic organizations including the Women's Christian Temperance Union stoked the public's outrage against Roosevelt's plans for a Pacific outpost in Asia.[11]

The Philippine-American War was so unpopular that Roosevelt was forced to prematurely declare the end of conflict on July 4, 1902. Over the next two years, the United States reduced its troops levels in the Philippines to a mere 18 percent of what they had been in 1900. However, counterinsurgency campaigns continued throughout Roosevelt's presidency and beyond. Governor-General of the Philippines William Howard Taft established the Philippine Constabulary in 1901 and relied on this national police force, staffed by Filipinos who were trained by US army officers, to surveil and suppress anticolonial guerrilla fighters.[12]

Nonetheless, Roosevelt was determined to convince the American people that imperial expansion across the Pacific was America's destiny. During his tour across the country from April to June 1903, Roosevelt stopped in San Francisco where he dedicated a monument honoring Admiral George Dewey's victory in the Battle of Manila Bay (1898). There, he argued that the "inevitable march of events gave us the control of the Philippines at a time so opportune that it may without irreverence be called Providential." Following what historian Frederick Jackson Turner famously described in 1893 as the closing of the "American frontier" in the continental United States, Roosevelt suggested, the American people were given an opportunity to continue expanding westward and annex the Philippines, Guam, and Hawai'i. The annexations had more than just national significance. The United States, he said, was ready to write a new chapter in human history by making "East and West finally become one."[13]

The first step toward connecting East and West was solving an unresolved issue in the Caribbean. While Roosevelt was on his tour, the US Senate ratified the Hay-Herrán Treaty, granting the United States the right to build a canal across the Panama isthmus in Colombia and thereby create a shortcut between the Atlantic and the Pacific. But the treaty never went into effect because the

Fig. 1.1 Theodore Roosevelt standing beside his large globe, 1903. Rockwood Photo Co. Library of Congress Prints and Photographs Division, LC-DIG-ppmsca-36041.

Colombian Senate rejected it. Understandably, when Roosevelt returned to Washington the canal issue became his priority. But it was not easy for the president to convince the US Congress to follow his lead. After a group of separatists declared independence from Colombia to form the Republic of Panama in November 1903, the Roosevelt administration recognized the new country in three days, scrapped the old treaty it had agreed to with Colombia, and signed a new treaty with a French citizen named Philippe Bunau-Varilla. A large shareholder in the New Panama Canal Company, Bunau-Varilla was so eager to sell the concession and equipment to the United States that he essentially financed the separatists in order to buy his right to represent the newly independent Panama in its negotiations with the United States. Some of the same politicians who criticized US rule over the Philippines, including Hoar, Williams, and Tillman, prolonged the ratification process by arguing that it was unbecoming for the United States to acquire its right to build the canal through such questionable means.[14]

The Senate eventually ratified the Hay–Bunau-Varilla Treaty in February 1904, and a few weeks before ratification, Roosevelt received an unexpected opportunity to start thinking about how to secure US interests in East Asia. On February 8, Japan declared war against Russia and began battling on the shores of Korea and Manchuria. Given the president's reaction to the two empires' record during the Boxer Expedition, it was not surprising that he rooted for the Asian power. Immediately after Japan's first naval victory at Port Arthur, Manchuria, he told his son, Theodore Jr., that he was "thoroughly well pleased" with the victory, "for Japan is playing our game." The Japanese were "non-Aryan and non-Christian." Yet "we who speak English," he recommended to Spring Rice, should be ready to recognize these "newcomers" as part of the world's greatest powers. Though they might interfere with US and British interests in the future, it was just as possible that they would "develop" China for the benefit of all interested empires.[15] Indeed, the latter possibility was exactly what Japanese elites attempted to highlight in English. Kaneko Kentarō, the special envoy who had been dispatched to the United States to influence American public opinion, promised in the *International Quarterly* that Japan would "clear the way for the American people in their Chinese enterprises." Although the Anglo-Japanese Alliance (1902) had played a role in "securing peace," he said, an "economic alliance" between the United States and Japan would develop the "world's commerce in China." When Roosevelt received this article from Kaneko, the president replied that he had "long felt that Japan's entrance into the circle of the great civilized powers was of good omen for all the world," and asked the Japanese envoy to let him know when he reached Washington so that they would talk "at length" about the next steps along with Japan's minister Takahira Kogorō.[16]

Roosevelt met with Kaneko and Takahira at the White House in June, and the president explained that Japan's inclusion in the circle of great powers was conditional. To secure full inclusion, Japan would have to demonstrate its self-restraint toward the "strong" as well as the "weak," a quality, according to Roosevelt, that defined the character of the truly "civilized" nations. As he confided to Spring Rice, the president told the Japanese dignitaries that Japan could showcase its self-restraint to the great powers by using the US policy toward the Caribbean as a model for its own relationship with the countries surrounding the Yellow Sea.[17]

The image of the US empire that Roosevelt conveyed to Japanese diplomats was, of course, based on selective memory. After taking Puerto Rico and Cuba as spoils of the Spanish-American War, the Roosevelt administration took various steps to secure the Caribbean as the American sphere of influence, steps that were anything but restrained in the eyes of both the weak and the strong. While the United States did not challenge British and French rule in the West Indies, it did rely on its military to intimidate the European powers. When Britain, Germany, and Italy imposed a naval blockade against Venezuela in 1902–1903 after the country refused to pay its foreign debts, Roosevelt sent the navy to en-sure that no European power would use this as an opportunity to establish a stronger military presence in the Western Hemisphere. The American attitude toward nations considered weak was not exactly reserved, either. After all, the United States prevented Colombia from suppressing the Panama independence movement so that it could lease the land necessary to build the canal without Colombia's consent.[18]

In selecting his example of American attitudes toward nations considered weak, there was a reason why—instead of Puerto Rico, Venezuela, Colombia, or Panama—Roosevelt chose Cuba as the model for Japan to follow in Korea. Just two weeks before his meeting with Japanese officials, Roosevelt composed a speech celebrating the two-year anniversary of Cuba's independence. As he put it, the 1904 occasion was to "congratulate not only Cuba but also the United States." In what is considered a prolegomenon to his corollary to the Monroe Doctrine, Roosevelt, who had the former secretary of war Elihu Root read the speech in New York, declared:

> We freed Cuba from tyranny; we then stayed in the island until we had established civil order and laid the foundations for self-government and prosperity; we then made the island independent, and have since benefited her inhabitants by making closer the commercial relations between us. I hail what had been done in Cuba not merely for its own sake, but as showing the purpose and desire of this nation toward all the nations south of us. It is not true that the United States has any land hunger or entertains any projects as regards other nations, save such as are for their welfare.[19]

In Roosevelt's mind, Cuba was a place to showcase both American virility and American humanitarianism.

It is difficult to read Roosevelt's statement without cynicism. After all, the reason why Cuba became the only independent nation among overseas possessions acquired through the Spanish-American War was that, when the war was declared, an anti-McKinley Republican senator named Henry Teller proposed an amendment precluding the United States from annexing the island after the war, and Congress adopted it as a joint resolution. There was no equiva-lent amendment for Puerto Rico, Guam, or the Philippines, all of which became US possessions. Furthermore, Cuba was granted nominal independence under the condition that it modify its constitution to include the Platt Amendment, authored by Elihu Root, which prohibited Cuba from entering into treaties with a third country without the United States' consent. "There is, of course, little or no independence left in Cuba under the Platt Amendment," Leonard Wood, the military governor of Cuba, put it in a letter to Roosevelt in 1901. Even as he celebrated the two-year anniversary of Cuba's independence, the president made clear that the country's continued independence depended on its ability to act with "decency in industrial and political matters," keep "order," and pay its "obligations." Should Cuba be found guilty in any "[b]rutal wrongdoing" or an "impotence which results in a general loosening of the ties of civilized society," Elihu Root intoned, the United States would intervene.[20]

Still, the American rule of Cuba generated widespread support in the United States, for it was where the American impulses for domestic reform and overseas expansion coalesced to create an empire of reform. Under the governorship of Leonard Wood, Cuba became, in the words of historian Howard Gillette, a "workshop for American progressivism." Wood applied the lessons of domestic reform to Cuba: he reorganized the school administration after the state system in Ohio, carried out public works and civil service reform, increased the efficiency of the municipal government, created a railroad commission, and improved sanitation. Wood's reform projects secured important allies at home. He gained the support of Jacob Riis, the social reformer most famous for his reports on the poor living conditions of New York City tenements, and the prominent intellectual and writer Herbert Croly, who argued in *The Promise of American Life* (1909) that the imperial project in Cuba provided "a tremendous impulse" to the domestic reform movement.[21]

US imperialism in Cuba even found support among politicians who opposed Roosevelt's Philippines policy. Carl Schurz, a former Republican senator who led the Mugwumps against the Republican establishment represented by McKinley and Roosevelt, lamented the prolonged American violence in the Philippines. But he expressed his disapproval by predicting that the American people would one day "deplore" how "we turned our arms against the Filipinos" instead of "treating the Philippines as we have treated Cuba." Indeed, when Alton B. Parker accepted the Democratic Party's nomination to challenge Roosevelt for the presidency in 1904, he declared that he would do for the Filipinos what the United States had "already done for the Cubans."[22]

After Roosevelt defeated Parker by a wide margin of electoral votes, he returned his attention to the Russo-Japanese War. There was no shortage of reading material. In addition to various reports from US diplomats and military attachés stationed in Asia, he had access to numerous newspapers and magazines that had been capitalizing on popular interest in the war. Magazine editors hired former missionaries like William Elliot Griffis (a leading expert of Japan who wrote the introduction to the 1905 edition of Nitobe's *Bushido*), and they also provided space for Japanese elites, like Kaneko, to explain Japan's actions directly to readers.[23]

But Roosevelt was particular about his source of information. He chose to learn about the war, and Japan, from a small number of personal friends who had known him in Cuba during the Spanish-American War and then traveled to Japan to cover the Russo-Japanese War. What he learned from these friends was disappointing. To be sure, Japan continued to demonstrate its military might. It seized Port Arthur, considered one of the best-fortified Russian ports, and destroyed Russia's Pacific Fleet. But Japan's attitude toward the "strong," as Roosevelt liked to say, became a cause for worry. While the Japanese government "treated us well," Roosevelt learned from his friends, the Japanese "down at bottom" did not. They seemed to "lump Russians, English, Americans, Germans, all of us, simply as white devils inferior to themselves," he vented to Spring Rice. The president hoped this would be a "passing phase," but he began to rethink whether Japan's entrance into the circle of the great powers would prove to be a good omen as he initially thought. In contrast to Japan's "rulers," Roosevelt said to his minister to Italy, George von Lengerke Meyer, in confidence, the Japanese people "doubtless . . . believe their own yellow civilization to be better" than those of the "white men" whose "past arrogance they resent."[24]

Despite his growing reservations about Japan's attitude toward the "strong," Roosevelt expressed little concern about its attitude toward the "weak." His friends who reported from Asia told him that Japan would do for Korea what the United States had done for Cuba. Or at the very least, they convinced him that Koreans needed a benevolent imperial power to guide them toward "reform" and self-government, just like Cubans.

From Cuba to Korea

Like Roosevelt, several veteran journalists of the Spanish-American War believed that the Russo-Japanese War provided an unprecedented opportunity to observe Japan. Several of them were close enough to the president that they provided him with information through direct correspondence. During the Spanish-American War, Richard Harding Davis and John Fox Jr. had traveled with the Rough Riders to report from San Juan Hill. George Kennan had followed Clara Barton's Red Cross to Cuba, where he crossed paths with the Rough Riders. Through their words, Roosevelt—in fact, many Americans—made sense of the distant place and assessed whether Japan had what it would take to turn the Yellow Sea into their Caribbean.

Because the Japanese government restricted what the journalists could see, the information they gathered was limited. As Davis personally explained to Roosevelt, war correspondents were held in Tokyo for ten weeks during the late spring of 1904 without being able to see the battlefront. Jack London, the novelist who had been hired by the Hearst newspapers, secretly traveled to Korea on his own, but he was arrested by the Japanese military and brought back to Japan. Davis, Fox, and Kennan eventually got to see Korea and Manchuria as part of a carefully arranged tour, but the Americans still saw little action. While Kennan seemed content to watch the blockade of Port Arthur, Manchuria, from a steamship, Davis and Fox grew more frustrated. Davis barely wrote anything about the war and left early to return to Cuba. Fox, who had wished to see how Japan would "Saxonize" China, concluded that after the seven months in Asia he learned "no more than I should have known had I stayed home."[25]

After Davis and Fox left Asia, Kennan's articles in *Outlook* magazine became the single most important lens through which Roosevelt perceived the war. But even before they left, Kennan was eager to deploy references to Cuba in order to make the Japanese resemble the Americans who fought in the Spanish-American War. Describing the Japanese soldiers who seized Port Arthur, Kennan noted their courage was not much different from "Anglo-Saxon courage" and compared it to that of "the men who charged up Kettle Hill and the battery-crowned heights of San Juan." In some ways, Kennan declared, the Japanese were even better than the Americans. In contrast to his countrymen during the Santiago campaign, he wrote, the Japanese demonstrated "strategical ability of the highest order," as well as a "wonderful system and thoroughness in the management of details" in their Manchurian campaign.[26]

As it was for many Americans at the time, it was not Manchuria but Korea that Kennan imagined as Japan's Cuba. As in the Caribbean, the sanitation level served as the barometer of the state of affairs in Asia. In his first article on Korea, Kennan claimed that the Korean port city of Chemulpo (present day Incheon) begged for comparison with Santiago, which had served as his standard for "maximum filthiness." The "choked drains, the rotting garbage, the stinking ponds, the general disorder, and the almost universal filthiness of Korea are not only surprising and disgusting, but [also] absolutely shocking," he argued. Six years earlier, Kennan had similarly described wartime Santiago as a city of "dirt, disorder, and neglect," as evidenced by its "open drains" and "dirty, foul-smelling water." Partially based on his observation of Cubans' unsanitary "character and habits," Kennan had concluded that they were neither "fit" nor "capable of intelligent self-government."[27] During the Russo-Japanese War, he carried over the association between sanitation level and capacity for self-government from Cuba to Korea. After seeing the "perfect order and immaculate neatness of Japan," Kennan reasoned, the unsanitary conditions of Korea created in him "a prejudice against the Koreans" from which he found it "extremely difficult to divest."[28]

In his comparisons between the Japanese and Koreans, Kennan explained that the differences did not stem from the environments they inhabited, but from human agency. "So far as climate and fertility of soil are concerned, Korea equals and perhaps surpasses Japan," he argued, "but in all the characteristics that are the outgrowth and flower of human endeavor, [Korea] is ages behind its wide-awake, energetic, and progressive neighbor." In addition to the unsanitary conditions, what struck Kennan as evidence of the country's lack of progress was the character of government officials and the emperor, Kojong. In the summer of 1904, Kennan, along with other foreign correspondents, attended a reception hosted by the Korean emperor in his palace. Describing the government officials he encountered in Rooseveltian terms, Kennan declared, with "few exceptions," they appeared to be "lacking in virility and in that combination of strong mental and moral qualities which we call *character*." In Kennan's assessment, the emperor was even worse than the officials. The best compliment he could offer the emperor was his "extraordinary discernment" in the choice of the caterer for the reception. If the emperor's Treasury Department were "as well managed as his kitchen," Kennan suggested, the country would have been far better off as a whole.[29]

Kennan so impressed Roosevelt that, after reading all of his articles, the president, through a mutual friend, instructed the journalist to communicate the president's "personal bias" to "a few men of influence of Japan." Kennan was asked to tell Japanese government officials that the president had "favored" Japan from the beginning and believed that "Japan must hold Port Arthur and she must hold Korea." The only warning Roosevelt had for the Japanese was the problem of possible insolence he had mentioned to Takahira and Kaneko at the White House: that Japan should not try to "gain from her victory more than she ought to have." When Kennan delivered this message to Prime Minister Katsura Tarō in March 1905, the prime minister replied through Kennan that he was "extremely grateful" to Roosevelt "for [his] personal sympathy with Japan" and, interpreting the president's warning as a statement about China, assured him that Japan "demand[ed] the 'open door' and equal opportunities for all" in the area.[30]

Kennan's exchange with Katsura set the stage for a meeting between the prime minister and US secretary of war William Howard Taft, in July 1905. The conversation Taft had with Katsura was similar to what Roosevelt and Katsura had said through Kennan. After clarifying that Japan had no interest in the Philippines—except that it did not wish to see the islands under the "misrule" of the Filipinos who were "unfit for self-government" or an "unfriendly European power" that would threaten Japan's geopolitical interests—Katsura and Taft described Korea as a country that shouldn't be conducting its own foreign relations. Korea, Katsura explained, had a "habit of improvidently entering" into agreements and treaties with other powers. Since this habit had served as a "direct cause" of the Russo-Japanese War, Katsura argued, it was necessary for Japan to take a step toward "precluding" Korea from conducting its foreign affairs "improvidently" again. Taft agreed. He recommended that Japan establish a "suzerainty" over Korea so that the Korean government could not enter into agreements or treaties with a third power without Japan's "consent"—an arrangement that Taft believed would "contribute directly to permanent peace in the East." When Roosevelt received a telegram from Taft, he was delighted by the wording of this "agreed memorandum." He wished that Taft would tell Katsura that he "confirm[ed] every word" the secretary had said on the subject.[31]

Although historians have often interpreted this memorandum as a secret treaty that enabled Japan to gain Korea in exchange for staying away from the Philippines, the effect of this agreement was more modest in Roosevelt's view.[32] As he explained to Taft, the statement about the American colony was merely meant to "clear up Japan's attitude," in response to the rumors spread by "pro-Russian sympathizers" in the United States that Japan planned to attack the Philippines. Even if the rumors were true, Roosevelt maintained, there was no need to negotiate for a way to prevent Japan's "meddling with any American territory." He was confident that the United States was "entirely competent" to prevent such a meddling on its own.[33]

The juxtaposition of the Philippines and Korea in the Katsura-Taft memorandum deserves close attention because it reveals how American and Japanese policymakers justified their decision to strip Korea of its right to conduct foreign affairs by making comparisons with other nations that they deemed unworthy of self-government. Taft's recommendation of establishing a suzerainty over Korea was consistent with the Roosevelt administration's mission to reshape the world through paternalistic imperialism. "[F]reedom," Roosevelt explained to Harvard president Charles William Eliot in April 1904, "does not mean absence of all restraint. It merely means the substitution of self-restraint for external restraint, and therefore, it can be used only by people capable of self-restraint." Races incapable of self-restraint, Roosevelt believed, required a stronger power to restrain their actions, but the stronger power should not treat all subjugated races the same. The Filipinos, whom Roosevelt believed were "not fit to govern themselves," required external restraint in the form of colonialism. The Cubans, whom he believed "fit" after "a short preliminary training," were entitled to their national independence, even if this independence was nominal.[34]

Rather than colonizing Korea as the United States did in the Philippines, however, Japanese policymakers declared a protectorate over Korea as if it were their own Cuba. Kennan thought that this decision was a mistake, for he believed that Koreans were closer to the Filipinos than Cubans in terms of their ability to self-govern. The Korean people, he argued upon revisiting the country in the summer of 1905, had been "corrupt[ed] and demoralize[d]" through years of bad government, which had provided its subjects only with examples of "untruthfulness, dishonesty, treachery, cruelty, and a cynical brutality in dealing with human rights." The task of "regeneration" would be difficult because the Japanese used a model that was better suited for a group of people closer to Cubans. There was a reason why the United States had not declared a protectorate over the Philippines. It would mean that Americans would be "compelled to govern and civilize the Philippines through a Filipino Emperor, aided by a Filipino Cabinet," a task that would be as difficult as what Japan was promising to do in Korea.[35]

In describing the Korean government in these negative terms, Kennan deployed the rhetorical strategy of what Roosevelt would call, somewhat pejoratively, "muckrakers": the journalists who exposed corruption, exploitation, and other sources of inequality and immorality in American cities. By measuring the efficacy of the Korean government using the same standards as American municipalities, Kennan turned Korea into a place familiar to many American readers, a place in need of reform. The government afforded "no adequate protection to life or property," provided "no educational facilities that deserve notice," took "no measures to prevent or check epidemics," and did not "attempt to foster national trade or industry." Yet these observations did not strike American diplomats as the words of a journalist who ignorantly imposed domestic categories of analysis onto a foreign country. The highest praise within the diplomatic community came from W. W. Rockhill, the author of the Open Door notes (1899) and the State Department's leading expert on the Far East. Upon reading the article, Rockhill expressed to Kennan that Korea "or I should rather say, the sovereign and the officials, have not changed, except for the worse, since my sojourn there . . . 18 years ago."[36]

Not all diplomats endorsed Kennan's views, of course. Horace Allen, a longtime American Presbyterian missionary who served as US minister to Korea for most of the Russo-Japanese War, wrote another diplomat that he was "disgusted" by Kennan's "sensational" article. Yet even he agreed with Kennan's diagnosis of Korea's problems, as revealed in his correspondence with Durham White Stevens, an American adviser to the Korean Foreign Office. "Kennan may be sensational but at least he is right in one thing," Stevens wrote, "and that is that Corea [*sic*] can never hope for good government under the auspices which have existed during the past two decades." Allen's anger seemed to have subsided after reading this letter. After all, even as the minister criticized the journalist, he admitted there was "truth enough for such a sensational article."[37] Whatever disagreements the diplomats had with Kennan's portrait, they agreed on the most important point about the Korean government. This was no coincidence. The journalist had only articulated for the American public what the diplomats had said in private.

Unworthy of Self-Government

After Horace Allen was recalled from his post as US minister to Korea in 1905, he told his Korean friends that he had been dismissed because he had stood for Korea, against President Roosevelt. This was not exactly true.[38] Certainly, Roosevelt might have decided to recall Allen after a heated conversation they had at the White House back in 1903, but the subject of that conflict was the country's policy toward Manchuria. In contrast to Roosevelt, Allen believed that Russian control of Manchuria would be more beneficial to US economic interests.[39] But Allen did not disagree with Roosevelt's assessment of Korea as a nation unworthy of self-government. Even before the Russo-Japanese War began, Allen recommended to Rockhill that the United States should close its legation in Seoul and represent Americans in the country with a consulate supervised by the US legation in Tokyo. "Let Japan have Korea outright if she can get it and she will have to take charge of everything here," he wrote to Rockhill a month before the war began in 1904. None of his Korean friends knew, after two decades of friendship, that the minister had told Washington, "These people cannot govern themselves."[40]

Horace Allen had first arrived in Korea as a missionary in 1884, at a time when the country was still hostile to Christianity, and he emerged as the most powerful American in Seoul due to his medical training, business instincts, persistence, and luck. When he first arrived, the American minister, Lucius Foote, had to introduce him to the king as a physician at the legation, rather than a missionary, in order to avoid suspicion. Three months later, Allen won the trust of the Korean royal family by treating queen Myŏngsŏng's nephew, who had been attacked at a banquet. This attack was the beginning of a failed coup d'état (known as the Kapsin Coup) orchestrated by a group of young radical reformers discontented with the royal family, whom they blamed for the slow pace of political and economic reform. As the capital of Korea descended into chaos, Foote left the country, but Allen decided to stay and continue to look after the wounded nephew for three months. This decision changed his life, and perhaps even US-Korea relations, forever.[41]

At the request of the queen, the Qing army crushed the coup d'état and then dominated the Korean peninsula for the next decade. The Qing empire appointed an adviser to the Korean government, Yuan Shikai, who oversaw much of Korea's domestic affairs, but Allen's stock in Korea continued to rise during the years of Chinese dominance. In recognition of his work in treating the queen's nephew, Allen was made the king and the queen's physician, and in 1885, he solidified the trust of the Korean royal family by advising the king on a sanitation campaign that successfully contained a deadly cholera outbreak. King

Kojong's high opinion of him eventually enabled the medical missionary to become a diplomat representing the United States without having the personal or political connections that were usually necessary in the United States to receive such an appointment during this period. In 1890, after King Kojong petitioned to President Benjamin Harrison, the State Department named him secretary of the US legation in Seoul. In 1897, he became the US minister.[42]

Allen's unusually close relationship with the Korean royal family drew the attention of not only missionaries and diplomats but also financiers and businessmen. Allen had a talent for delivering many of their desired concessions every time Korea faced a crisis. In 1894, when the Sino-Japanese War began in Korea, Allen took advantage of the insecure royal family to gain the long-coveted Unsan gold mine for the American financier James R. Morse. The queen, who triggered the crisis by requesting Qing assistance to suppress a countrywide peasant rebellion, believed that significant American economic interest in Korea would prevent the domination of her country by the Japanese, who had deployed its military in Korea to fight the Chinese. After the Japanese assassinated the queen in 1895, Allen helped the distressed king escape to the Russian legation in Seoul and used the king's insecure position to help Americans gain more concessions. In 1896 he helped an American railroad company receive a contract to build a line between Seoul and Incheon. After the king left the Russian legation and declared himself emperor in 1897, Allen helped an American company win a waterworks concession and a streetcar concession. In essence, Allen enabled the United States to subjugate a foreign country without territorial conquest, through strategic control of key resources and infrastructure.[43]

Allen's work with American financiers and businessmen eventually brought Korea into the plans of labor recruiters across the Pacific, as he arranged for the first large-scale emigration of Korean laborers to Hawai'i in 1902. The Hawaiian Sugar Planters' Association had approached him, seeking a new source of cheap labor to replace the Chinese, who had been prohibited from immigration, and the Japanese, who were striking for higher wages with a near-monopoly of the labor market. Using his position of power, Allen convinced the Korean emperor to permit emigration. Some 7,000 Korean laborers migrated to Hawai'i over a two-year period.[44]

In light of such economic ties, it is all the more surprising that Allen recommended the Japanese takeover of the Korean peninsula. But a particular episode on the eve of the Russo-Japanese War made him decide that Korea should no longer be sustained the way it had been the previous two decades. As he pointed out in letter after letter, Allen believed that the Korean government's refusal to open Ŭiju, a port city on the Korean-Manchurian border, to international trade was the turning point in Korea's foreign relations, as well as in his own career.[45]

Although Ŭiju itself was "useless for commerce," Allen explained, the episode was symbolic of how poorly the government handled foreign policy. Allen declared that the emperor, who had gone from "bad to worse" since the queen's assassination, was an "awful curse and blight" to Korea. When the Japanese minister, with the support of the British and American diplomats, demanded the Korean emperor maintain a balance of power by asking him to open Ŭiju to international trade, the emperor decided not to make the decision himself but instead left it up to the acting minister of foreign affairs, Yi Ha-yong.[46] But when Yi Ha-yong, a personal friend of Allen's, declared the opening of Ŭiju, he was promptly removed from his position. The port remained closed to trade. According to Allen, the emperor changed his mind after heeding the advice of Yi Yong-ik, the minister of the royal treasury, who was well known as the leader of the pro-Russian faction in the cabinet. "There is no government here," Allen concluded. The United States would make "a great big mistake" if it attempted to "bolster up this 'Empire' in its independence" for "sentimental reasons," he told Rockhill. Two weeks into the Russo-Japanese War, Rockhill replied in agreement: "I cannot see any possibility of this Government using its influence 'to bolster up the Empire of Korea in its independence.'" As for the Japanese takeover of Korea, Rockhill agreed that it would "be better for the Korean people," as well as "for the peace in the Far East."[47]

Hence Allen raised no objections in February 1904 when the Japanese government signed what he described to Secretary of State John Hay as a "very strong" protocol with the Korean government.[48] Although Japan and Korea would not sign the official protectorate treaty for another twenty-one months, in Allen's view, the February 1904 protocol already established the "Japanese Protectorate of Korea." In exchange for maintaining the nominal independence and territorial integrity of Korea, the February 1904 protocol asked the Korean government to follow Japan's "advice" in making "improvements" in the Korean administration. It also enabled the Japanese military to occupy the country. In addition, the two countries agreed not to enter into any arrangement with a third power that would undermine the conditions outlined by the protocol, at least not without "mutual consent."[49]

Allen's view resonated with officials in Washington all the way up at the top of the State Department. Curiously, the existing scholarship on why the US government supported Japan's imperial expansion does not give much weight to the agreements Korea and Japan made at the beginning of the war, long before Taft and Katsura met in Tokyo. While the aging John Hay, who had begun his career in Washington as Abraham Lincoln's secretary in 1861, left behind few records of his views on Korea, Elihu Root, who succeeded him as secretary of state in July 1905, made clear in his official communications that Korea had already become, in effect, a protectorate of Japan in 1904. Root had served as secretary of war during the Philippine-American War and stepped down a few days before the beginning of the Russo-Japanese War to practice law. But as his public reading of Roosevelt's message on US-Cuba relations demonstrated, he remained an important voice in defense of imperialism even as a public citizen. In fact, when he became secretary of state, Root conceptualized Japan's relationship with Korea the same way he thought of the US relationship with Cuba. A month after Korea and Japan signed the Treaty of November 17, 1905, Korea's minister to France, Min Yŏng-ch'an, arrived in Washington to tell Root that Emperor Kojong did not consent to the signing of the treaty and that Korea's foreign minister only signed it due to Japan's threat of violence. Root replied that, regardless of what happened during the signing of the "latest treaty," the treaty represented only "a slight advance upon the relations of control" already established by the two protocols Korea voluntarily signed with Japan in 1904. In his view, Korea had given Japan "such extensive control over her affairs and put herself so completely under the protection of the Government of Japan" with these protocols that the November 1905 treaty merely made Korea's protectorate status official.[50]

In addition to the February 1904 protocol, the State Department paid close attention to the second protocol, signed in August 1904, that enabled Japan to assign two foreign advisers, one to the Korean Finance Ministry and the other to the Foreign Ministry. For both positions, Japan selected two men US diplomats knew well. The US minister to Japan, Lloyd Griscom, emphasized to John Hay that the Japanese adviser to the Korean Ministry of Finance, Megata Tanetarō, was "a graduate of Harvard University."[51] When Durham White Stevens was named the adviser to the Korean Foreign Ministry, Allen admitted to Rockhill that he had "liked the idea all along." Allen saw much in Stevens, who had first arrived in Japan in 1873 as a legation secretary and, like the minister himself, became an employee of a foreign government through decades of friendship, serving as a counsellor to the Japanese legation in Washington. Once in Korea, Stevens saw eye to eye with Allen on many matters. Stevens considered Allen and his wife his "only personal friends" in Korea, a country he described as a "mephitic atmosphere" run by "rascals."[52]

Indeed, the reason why Kennan's article had striking similarities with Allen's private statements was that Stevens essentially told the journalist what Allen had shared with him. Stevens described the country he had known little about prior to his appointment in 1904 as showing an "inability to regenerate [it]self" ever since the "murder of the queen." The emperor was "weak [and] incapable." In explaining the emperor's weakness, Stevens told a story that was noticeably similar to what Allen had recounted when he failed to get the emperor to open Ŭiju. "[W]hen you go to the Emperor [and] ask to get something done," Stevens told Kennan, "he agrees with you as to the necessity for it, says certainly it shall be done [and] publicly order[s] the ministers or a minister to do it, at the same time he tells ministers privately that if they do it they'll lose their heads. There[fore] they all resign." Kennan slightly modified these observations and published them as part of his articles in *Outlook*. Upon receiving copies of these articles, Stevens circulated them in the Japanese Foreign Ministry and praised the journalist for his "impartiality and fairness."[53]

After the US legation withdrew in late November 1905 in recognition of the protectorate treaty, Allen revealed his true opinion of Korea to one of his closest Korean friends, Vice Minister of Foreign Affairs Yun Ch'i-ho. In a letter that described Kennan's article as "most abominable" and explained the reason for his own dismissal as "being too pro Korean," Allen frankly told Yun that the Japanese protectorate of Korea "may all be for the best." "Now, under the regime," Allen attempted to comfort Yun, "it is to be expected that life and property will be safe." "Officials will be given a living salary and the people will be encouraged to better their condition and produce all the land will." Yun agreed, or at least that is what Allen said when he delivered a speech at the Naval War College in 1906. "[W]hat else could have been expected from such a reign of corruption, imbecility and vanity as you and I have known during the past twenty years[?]" Allen quoted Yun.[54]

Privately, however, Yun found the American approval of the protectorate difficult to accept. In his diary he expressed his frustration. "Well, I like the Americans. I loved Dr. Allen," he vented, "But that doesn't blind me to the fact that it was, and is, all nonsense that the investment of the American capital in Korea will secure for us the support of America." In spite of all the concessions granted to the Americans, the United States became the first nation to recognize the protectorate treaty and the first to withdraw its legation from Korea.[55] Yun was well aware of the logic behind the American decision-making. Yet even for him, it was difficult to repress his bitter feelings toward the Americans, who had deemed Korea unable to reform itself and entrusted the Japanese with "regenerating" the Koreans by stripping them of their diplomatic sovereignty and much else.

Surviving the Age of Empires

More than any other Korean of his time, Yun Ch'i-ho was familiar with the way Americans spoke about Korea, both in Seoul and Washington. Yun spoke their language, not just English but the language of imperialism and reform that shaped the American responses to the Japanese protectorate of Korea. Well before coming into regular contact with Allen and Stevens as the vice (and oftentimes acting) minister of foreign affairs, Yun had spent years in the United States studying the very set of ideas that had inspired Roosevelt's generation to build an extensive overseas American empire, ideas that would naturally roll off his own pen.

Born in 1865 as the eldest son of a military official in Korea, Yun was forced to learn, from his adolescence, how to survive the ubiquitous tides of imperialism. His first encounter with imperial aggression was with Japan, which used gunboat diplomacy to open Korea to international trade in 1876. In 1881, Yun became one of the promising students selected by the Korean government to study in Japan how the neighboring country had modernized its military and economy. While studying there, he met Lucius Foote, who was on his way to becoming the first US minister to Korea in 1883. After returning to Korea with Foote, he learned the workings of American diplomacy as a translator and secretary in the US legation in Seoul. Like Allen's, Yun's life was forever changed by the Kapsin Coup of 1884, leading to a decade spent in exile. He had been associated with the leaders of the coup, whom he had known from his days in Japan. When Foote left Korea in early 1885, Yun followed him, eventually ending up at the Anglo-Chinese College, an American missionary school in Shanghai, with Foote's assistance. During his three years in China, he became the first Korean converted to Methodism, and he performed so well in his studies that the head of the school eventually sent him to study in the United States from 1888 to 1893.[56]

The university education Yun received was not simply on Christianity but on the providential right of the strong nations such as the United States to subjugate the nations "unfit" for self-government. Yun was exposed early to Josiah Strong's *Our Country* (1885), an immensely popular tract auguring the coming supremacy of the Anglo-Saxon race around the world. He became so affected by the prevalent imperialist ideas that, in late 1889, he began to repeat the imperialist ideas himself: "When a nation is unfit to govern herself," he jotted down in his diary, "it is better for her to be governed and protected and taught by a more enlightened and stronger people until she is able to be independent." Two years later, using examples of the British conquest of India and the American treatment of "the Negro and the Indian," Yun expressed his faith in Western empires' mission to change the world. "The ultimate betterment of the whole race is [the] end of Providence," he declared in a statement strongly resonant of Strong's. "The follies and crimes committed by the strong against the weak in training the latter for self[-]government ought to be looked at as necessary evils unavoidable in such a gigantic work."[57]

Yet Yun did not take the imperialist ideas of conquest uncritically. He could not overlook how Western empires, especially the United States, behaved in contradiction of their professed "philanthropy and civilization and morality and liberty." It was "foolish" to be deceived by the "boastful pretensions" of Americans who spoke of the equality of men, when this doctrine of equality was obviously only applicable to white Americans. "The persecution of the Chinese in the West, the treatment of the Negro in the South, and the dealing with the Indian by the whole nation," Yun observed in 1890, were "fair commentaries on the bragged about 'American doctrine' of the 'inalienable right[s] of man.' "[58]

Yun's writings about these three groups—the Chinese, the African Americans, and the Native Americans—provide a glimpse of the way in which he placed importance in the agency of the nonwhite peoples in surviving the world of empires. Even as he criticized the United States, Yun did not defend the Chinese laborers who, in his estimation, were a "hard element to be assimilated." He supported the American restriction of Chinese laborers, as he believed that it would save China from having its name "daily soiled" by "miserable coolies."[59] To be sure, he was fond of Chinese Christian converts, and he even married a Chinese woman named Laura Ma, whom he met while teaching in Shanghai in 1894. Yet he had little sympathy for the Chinese in general. When the Chinese Boxers attacked missionaries and converts with hopes of driving out Western influence from their country, Yun later scorned the anti-imperialist movement for demonstrating what he called the Chinese people's "aversion to improvement."[60]

By contrast, Yun was impressed by the way African Americans embraced Christianity and attempted to remake themselves through education. Yun first became interested in African Americans upon hearing a Vanderbilt classmate say that he would "sooner pull down his church than to admit a colored member to the congregation." This comment prompted him to embark on an intellectual journey to find out whether this prejudice was "compatible with the boasted civilization, philanthropy, [and] religion" of Americans. To investigate this question, Yun often visited a nearby Black church, went to hear lectures at Fisk University, and befriended a Black man working as a waiter to learn more about the state and local racial segregation regulations known collectively as Jim Crow laws. After moving to Emory College in Georgia, Yun likewise frequented a nearby Black church, closely read Harriet Beecher Stowe's *Uncle Tom's Cabin* (1852), and befriended two formerly enslaved men at a local almshouse where he taught Bible study every Sunday. It was from these two men that he verified the information on slavery he learned from the novel. In each encounter with African Americans, Yun became more convinced of their humanity and determination for upward social mobility.[61]

For Native Americans, however, Yun had very little sympathy. In his diary he recounted only one encounter with Native Americans, in Vancouver, on his way back to Shanghai following the five years of American education. During this trip Yun witnessed Native Americans at train stations and remarked that they constituted a "sad and somewhat contemptible sight": "sad because of their past history, but contemptible because of their inability to improve their condition." Echoing the Social Darwinist dictum "survival of the fittest," Yun declared that a "race that fails, from voluntary laziness and ignorance, to avail itself of the advantages of civilization brought so close to its reach isn't worth-while to live." His contempt for Native Americans matched that of many US policymakers like Theodore Roosevelt who relied on racist ideas about Indigenous people to strip them of property, separate children from their parents, and force the younger generation to attend federal boarding schools in the name of "assimilation."[62]

Where, then, did Koreans stand in this struggle for survival? As a student, Yun was not sure, but he was not pessimistic about the future. He thought that Koreans had not yet received a "fair chance" to prove their "fitness." He believed that establishing "an intelligent and manly ministry" would "awaken the slumbering faculties" of his countrymen. He therefore made it his duty to do his part in "making them fit to live."[63]

Yet because of his association with the Kapsin Coup, Yun remained exiled during his postgraduate years teaching at his alma mater in Shanghai for two years. When a group of Korean reformers established a new cabinet with the support of the Japanese army, Yun returned to his country in May 1895 to take the position of the vice minister of education and ten days later the vice minister of foreign affairs.[64] But even as a cabinet member, he remained unable to realize his dream. After the Japanese assassinated the Korean queen and the king fled to the Russian legation, the cabinet collapsed. Only after the king left the Russian legation and declared himself an emperor did Yun get a true opportunity to re-shape his country. Along with several key reformers from the collapsed cabinet and an organizer of the Kapsin Coup, Yun became a leader of the Independence Club (Tongnip hyŏphoe), which sought complete national independence by de-manding that the Korean government stop granting foreign concessions. Just as important, the Independence Club sought unprecedented political partici-pation of the Korean people by asking the government to convert the largely nonfunctional Privy Council into a national assembly consisting of two different types of representatives, one chosen by the emperor and the other elected by the members of the club.[65] The emperor initially assented to this idea of a national assembly, but on the day of the planned election, he changed his mind, and the police arrested 340 members of the Independence Club. Yun was exiled to serve as a local director general (*kamni*) and district governor (*kunsu*) in northern Korea. "While it is by the grace of international jealousies that the nominal inde-pendence and integrity of Korea are kept on their legs," Yun lamented in a letter to his mentor at the Anglo-Chinese College in 1902, "it is by the same grace that Korea's reformation and regeneration are so hopeless."[66]

With the beginning of the Russo-Japanese War, however, Yun was suddenly called up to the Korean cabinet in March 1904 as vice minister of foreign af-fairs. It is not clear if his father, Yun Ung-nyŏl, who had been promoted to min-ister of war the previous month, had anything to do with this appointment. Yun Ch'i-ho was excited to return to Seoul. He was encouraged by Japan's

Fig. 1.2 Vice Minister of Foreign Affairs Yun Ch'i-ho standing behind his father, Minister of War Yun Ung-nyŏl, and his four children, 1904. Underwood & Underwood. Library of Congress Prints and Photographs Division, LC-DIG-stereo-1s32318.

promise, as made explicit in the February protocol, to advise Koreans on administrative reforms. Yet once he began working in the Ministry of Foreign Affairs, he quickly realized that the so-called advice for "improvement," far from persuading the emperor to introduce the much-needed reforms, ended up mostly serving Japan's own interests. Two months after the protocol was signed, Yun observed that the Japanese had only accomplished "peremptory occupation of strategic points all over the country," demanded extension of "fishing concessions," and recommended and supported "notorious rascals" for various cabinet positions.[67]

Nothing infuriated Yun more than the plan to grant a Japanese syndicate the right of leasing "wastelands" with the alleged goal of development. While Horace Allen explained to John Hay that this plan would plant trees on "barren hills" and improve the "vacant lands" with a system of irrigation, Yun believed that the scheme, which proposed to lease the lands for fifty years, would allow the Japanese to "swallow" Korea "in one mouthful." A brainchild of Nagamori Tokichirō, the former minister of finance, this plan sought to solve the problem of population increase and rural poverty in Japan by subleasing Korean lands to Japanese emigrants, who would produce food for the people back home.[68] From Yun's perspective, it revealed Japan's true plans for Korea. "The Japanese professing to be fighting for the welfare of Korea don't even disguise their well-known intention and policy of making Koreans their slaves," he criticized them in his diary. In another comparison, Yun wondered if Japan would reduce Koreans to the "condition of an American Indian on [a] reservation."[69]

Yun believed the Koreans avoided the fate of Native Americans for the time being. Due to popular protests, the Nagamori plan was aborted in the summer of 1904. But the Japanese government pressured the Korean government to sign another protocol in August 1904, yet again in the name of reform. Yun was particularly bitter about this protocol because his superior, the minister of foreign affairs, filed for a leave of absence just in time for the signing event. As the acting minister and, by order of the Korean cabinet, Yun reluctantly signed the document that he described as "derogatory to the dignity of Korean independence."[70] The protocol required the Korean Ministry of Foreign Affairs and the Ministry of Finance to hire foreign advisers, and it prohibited the Korean government from entering into treaties with foreign powers or granting concessions without previous consultation with the Japanese government.

When Durham White Stevens arrived as the adviser to the Ministry of Foreign Affairs, Yun was initially skeptical but eventually became fond of the American. He was particularly impressed by how Stevens strove to make an American company "disgorge some of the extraordinary privileges [it had acquired] through bribery and intrigue in their contracts for water works, electric plants, and for a mine." In his eyes, Stevens was slowly undoing Allen's concession diplomacy, a development that Allen attributed to Japanese "instigations."[71]

Yet not even Japan's hiring of Stevens could convince Yun that the Japanese had a genuine interest in helping Koreans. After his trip to Hawai'i, where he spent the final months of the Russo-Japanese War, Yun was sure that Koreans would have to struggle against the Japanese to survive. The original purpose of this trip was to deal with his depression. When Yun's wife died suddenly in early 1905 from an ectopic pregnancy, Allen arranged for her burial in the foreign cemetery alongside Americans, and Stevens recommended to the Korean emperor that he send Yun on an investigative trip to clear his mind.[72] The emperor approved this plan, as he needed someone to go inspect the conditions of Korean laborers abroad. Earlier in the year, the Korean government had temporarily suspended all overseas labor migration after receiving reports that Korean laborers recruited to Mexico were working under inhumane conditions. When Yun stopped by Japan on his way to Hawai'i, he learned that the Japanese government planned to permanently prohibit Korean migration to the US territory so that they could not undercut Japanese laborers' demands for higher wages. Yun then became determined to transform the Korean immigrants into respectable members of the American empire. He believed that this was the only way to convince the American government that it should continue accepting the Korean working class who were moving to the islands in search of economic opportunities. He also hoped that this would disprove Americans' lowly view of Korea.[73]

In Hawai'i, Yun preached to approximately five thousand Korean workers across thirty-two plantations, encouraging them to stop gambling, go to church, and teach their "more ignorant brethren in the plantations, the habit of industriousness, of thriftiness, of cleanliness and of steadiness." It paralleled the campaign of the Japanese diplomats and immigrant elites who, in an effort to blunt anti-Japanese racism, endeavored to reform the working-class immigrants in line with the tenets of white Progressivism. Because Korean immigrants were more vulnerable to exclusion and anti-Asian violence without the support of a strong home government such as Japan's, Yun believed that they must work particularly hard to survive in Hawai'i. Between the American and Japanese empires, he augured, unreformed Koreans could face the fate of the native Hawai'ians who, in his view, had been seemingly wiped off their own land.[74]

But what about the Koreans back home? Yun was forced to address this question on the transoceanic voyage from Hawai'i to Japan when he encountered, by great coincidence, the prominent American politician William Jennings Bryan. Bryan asked Yun what Koreans thought about the terms of the peace negotiated by the president the previous month. Yun believed that it would be impolitic to honestly respond to Bryan about how he felt about US support for Japan, so he just replied, "the weak nations of the earth have to take things as they come and not as they like."[75] Yun correctly predicted that Bryan would see Korea no differently than did other Americans. After touring Japan, the Democratic leader spent several days in Korea, where Yun translated his speech at the Seoul YMCA. Bryan then wrote an article for the *Washington Post* reminiscent of George Kennan's articles in the *Outlook*, pointing out the "foul odors" of the open sewers and the corruption of the Korean government. He also suggested that the Japanese, through the terms of the protectorate, might be able to "purif[y]" the government and work toward the "advancement of the Korean people."[76]

Even as Yun accepted the fact that Korea would in effect lose its sovereignty by becoming a Japanese protectorate, he refused to acquiesce to the changes. In his diary, he began to express some signs of resistance, if not resentment toward Japan and the United States. As a student, he had written that the "follies and crimes committed by the strong against the weak in training the latter for self[-]government ought to be looked at as necessary evils." Yet once Korea became the subject of such "training," he became much more critical of the "strong" nations that allegedly carried out God's plan. "Korea was made to enable Japanese to practice the meanness they have learned from their American and European teachers," he vented in October 1905. Under the guise of providing reform and tutelage, Japanese imperialists were following the examples in "Hawai'i, Cuba and the Transva[a]l Republic" to exploit Korea's land and labor and join the circle of great world powers at the expense of the Koreans.[77]

The public reaction to the protectorate treaty was overwhelmingly negative in Korea. Particularly important in galvanizing the people to action was the Seoul-based newspaper *Hwangsŏng Shinmun*. Its articles openly criticized Japan, and it was particularly angry at Japan's first prime minister (1885–1887), Itō Hirobumi, who had visited Korea at the beginning of the Russo-Japanese War and had secured the Korean government's cooperation with a promise of Korea's continued self-rule. The editors of *Hwangsŏng Shinmun* initially supported Japan, even urging Korean officials to work with their Japanese counterparts so that Korea, Japan, and China could form an alliance against Russia. But like Yun, the editors were quickly disillusioned by Japan's unfulfilled promise of reform. In response to the news of the protectorate treaty, *Hwangsŏng Shinmun* decried Itō, who had returned to Korea to complete the treaty, for betraying his original promise. Japan, in turn, incarcerated the author of the editorial, Chang Chi-yŏn, and censored the newspaper.[78]

Yun remained publicly silent. But once it was announced that the US legation would withdraw, he divulged his true feelings to Durham White Stevens. Japan, he contended, had shown little interest in reforming Korea. In addition to exacerbating the "corruption and bribery" within the Korean government, the Japanese government showed its true colors by allowing its "surplus coolies" to "pour into Korea" while simultaneously seeking to prohibit Korean immigration to the United States, in "grudge [of] the few miserable dollars which the Korean laborers may pick up" in the cane fields. Why should Koreans believe in Japan's promise when the Japanese settlers "grab everything in sight" and "cuss the Koreans as ingrates and savages for not being grateful"?[79]

Yun did not record in his diary how Stevens responded. But Stevens was already aware of this problem. In fact, many Americans—from journalists to diplomats, all the way up to President Theodore Roosevelt—became aware of the failed promise of Japan's "reform" on the eve of the signing of the official protectorate treaty on November 17, 1905. The Americans did not decide to endorse Japan's declaration of a protectorate over Korea based on any proof of Japanese reform efforts. Instead, they decided to welcome the Japanese protectorate in spite of the uncertainties about Japan's capacity as a "civilizing" power.

The Problem of Japanese Settlers in Korea

Well before Yun confronted Stevens about Japanese exploitation, Theodore Roosevelt and the American public had become aware of the problem. In a widely reported meeting in the summer of 1905, Roosevelt granted an audience to a Korean pastor from Hawaiʻi named P. K. Yoon and a Korean student named Syngman Rhee, who had been a member of Yun's Independence Club. According to the *New York Sun*, which reported on the Koreans' journey from Hawaiʻi to New York, Yoon hoped to ensure through the terms of the peace that Japan would give "assurance" of Japanese withdrawal after a period of occupation, just as "the United States gave to Cuba."[80]

But the letter they presented to Roosevelt asked for something different. Written on behalf of the "common people of Korea," it asked for immediate US intervention against Japan in Korea. When the war began, Yoon and Rhee explained, Koreans had "fully expected that Japan would introduce reforms into the [Korean] administration along the line of the modern civilization of Europe and America." But to their "disappointment and regret," the Japanese government had not done a "single thing in the way of improving the condition of the Korean people." It had only turned loose "several thousand rough and disorderly men of her nationals" in Korea who exploited the opportunity for their own interests. Strategically couched in the prevalent language of Progressivism, Yoon and Rhee asked for American intervention against a people who had broken the promise of reform. They asked the president for "a square deal" in international relations as in domestic politics.[81] Although the letter never had much effect beyond generating short-lived publicity, in large part due to the refusal of the Korean legation in Washington to submit it as a message to the US State Department, the issue of Japanese colonial exploitation only became more prominent in Washington upon the end of the Russo-Japanese War.[82]

Exposing the problem of Japanese colonialism to the American public was none other than George Kennan, whose view of the Japanese empire had changed significantly since his first visit of Korea in 1904. In the summer of 1905, Kennan returned to Korea on a journalistic assignment for *Outlook* to investigate Japan's "capacity for leadership," as seen in its "experiment" to "uplift and civilize the degenerate nation" of Korea. Lawrence Abbott, the president of the Outlook Company, approved this project with the prediction that the postwar "reconstruction period" would be of "deeper interest to thinking people than the war itself."[83] The results of Kennan's trip, however, were disappointing.

Kennan highlighted three ways in which the Japanese imperialists had failed to live up to Americans' expectations. The first was that the Japanese had done nothing in "weeding out corrupt ministers" or "making a vigorous effort to improve Korean administration." Contrary to the promises made in the protocol of February 1904, Japan had not done much in the way of reform. Instead of appointing "a capable and absolutely incorruptible Korean statesman—a man like Yun-Chi-Ho [*sic*]" (whom Kennan probably met at the 1904 reception for foreign correspondents held at the emperor's palace), the Japanese had appointed to the cabinet Korean politicians they could easily influence.[84] Since the beginning of the war, Japan's favorite member of the cabinet, Yi Chi-yong, had been appointed, in succession, the minister of justice, the acting minister of foreign affairs, the minister of agriculture, the minister of home affairs, and the minister of education, all within the span of nineteen months.[85] The Korean cabinet was still in a state of chaos a year and a half after the February 1904 protocol was signed.

The second subject of Kennan's criticism was the Nagamori plan. This "scheme for the reclamation and utilization of unoccupied and uncultivated land," Kennan concluded, only exacerbated Korean "hostility to the Japanese." The plan, according to Kennan, was as corrupt and counterproductive as the idea of the US government granting the railroad tycoon E. H. Harriman or the oil tycoon John D. Rockefeller—well-known symbols of corporate monopoly— "a fifty-year right to reclaim and utilize all the unoccupied and uncultivated land" in the Philippines. This was not reform. It was understandable that the Koreans distrusted the Japanese, for planning something similar in the Philippines would have led the Filipinos to see the American colonization as nothing but "a policy of wholesale exploitation and confiscation."[86]

Finally, Kennan condemned the Japanese settlers, who seemed to regard the rights of the Koreans as some Americans regarded the "rights of the Indians." With the protection of their own military, many Japanese civilians were violently confiscating Korean property. The Japanese government, Kennan argued, should have kept its civilians at home until the Korean administration was improved, so that there would have been a state mechanism to settle the disputes between the "horde of more or less unscrupulous immigrants" from Japan and the "hostile native population."[87]

Kennan's assessment of the Japanese activities in Korea was remarkably similar to Yun's. But Yun was not the source of this information. It was an American missionary named Homer Hulbert. When the Japanese gained influence over the administration of Korea during the war, Hulbert was cautiously optimistic that Japan would be able to rise as a progressive empire akin to the United States. Even at the beginning of 1905, he was still "waiting to see" what Japan would do "to establish the independence and autonomy of Korea in any such sense as America established that of Cuba." But by the time Kennan arrived to interview foreign residents in Korea, Hulbert was just as critical of the Japanese government as he was of the Korean government. Kennan's diary entries reveal that Hulbert was the one who informed him of the Japanese appointment of corrupt Korean ministers, the Nagamori plan, and the activities of the Japanese settlers. It was because of his disillusionment with Japan that, in November 1905, the missionary traveled to Washington with a letter from the Korean emperor appealing for US intervention, a letter that the US State Department refused to consider.[88]

It is important to note that Hulbert was not exactly an anti-imperialist but an opponent of what he considered the worst forms of imperialism, as his response to Kaneko Kentarō illustrates. In the wake of the Treaty of Portsmouth, Kaneko gave an interview to American newspapers in which he declared that the "great political question" of the twentieth century was colonization and that Japan was studying what the United States was doing in the Philippines. Never mind the fact that Japan had declared a protectorate over Korea; Hulbert took offense at Kaneko's suggestion of the similarities. He argued that the work of the United States in the Philippines did not indicate "any desire to colonize those islands." Although the Philippines was a colony, Hulbert believed that the American imperial project in the islands did not deserve the epithet of "colonization." Unlike Japan in Korea, the United States never had plans to send a large number of settlers to the Philippines. As evinced by the "enormous number of teachers sent there," Hulbert argued, the United States aimed to lead the Filipinos to "develop the resources of their land themselves."[89]

US diplomats found Hulbert irritating, but they agreed with his assessment that Japan had failed to live up to its promise. The most vocal State Department critic of the Japanese settlers was Willard Straight, who had come to Korea as a war correspondent but eventually became a vice consul there in 1905. Like many Americans, Straight was initially excited by the prospect of Japanese victory and the protectorate of Korea. When he first arrived, he described the February 1904 protocol as an arrangement that would enforce reforms "in a manner even more aggressively paternal than that which we assumed toward Cuba at the close of the Spanish War." Under Japanese control, he predicted, the "old corruption and extortion" in Korea would cease and the Korean people would become "industrious and prosperous as they are on the sugar plantations of Hawaii."[90] Yet by the time he became vice consul, his opinion of the Japanese in Korea, and in fact Japan itself, had completely changed. "Come to Korea, and see the rapacity of his minions where there is no one to interfere," he wrote a friend in the United States. In Korea one would see "the real yellow man." "Not the pleasant fellow you met at Harvard, not the very likeable one I knew in Tokyo, in the Foreign Office, but the real Jap. The kind there are pretty nearly thirty nine millions of."[91]

Straight's superior, Edwin Morgan, did not describe the situation in such colorful language, but he did advise Elihu Root that the Japanese settler question demanded attention at the highest level of the US government. Morgan reported to Washington in October 1905 that the attitude of foreigners in Korea, especially the missionaries, had changed over the past year due to the "insolence of the coolie class." The Japanese regarded the Koreans as a "weak and inferior race, incapable of reforming or defending themselves," Morgan explained. And the Japanese who had come to Korea to "seek their fortune" "readily resort[ed] to violence in their treatment of a people whom they respect as little as they fear."

Morgan also cautioned that the Japanese elites were "utilizing" the Ilchinhoe, a populist Korean organization that aimed to radically reform the country through collaboration with the Japanese, to "secure an appearance of popular support" for the protectorate treaty.[92]

Roosevelt learned about this problem from the US minister in Tokyo, Lloyd Griscom, who had hosted the president's daughter Alice twice that year, once on her way to tour the Philippines and again after her visit to Korea, where she even dined with the emperor. "As conquerors," Griscom explained to the president in a private, confidential letter, the Japanese civilians were "very different from the disciplined Japanese Army." They were the "scum" of Japan. They were in Korea to "get all there is to be got." The activities of the Japanese settlers made Griscom reconsider the American policy toward the Japanese in Korea. "I think we ought to throw our whole moral weight onto the scales to prevent the Japanese from abusing the Koreans," Griscom wrote. "The Koreans don't deserve much good treatment but we should try to prevent the Japanese from going too far."[93]

Following Griscom's advice, Roosevelt directly communicated his concerns regarding the Japanese settlers in Korea during a White House meeting with Japan's minister in Washington Takahira Kogorō.[94] It is possible that Roosevelt's view of the Korean situation was colored by how negatively the Japanese people reacted to the terms of the peace he helped broker. Although the president believed that Japan received what it deserved from the Treaty of Portsmouth, numerous Japanese politicians, journalists, artisans, and factory workers were disgruntled that, despite being victorious, Japan received no indemnity from Russia to cover the cost of the war. They did not agree with the Katsura cabinet's decision to end the war at the earliest opportunity to stop the bleeding (over 80,000 members of the Imperial Japanese Army died, with the "successful" campaign to seize Port Arthur resulting in a casualty rate of 46% and a death rate of 11.5%).[95] Over three days, popular unrest centering on Hibiya Park in Tokyo resulted in the deaths of seventeen people and destruction of fifteen streetcars and some 70 percent of small neighborhood police stations. Politicians such as Katō Takaaki, who had served as Japan's minister to England and a minister of foreign affairs in a previous cabinet, used this as an opportunity to demand the resignation of the Katsura administration. In addition to public disorder, Katō blamed the Katsura cabinet for failing to gain the entirety of the Sakhalin Island, which would have allowed the Japanese empire to expand further north.[96] Roosevelt was of course unhappy to hear this news. Days after Griscom mailed his letter about Japanese settlers in Korea, the president wrote Lyman Abbott, *Outlook*'s editor in chief, criticizing Japanese protestors as well as George Kennan, who portrayed the protesters in a sympathetic light.[97] By the time Roosevelt spoke with Takahira about Korea at the White House, the president's enthusiasm for Japan had considerably subsided.

The records of the Japanese legation in Korea show that Roosevelt's words exerted tremendous influence, trickling down all the way to Japanese consuls in Korea. Soon after Roosevelt met with the Japanese minister in Washington, the Japanese minister in Seoul, Hayashi Gonsuke, received a telegram from Prime Minister Katsura informing him of the meeting between the president and Takahira. The prime minister explained that Roosevelt mentioned the "cruelty" of the "lower-class" Japanese in Korea and that Japanese officials should do all they can to provide a "just rule" and prevent antagonizing the Koreans. Hayashi replied that Roosevelt's advice was worthy of "serious consideration." He contacted all consuls to use the police to make the Koreans feel that the Japanese government was giving the Koreans and Japanese "equal protection."[98] This was in stark contrast to how the Katsura administration had responded to criticism within Japan. When the socialist pacifist *Heimin Shinbun* (The Commoner's Newspaper) carried articles and editorials that named the war "robbery" and the Nagamori plan "exploitation," the Japanese government silenced it by shutting down the paper and incarcerating its editor.[99] But when the president of the United States expressed his concerns about the behavior of Japanese settlers in Korea, Japanese politicians and diplomats decided to do all they could to address them.

The news of Hayashi's instruction to Japanese consuls reached Roosevelt's minister in Seoul Edwin Morgan, who, only a week before he closed the legation, reported to Washington that the matter was settled. He received assurance from the newly installed Resident General Itō Hirobumi that Japanese officials would punish their own countrymen who had been found "guilty of improper conduct" in Korea. When Morgan was in transit to his next diplomatic assignment—as US minister to Cuba—he gave an interview with American newspapers saying that Korea under the Japanese would have a "better government than it has ever had."[100]

What is interesting about Roosevelt's decision, though, is that in his conversation with Takahira he did not criticize the Japanese but seemingly sympathized with them. Drawing a comparison with the Philippines, Roosevelt explained that controlling the civilian settlers was a problem common in imperial projects. According to Takahira, the president explained that when the Americans first occupied the Philippines, the US colonial government had to "reprimand" the "lower-class" Americans for their attitude toward the native people, and that it was possible that Japan was experiencing something very similar in Korea.[101] Overcoming this difficulty was part of Japan's, as well as America's, own development as progressive empires, and the president believed that both the United States and Japan would eventually improve their own methods of colonial administration.

Roosevelt's logic was strikingly consistent with that of Americans who watched Japan's imperialism at work in Korea. When Durham White Stevens, who was generally positive about Kennan's articles, took issue with the journalist's portrayal of the Nagamori plan, he told Kennan that Americans should condone the Japanese usurpation of Korean land because Americans had done "something of the same sort in the Philippines." Indeed, as much as Kennan criticized the Japanese, he stopped short of calling for US intervention. "When a new and undeveloped country is suddenly thrown open to business enterprise, it is likely to be invaded first by speculators, exploiters, and adventurers," Kennan explained to readers of *Outlook*. "Such has been the case in some of our own colonial dependencies, and such was the case in Korea."[102]

Yet Kennan did not justify Japanese rule out of self-deprecation. He was confident about the future. Echoing Stevens, Kennan declared that Japan would "learn how to govern in Korea just as we are learning how to govern in the Philippines—by example and practice."[103] In the decades to follow, many Americans would look upon the Japanese control of Korea with sympathy, often overlooking the actual experiences of the subjugated peoples, with their eyes focused on whether the nonwhite colonizers would, in the end, showcase the "civilizing" capacity long assumed to be an exclusive trait of the "white" races.

By the time Japan and Korea officially signed the protectorate treaty, much of the enthusiasm for Japan at the beginning of the Russo-Japanese War had tapered off. The whole world found out that Japan possessed the might to defeat a European empire, but Roosevelt never got answers to his questions about Japan's ability to turn the Yellow Sea into its own Caribbean, whether its leaders had the capacity to restrain their desires for the conquest of the weak and war against the strong. Yet Americans confidently believed that Japan would emerge as a partner in the Pacific, and, for the next three decades, they would continue to justify Japanese control of Korea through a comparative mode of imperial argument, declaring that both the United States and Japan would emerge as progressive empires through reform, uplift, and tutelage.

Americans' confident outlook willfully ignored the actual experiences of the Koreans, Filipinos, Cubans, and others living under the two empires' colonial and semi-colonial rules. No matter how "progressive" the imperialists believed themselves to be, both American and Japanese empires inevitably brought violence and suffering to the vast majority of the populations they allegedly sought to reform, perhaps with the exception of the opportunistic elites who took advantage of foreign invasions to secure their own interests. Yet there was no uniform response among those who resented imperial expansion. While radicals

took up arms against empires, moderates and conservatives chose to resist not
by demanding the end of imperialism but by pressuring empires to live up to
their promise of reform. This was not the result of their naiveté. Many subjugated
peoples, like Yun Ch'i-ho, believed that a world without empires remained too
distant a future. Therefore, they worked to ameliorate the severity of imperial
exploitation in their immediate surroundings and prepare themselves toward
the eventual goal of self-government within a world of empires. Ironically, many
of these people would attempt to prove their capacity for self-government by
reforming themselves in the image of the world's colonizers.

Between Empire and Exclusion

*The Professional Class at the Helm of Anti-Japanese Politics,
1905–1915*

In spring 1905, when Japan appeared close to winning the Russo-Japanese War,
Theodore Roosevelt received some disconcerting news from California. The
state legislature had passed a resolution demanding that the federal government
"limit and diminish" the immigration of Japanese laborers to the United States.
In private, Roosevelt called the California politicians "idiots." It made little
sense to him that they thought it was a good time to provoke an empire that had
demonstrated its military might on the world's stage.[1]

Yet these "idiots" proved difficult to ignore. Roosevelt eventually devised a
policy to reduce Japanese immigration. Why he did so has been subject to various interpretations that, with few exceptions, share a common assumption,
that the president pursued this policy in order to prevent domestic racism
from causing international complications. According to existing narratives, the
Roosevelt administration recognized that it could not disabuse Californians
of their racial prejudice, so it negotiated an immigration restriction agreement
with the Japanese Foreign Ministry to stop the nativist movement from further
provoking the Asian empire and jeopardizing American economic and security
interests across the Pacific.[2]

But what if it was international relations that created a problem for Roosevelt's
domestic agenda? After all, well before the Russo-Japanese War, his administration began planning for a comprehensive immigration reform. Roosevelt became president because William McKinley was assassinated by a US-born Polish
American anarchist. In response, the Rough Rider induced Congress to pass the
Immigration Act of 1903 to prohibit "the insane, the impoverished, prostitutes,
and anarchists" from entering the United States. In 1904, when Congress sent
him a bill to extend the Chinese Exclusion Law indefinitely, without negotiating

The Allure of Empire. Chris Suh, Oxford University Press. © Oxford University Press 2023.
DOI: 10.1093/oso/9780197631614.003.0003

the terms of exclusion with the Chinese government as the United States had done since 1882, Roosevelt signed it without a blink of an eye. Before his administration began negotiating Japanese immigration restriction, Roosevelt signed the Immigration Act of 1907 that denied entry to people with mental and physical disabilities. The Act also created the US Congress Joint Immigration Commission, better known as the Dillingham Commission, which conducted a large-scale study of various immigrant groups so that the federal government could use the findings to reshape the racial and ethnic composition of the US body politic.[3]

From this perspective, the American restriction of Japanese immigrants stands out because the executive branch went to great lengths to take care of this issue on its own rather than working with the legislative branch to meet its goal. Against nativist organizations' demands, the US government refused to expand the Chinese Exclusion law to cover the Japanese. Instead, it entered into what became known as the "Gentlemen's Agreement" with a willing Japanese government that promised to restrict the outmigration of its laborers bound for the United States. As subjects of an imperial partner, Japanese immigrants avoided the treatment of other Asian people under federal jurisdiction.

This was not the case under state jurisdiction. After the Gentlemen's Agreement went into effect, the California state legislature deliberated over anti-Japanese bills at every one of its biennial sessions through 1913, when it passed the Alien Land Act. The resulting law prohibited Japanese immigrants from purchasing agricultural property, and, symbolically, it grouped them with other Asian immigrants as "aliens ineligible to citizenship." Thus the Act, which was instituted against the wishes of the newly inaugurated president Woodrow Wilson, represented the victory of California's state government over the US federal government, as well as the vindication of the state's exclusionists who had long maintained that Japanese and Chinese immigrants must be treated the same. Even if Japanese immigrants could not be excluded at the border like their Chinese counterparts, the Californians reasoned, those already in the United States would be treated no differently from other Asians, at least within their own state.

This chapter explains how the inter-imperial relationship shaped US federal immigration policy toward Japan, and how the local nativists in California changed the lives of Japanese immigrants already in the United States. On the surface, California's institution of the Alien Land Law in 1913 appeared to be the culmination of a single anti-Japanese movement that began during the Russo-Japanese War.[4] In reality there were multiple anti-Japanese movements, some of which conflicted with one another. The most successful movement was led by a group of lawyers, journalists, and other white-collar professionals who sought to protect the white working class from Japanese immigrants but who were nevertheless distrustful of the very people they sought to protect. Many of these professionals were members of the Lincoln-Roosevelt League, a Republican club that emerged to purge California of the political influence of big businesses. The League played a pivotal role in the creation of the Progressive Party, which would nominate Roosevelt for the presidential election of 1912 to compete against the Republican William Howard Taft and the Democrat Woodrow Wilson.[5] In fact, after corresponding with the California Progressives for years, Roosevelt privately came to support the Alien Land Act. He no longer saw the California politicians as "idiots."

The Lincoln-Roosevelt League succeeded where other nativist organizations failed because the professional class was able to fit its anti-Japanese messages seamlessly into the broader Progressive Era conversations about "social politics," conversations about how to promote the public good in a society that had been badly damaged by decades of unbridled capitalism.[6] To members of the Lincoln-Roosevelt League, the Alien Land Law mattered primarily because it was a preventive measure against the formation of Japanese land and labor monopolies that, in their view, would create various social problems including poverty, political corruption, and what they called "race suicide," the decline of the white race.

Against the East Coast elites who criticized them as parochial racists undermining the nation's cordial relations with Japan, Californians attempted to enlist national support by describing the anti-Japanese movement in terms they would understand—as a movement to prevent the race, labor, and land conditions existing in Hawai'i and the American South from being replicated on the Pacific Coast. Comparing Japanese immigrants with African Americans said a lot more about the nativists than the two minority populations. Many white supremacists in the South complained that this comparison was overblown. Nevertheless, by 1913, members of the Lincoln-Roosevelt League convinced many Americans outside their state that the Japanese problem was not just a local and an international issue but also a national one.

Yet in an unexpected turn of events, the very group of Californians who led the campaign for the Alien Land Act prevented additional anti-Japanese bills from being considered in the state legislature after instituting the law. The outbreak of the Great War in 1914 caused European markets to decline and made US trade with Asia, especially Japan, more important. The beginning of the war also coincided with the completion of the Panama Canal, and Californians capitalized on the fact that San Francisco was chosen to host the Panama-Pacific International Exposition in 1915 to celebrate the opening of this new gateway to the Pacific.

Meanwhile, in Washington, DC, the Wilson administration continued to uphold the Gentlemen's Agreement. When Congress passed the Immigration Act of 1917, which reduced immigration from Europe by requiring literacy tests and prohibited immigration from almost the entirety of Asia by creating the "Asiatic Barred Zone," it made sure to leave Japan out of this zone. Federal policymakers refused to group the Japanese together with various Asian colonial subjects of Britain, France, and the Netherlands as well as the already-excluded Chinese.

Japanese immigrants navigated through this shifting terrain of international relations and domestic politics to make California their home. In their political battles against the state's nativist campaigns, Japanese immigrant elites made many accommodations to meet the demands of the white American reformers who led the Lincoln-Roosevelt League, emphasizing their ethnic difference from the Chinese and even policing the "immoral" behavior of the working-class Japanese. Yet no matter how much they reshaped their own image and behavior to meet white reformers' expectations, they saw a drastic decline in their opportunities for social inclusion and material prosperity, a decline that was halted only by a catastrophic world war that paused the white rage against the Japanese immigrants in the United States.

"Gentlemen" and "Coolies"

When Roosevelt first heard of the Californians' demands for Japanese exclusion during the Russo-Japanese War, he was appalled by the Californians' refusal, or perhaps their inability, to see the difference between the Chinese and the Japanese. "I am utterly disgusted at the manifestations which have begun to appear on the Pacific slope in favor of excluding the Japanese exactly as the Chinese are excluded," he vented to Senator Henry Cabot Lodge, a prominent Republican imperialist serving on the Senate Committee on Immigration. As he told John Hay, it was "nonsense" to speak of the Japanese and Chinese as the "same race."[7]

Extending the Chinese immigration restrictions to the Japanese appeared all the more impractical given how much difficulty the Roosevelt administration had the previous year. In April 1904, Congress made an unprecedented move of making the Chinese Exclusion Act permanent. The original act, passed in 1882 to prohibit all immigration of Chinese laborers, was intended to last ten years but was renewed in 1892 and again in 1902. When Congress renewed the Exclusion Act for the second time, it made explicit that the law would be only "enacted, extended, and continued so far as the same are not inconsistent with treaty obligation." Yet two years later, in 1904, Congress decided to eliminate this clause and make renewal unnecessary. The Chinese government was upset by American treatment of officials and diplomats attending the St. Louis World's Fair, and it demanded a new treaty that would better protect the exempt classes—government officials, teachers, students, merchants, and travelers—from harassment and mistreatment upon arrival. But Congress, emboldened by the declining international stature of the Qing dynasty following the Boxer Rebellion, decided that it would exclude Chinese people however it wished, and as long as it wished, without considering the views of the Chinese government.[8]

Roosevelt swiftly signed the exclusion act when it arrived at his desk, but he underestimated its effect. In December 1904, the Chinese government revoked a key concession it had granted to the American China Development Company, which had been contracted to construct a railway from Guangzhou to Hankou. In the summer of 1905, Roosevelt successfully convinced the Chinese government to reach a financial settlement with the American company for the loss of concession. By then, however, Chinese merchants had begun a coordinated boycott of American exports in Shanghai, Guangzhou, Fuzhou, Singapore, Thailand, and Japan. They hoped to use the US commercial interests as a bargaining chip to modify the terms of the exclusion, in particular its treatment of the exempt classes.[9]

The boycott posed the greatest threat to the American business community. Following the end of the Russo-Japanese War, Roosevelt attempted to convince members of Congress, especially those representing the American South, to protect the Chinese exempt classes. Speaking in Atlanta, during his tour of the South in October 1905, Roosevelt implored Southerners to assist him in showing "every courtesy and consideration and every encouragement to all Chinese who are not of the laboring class," so that American cotton producers would not lose their greatest export market in China.[10]

Roosevelt built on this speech to declare in his State of the Union address two months later that Chinese of the exempt classes should be treated "on precisely the same footing" as the students, businessmen, and officials from European nations. This was a remarkable statement for someone with such a low opinion of the Chinese. Regardless of one's national origin, he suggested, a foreigner's class status was what merited one's entry to the United States. He argued that the United States should reframe its laws and treaties so that the exempt classes would not have to prove their worth upon arrival. Rather than considering all Chinese as "coolies" until proven otherwise, Roosevelt suggested, all Chinese arriving in the United States should be considered as admissible until proven otherwise.[11]

The sincerity of Roosevelt's remarks went unproven. By the time he made this statement, the boycott movement was already dwindling in China, except in Guangzhou. The Chinese government, concerned that the merchants were undermining the power of Chinese officials, began suppressing the boycott movement. But the final blow to the movement was dealt by the massive earthquake in April that destroyed much of San Francisco, including its Chinatown.

Chinatown had been the movement's most important overseas source of financial support, and its destruction evaporated the remittances sent back to China. The United States no longer had the incentive to modify the terms of Chinese Exclusion.[12]

To Roosevelt's great irritation, the San Francisco earthquake also led to a resurgence of the anti-Japanese movement in the city. In its immediate aftermath, white residents boycotted Japanese-owned businesses, and mobs violently assaulted dozens of Japanese residents. Most controversially, the San Francisco Board of Education used the destruction of various school buildings as an excuse to justify the segregation of Japanese and Korean students from white students. It ordered these students to attend the "Oriental Public School," where Chinese students already had been studying in a racially segregated environment since 1885. According to Secretary of Labor and Commerce Victor Metcalf, who had been dispatched to San Francisco by Roosevelt to investigate the situation in 1906, the school board's decision "was undoubtedly largely influenced by the activity of the Japanese and Korean Exclusion League."[13]

Founded in May 1905, the Japanese and Korean Exclusion League aimed to extend the Chinese Exclusion Act to the two ethnic groups, essentially in an effort to relegate the Japanese to the status of the already excluded and segregated Chinese. Headed by Olaf Tveitmoe, the Norwegian-born editor of the San Francisco Building Trades Council's newspaper, *Organized Labor*, the League did not exercise the level of influence that Metcalf imagined. Yet it was true that the school board, which was composed of mostly the mayor's personal associates, stood together with the League for segregation. Two days before Christmas, Mayor Eugene Schmitz attended a mass meeting organized by the League to denounce Roosevelt's State of the Union address.[14]

In his address, Roosevelt had described the school board's segregation order as a "wicked absurdity." Even "first-class colleges" in the United States admitted Japanese students. In fact, Roosevelt contended, Japan won in a single generation the right to stand next to the "foremost and most enlightened peoples of Europe and America," and not just with its military might. The Japanese people had sent through the Red Cross $100,000 to San Francisco's relief. Furthermore, given that securing American commercial interests in East Asia depended on maintaining cordial relations with Japan, the treatment of the Japanese in the United States directly affected the United States' development as a Pacific nation. Yet he did not conclude by calling for amicable relations. Roosevelt recommended that Congress pass an act "specifically providing for the naturalization of Japanese who come here intending to become American citizens."[15]

Roosevelt's speech outraged the exclusionist leaders. "Make American citizens out of Japs!" Tveitmoe exploded in *Organized Labor*. In his mind Roosevelt was not the man that many thought he was. The Rough Rider was "afraid" of the Japanese navy, "love[d]" the Japanese more than Americans, and worked to appease the "Wall Street money-lenders" who had invested heavily in Japan. Horrified by the prospect that the United States might place the Japanese in the "same class" with Europeans, Tveitmoe defiantly declared in his editorial, "Understand, Mr. President, that America is the White Men's Country, and that it is going to remain so."[16]

While local newspapers in San Francisco joined Tveitmoe in denouncing the president, Roosevelt enjoyed public support from the East Coast establishment. In particular, the periodicals that celebrated Japan's victory against Russia and its conquest of Korea praised the president's message. As it did during the Russo-Japanese War, the *Outlook* dispatched George Kennan to the scene of action, where the journalist conducted extensive interviews and concluded that labor unions fanned racial animosity. There was a "rapidly growing conviction" in the Atlantic states that maintenance of cordial relations with Japan and China was critical to the United States' commercial development, the editors of *Outlook* argued. They claimed that San Franciscans' fear of Japanese invasion was misplaced, for Japanese migration to Korea and Manchuria made the prospect of invasion of California "improbable." In fact, this is exactly what Kennan and Durham White Stevens claimed when they were in Korea. The *Independent* magazine went one step further by welcoming the president's proposal to extend US citizenship to the Japanese.[17]

Privately, Roosevelt expressed a more qualified view of Japanese immigration. The proposal to extend naturalization rights to the Japanese, as revealed by the State Department documents, was a bargaining chip that US diplomats considered using to secure Japan's voluntary restriction of emigration bound for the United States. A week before the State of the Union, the president met with the Japanese minister in Washington Takahira Kōgorō and told him that it was necessary to prevent "all immigration of Japanese laboring men—that is, of the coolie class—into the United States." Days after the address, Roosevelt confessed to British Foreign Secretary Edward Grey that he thought laborers in San Francisco were right in objecting to the immigration of Japanese laborers. Even "the Japs would object at least as much to any great number of foreigners coming into their territory and exercising industrial pressure as competitors with their people." So instead of quashing his opposition, the president invited the San Francisco Board of Education and the mayor to meet him at the White House.[18]

At this crucial juncture, Roosevelt consulted David Starr Jordan, president of Stanford University. Because Jordan was a well-known anti-imperialist who opposed the American colonization of the Philippines, this move might seem illogical. Yet Jordan personally admired the imperialist president, so much so that he named two fish he discovered in Hawai'i after Roosevelt.[19] Like Roosevelt,

Jordan celebrated the Japanese victory over Russia, regarded Japan as a modern nation distinguished from China, and believed that the Japanese deserved to be treated no differently from the Europeans. "The most unpatriotic type of man in America is the man who believes that this is a 'white man's country,' and that all men not white are niggers without rights, personal or international," Jordan publicly argued in the wake of the California legislature and the Exclusion League's demand for extension of the Chinese Exclusion Act to the Japanese. Ever since his first trip to Japan in 1900, Jordan the eugenicist hoped to confirm his hunch that Japanese people were "white." But he could never arrive at certainty. While he was able to state with confidence that the Ainu people (indigenous to Japan's northern islands) belonged to a "branch of the Aryan race," he could only conjecture that the Yamato people "too were Aryans allied to the Greeks." He ultimately conceded to a Japanese authority on the subject who argued the relationship between the Yamato and Aryans remained "not conclusive."[20]

Regardless of the question of whether the Japanese were white, Roosevelt listened to Jordan because he provided him with a solution to restrict Japanese immigration without relegating Japan to the second tier of the hierarchy beneath European powers. Japan was a "nation of the first class," Jordan wrote in response to Roosevelt's State of the Union, "and we can no more turn the Chinese exclusion act against her than we could against France or Germany." Yet given that Japanese laborers' "scale of living" was low, Jordan explained in January 1907, labor unions still had some "valid objections." The solution, then, was specifically excluding Japanese laborers, and laborers only. Japan should not be insulted by the proposal, he insisted. "Man for man, the Japanese of each class is fairly the equal of the European immigrant," he explained. "But the unskilled roustabouts from Osaka and Okayama are the least desirable of the Japanese, just as the victims of the sweatshop and the beef-packing jungles are the lowest of Europeans."[21]

Roosevelt was entirely in agreement. He also regarded the immigration matter primarily as a class issue that could be resolved by removing laborers from binational relations. "If a hundred thousand American miners streamed into Sa[k]halin, or if we sent great masses of Americans into Japan proper," he replied to Jordan, "Japan would be quite right in keeping them out." Reminding Jordan that a nation should be a "gentleman" in dealing with other nations, Roosevelt expressed that he earnestly hoped Japan would propose a "reciprocal arrangement" by which American and Japanese laborers would be kept out of each other's countries.[22]

Such was the thought process behind the decision to formulate what would become known as the Gentlemen's Agreement, a series of notes the State Department exchanged with the Japanese Foreign Ministry during 1907 and

1908 to restrict the migration of Japanese laborers to the United States. The agreement convinced the school board to rescind the segregation order in San Francisco and, more important, enabled the Japanese Foreign Ministry to self-regulate the emigration of Japanese laborers by refusing to issue passports to working-class Japanese bound for the United States. The practical result differed little from the Chinese Exclusion Act: both stopped working-class immigration to the United States, and both allowed the exempt classes (including merchants, students, teachers, and tourists) to continue entering the United States.[23] But from the perspective of the Japanese government, the US government conveyed respect to Japan by refusing to resort to a unilateral action of Congress. Immigration restriction was usually a matter of US national sovereignty, but this exceptional case put the power of restriction in the hands of the Japanese government and enabled it to avoid the fate of China, which no longer could negotiate the terms of exclusion with the United States. This arrangement also allowed the Foreign Ministry to police the working-class emigrants whom it saw as an embarrassment to the rising power. What is more, the Foreign Ministry used emigration restriction as a bargaining chip to negotiate for alternative forms of Japanese expansion, especially commercial expansion to the United States.[24] Meanwhile, the Japanese government redirected working-class migration to Korea, where a state-supported emigration company—Tōyō Takushoku Kabushiki Kaisha (Oriental Development Company)—facilitated the growth of Japanese settler communities.[25]

The significance of the decision to rely on a bilateral agreement rather than a unilateral act was not lost on the Japanese and Korean Exclusion League. "Treaty will not exclude," declared Tveitmoe, who demanded "exclusion by Act of Congress." "We will not yield one iota of our rights as a sovereign people, regardless of cost or consequence." The League continued to advocate the abrogation of the Gentlemen's Agreement for years, even though the practice of entering into such an agreement to restrict Japanese immigration became adopted by Canada as well. In 1908 Canada restricted Japanese labor migration to 400 per year through the Hayashi–Lemieux Agreement.[26]

Roosevelt remained committed to the Gentlemen's Agreement through the end of his presidency in 1909, but privately he began to express doubts about the very policy he had set up. A month before he left the White House, Roosevelt confided to a personal friend in California that he "did not clearly see this at the outset," but came to see that "the Japanese should, as a race, be excluded from becoming permanent inhabitants of our territory." "This is the wise and proper policy," he explained. "It is the policy we already pursue as regards the Chinese."[27]

Such a drastic turn suggests that Roosevelt came around to the position of the Exclusion League. In fact, one Japanese immigrant observer believed that the president "accepted, willingly or unwillingly, the main contention of the Exclusion League after he conferred with the California delegates" at the White House.[28] Yet even if he did accept this contention, it was not because he respected the Exclusion League. The League, in spite of all the effort it put into anti-Japanese campaigns, never got to exercise the kind of power it wished for, because white elites and professionals prevented it from shaping policy.

Holding Back the "Hoodlums"

The Japanese and Korean Exclusion League was founded in 1905 with the explicit goal to "mold public sentiment so as to force Congress to exclude all coolie immigrants, no matter where they come from."[29] In subsequent years, the League made significant headway in spreading its messages of hate. But the working-class nativists ultimately failed to shape federal immigration policy, or even the state-level anti-Asian policy, as the class barrier proved too high to overcome.

In its initial years of existence, the League enjoyed strong support from the white working class. In San Francisco, where labor leaders associated with Building Trades Council dominated the municipal government, the League worked easily with local politicians as well as the conservative *San Francisco Chronicle*, which regularly fanned the fear of the "Yellow Peril" with its sensationalist articles on Japanese immigrants. The League also secured a strong ally in Seattle, though the nativists in the Pacific Northwest at this time were primarily concerned about South Asians who entered the United States through Canada. In September 1907 members of the Seattle Exclusion League organized a march against Indian immigrants, mostly Sikhs, in the nearby town of Bellingham, assaulted the immigrants, and destroyed their barracks. When the Indian workers crossed the US-Canada border in search of safety, the Seattle Exclusion League's leader, A. E. Fowler, traveled to Vancouver, where he helped organize another demonstration that turned violent, this time resulting in the destruction of Japanese and Chinese communities. After the Bellingham and Vancouver riots, the Japanese and Korean Exclusion League of San Francisco decided to broaden the scope of its nativism to include "Hindoos" and adopted the name Asiatic Exclusion League to reflect this change.[30] Most significantly, toward the end of Roosevelt's presidency, the Exclusion League gained the support of the American Federation of Labor (AFL), which, at its annual convention in November 1908, resolved to ask Congress to extend Chinese exclusion to other "Asiatics."[31]

But the Exclusion League faced a formidable class barrier in its home state. Tveitmoe frankly declared at the first meeting that the success of its anti-Japanese movement depended on proving that its anti-Asian campaign was not a labor movement but "one in which all classes are interested." They had to prove that the white working class and the professional class had a common interest, a mission that the populist movement of the late nineteenth century had failed to achieve.[32] Like the populists before them, the Exclusion League failed as well.

With hopes of breaking down the class barrier, Tveitmoe's *Organized Labor* often featured experts from the professional class to legitimate his anti-Japanese sentiments. To spread the fear that Japanese immigrants were responsible for bringing infectious diseases like trachoma to San Francisco, he referred to the statements of the Surgeon General of the United States. To claim that Asian immigrants were responsible for spreading the bubonic plague on the West Coast, he extensively quoted a bacteriologist employed by the Oregon State Board of Health.[33] But Tveitmoe's favorite was a former Stanford sociologist named E. A. Ross. When Ross delivered a speech at an anti-Japanese immigration rally held in San Francisco's Metropolitan Temple in 1900, Tveitmoe was convinced he found the primary channel through which the working class could convince other Americans to exclude Japanese immigrants. Ross publicly validated the San Franciscans' fear of Japanese "invasion" by claiming that it was based on the "soundest of economic principles." It was not a matter of race prejudice, Ross argued. "The root of our objection to the Japanese emigrant is not that he is brown," he insisted. "What American labor objects to is exposure to competition with a cheaper man."[34]

Yet this was a disingenuous argument. The rest of Ross's speech showed the economic and racial reasons were one and the same. The issue was not just that competition with the "cheaper man" led to the decline of the American standard of living. It also led to the decline of the white race. Asians, Ross argued, "multiply like rabbits in good times and die like flies when there is drought." If they were allowed to put their roots down in the United States, so the logic went, the Japanese would eventually outnumber white Americans. Hence, Ross argued that Japanese immigration was not just a problem for the white working class. "To let this go on, to let the American be driven by coolie competition, to check the American birth-rate in order that the Japanese birth-rate not be checked," Ross predicted, "is to reverse the current of progress, to commit race suicide."[35]

This was the first time Ross mentioned "race suicide," a phrase that would define his long career as one of the most distinguished sociologists of his generation.[36] Yet in 1900 Ross lost his faculty position at Stanford for making these remarks. Jane Stanford, the university's cofounder then serving as a one-person board of trustees, believed that Ross's speech was nothing more than a "repetition of Kearneyism." To her there was little difference between his words and those of labor leader Denis Kearney who, during the long economic depression caused by the Panic of 1873, had galvanized the San Francisco working class by delivering speeches at a vacant lot adjacent to City Hall. Kearney, best known for his infamous slogan "The Chinese Must Go," specifically blamed railroad companies for employing low-wage "coolies" to drive up profit and impoverish the white working class. For Stanford, whose husband had been the president of the Central Pacific Railroad and the Southern Pacific Company, it was difficult not to take Kearney's attacks personally. At the height of his popularity, Kearney threatened, "I will give Central Pacific just three months to discharge their Chinamen, and if that is not done Stanford and his crowd will have to take the consequences."[37] Consequently, Stanford dismissed Ross over the protest of David Starr Jordan who, in spite of his high regard for the Japanese, publicly defended Ross as "the most effective worker" in the field of social science whose arguments were "scientific and fair."[38]

Given Jordan's support of Ross, it seems ironic that, when the Exclusion League reiterated Ross's "cheaper man" speech as its rallying cry five years later, the organization only received condescension from Stanford's president. The "hoodlums" of San Francisco, Jordan said in response to the 1906 anti-Japanese incidents in San Francisco, did nothing but jeopardize the amicable relations between the United States and Japan, which were hoping to come to a bilateral agreement that would limit "coolie" immigration. Tveitmoe read Jordan's use of the word *hoodlum* as a reference to himself. In response he declared, perhaps too frankly, that this was "more than a labor problem—it is a race problem." But Jordan's view was espoused by the professional class at large. In July 1907, *Harper's Magazine* ran a cover that illustrated Uncle Sam restraining the "hoodlums" in the American West to prevent war with Japan, where Emperor Meiji restrained the "jingos" for the same reason. Notably, Ross himself remained distant from the League. Although Tveitmoe asked Ross to meet with him, there is no evidence that Ross answered the call.[39]

Yet class was not the only factor that bothered certain Americans about Tveitmoe. To Jordan, he represented what Ross infamously identified as the "lesser breeds" of European immigrants. Although Ross believed that not all Europeans were of the same "stock" (for example, he believed Scandinavians were superior to the Irish and Italians), Jordan despised all "proletariat of Europe." As he declared in his commencement speech at Stanford in 1907, they represented the "beaten men of the beaten races" who caused the degeneration of the American body politic. Even their American-born children created problems. "The problem of the European proletariat does not disappear with the loss of the immigrant's language or the change of his dress," Jordan warned. "If his stock is bad, it stays bad; still worse, if it mixes with the stock of freeborn races, for it leaves upon this stock a mulatto taint." Jordan did not hold back his criticism of the city's mayor, Eugene Schmitz, a child of Irish and German immigrants, in the commencement speech and in his letter to Roosevelt. In anticipation of Roosevelt's meeting with Schmitz and his associates at the White

House, Jordan warned the president that these "foreigners" were holding San Francisco "by the throat."[40]

In fact, when Roosevelt hosted the San Francisco delegation to solve the school board segregation order in February 1907, the Japanese immigration question intersected with congressional debates about the need for restriction of European immigration. In addition to negotiating the Gentlemen's Agreement, the Roosevelt administration put pressure on Congress to pass a deadlocked immigration bill that aimed to exclude various "undesirable" people who, as the Boston Brahmins of the Immigration Restriction League described them, menaced the American citizenship. These included prostitutes, "imbeciles," and aliens who contributed to a "detriment of labor conditions" in the United States.[41] During the debates, Roosevelt had his ally and a prominent member of the Immigration Restriction League, Senator Henry Cabot Lodge of Massachusetts, introduce an amendment to the immigration bill so that the president could prohibit foreigners' entry into the continental United States if their passports had been issued for travel to Canada, Mexico, or Hawai'i. Although the amendment did not explicitly mention any nationality, it was clearly aimed at Japanese and Korean laborers entering the continental United States through these three channels. Less than a month after Congress passed what became the Immigration Act of 1907, Roosevelt signed Executive Order 589 specifically to prohibit Japanese and Korean laborers bound for Canada, Mexico, and Hawai'i from entering the continental United States.[42]

Before its passage, however, the immigration bill faced stiff opposition in Congress from its Southern members. Why should the president be allowed to "dicker" with San Francisco's labor unions for a political bargain? asked Democratic senator Benjamin "Pitchfork Ben" Tillman of South Carolina, who led the opposition. The Lodge amendment, however, was not the focal point of the debate. Rather, it was the bill's exclusion of "contract laborers" recruited from abroad, including Europe. From Tillman's perspective, the bill allowed the interests of the Pacific Coast states to outweigh that of the South. To be sure, he said, every Southerner sympathized with the West Coast's hope to exclude the "undesirable" Japanese. Yet unlike the West, the South was "languishing" due to "want of labor." States such as South Carolina, which had recently recruited laborers from Belgium, needed access to the European labor market. Upon being asked by Republican senators why the South faced a labor shortage, Tillman's supporter, Senator Augustus Bacon of Georgia, declared that racial prejudice "naturally keeps white men away" from the South because it made them believe they would have to compete with "negroes." Overseas labor recruiting was necessary because white men did not come to the South "voluntarily." "You have to go and seek them in order to secure them," Bacon argued.[43]

The Immigration Act of 1907, signed into law in February, disappointed the Southern politicians and the Exclusion League alike. But to Tveitmoe, the absence of Japanese exclusion in the Immigration Act was not the most pressing concern. It was his deteriorating power base in San Francisco. In May, Mayor Schmitz was convicted by the grand jury of extorting money from French restaurants in the city's Tenderloin District, though his crimes reached far beyond the businesses that served as fronts for a prostitution ring. Through the Union Labor Party's attorney, Abe Ruef, Schmitz and his board of supervisors had received large sums of money from the Pacific Gas and Electric Company, the Home Telephone Company, the United Railroads, and the Bay Cities Water Company, all in exchange for contracts that clearly undermined the city's public interest. After Schmitz was removed from office, Tveitmoe was publicly humiliated and scrutinized as well. Local newspapers published his mugshots from a Minnesota prison where he had spent eight months for forgery decades earlier and tarnished the name of the Exclusion League. In December 1912, Tveitmoe was convicted and sentenced to six years in prison for his involvement in the bombing of the anti-union *Los Angeles Times*'s building that killed twenty-one employees.[44]

But the year 1913 began auspiciously for the Exclusion League. Tveitmoe posted bail thanks to his friendship with P. H. McCarthy, who had become mayor of San Francisco in 1910. More important, the California state legislature passed a bill that would prohibit Japanese and other "aliens ineligible to citizenship" from purchasing agricultural land in the state. Although this would not change the flow of Japanese immigration, it would prevent Japanese immigrants already in California from becoming landowners. The Exclusion League declared that its own "eight years' agitation" was finally "bearing fruit."[45]

Organized Labor was mistaken. The state assembly passed the bill in spite of, not because of, the Exclusion League. "I desire to say that in touch with myself are at least fifteen members who treated the communication from the Japanese Exclusion League [*sic*] the same as I did, dropped in unanswered and unpledged into the waste paper basket," a state senator said before he voted for the passage of the Alien Land Law. The law's official name was the Webb-Heney Act.[46] Francis Heney was the special prosecutor in the case against Schmitz and his political boss, Abe Ruef. Heney could not finish prosecuting them because he was shot, in the courtroom, by a juror he dismissed. The prosecutor who then took over the case and sent Schmitz and Ruef to jail was Hiram Johnson who, as governor of California, signed the Alien Land bill. In fact, it was in part due to his celebrity created by the graft case that Johnson was elected governor in 1910. Thus, it was not surprising that Johnson, even as he signed the Webb-Heney bill into law, repeatedly ignored the letters from the Asiatic Exclusion League.[47] Far from being the fruition of the Exclusion League's labor, the Alien Land Law was the culmination of a separate anti-Japanese movement led by the professional class, whose interest in legislating against the Japanese dated back to Roosevelt's presidency.

To Prevent the "Hawaiianization" of California

In 1909, California journalist Chester Rowell published a provocatively titled article "Orientophobia" in the prominent national muckraking magazine *Collier's*. Rowell was a founding member of the Lincoln-Roosevelt League, organized in 1907 to cleanse California politics of the monopolizing influence of the Southern Pacific Railroad Company. As the club's name suggested, the League aimed to destroy this special interest by reforming California according to Abraham Lincoln's famous dictum, a government "of the people, by the people, for the people." To create such a government, the Lincoln-Roosevelt League supported Theodore Roosevelt's domestic reform projects, from regulation of the market and conservation of forests to the protection of women and children. Many Lincoln-Roosevelt League members, such as Francis Heney and Hiram Johnson, rose to fame by attacking political machines that monopolized municipal and state politics. In "Orientophobia," Rowell described the anti-Japanese movement as a logical extension of this antimonopoly campaign. He identified "short-sighted capitalists" who brought "Oriental" immigrants as enemies of the people. The problem was not simply California's. If the United States would "repeat in California the Hawaiian experiment," he warned, the "frontier of the white man's world" would retreat from the Pacific Coast across the Rockies.[48]

The Asiatic Exclusion League also pointed to Hawai'i as an example of what they were working to prevent in California. "Unless relief is obtained by legislative action," it argued, "two or three decades hence [we] will see California as much Japanized [*sic*] as is Hawaii to-day."[49] Yet the Lincoln-Roosevelt League used Hawai'i as a model to avoid much more effectively by neatly folding its anti-Japanese movement into the broader antimonopoly movement with which many Americans elsewhere sympathized. To them, Hawai'i was a case study of what happened to a society when the local government did not take initiative to check the power of businesses. The islands' "Big Five" sugar companies controlled the land, machinery, and labor, to the point that Hawai'i had become an undemocratic society where the great majority of its inhabitants were non-white laborers who could not vote in elections.

To Northern Californians, "Orientophobia" was only the latest iteration of the arguments that Rowell had been making in the local press since the turn of the century. Illinoisian Rowell had moved to California in 1898 to become an editor of his uncle's newspaper, the *Fresno Republican*. After identifying the Japanese as the "New Race Problem" in 1900, possibly in reference to the anti-Japanese rally where Ross galvanized the San Francisco working class, he regularly wrote in the *Fresno Republican* that Hawai'i was a lost cause and that California needed to protect itself from turning into another Hawai'i. "As a business proposition, Japanese are as valuable in California as in Hawaii," he argued in 1905, but "we would rather [see] its resources were twenty years slower in developing, and meantime develop our American civilization than to have a great business boom at once and forever establish a Hawaiian civilization."[50] In his view, the preservation of the white race should always come before the pursuit of profit.

When Roosevelt read Rowell's "Orientophobia" article, the president was so impressed that he sent the author a personal congratulatory note. In fact, Roosevelt himself often referred to Hawai'i as the prime example of American "race suicide," a term he adopted from Ross. In 1903, after reading a report on labor conditions in Hawai'i, Roosevelt told his secretary of agriculture James Wilson that he would like to "discourage by every method the race suicide" that the planter class had caused in Hawai'i by "bringing every kind of Asiatic to help them to make fortunes for a moment and insure the extinguishment of their blood in the future." A month before Taft entered the White House, Roosevelt confessed to a politician in California that he would rather see the sugar plantations in Hawai'i fail than "see them a success at the cost of being tilled by coolie labor."[51] The contrast between his enthusiasm for the Japanese imperial enterprise in East Asia and his apprehension about the increasing Japanese presence in the American territory was hard to miss. As much as he respected Japan, he hoped to limit its activities to its end of the Pacific Ocean. He never wanted the Japanese to migrate across the Pacific at a scale that would change the racial composition of the American body politic.

Though he did little to curb Asian immigration to Hawai'i during his presidency, Roosevelt translated such views into a policy recommendation memo for the incoming secretary of state, Philander Knox, who had served as his attorney general from 1901 to 1904. Due to the "shortsighted greed of the sugar planters and of the great employers," Roosevelt explained to Knox, Hawai'i had already become "an island of coolie-tilled plantations." As a remedy, he recommended that the American government encourage the emigration of Europeans, "no matter of what ancestry," to settle in Hawai'i so that "the islands may be filled with a white population of our general civilization and culture."[52]

Despite the fact that Roosevelt agreed with Rowell's view, he publicly discouraged the passage of the Alien Land bill, proposed by a Lincoln-Roosevelt League member representing Fresno, A. M. Drew, in 1909. It was a matter of practicality. In addition to Drew's land bill, a school segregation bill proposed by Assemblyman Grove L. Johnson from Sacramento greatly bothered Roosevelt. As he declared in his public letter to the speaker of the assembly, Roosevelt believed that such measures would derail the Gentlemen's Agreement, which had proven effective in getting more Japanese to leave the United States than enter the country during the previous six months. In Roosevelt's view the school bill would accomplish "literally nothing whatever" and would only cause "irritation" by combining "the very minimum of efficiency with the maximum of insult."[53] To the outgoing president's relief, the California assembly defeated both the Alien Land bill and the school segregation bill.

The next time the California assembly considered an Alien Land bill, in 1911, Roosevelt had little reason to make a public statement. In 1910 the Lincoln-Roosevelt League had successfully campaigned for the gubernatorial election of Hiram Johnson, son of Grove L. Johnson, and Roosevelt trusted both the new governor in California and his successor in the White House to do the right thing. Putting practicality over ideology, Johnson made sure the Alien Land bill would not pass, for he was asked, in a "strictly confidential" telegram from Taft's secretary of state, Philander Knox, to discourage any public discussion of the bill. Knox explained that the bill would be "most inexpedient and detrimental to the interests of the United States as a whole" since the two nations were in the middle of negotiating the Treaty of Commerce and Navigation.[54] Knox, who had previously worked as a director of the Fifth National Bank of Pittsburgh and a counsel for the Carnegie Steel Company, prioritized international trade and finance above all else, and he made sure that the California land question would not get in the way of completing the new treaty. Soon after the Alien Land bill was defeated, the United States and Japan signed the Treaty of Commerce and Navigation in Washington, in February 1911, to signal a new chapter in their friendly relations.

Roosevelt eventually became displeased with Taft and challenged his successor in the presidential election of 1912 as the candidate for the new Progressive Party, with Hiram Johnson as his running mate. Among the many aspects of Taft's presidency that infuriated Roosevelt was his successor's refusal to include a clause in the Treaty of Commerce and Navigation "reserving our right to exclude by law Japanese laborers." Roosevelt was already concerned by the administration's close relationship with Wall Street. He disliked Taft's "dollar diplomacy," which enabled a group of US banks headed by JP Morgan & Company to enter into a consortium with their British, French, and German counterparts in hopes of jointly financing a loan to China for railroad construction. He also despised Knox's failed plan for the "neutralization" of the railways in Manchuria (which the secretary of state tried to accomplish by asking China to purchase Russia and Japan's railways and then allow the United States and other powers to jointly administer them). But Roosevelt seemed especially concerned that his own handpicked successor prioritized the interests of Wall Street over the interests of the progressives on the West Coast. "[W]hereas our interests in Manchuria are really unimportant," Roosevelt wrote Taft, "our interest in keeping the Japanese out of our own country is vital."[55]

By this time, Roosevelt was no longer optimistic that the Gentlemen's Agreement could forever function as an effective way of restricting Japanese immigration. In his first documented meeting with E. A. Ross, in November 1911, he agreed with the sociologist that the strength of the US Navy was the primary reason why the Japanese government hadn't broken its promise. Roosevelt was greatly irritated by the critics of his naval expansion program, and on the particular day when he met with Ross, it was muckraking journalist Ray Stannard Baker who incurred the Rough Rider's wrath. Best known for his exposé of racial violence in the American South, *Following the Color Line* (1908), Baker had recently toured Hawai'i and written a series of articles about the islands for the *American Magazine*. Although he agreed with Rowell and Roosevelt that the Big Five's monopoly of land, labor, and politics made the islands an example of an undemocratic society, Baker contended that the Gentlemen's Agreement had irritated Japan to the point of possible military retaliation and thus led to US fortification of Hawai'i and Panama.[56] Baker misunderstood the causality of events. With Ross's approval Roosevelt wrote Baker that US militarization in the Pacific was necessary not primarily to defend against Japan's retaliatory attack but to protect the white working class from further Asian immigration. Without military force, Roosevelt explained, the Gentlemen's Agreement would not be able to "stand for five minutes in the face of Japan."[57]

This was an exaggerated claim, but the US Navy did demonstrate its power to Japan after entering into the Gentlemen's Agreement. The navy began preparing War Plan Orange in the summer of 1907 for a possible war with Japan (it also prepared War Plans Red with Britain, Black with Germany, and Brown for a possible uprising in the Philippines). The following summer Roosevelt had sent sixteen US battleships from the Atlantic Fleet, popularly known as the Great White Fleet, on a transpacific tour, stopping by New Zealand, Australia, and the Philippines before arriving in Japan. Rear Admiral Alfred Thayer Mahan, the preeminent American naval strategist of his generation, publicly supported this demonstration of power. It represented the fruition of Mahan's lasting influence on the president, which dated back to the time when Roosevelt served as William McKinley's assistant secretary of the navy.[58]

Simultaneously, the Japanese Navy devised its own plan to deter the US Navy. After Emperor Meiji sanctioned the Imperial National Defense Policy in 1907, Japan's naval officers drafted a building program to attain 70 percent of US naval strength, a percentage that was calculated as sufficient enough to defend Japan since the US fleet was likely to lose some of its fighting power during its journey from Hawai'i to Asia. Japan's minister of navy Saitō Makoto justified his proposal for a naval increase by arguing that, as seen in US interference in Manchuria, the United States had moved far beyond its traditional focus on defending the Western Hemisphere with the Monroe Doctrine.[59]

From the opposite side of the Pacific, many Americans accused Japan, more specifically Japanese immigrants, of threatening the security of the Western Hemisphere. Alarming the nativists was Japanese American elites' attempt to purchase land in Magdalena Bay, located in the Baja California Peninsula, Mexico. In early 1911, the Chartered Company of Lower California, a US company based in Maine, offered Abiko Kyūtarō, the owner of the San Francisco-based newspaper *Nichibei Shinbun*, and Noda Otosaburō, the co-owner of a Monterey Bay–based fishing and canning company, the opportunity to acquire two thousand acres in Magdalena Bay. Various newspapers in the United States sensationalized this development by stoking the popular fear of the "Yellow Peril," with the *New York Times* arguing that this was part of Japan's plan to establish its own naval base within the Western Hemisphere. The land transaction never materialized, but the possibility of a conflict with Japan continued to captivate not only the general public but also the former president. In a letter to Taft, Roosevelt wrote that on the remote chance that "Japan or some other big power were to back Mexico" in a war against the United States, he would like to raise a cavalry similar to the Rough Riders and personally take part in the battles.[60]

Fortunately, this never happened. Neither the immigration question nor the navy question was important in the election of 1912, and neither Roosevelt nor Taft seized on the anti-Japanese sentiment. But the winner of the election, Woodrow Wilson, did. During his campaign in California, the New Jersey governor made a statement, written by former San Francisco mayor James D. Phelan, against the "Chinese and Japanese Coolie immigration." Asians' lower standard of living presented a "serious industrial menace," Wilson's statement read, and something must be done before they "crowd out the white agriculturalist" from the country.[61]

Wilson's victory had little to do with California's anti-Japanese sentiments, but both Roosevelt and Johnson were eager to see whether the first Democrat elected president in twenty years would change the national policy set by his Republican predecessors. When the California assembly met the next time in 1913, the Alien Land bill became Wilson's litmus test. The logic of the bill was the same as before. "The law must be passed ultimately, if California is not to be Hawaiianized," Rowell wrote Johnson. When Johnson signed the bill, against Wilson's public pleas, Roosevelt could not repress his joy. "It seems to me that Wilson made a mighty poor exhibition of himself," he wrote Johnson. "If he was sincere in what he said before the election, then his conduct after [the] election was an outrage; if on the other hand he was sincere in what he did after [the] election, his conduct before [the] election represented a peculiarly offensive and demagogic as well as insincere bid for votes."[62] Either way, Wilson had embarrassed himself in the first months of his presidency.

While partisan politics certainly played a role in California politicians' legislation of the Alien Land Law, it was not the only factor that contributed to their victory. Neither was the desire to prevent the "Hawaiianization of California."[63] In addition, many Californians declared that they were working to prevent the replication of the race and labor conditions in the American South. The comparisons went hand in hand. After all, as Ray Stannard Baker had argued, the problem of the Hawai'ian model of society was that "Sugar is King in Hawaii to a far greater extent than cotton was in the old South." Although Roosevelt did not endorse the Southern comparison, it proved effective in convincing many Americans that Californians were justified in their action against the Japanese. As Rowell warned in "Orientophobia," many Americans believed that preemptive action was necessary to prevent the rise of Japanese communities in California for the Asians, unlike the "negros," would "submit to no imputation of racial inferiority." Indeed, one Japanese man publicly warned in a letter to the *New York World*, republished in the influential African American newspaper the *Boston Guardian*, that "Japanese men are not good-natured black Negroes, glad to smile and laugh at white oppressors."[64]

Yellow Is the New Black?

Like the Hawai'ian comparison, the Black-Japanese comparison was nothing new in 1913, but it became more prominent as Woodrow Wilson became the first president native to the South since the Civil War. When Wilson belatedly dispatched his secretary of state, William Jennings Bryan, in April with hopes of dissuading Californians from instituting the law, it was too late to turn the tide of nativism that justified its logic as a measure to prevent another "race problem" that could be even more difficult to solve than the one in the American South.

No one in California deployed the Black-Japanese comparison more eagerly than Rowell. He had become familiar with the problems of the post-Reconstruction South when he served as a clerk of the House Elections Committee in Washington, DC, before moving to California. Blaming slavery as the origin of Southern problems, he believed that Californians should prevent a repetition of the "blunder" committed by the founding fathers who had allowed Southern planters to acquire labor through the transatlantic slave trade centuries earlier. Because of this blunder, he insisted, there existed a permanent "caste" of Black Americans who created an "incurable" condition in the South. The Pacific Coast, "the ideal region of the world for the small farmer," was facing a similar problem with the rising Japanese population. The class of "free white farm laborers" was already "disappearing," Rowell argued, and if the "policy of *laissez faire*" continued, it would end the project to uplift the white laborers into landowners.[65]

Not all Californians agreed, of course, and the most vocal opponent of the Black-Japanese comparison was David Starr Jordan. Writing in the wake of the Alien Land bill proposed in 1911, Jordan lamented how many "honest men" feared that Japanese immigrants would provoke "racial troubles similar to those which exist in the South." Californians' fear was misguided, he said. Jordan, a eugenicist, believed that the problem of the South had much to do with the racial traits of African Americans themselves. Speaking at a conference held at Clark University in Massachusetts, following a tour of the American South that included a stop at Booker T. Washington's Tuskegee Institute, Jordan argued that a great number of Black Americans were actually "half-white" people who possessed "diverging instincts of two races." Because of this, he suggested, they had not seized the opportunities provided by their US citizenship acquired through the Fourteenth Amendment. Jordan believed that lower-class Japanese would not make good American citizens, either. Yet the Gentlemen's Agreement already prohibited the "rice-field coolie" class from leaving Japan for the United States, so debating that point was moot. No race was "more readily at home in our civilization than the cultivated Japanese," he argued.[66]

Californians were not interested in this argument. Their problem with the Japanese was not that they believed Asians were racially inferior. Most exclusionists saw the Japanese as distinct from other nonwhite peoples. As early as 1900, Rowell argued that Japanese civilization was "absolutely on par with white civilization," and because of this, the United States could not treat the Japanese as "incorrigible outsiders, like the Chinese, nor inferiors like the negroes."[67]

In fact, as a prominent Black newspaper in Los Angeles, *The Liberator*, observed, white Americans in power treated Japanese and Black Americans differently. During the 1906 school board crisis, the Roosevelt administration intervened on behalf of Japanese immigrants who were not US citizens, yet it refused to do the same when Black children were prohibited from attending school with white children, noted *The Liberator*'s editor Jefferson L. Edmonds. During the 1913 Alien Land Act crisis, Edmonds complained that Wilson listened to the Japanese government's pleas while ignoring its own Black population.[68]

African Americans' resentment toward Japanese Americans was clearly visible to W. E. B. Du Bois, who visited California for his first time in the summer of 1913. Du Bois, one of the most vocal African American champions of Japan during the Russo-Japanese War, had left his teaching position at Atlanta University in 1910 to join the National Association for the Advancement of Colored People (NAACP) as its Director of Publicity and Research. In *The*

Fig. 2.1 W. E. B. Du Bois. Photo taken in Boston, Summer 1907, in conjunction with the Third Annual Meeting of Niagara Movement. W. E. B. Du Bois Papers, Robert S. Cox Special Collections and University Archives Research Center, UMass Amherst Libraries.

Crisis, the NAACP's organ he edited, Du Bois reported that the majority of Black Californians had not yet arrived at "their own logical position." In contrast to the "more cultured colored people," he lamented in a speech, working-class African Americans in California were "decidedly against the yellow man." He was so disappointed that he publicly declared that, "at this time," he did not think it was possible for "all the darker peoples" to join forces "against the whites in a world conflict."[69]

One of the Black Americans who had arrived at what Du Bois considered the "logical" position was his rival, Booker T. Washington. In March 1913, the renowned champion of Black industrial education visited the Pacific Northwest. In Seattle, he observed that Black workers in the hotel industry faced stiff competition from Japanese immigrants because the Japanese were "steady, reliable, sober and already on the job." Yet Washington was also unexpectedly presented with a financial gift from the Japanese consul in Seattle for a scholarship at the Tuskegee Institute, where he carried out his vision of racial progress with a curriculum that encouraged Black students to focus on learning industrial skills to improve their economic conditions rather than demanding racial equality, as more radical race leaders like Du Bois did.[70] The financial gift was a fitting tribute to the man who publicly responded to Japan's rise as a great power by writing in his book, *Putting the Most into Life* (1906), "The Japanese race is a convincing example of the respect which the world gives to a race that can put brains and commercial activity into the development of the resources of a country." During his return trip to Alabama, Washington decried the West Coast racism against Japanese immigrants in public forums on multiple occasions. Washington's defense of the Japanese reached a point where Nettie J. Asburry, a corresponding secretary of the Tacoma branch of the NAACP, sent him a letter criticizing his work. "You have noted (and replied to) how the Americans discriminated against the Japanese in the California [A]lien Land Law," she wrote, "Don[']t you think it is about time you lifted your voice in defense of the American Negro?"[71]

The frustration of the Black Americans on the West was not unique. Exclusionists in California were also disgruntled that white Americans outside the Pacific Coast had not taken their side on the Japanese question. This is precisely why they made the Black-Japanese comparison, to draw the sympathy of white Americans from other regions who condoned the Southern repression of African Americans. The executive board of the Asiatic Exclusion League declared, in February 1913, that just as the "Southern man" knew far more about the "negro" than "all the theorists and idealists ever born in Massachusetts," so did the Western man about the "Asiatics." When the state legislature considered the Alien Land bill in 1913, elected officials in California deployed the Black-Japanese comparison as well. US Representative William Kent directly explained to Secretary of State Bryan, who arrived in California with hopes of dissuading Johnson from signing the bill, that the "negro problem" had already proven that crossing "racial lines" resulted in "racial friction." Opponents of Wilson and Bryan were not the only ones deploying this parallel. James D. Phelan, the Democrat who composed Wilson's anti-Asian campaign speech, wrote in the *Independent* that the founding fathers who "originally opposed the introduction of negro laborers took the same ground, that being essentially foreign and unassimilable, the negro would create a race classification, which would be repugnant to American institutions and would destroy the idea of equality."[72]

The Alien Land bill found supporters in the American South, but Southerners thought the comparison showed how little Californians understood the "race problem" on the opposite side of the continent. Senator Tillman, who had already opposed the 1907 Immigration Act because of its refusal to represent the interests of the American South, claimed the economic reason, "That the 'Japs' can outwork you and underlive you," was not the real reason for racial hostility.

Fig. 2.2 William Jennings Bryan, Hiram Johnson, and Robert F. Rae outside the Governor's Mansion in Sacramento during the Alien Land Law controversy in 1913. Library of Congress Prints and Photographs Division, LC-USZ62-78364.

In a letter to Kent, he said that the anti-Japanese argument "ought to rest on its real basis—caste feeling and non-assimilability." Likewise, Clarence Poe, the prominent North Carolinian publisher of *The Progressive Farmer*, argued that Black Americans presented a much more urgent "race problem." Because they were not "handicapped" like Asian immigrants who lacked US citizenship, they were free to "live and work and buy land without let or hindrance," all the while they stood as "Hindrances to White Progress."[73]

Rowell was well aware of the Southern criticism and publicly defended the comparison in the *Fresno Bee*. Arguing against an editorial that appeared in South Carolina, Rowell wrote that the relatively small number of Japanese in California did not mean that white Californians were overreacting. After all, he said, Californians were trying to be proactive rather than reactive to the problem. "The very importance of California's problem is that it is now in a condition in which South Carolina's problem was in the sixteenth century, when it began," he argued. "If Californians do not deal with it now, they, like South Carolinians, will leave a race question which their descendants will have to deal with, and against which they will be helpless."[74]

This argument, however, had little basis in fact. Japanese labor was not cheap. It certainly cost more than enslaved labor. For all the rhetorical appeal E. A. Ross had among exclusionists, he was wrong to claim that the Japanese immigrant was the "cheaper man." As Rowell himself admitted in the *World's Work*, "underbidding" was the "least part of the Japanese problem in California." Statistical studies commissioned by the US government demonstrated that the Japanese brought home more money per capita than any other immigrant group except the English and the Germans. Furthermore, the Japanese showed higher levels of literacy than immigrants from southern Europe and demonstrated their high potential for "assimilation."[75]

What, then, was Rowell's problem with the Japanese laborers? The issue was that the Japanese could "monopolize almost any occupation . . . even without underbidding." According to Rowell, they could consolidate labor monopoly by converting any occupation into a "Jap job [*sic*]" in the West, just as African Americans had converted certain occupations into "niggers' work [*sic*]" in the South. Even if the pay were high for such jobs, he said, white workers would not take these jobs for fear of becoming degraded to the nonwhite laborers' level. This was a serious social problem, Rowell augured, for the unwillingness of the white laborers to enter into agricultural and horticultural sectors in California would enable the Japanese to monopolize those sectors, if not the whole state's economy. Rowell was not alone in expressing his fear. In May 1913, when Johnson was about to sign the bill into law, a man from Long Beach expressed his fear directly to the governor. As Japanese laborers come to dominate agricultural labor, the Californian wrote, the average "white men [would] look upon manual labor with aversion," and soon the whole society would be divided into "a few 'aristocratic land holders[,]' poor white trash[,] and slaves." What was worse, he said, there was the "possibility that the 'Asiatics' might conclude to be the master."[76]

Yet strangely, the Alien Land bill did not aim to break up or prevent the Japanese monopoly of agricultural labor. Instead, it aimed to illegalize Japanese ownership of agricultural property, which Rowell admitted was small in scale. This was not a mistake. During the debates over the bill in the California legislature, it became obvious that Japanese laborers were necessary to sustain the state's agricultural production, just as wealthy landowners had proclaimed. White men were unwilling to do the difficult manual labor that the Japanese were already doing. A California assemblyman named W. C. Wall from San Joaquin, where George Shima, the "Potato King," had built an empire, conceded that white landowners were compelled to hire nonwhite, especially Japanese, laborers because no white workers would work there.[77]

This is why, in its final form, the Alien Land Law contained a clause allowing aliens ineligible to citizenship to lease agricultural land up to three years. It is not clear who exactly slipped in this clause before passage, but the clause outraged many white Californians, including the Asiatic Exclusion League. Olaf Tveitmoe denounced Johnson for enabling a "small group of land owners" to continue profiting at the expense of landless white workers. Hence, the Asiatic Exclusion League resolved to go directly to the people to "prevent the ineffective land bill from finding a place in the statutes of the State of California."[78] By reaching out to the California electorate directly, the Exclusion League hoped to introduce a referendum to prevent the adoption of the Alien Land Law.

But Johnson and other California progressives prevented the question of the law's adoption from going to the people. The truth is, they did not trust the people. As Chester Rowell explained directly to William Jennings Bryan, a referendum would "turn loose every irresponsible agitator in California, and give us two years of unregulated turmoil on the hustings in place of two months of restrained discussion in the legislature." "No man who really wishes an alien land law [would] find a referendum as to this law," declared Hiram Johnson when he signed the law in May, making it effective as of August 10.[79]

In this view, the 1913 Alien Land Law was a largely symbolic gesture toward securing the future of the white race without immediately undermining the agricultural economy dependent on Asian labor. Yet even as a symbol, it mattered a great deal to white Californians. The law put a ceiling on the Japanese farmers' upward social mobility. No matter how hard Japanese immigrants would work and no matter how much capital they would accumulate, they could not attain the goal reserved for white farmers. "[I]f we must have the Japanese," W. C. Wall contended, "we want him as an underling, we do not want him as an equal, because at all times, in my county, it is like attending a masquerade. The Japanese are in our midst and are pretending to be our equal[s] all the time."[80]

Of course, the Japanese, like all other peoples, had no desire to live as underlings. In fact, as many Japanese immigrant elites pointed out, the Alien Land Law would not deter their desire for upward social mobility. In the years following, they demonstrated that they had what it took to be equals and successfully stopped the tide of anti-Japanese legislation in California.

Japanese Americans Respond

A month after the California Alien Land Law went into effect, George Shima sent Chester Rowell a sack of potatoes. Rowell interpreted this as a gesture of appreciation. After all, Shima had been able to purchase a large house in Berkeley overlooking the San Francisco Bay in an all-white neighborhood because Rowell's brother, against local residents' protest, sold it to the Japanese American millionaire. Yet, seen another way, the potatoes appeared to be a reminder that

Japanese Americans would persevere in spite of the legal restriction imposed on them. Although Shima's note did not survive the passage of time, Rowell's reply suggested that the Japanese immigrant millionaire remained confident about the future. "The potatoes will taste equally good whether they came from owned or rented land," Rowell wrote Shima in reply.[81]

Shima wasn't just a rich man. He was the president of the Japanese Association of America and a key member of Issei (first-generation) elites engaged in campaigns to "uplift" working-class Japanese Americans. Since the turn of the century, when the San Francisco municipal government falsely accused the city's Chinese residents of carrying the bubonic plague, Issei elites had engaged in their own version of the progressive movement that emphasized hygiene, industry, and moral virtues. The idea was that, if they could remake the Japanese immigrants to satisfy the expectations of white progressives, white Americans would distinguish them from the Chinese and see them as a "race" worthy of respect. As racist as this campaign was, it had a counterpart within the Chinese elite community, which attempted to distinguish itself from the working-class Chinese. Both elite communities looked down on the same set of "problems" as their white counterparts. In 1911, when the Japanese Association of America inaugurated a statewide moral reform campaign, Shima singled out the Chinese gambling dens as sites that Japanese Americans must avoid in order to "elevate our individual character and our community."[82]

One of the central pillars of the moral reform campaign was the anti-prostitution campaign. Responding to the fact that exclusionists often attacked Japanese and Chinese laborers as "immoral" men who frequented prostitutes, Issei elites and Japanese church women began collaborating as early as the 1890s to deport and discipline prostitutes to create a "respectable" image of the Japanese that appealed to Americans. With the institution of the Gentlemen's Agreement, which prohibited the emigration of laborers from Japan but allowed the Issei men to bring "picture brides" to the United States, the Issei elites and Japanese church women took an expanded role. They mobilized themselves to make sure that these brides, who previously had only interacted with their husbands by photographs and letters that traversed the Pacific, would not "fall" into prostitution upon arrival or elope with other men after getting divorced in the United States.[83] This was a move to dispose exclusionists of their ammunition against Japanese immigrants. After all, for all the disrespect the Exclusion League received from various levels of American society, the organization did successfully bring the existence of Japanese brothels in California to the attention of the Immigration Bureau.[84]

Such efforts to self-police immigrant behavior proved ineffective in blunting the white racism that led to the passage of California's Alien Land Law, which, broadly defining its target as "aliens ineligible to citizenship," refused to distinguish the Japanese from the Chinese. Yet the passage of the law also wrought profound changes in the Issei community as it led to greater cooperation with Japanese elites across the Pacific. The Japanese Association of America received support from Shibusawa Eiichi, the head of the leading Japanese financial-industrial conglomerate, who allowed Issei leaders to use his office in San Francisco as their headquarters. To prepare Japanese "picture brides" for American life, Shibusawa set up in Yokohama a center for emigrant training within his Japan Emigration Society, so that emigrants destined for the United States could be educated in various skills that white progressives valued, such as hygiene, sanitation, child rearing, and proficiency in the English language. During the Alien Land Act crisis in 1913, Shibusawa led a group of businessmen and politicians to form the Japanese-American Friendship Society (Nichibei Dōshikai), which joined a chorus of newspapers and mass rallies to criticize the Japanese cabinet led by Prime Minister Yamamoto Gonnohyōe. The Yamamoto cabinet was preoccupied with a series of political upheavals that followed the passing of Emperor Meiji in the summer of 1912 (the "Taishō political crisis," as it was called in reference to the new emperor's name, was energized by the popular discontent at the continuing rule of the Meiji oligarchy). Distrustful of this cabinet, Shibusawa had the Tokyo Chamber of Commerce dispatch two of his own protégés to San Francisco during the Alien Land bill crisis, and they even got to meet, along with Shima, Secretary of State Bryan in Washington. Their approach was so conciliatory that they accepted anti-Black racism. In their report of the trip, the two Japanese elites appealed to white American sentiments by declaring that "the country that even fought for the negroes cannot deny the admission of the Japanese on mere racial grounds."[85]

More significantly, Issei elites collaborated with the Japanese government through the San Francisco consulate, where Consul Numano Yasutaro provided institutional support to combat anti-Japanese racism. Numano, who took up his post just as the 1913 Alien Land bill was being discussed in the state legislature, had brought with him to California extensive experience in imperial politics. During the Russo-Japanese War, he worked in Korea as an aide to Durham White Stevens. Numano was particularly skilled at surveilling those who challenged Japan's imperial rule. When he was stationed as a consul in Poland in 1909, he submitted reports to Tokyo on anti-Japanese speeches that Homer Hulbert delivered while attending a conference there. Upon arriving in San Francisco, Numano continued to tighten his grasp over Japan's imperial subjects, including the Japanese socialists and Korean immigrants who openly criticized the Japanese empire. When a group of Korean farmers were chased out by a white mob in Hemet, California, Numano and the Japanese Association of Southern California acted quickly to represent Korean immigrants, only to have the Korean National Association balk at the consulate, saying that this was a "purely Korean problem." The Korean National Association was so invested in claiming its own sovereign rights that it rejected Numano's attempt to receive reparations from the US government on behalf of the Korean farmers.[86]

The most visible collaboration between the Issei elites and the Japanese consulate was the publicity campaign coordinated by an agency called the Pacific Press Bureau (PPB). Although it claimed to primarily supply news cables between American and Japanese newspapers, the PPB, as its letterhead made clear, was focused on improving US-Japan relations ahead of the Panama-Pacific International Exposition, scheduled to be held in 1915 in San Francisco in honor of the opening of the Panama Canal. Japan, including Japanese immigrants in the United States, had great success convincing white Americans at the Alaska-Yukon-Pacific Exposition, held in 1909 in Seattle, that cordial bilateral relations would directly contribute to the development of the Pacific Northwest. Japanese diplomats wished to replicate this success in San Francisco. Numano originally wanted to hire a white American to direct the bureau, but he eventually settled on an American-educated Issei named Kiyoshi Karl Kawakami, who would spend the next two decades working as the leading Japanese propagandist in the English language.[87]

Kawakami was the perfect person for the job. Perhaps more than any other Japanese in the United States at the time, he was familiar with the way white Americans, especially experts of "social politics," spoke about the Japanese. Born in 1873, Kawakami initially came to the United States in 1901 to study political economy. As he explained in the *International Socialist Review*, the "Occidentalization" of Japan had brought not only material progress but also social conflict caused by the widening gap between the rich and the poor. With hopes of finding solutions to societal problems, Kawakami converted to Christianity, gave himself a middle name after Karl Marx, joined the first socialist party of Japan, and fled the state's persecution of socialists by leaving to study at the State University of Iowa, where he wrote a master's thesis on the development of political ideas in Japan. He then received a scholarship to study with Richard T. Ely at the University of Wisconsin.[88]

Had he stayed in Wisconsin long enough, he might have crossed paths with E. A. Ross, but Kawakami left graduate school after one year, became disillusioned with socialism, and devoted his career to defending Japan and its immigrants in the United States. After assisting the Japanese government at the 1904 St. Louis World's Fair, he worked as a correspondent for the Japanese newspapers *Tokyo Asahi* and the *Daily Yorodzu*, traveling to New Hampshire to report on the Treaty of Portsmouth. By the end of that year, his focus had shifted from the working class to the Japanese empire and its immigrants, as Kawakami had grown bitter about the racism of the white working class. In the United States, he lamented later, even the socialists were "not true to their professed internationalism."

Fig. 2.3 Newspaper correspondents and artists gathered in Portsmouth for the signing
of the peace treaty to end the Russo-Japanese War in 1905. Kiyoshi Karl Kawakami is
the man with a middle part on the front row, next to the man holding a cat. Library of
Congress Prints and Photographs Division, LC-DIG-ppmsca-08820.

From a small rural town in Illinois where married a white woman named
Mildred Clarke, he wrote article after article on Japan and Japanese immigrants
for widely read journals such as the *North American Review, Independent,* and
Forum. In the *Pacific Monthly,* the same magazine where David Starr Jordan
defended Japanese immigrants by differentiating them from African Americans,
Kawakami defended Japanese imperialists by comparing the Philippines with
Korea. He quoted Roosevelt's 1903 speech in San Francisco that described the
US colonization of the Philippines as "Providential" and argued that the "same
may be said with regard to the Japanese control of Korea."[89]

When Kawakami headed the PPB, he developed a close relationship with
Chester Rowell. This might seem unexpected, but they bonded over the
common assumption that elites from Japan and the United States would serve
as the best bridges of understanding. Rowell saw Kawakami as the exact kind
of Asian that the United States must embrace. In response to Kawakami's letter
recounting his difficulty buying a house in an all-white neighborhood in San
Francisco, Rowell replied that "racial prejudice" was "entirely ridiculous to apply
it to you or to any one of your class." Kawakami agreed. After all, before he took
the job with the PPB, he had written an article that was just as damning of the
Japanese working class as it was of white racists. Upon visiting the Sacramento

Valley in 1913, Kawakami expressed his disappointment that Issei farmers did not live in "houses but huts." He falsely accused them of moving into the "huts vacated by the Chinese" and publicly wished that the Issei had "built more respectable dwellings." As he prepared the PPB for the Panama-Pacific International Exposition, his focus lay on protecting the Japanese elites. "It was unfortunate that the first-class Japanese passengers" arriving in San Francisco were transported to Angel Island, Kawakami wrote in a letter to the *San Francisco Chronicle* that he shared with Rowell. To Kawakami it was outrageous that Japanese elites were subject to physical examination at Angel Island immigration station, "as if they were common immigrants of the laboring class."[90]

The greatest blessing to US-Japan relations during these years was the outbreak of the Great War. As Europe descended into the chaos of war in the summer of 1914, the PPB did not need to work very hard to convince Americans of the importance of Japan's participation in the exposition. "With the temporary suspension of European civilization and industry," Rowell wrote in the *California Outlook*, "the Oriental character and significance of this Exposition become more than ever important." China planned on participating in the exposition and, given that the 1911 Revolution put an end to the Qing dynasty that had ruled China longer than the United States had been a nation, there was great anticipation for the China exhibition. Yet Rowell was more invested in Japan, which had gone through its own transformation with the end of Emperor Meiji's reign and the beginning of Emperor Taishō's in 1912. He singled out Japan's participation as "the key to the whole Oriental significance of the Exposition."[91]

So invested in Japan's participation in the exposition, Rowell and his associates, including Hiram Johnson, made sure that there would be no discussion of anti-Japanese legislation in the California state assembly when it convened for a new session in early 1915. Labor unions, represented by Paul Scharrenberg of the American Seamen's Union, continued to put pressure on the state assembly to eliminate the three-year lease clause from the Alien Land Law. Yet when an assemblyman introduced a bill to do exactly that, it died without a vote. As Rowell requested in the *California Outlook*, the state legislature decided to hold the lease clause question "in abeyance" in light of international developments.[92] Japanese Americans' right to lease land in California would remain unchanged for the rest of the war.

The Great War and Interracial Collaboration

The Panama-Pacific International Exposition opened in February 1915, about seven months after the outbreak of the Great War, with the mayor of San Francisco delivering a speech in front of various Japanese dignitaries to celebrate

Japan's participation. Both American boosters and the Japanese commission wanted to ensure the exposition's success. While the fair officials guaranteed that the welcoming band would not play any offensive music, such as highlights from *The Mikado*, in front of the dignitaries, the Japanese delegation provided a tea room (where Japanese women clad in kimonos served white patrons), a large-sized Buddha statue, replicas of the streets of Tokyo and Kyoto, sumo wrestlers, and a Red Cross exhibit.[93] For the exposition's Japan Day, former president William Howard Taft delivered a speech asking the two nations to "maintain the strongest kind of friendship." In November the seventy-five-year-old Shibusawa Eiichi arrived in San Francisco to visit the exposition. As Kawakami reported in the local Japanese American newspaper *Nichibei Shinbun*, the fact that he came to the United States was "a compliment to America for which he cherishes admiration and affection."[94]

Yet bilateral relations did not develop as smoothly as Shibusawa or Kawakami hoped. This time a problem emerged on the other side of the Pacific. In January 1915 the Japanese minister in Nanjing presented the nascent Republic of China with what came to be known as the Twenty-one Demands. Taking advantage of the world's preoccupation with the war in Europe, Japan had already occupied the German operations in the port of Shandong. In addition to China's recognition of Japanese rights in Shandong and granting of new concessions to Japan in Manchuria and Central China, the Japanese minister demanded, among other things, that the Chinese government accept Japanese advisers for its internal political, military, and economic affairs.[95] To those who had watched Japan's rise as an imperial power during the previous ten years, these latest demands signaled what had happened in Korea during the Russo-Japanese War. In effect, Japan proposed to make China its protectorate.

During the Panama-Pacific International Exposition, it became Kawakami's job as the head of the PPB to publicly defend Japan's actions. Kawakami, who had already declared that "[i]n the whole Orient Japan is the one standard bearer of modernism and liberalism," wrote in *Sunset Magazine* that Japan was simply doing its job to maintain order. Like a "minor" who does not "always like the way his wise and experienced guardian treats him," Kawakami argued, China "misunderstands and dislikes the measures which Japan" provides. The so-called Monroe Doctrine of Japan, he said, had to be more aggressive than what Americans instituted in the Caribbean because the Chinese had "repeatedly invited Western aggression." Rather than closing the "open door," as many warned, Kawakami continued, the policy would stabilize China for European and American access to the market.[96]

Kawakami's argument ran counter to the official US position, especially that of the US minister in China, Paul Reinsch. Reinsch, who had been on the faculty at the University of Wisconsin when Kawakami was there as a student, was far from an anti-imperialist. He was one of the country's leading experts on colonial administration, and he lauded the Japanese during the Russo-Japanese War. Yet Reinsch began to criticize Japan after the war, and by the time he was appointed minister in 1913, he advocated for a stronger American stance toward Japan to ensure the Open Door policy and guarantee China's territorial integrity.[97]

Although Kawakami was teetering on a line between publicity and prop-aganda, his words were strikingly similar to what former president Theodore Roosevelt said upon arriving in San Francisco to celebrate the Panama-Pacific International Exposition. In contrast to Wilson, who merely sent a congrat-ulatory message, Roosevelt was excited to make this an opportunity for him-self. After all, the United States was able to attain its rights to the canal, and the Panama Canal Zone, because he had provided military support to the Panamanian nationalists when they ceded the isthmus from Colombia in 1903. However his views of Japanese immigrants might have changed since his presidency, Roosevelt continued to see China less as a victim of Japanese and European imperialism and more, as he did during the Russo-Japanese War, as a disorderly country that needed outside help. In his speech at the exposition, Roosevelt claimed that China, even after the end of the Qing dynasty, continued to suffer because it had not prepared for war. It had "province after province lopped off her, until one-half of her territory is now under Japanese, Russian, English and French control."[98]

Eyeing the possibility of another presidential run, Roosevelt used the expo-sition as an opportunity to blast his political opponent who, in his words, was "seeking to Chinafy [sic]" the United States by refusing to prepare the country for war. Roosevelt disliked pacifists, but he despised Wilson, who responded to Germany only with words when a German submarine sank the *Lusitania* earlier in May and killed over a thousand passengers, including 128 Americans.[99]

For Kawakami, it was too risky to openly agree with the disgruntled ex-president. By preparing the country for war, Kawakami explained to American readers in the *North American Review*, the US government might possibly identify Japan as its potential enemy on the Pacific. If this were to be the case, Japanese immigrants, like many "hyphenated" Americans, would be vulnerable to another wave of xenophobic attacks. Anti-Japanese movements in California could reemerge with the slightest complication in international relations. After all, as Kawakami reminded readers, Roosevelt had publicly argued in the *Outlook* after leaving the White House that it was America's "first-class fighting navy" that empowered the US government to "enforce" its "right to say what immigrants shall come to our shores."[100]

Fortunately for Japanese immigrants, the Great War did not bring the United States into combat with Japan, and the Gentlemen's Agreement held up well throughout the war. In fact, policymakers in Washington went out of their way

to ensure that the bilateral relationship would not be affected by new immigration laws passed during the war. Most revealing of the State Department's
commitment to this relationship was its intervention during a year-long debate
in Congress about what would become the Immigration Act of 1917, a comprehensive law that aimed to limit wartime immigration, including European
immigration. In addition to expanding the list of unwelcome foreigners to encompass alcoholics, anarchists, and polygamists, the law instituted literacy tests
to exclude those who did not have educational opportunities. It also created a
geographical area called the Asiatic Barred Zone from which the United States
refused to accept immigrants. Originally conceptualized to prohibit the entry of
Britain's colonial subjects in India, the zone covered almost the entirety of the
Asian continent and more, stretching from Afghanistan to Polynesia. But it conspicuously left out not only the US colony in the Philippines (which was under
US jurisdiction) but also Japan and its colonies.[101]

Leaving Japan out of the Asiatic Barred Zone was a deliberate choice. Initially,
the House Committee on Immigration and Naturalization proposed to exclude
"Hindus and persons who can not become eligible, under existing law, to become citizens of the United States by naturalization." But after receiving protest
from the Japanese embassy in Washington, which was well aware that California
prevented Japanese immigrants from purchasing land as "aliens ineligible to citizenship," the State Department asked key members of Congress to substitute the
racial category with a geographical boundary defined by longitudinal and latitu-
dinal lines.[102] Predictably, not everyone in Congress was happy about this change.
Senator George W. Norris of Nebraska called the use of longitudinal and latitu-
dinal lines an "illogical method" of exclusion. Interestingly, it was Senator Henry
Cabot Lodge of Massachusetts, the most infamous member of the Immigration
Restriction League, who explained in Senate that the State Department created
the zone because it believed that the original wording would be "extremely offensive" to Japan. In the House, Representative John Burnett of Alabama, chairman
of the Committee on Immigration and Naturalization who sponsored the exclusionary bill, explained that the committee struck out all mention of immigrants'
eligibility to citizenship from the bill in order to remove any doubt that the bill
was intended to insult Japan.[103] In spite of the increasing xenophobia around the
country, American policymakers in Washington ensured that Japan would not
be treated like Europe's colonial subjects in Asia, at least for the time being.

The decade following the end of the Russo-Japanese War revealed how quickly
Americans could transform an Asian people from a member of the "great
civilized nations" to one of the most dangerous threats to the future of the white
races. More precisely, the decade showed how these two contrasting views

could coexist. While American policymakers in Washington, DC, success-fully maintained the cordial relationship with Japan forged during the Russo-Japanese War, American political activists in California, first the working class that dominated San Francisco and later the professional class that ruled the state from Sacramento, made significant headway in challenging the monolithic view of the Japanese as Americans' partner in the Pacific. As the professional class in California grew stronger in shaping the trajectory of US-Japan relations, the working class of San Francisco were not the only ones who lost their ground. The executive branch of the US government, so strong during Theodore Roosevelt's second term that it could quash any anti-Japanese proposal in Sacramento, was humbled and humiliated by California's state government when Hiram Johnson signed the Alien Land Law against Woodrow Wilson administration's pleas in 1913. Indeed, the story of the anti-Japanese movements in California was as revealing about the changing American ideas about race as it was about the changing power dynamics in US politics.

The trajectory of events from the Russo-Japanese War to World War I also revealed how capitalism shaped inter-imperial relations and domestic politics. While the United States and Japan became more competitive over the China market during this period, white American Progressives and Japanese American elites in California gradually converged in their visions of a desirable future. The addition of the lease clause in the Alien Land Act and the subsequent efforts by the members of the Lincoln-Roosevelt League to prevent the state legislature from considering anti-Japanese bills after 1913 demonstrated that, despite the white Progressives' earlier calls to prioritize the preservation of white supremacy over the pursuit of profit, the white professional class of California could not resist the prospect of rapidly developing the state's agricultural economy and taking ad-vantage of the country's increasing trade with Japan, which would remain larger than US trade with China until the eve of World War II.[104] Japanese American elites strategically cast themselves as the white Progressives' economic and polit-ical partners through the Japanese Association of America and the Pacific Press Bureau. Instead of confronting white supremacy, the Issei elites exploited the existing divisions between the white working class and the white professional class by convincing the white professionals that Japanese Americans would con-tribute to the state's economy without disrupting the existing racial hierarchy. Even after the Alien Land Act put a ceiling on the Issei working class's upward socioeconomic mobility, the Issei elites sought a common ground with their white counterparts with hopes that Japanese American and white communities would become prosperous in mutually beneficial ways. They achieved peace by accommodating to the white professional class's racialized vision of "progress" that precluded economic equality.

Uplifting the "Subject Races"

*American Missionary Diplomacy and the Politics of
Comparative Racialization, 1905–1919*

In February 1915, a week before the Panama-Pacific International Exposition
opened in San Francisco, Yun Ch'i-ho was released from prison in Seoul, in
the Japanese colony of Korea.[1] The former vice minister of foreign affairs had
spent three years behind bars for allegedly organizing a failed assassination attempt on the Japanese colonial governor. The presumed reason for his arrest
and incarceration was something else. After Japan dissolved the Korean foreign
ministry, Yun built a Christian industrial school with the support of American
missionaries. He then returned to the American South in 1910 for an extended
tour, becoming the most prominent Korean in the missionary network. While
American missionaries believed the school served as a haven for future Christian
leaders of Korea, Japanese colonial officials became concerned that Yun's school
was a training ground for future anti-colonial nationalists.

When Yun faced public trial in the summer of 1912 alongside several hundred other Korean converts, missionary leaders in the United States mobilized
themselves and their political connections to address what appeared to be an
act of religious persecution. They publicized Yun's ordeal in local and national
newspapers, and they put pressure on the Japanese embassy in Washington
through several US senators to prevent his execution. In the United States,
the news of Yun's incarceration captured people's attention far beyond the
missionary community. Korean immigrants, who had been disappointed in
American missionaries' previous discouragement of an anti-colonial revolution
led by Korean Christians, hoped this incident would finally lead to US intervention against Japanese imperialism.[2] Japanese American elites and their white
American allies, who had been battling against nativist groups in the American

The Allure of Empire. Chris Suh, Oxford University Press. © Oxford University Press 2023.
DOI: 10.1093/oso/9780197631614.003.0004

West, worried that such a strong reaction by the missionary community would contribute to the growing anti-Japanese sentiments in the United States.[3]

By the time Yun was released, however, few Americans expressed concerns about Japan's colonial project in Korea. While Korean immigrant communities continued to denounce Japan's colonial rule, Japan appeared to have success-fully convinced various American observers—from academics to journalists to politicians—that Japan had "reformed" Korean society to American standards. In spite of the anti-Japanese movements in California, the inter-imperial relation-ship between the United States and Japan remained strong. While US competi-tion with Japan over the Manchuria and China markets tested the relationship, many Americans believed that Japan had successfully emerged as a "progressive" empire.[4] They praised the Japanese colonization of Korea by comparing it to the American colonization of the Philippines, which had replaced Cuba as a meas-uring stick for success in colonial administration.

It is easy to assume that missionaries became overpowered by academics, journalists, and politicians in the United States. But the missionary archives tell a different story. The narrative of "progress" prevailed not because the missionaries were weak, but because they privately shared the belief that Koreans, even the converts, were incapable of self-government and needed to be placed under the "tutelage" of a more "advanced" race. Missionary leaders compared Koreans to Filipinos as well as Black Americans, whose subjugation was likewise rationalized with the argument that they were incapable of self-government. In fact, when missionaries criticized Japan's incarceration of Korean converts, what they demanded was "reform" of the colonial rule, not its abolition.

This chapter examines how the American missionary enterprise helped shape the imperial order in the Pacific, in particular how American ideas about "race," often articulated through comparative exercises, determined the missionaries' decision to support Japan's continued colonial rule in Korea. Unbeknownst to many Korean Christians, there was a wide gap between how the missionaries and the converts perceived one another.

This gap provides a useful entry point to reinterpret the US government's re-sponse to the nationwide Korean independence movement in 1919, popularly known as the March First Movement, which attempted to restore Korean sover-eignty by appealing to then US president Woodrow Wilson. A son of a southern Presbyterian minister, Wilson appeared to present an alternative trajectory of US foreign policy from his predecessors' by engaging in what his biographer Arthur Link has called "missionary diplomacy," an effort to bring the blessings of Christianity and democracy to the world.[5] When Wilson appeared at the Paris Peace Conference to help reconfigure the world order after World War I, many colonized subjects around the world, including Koreans, attempted to seize the opportunity and articulated their aspirations in response to Wilson's wartime speeches.[6] But like missionaries of his time, Wilson's worldview was colored by the prevalent ideas about race and self-government that had sustained the imperial order in the Pacific. He ignored Koreans' pleas and Korea remained Japan's colony.

Yun Ch'i-ho, based on his intimate knowledge of American ideas about race and progress, attempted to dissuade his countrymen from appealing to Wilson. But Koreans were not as naive as Yun believed they were. Koreans in the United States paid close attention to how Filipinos attempted to take advantage of the US Democratic Party's promise to provide the Philippines more autonomy than the previous Republican administrations. They also followed the path of radical Black Americans who sought to make Wilson, while the world's attention was on him, live up to his wartime declaration that the postwar world would be different for colonized peoples. Their vision contrasted starkly with Yun's moderate stance, which was heavily influenced by his reading of the African American leader Booker T. Washington.

By the end of the Peace Conference, Filipinos, Koreans, and Black Americans all faced tragic ends to their struggles. Wilson was the least of their problems. In the Philippines, food shortage and the soaring price of rice led to social unrest, which was subdued by the US-trained Philippines Constabulary. The Japanese colonial government violently suppressed Korean anti-colonial demonstrations. In the United States, anti-Black violence swept the country during what would become known as the Red Summer of 1919. The Japanese government deployed stories of lynching and other forms of white-on-Black violence to discourage Koreans from seeing the United States in a positive light.

The collective history of missionaries, converts, and US policymakers brings into view how these comparative exercises—of Koreans and Filipinos, of Koreans and Black Americans, and, perhaps most important, of Japanese and white Americans—sustained the imperial order in the Pacific. These comparisons are what enabled white Americans and Japanese to imagine themselves as akin in spite of the rising anti-Japanese immigration movements, all the while keeping Koreans, Filipinos, and African Americans subjugated, ironically, for the sake of their "development" toward self-government.

Narratives of Progress in Korea and the Philippines

When the US government withdrew its legation from Korea at the end of the Russo-Japanese War, Americans did not withdraw their interest in Korea. The president of the *Outlook* company correctly predicted that the postwar "reconstruction" would interest the "thinking people" more than the war itself.[7] The interest, however, had less to do with Koreans than the Japanese. Various

American journalists followed George Kennan's path to Korea to investigate whether Japan possessed the civilizing capacity long assumed to be an exclusive trait of Western nations. After Japan's annexation of Korea in 1910, prominent groups of academics took interest in Japan's colonization.

During the initial years of Japan's rule of Korea, however, it was more common to read about Japan's shortcomings than its success. Contrary to war correspondent George Kennan, Korean Foreign Office adviser Durham White Stevens, and Theodore Roosevelt, who saw Japan's shortcomings as akin to those of the United States in the Philippines, various journalists who wrote about Korea after the Russo-Japanese War refused to overlook signs of imperial exploitation. Homer Hulbert, an American missionary who published the *Korea Review*, criticized Japan's "broken promises" in his book *The Passing of Korea* (1906). Frederick A. McKenzie, a Canadian journalist who had once welcomed the Japanese protectorate, explained that Japan had squandered the "golden opportunity" to demonstrate its capacity for reform by refusing to restrain its settlers. Thomas F. Millard, an American journalist who had covered the Russo-Japanese War for *Scribner's*, concluded upon visiting Korea that Japan did not have the "slightest intention of restoring the independence of Korea." Millard was particularly concerned by the Japanese settlers in Korea, and he attempted to draw the attention of American exclusionists by predicting that, "should circumstances permit," Japanese settlers would do to California what they had done in Korea.[8]

Japan's reputation as a progressive empire came under international scrutiny in 1907 when Emperor Kojong sent emissaries to the Second Peace Conference held in The Hague. Although the three former Korean government officials who had been sent there to protest the legality of the 1905 protectorate treaty failed to gain entry into the conference, Hulbert successfully made the emperor's plea public. He convinced prominent British social reformer W. T. Stead, a household name among American progressives, to publish the emperor's pleading letter as well as interviews with the Korean emissaries in the daily journal of the conference. By helping Koreans testify against the Japanese, *Harper's Weekly* declared, Hulbert had delivered a "severe blow to Japan's international prestige."[9]

Yet few Americans protested when Japan responded to The Hague emissary affair by forcing the Korean emperor to abdicate. The *Outlook* reiterated Kennan's critical description of the Korean imperial government during the Russo-Japanese War and declared that "any revolutionary movement" to reestablish the independence of Korea was as "hopeless" as it would be in Egypt, since both Koreans and Egyptians were "totally incapable" of maintaining strong governments dedicated to reform.[10] The US State Department willingly accepted the Japanese government's argument, that the emperor had to be removed from his position for Japan to better carry out the "comprehensive administrative re-form" of Korea.[11]

American views of Koreans then took a negative turn when two Korean Americans killed Durham White Stevens in San Francisco. Stevens was on his way to Washington, DC, to speak with American politicians about the rising anti-Japanese movements in the United States at the request of the Japanese government.[12] Upon arriving in San Francisco in 1908, he declared that Japan was doing for Korea what the United States was doing for the Philippines. In response, local Korean representatives physically confronted him at his hotel and, later, shot him at the city's port. Stevens's murder proved to be a decisive moment in the development of Korean diasporic nationalism. The trial of the Korean anti-colonial activists served as an impetus for disparate Korean immigrant organizations to join forces for their defense, which ultimately led to the formation of the Korean National Association (KNA).[13] For white Americans, however, the assassination of Stevens only solidified the case for Japanese rule of Korea. The "cowardly murder" of Stevens, the *Outlook* argued, was the "best possible proof of the fact that Korea is not able, in spite of high-sounding proclamations, to govern itself in accordance with the standards and laws of modern civilization."[14]

Stevens's murder also provided an occasion for Japan's minister in Washington to justify the aggressive Japanese military campaign that the colonizers had launched, in the wake of the abdication, to suppress the growing resistance of Korean nationalists in Korea.[15] In his article memorializing Stevens in the *North American Review*, Minister Takahira Kogorō argued that Korea occupied the "same relation to Japan" as Cuba to the United States. But the comparison had a different meaning than when Theodore Roosevelt used it during the Russo-Japanese War. After the pro-American government in Cuba collapsed following a rigged election, the United States deployed its military to occupy the country again in 1906, this time for three years. The United States demonstrated in Cuba that military violence was part of the effort to bring order to subjugated countries. Japan, Takahira explained, was similarly "compelled" to take aggressive action in Korea, in order to provide Korea with "a stable government."[16]

US officials in Washington appeared to agree. Later in 1908, Washington signed the Root-Takahira Agreement with Tokyo, as a confirmation of their vision of a shared future in the emerging transpacific imperial order. The agreement explicitly mentioned the preservation of China's territorial integrity, and it also promised mutual respect between the two empires regarding their sovereign rights in each of what the agreement mentioned as "territorial possessions": Korea, Taiwan, and the Kwantung Leased Territory in Manchuria for Japan; the Philippines, Guam, American Samoa, Wake Island, and Hawai'i for the United States.[17]

Yet there was a reason why Stevens used the Philippines, not Cuba, as a point of comparison when he arrived in San Francisco. And it was the same reason why Japanese colonial officials from Taiwan went on inspection tours to the adjacent US colony.[18] By the time Stevens died, the Philippines had emerged as a positive example of how the United States prepared colonial subjects for self-government. In 1907 the Roosevelt administration finally fulfilled the promise outlined in the 1902 Philippine Organic Act and administered the first general election for the Philippine Assembly, the lower house of the bicameral legislature, and turned the presidentially appointed Philippine Commission into the upper house. In reality, the election was far from democratic: it was held only in the Christian provinces, and suffrage was limited to men who could read Spanish or English and had held office in either the Spanish or American imperial regime. From Roosevelt's perspective, however, the Filipino political participation marked an "absolutely new" development in the history of colonial rule in the Pacific. The president propounded in the 1908 State of the Union address that the United States had given the Filipinos "the opportunity to develop the capacity for self-government," so that they may one day decide for themselves whether they should become independent or continue to live under the "protection of a strong and disinterested power." This, he contended, was "real progress."[19]

Korea's transition from Japan's protectorate to its colony represented a violation of the promise Japan made in 1905, that it would preserve Korea's nominal sovereignty and institute administrative reforms to help Koreans govern themselves. Yet Roosevelt contended that the promise was not worth keeping since not all subjugated people deserved the protectorate status. In his 1913 autobiography, published after the United States withdrew troops from Cuba, Roosevelt proudly expounded that his country had proven its skeptics wrong by keeping its promise of independence to the Cubans after relatively short periods of military occupation. As for the Filipinos, he explained, the United States made a deliberate choice not to promise them independence, for they were "quite incapable of standing by themselves" when the United States first entered the country. This was why the Philippines became a colony, not a protectorate. Roosevelt then argued that Japan had made an "unwise" decision in declaring a protectorate over Koreans who, in his estimation, were incapable like the Filipinos. But Japan annexed Korea five years after the protectorate treaty, and Roosevelt was pleased to report Japan had corrected the mistake it had made earlier.[20]

In 1915, Roosevelt publicly declared that he had been correct to predict that Japan would be able to reform Korea to US standards. In an essay wholly devoted to Japanese colonial rule in Korea, published in *Metropolitan* magazine, the former president explained how Japan had effectively combined imperialism and progressive reform to achieve parity with Western powers. "The Japanese have restored and enforced order, built roads and railways, carried out great engineering works, introduced modern sanitation, introduced a modern school system and doubled commerce and the agricultural output, substantially as the most advanced nations of Europe and America have done under like conditions," he noted. The Japanese, he concluded, had mastered the "difficult task of colonial administration."[21]

The basis of Roosevelt's confident assessment of Japan's work was a conspicuously titled series called the *Annual Report on Reforms and Progress in Chosen (Korea)*, a copy of which he received directly from Governor General Terauchi Masatake. These annual reports, produced in English by the colonial government, were part of Japan's response to the Korean emperor's attempt to secure foreign assistance at The Hague conference in 1907. Following his abdication, Japanese colonial administrators produced the heavy tomes every year to narrate how the Japanese were developing the various aspects of Korea—agriculture, industry, finance, commerce, communication, mining, forestry, fishing, sanitation, and education—so that Koreans could one day enjoy the "advantages of modern civilization."[22] The narratives were accompanied by quantitative data that made Japan's work legible to American progressive imperialists. Roosevelt expressed directly to Terauchi that he was glad this report was made available in English, for "our people" should understand the "really remarkable work that has been done by Japan in Korea." Roosevelt also wanted Japanese elites to know how much he publicly supported Japan's empire. So he sent a copy of his *Metropolitan* article to Baron Kaneko Kentarō, with whom he had conversed several times in the United States during the Russo-Japanese War. No recent book of the kind, Roosevelt said in his article, was "better worth the study of statesmen and of scholar interested in every kind of social reform."[23]

The *Annual Report on Reforms and Progress* neatly fit into prevalent narratives about "civilizing" missions legitimated by the *Journal of Race Development*, an academic journal that served as a clearinghouse for, in its own words, "the methods by which developed peoples may most effectively aid the progress of the undeveloped" around the world. Published from 1910 to 1919, the journal brought together the day's most prominent American academics as its contributing editors, including Franz Boas, W. E. B. Du Bois, and G. Stanley Hall.[24] As political scientist Robert Vitalis has uncovered, the *Journal of Race Development* was in effect the first journal in the field of international relations, and it would later become the leading international relations journal, *Foreign Affairs*. In its initial decade, it was clear that what academics would label "international relations" was in essence interracial relations, more precisely the unequal power relations within the world of empires.[25] The journal's geographical coverage encompassed Africa, Asia, Latin America, the Middle East, and the American South, yet the focus was overwhelmingly on European and American as well as Japanese efforts to "develop" the "underdeveloped" subjugated people, such as Filipinos, Koreans, and African Americans.

Given that the journal's editor, George Blakeslee, stated in its inaugural issue that Japan's "civilization" was on a "substantial equality with that of the nations of the West," it was not surprising that commentary about Japan's colonial project in Korea was generally positive. Several prominent American-educated Japanese intellectuals, including Nitobe Inazō (professor at the Kyoto Imperial University) and Iyenaga Toyokichi (lecturer at the University of Chicago) contributed articles describing Japan's success as a colonizing power.[26] The most vocal champion of Japanese colonization of Korea from the US side was Yale University professor George Trumbull Ladd. A former president of the American Psychological Association, Ladd had visited Korea in 1907 at the invitation of then resident general, Itō Hirobumi, who had received a law degree from Yale. Ladd also had a personal connection with the Japanese minister in Washington, and he described the *Annual Reports* as evidence of how Japan was engaged in "benevolent assimilation" of the Koreans. "Benevolent assimilation" was the phrase used by former president William McKinley in 1898 to promise how the United States would rule the Philippines with "justice and right," as opposed to "arbitrary rule." Following McKinley's death, Roosevelt pursued a policy of tutelage toward self-government rather than assimilation. Yet Ladd believed it was appropriate to compare Korea with the Philippines since the two projects, in his view, reflected the two empires' compatible visions of progress. To him, the *Annual Reports* made clear that Japan was not simply making "material improvements" for Koreans' benefit but, more important, guiding the development of their "social and moral character."[27]

What is so remarkable about such narratives of progress is that they even attracted several Asian intellectuals in the United States. Its appeal went far beyond Japanese immigrants like Kiyoshi Karl Kawakami.[28] The case of the prominent Bengali anti-colonial activist Taraknath Das is illustrative. Das, a key member of the Ghadar Party, spent much of his adult life in the United States advocating the end of British colonial rule in India. Toward the end of World War I, Das became known to the American public as a defendant in what the US newspapers named the Hindu Conspiracy trial, which indicted a group of revolutionaries for planning to recruit Indian men in the United States, train them with the help of German military officers, and ship them with guns to South Asia to start a military revolution within the British empire. But immediately before he became entangled in this trial, Das traveled to Japan, where he met a number of Pan-Asianists including Rash Behari Bose of India, Sun Yat-sen of China, and Ōkawa Shūmei of Japan.[29] In a pamphlet titled *Is Japan a Menace to Asia?*, published in Shanghai in 1917, the anticolonial revolutionary denounced the US and Canadian restrictions of Japanese labor migration and praised Japan's "conspicuous success" in erecting economic barriers to "restrain the whiteman [sic]" from interfering in Taiwan and Korea. Das didn't stop there. He also defended Japan's colonial project in Korea by writing, "Korea is being developed for the benefit of the Japanese and Koreans and other nations." "The Japanese government in Korea is not a perfect one," he noted, but given that production of opium in Korea was "less flagrant" than in India, he believed that Japan genuinely represented Koreans' interests. While there is no evidence that he read the *Annual Report*, prohibiting opium production and isolating opium addicts was something that Japan proudly noted in the propagandistic text as well.[30]

Such narratives of progress, backed by quantitative data in the annual reports and further legitimated by articles in the *Journal of Race Development*, did not go unchallenged. American missionaries in Korea exposed Japanese colonial violence. Yet missionary leaders in the United States were not entirely opposed to these narratives of progress, even as the Japanese colonial project seemed to undermine the missionary enterprise. Indeed, many missionary leaders subscribed to, and sometimes even contributed to, the prevalent ideas about "race" and "development" that sustained racial inequality both at home and abroad.

American Missionaries and the "Korean Conspiracy Case"

Years before the Hindu Conspiracy trial, US newspapers across the country reported on another trial of a foiled anti-colonial plan which they named the Korean Conspiracy Case. The tone of the US newspapers was remarkably supportive of those standing trial. From late 1911, from the time some seven hundred Koreans were arrested for allegedly plotting to assassinate the Japanese colonial governor, Terauchi Masatake, letters from American missionaries in Korea disrupted the narratives of progress. "Persecution" was a commonly used label by missionary publications and US newspapers to describe the conduct of the colonial government, which, almost exclusively based on confessions forcibly extracted from the prisoners, levied prison sentences on 105 of the arrested Koreans, the vast majority of whom were Protestant converts.[31]

At a time when Koreans in the colony could not print their own newspapers (the only Korean-language newspaper published from the time of annexation in 1910 to the second year of the "cultural rule" in 1920 was the colonial government's organ *Maeil Sinbo*), the American press exposed Japan's colonial violence and voiced support for the Koreans.[32] American public reaction was so strong against the Japanese colonial government in 1912 that Korean immigrants and exiles in the United States believed that they had an opportunity to re-establish Korean independence with US support.[33] But this did not happen, in part, because American missionary leaders decided against intervention in Korea, believing that Koreans, even the converts, should remain under the tutelage of the Japanese for the sake of their "development."[34]

When the news of the mass arrests was first reported, missionaries in Korea had good reason to be concerned. Christianity in Korea had grown at a rapid rate from the signing of the protectorate in 1905 to annexation in 1910. During those years, Protestant churches in Korea gained 79,211 converts in net, more than the total number of Christians in the entire mainland Japan in 1910. Koreans turned to Christianity in search of consolation and alternative modes of political organization in the face of increasing Japanese control of the country.[35] From the missionary perspective, what mattered most was that their enterprise was finally bearing fruit. As Presbyterian missionary Horace G. Underwood wrote during the Korean Conspiracy Case, the growth of Christianity in Korea was "a God-given opportunity which we should seize."[36]

Because the vast majority of the sentenced were Presbyterian converts, it was the Presbyterian Board of Missions that first approached Japanese officials in Washington. After the board met to discuss the letters from missionaries in Korea, its secretary, Arthur Judson Brown, immediately visited the Japanese embassy and later expressed the board's concerns in writing. While Japan "has made great administrative reforms and inaugurated many beneficial public enterprises in Korea," Brown explained, the mass incarceration of Koreans "awakened grave misgivings" about the Japanese rule of Korea, especially regarding its "reputation for the humane and enlightened rule of a subject race."[37]

Yet it was not the Presbyterian Church but the Methodist Episcopal Church, South (MECS) that put the strongest pressure on the Japanese government. The reason was simple: the accused ringleader of the conspiracy case was Yun Ch'i-ho. After the Korean foreign ministry was dissolved, Yun had been working as an educational leader, devoting most of his time to an industrial school he founded with the backing of the MECS in 1906. The Anglo-Korean School, as it was called, was the realization of a plan Yun had drawn up as a student at Emory College. Before leaving the United States in 1893, Yun had entrusted the college president, Warren Akin Candler, with his savings, which eventually became the nucleus for the fund that established the school.[38] Candler, who became a bishop of the MECS, visited Korea in 1906 and gave Yun his blessings to build the school. After returning home, Candler continued to support Yun's plan by raising money for the school from various MECS organizations and Emory alumni, as well as from his brother Asa Griggs Candler, the owner of the Coca-Cola Company. He also sent Yun seeds for pecans, apple trees, peach trees, grapevines, and cotton.[39] Although Candler's cotton seems to have never arrived

Fig. 3.1 Anglo-Korean School in 1910. Yun Ch'i-ho is the man with the mustache standing near the center of the fourth row from the bottom. C. F. Reid, *Yun Chi Ho, the Korean Patriot and Christian Educator* (Nashville, TN: Publishing House of the Methodist Episcopal Church, South, 1914), 24. Stuart A. Rose Manuscript, Archives, and Rare Book Library, Emory University.

in Korea, the students at the Anglo-Korean School later manufactured textile goods that would be sold under the name Korea Mission cloth.[40]

On the eve of annexation in 1910, Yun followed Candler's advice and returned to the United States for several months to raise money for the school.[41] Yet Yun's significance was larger than that of his school or his country. The greater purpose of this trip was to help the MECS galvanize the Laymen's Missionary Movement, which sought to reduce the gap between the money spent on churches within the United States and the comparably small amount given to foreign missions. After delivering a speech to the ecstatic Korean American crowd welcoming him in San Francisco, Yun spent three months traveling through the South, garnering major attention at public appearances in St. Louis, Memphis, New Orleans, Shreveport, Dallas, Houston, Fort Worth, Muskogee, Montgomery, and Atlanta. A wide range of newspapers from Idaho, Missouri, Texas, Louisiana, Oklahoma, Alabama, Tennessee, and Georgia provided sensational coverage of Yun's mission, most of them mistakenly calling the unusual visitor a member of the Korean imperial family, if not a "Japanese Prince."[42] Yun also spoke at the national conference for the Laymen's Missionary Movement in Chicago and the World's Sunday School Convention in Washington. At the request of the YMCA leader John R. Mott, he then traveled across the Atlantic to attend the World Missionary Conference held in

Edinburgh, before returning to Korea.[43] Yun Ch'i-ho became the best-known Korean within the missionary network.

Therefore, when Yun was arrested two years later by the Japanese colonial police, the MECS mobilized members of the US Senate to pressure the Japanese minister in Washington. At the request of Candler, three southern Democrats— Nathan P. Bryan of Florida and Hoke Smith and Augustus Bacon, both of Georgia—met with the Japanese minister in the summer of 1912. Bryan was a classmate of Yun's at Emory, but Smith and Bacon had no other reason to take an interest in the case except that they had a good relationship with Candler. Smith, a former governor of Georgia, was a well-known champion of Jim Crow laws; Bacon, a former Confederate soldier, was the president pro tempore of the Senate and the leading Democrat on the Senate Foreign Relations Committee. The three senators delivered Candler's letter to the Japanese minister and, according to Bacon, "did all in [their] power" to convince him that Yun was a "man of very high character" and warned the minister that "the Methodist denomination, constituting a large proportion of the people of the Southern States, was deeply concerned in his behalf." Bacon was hopeful that the senators' visit would influence the outcome of the trial.[44] But before the trial began, Candler grew nervous. After the Japanese minister publicly defended the colonial government's actions, three MECS bishops including Candler visited the Japanese embassy with Hoke Smith and Augustus Bacon. Should Yun receive a death sentence, the MECS missionaries in Korea were instructed to cable to the United States one word, "Candler."[45]

The day after the trial began, Candler joined forces with four other church leaders, including Arthur Judson Brown of the Presbyterian Board of Missions, and revisited Washington, this time to meet with not only the Japanese minister but also President William Howard Taft, Secretary of State Philander Knox, and the chair of the House Foreign Affairs Committee, William Sulzer. The missionaries acquainted the three US officials with relevant information and asked the government for counsel. Knox told the missionaries that they had been "pursuing the right course," manifesting their "solicitude for their friends" through the Japanese minister, and recommended that they should continue pursuing this path.[46]

After 105 Koreans were sentenced to prison, with Yun receiving the highest sentence of ten years, missionary leaders of various denominations met in New York to consult several "eminent laymen." Led by Arthur Judson Brown, the missionaries sought advice on whether they should change their course of action against Knox's recommendation. Powerful and well connected, these laymen were mostly academic experts on international law and the field of "race development."[47] Of the eight laymen consulted, five had experience at The Hague: former Columbia University president Seth Low and Rear Admiral

Alfred Thayer Mahan (who could not attend but contributed to the meeting with a letter) had represented the United States at the first International Peace Conference in The Hague in 1899, legal scholar James Brown Scott and economist Jeremiah Jenks had represented the United States at the second Hague conference in 1907, while the former secretary of state John W. Foster attended the same conference as a delegate plenipotentiary for China.[48] The other three contributors to the meeting were well-known intellectuals who had contributed to prevalent ideas about race and empire. As president of the *Outlook* company, Lawrence Abbott had overseen the publication of countless articles defending Japanese rule of Korea. Yale president Arthur Twining Hadley, a well-known economist, had provided Theodore Roosevelt with a definition of "freedom" that the president had used to justify the prolonged colonial rule over the Filipinos. Former Harvard University president Charles William Eliot, who had met with Governor Terauchi in Korea while touring on behalf of the Carnegie Endowment for International Peace that year, believed that the former Korean government embodied the "complete inadequacy of feeble, despotic government to modern needs."[49] Therefore, the missionaries decided not to change the course of their action.

For Arthur Judson Brown, consulting such academics only confirmed the view that had been established long before the missionaries gathered in New York. A contributor to the *Journal of Race Development* and *Outlook*, Brown firmly believed that Japanese rule would benefit the Korean people. After touring Korea in 1909, Brown made note of various problems caused by the Japanese settlers who descended on the country like "brutal and lustful Americans" in the Philippines. But he also quoted from one of Kennan's articles on Korea and relied on the *Annual Report on Reforms and Progress* to provide "indisputable" evidence of Japanese regeneration of the country. As for the various arguments against Japanese violence, he conceded, "it would be easy to show that the Japanese are not doing as well as England is doing in India and America in the Philippines." But "give them a chance," he contended in 1909.[50] In his report of the 1912 meeting in New York, Brown extended this argument to defend Japan from its critics. Given that the United States was still struggling to close the "social chasm" in the Philippines, he insisted that the missionary leaders should be patient and let Japan "prove to all the world" that it could develop benevolence toward a "subject race."[51]

Yet turning from his comparison of Koreans to the Filipinos, Brown drew another analogy to justify why, in spite of the frequent stories of violence from the Japanese colony, Americans should not criticize or intervene against the Japanese:

At present, when many Japanese are kind to the Koreans, as the best Japanese are, it is apt to be [compared] with the type of kindness which characterizes a Georgia gentleman towards a negro. The Georgian may be a friend and benefactor of the negro, but he does not consider himself on the latter's level. . . . We should therefore be slow to criticise the Japanese for an attitude which we also have to struggle to overcome.[52]

The comparison was remarkable, given how widely known it was that Jim Crow laws in the South systematically stripped African Americans of the legal equality and a certain degree of autonomy they had achieved under Reconstruction. Many Americans remained horrified by the terrorism of lynching that often enforced disenfranchisement and institutional segregation in public spaces. Yet Brown believed that such a comparison, focusing on the "kindness" of two respective oppressors, would discourage Americans from criticizing the Japanese.

Although Warren Candler was not present at the New York meeting, it is difficult to dismiss the possibility that Brown had aimed this comparison at the former president of Emory.[53] Candler bore a striking resemblance to the "Georgia gentleman." He was one of the cofounders and trustees of the Paine Institute, a Black college in Augusta, Georgia, that was established with funds from the church in the aftermath of Reconstruction. Yet Candler, the son of a slave owner, also remained one of the leading bishops standing against the reunification of the Methodist churches, which had split in 1844 over a controversy regarding a slave-owning bishop in the South. Even after the abolition of slavery, Candler still stood against reunification because he opposed integration of African Americans into the church, especially as high-ranking members of the clergy.[54] What better way was there to convince Candler that he should stop criticizing the Japanese? Candler's response to Brown's report went unrecorded, but it does not appear that the Georgian filed an official protest against the decision of the missionary leaders gathered in New York. Instead, Candler seems to have privately worked with MECS missionaries in Korea to check on Yun's health while his former student remained in prison.[55]

The effect of the comparison wasn't simply to make Americans like Candler self-reflect on their own shortcomings. It was also to blunt Koreans' cries for help by synonymizing their struggles with the prolonged sufferings of African Americans and condone the obvious signs of colonial violence in much the same way that Americans had been condoning the racism and violence of the American South.

It remains unknown if Yun ever encountered this report of the New York meeting. Yet ironically, he had been incarcerated precisely because he had identified with the struggles of African Americans in the South. The Anglo-Korean School was not just a Christian school. It was an industrial school modeled after the Tuskegee Institute in Alabama, the embodiment of African American leader Booker T. Washington's "self-help" ideology. During his 1910 tour of the United States, Yun made sure to visit Tuskegee, where he was given a guided tour by Washington himself.[56] He believed that abiding by the principle of self-help would enable Koreans to survive the tyranny of imperialism and prove to the world that they were capable of "developing" themselves without depending on the tutelage of a more "advanced" people. For Yun, the Black-Korean comparison had been a source of inspiration, not a mechanism of subjugation.

Yun Ch'i-ho's Vision of Racial Uplift

Well before Japan colonized Korea, Yun saw in Washington's model a pathway to Korean resistance against increasing foreign control of their country. It is unclear if he learned about Washington during his student days in the United States, but beginning in 1895, when he served as Korea's vice minister of education and then vice minister of foreign affairs, Yun repeatedly told Candler that industrial education should be prioritized for Koreans, for it would "not only encourage self-reliance but also give one means of self-reliance." This repeated emphasis on "self-reliance" was appropriate in the final years of the nineteenth century when various imperial powers were competing for railroad, utility, and mine concessions in Korea, enabled by the Korean emperor whose survival strategy appeared to be pitting various foreign powers against one another.[57]

From Yun's perspective, Washington's concept of self-reliance neatly complemented a non-Western concept, self-strengthening (*chagang*), that had already taken root in the minds of many Koreans. A few weeks after Korea and Japan signed the protectorate treaty in 1905, Yun received an audience with the Korean emperor and argued that their country would not be able to survive Japanese imperialism unless it learned to stand on its own. Korea's "path to independence," he explained, was "self-strengthening." He recommended that the emperor replace corrupt officials with "just ones" who could not be bought by foreign interests.[58] After Yun left the Korean government, he became the president of the newly founded Korea Self-Strengthening Society (Taehan chaganghoe) and the principal of the Anglo-Korean School.

Once Korea became a Japanese protectorate, Washington's educational model became important not only for the sake of self-reliance but also for the exigencies of self-preservation. "Shakespeare can wait," Yun explained to American missionaries in Korea, "but the land, under our present regime, may be seized, by the military necessity that knows no law and laws that have no necessity." Against the "steady, irresistible stream" of Japanese settlers "rapidly filling the land," Yun contended, only industrial education and accumulation of capital would enable Koreans to hold onto their land, without which achieving independence would be difficult.[59]

Indeed, as the Self-Strengthening Society's monthly bulletin made clear, Yun was joined by a number of Korean elites who similarly saw the protectorate era (1905–1910) as an opportunity to develop Korea's economic self-sufficiency and train a new generation of professional bureaucrats who would replace the older generation of Korean government officials. Many of these officials had risen to their positions due to their personal connections to the Korean emperor and the deceased queen's families and, from Yun Ch'i-ho's perspective, were "unworthy" to lead a nation that was struggling to maintain even its nominal independence, which made them useful to Japanese imperialists. "[O]ur protectors," as Yun sarcastically referred to Japanese imperialists, were willing to work with the Korean emperor and his cabinet as long as Japan could economically exploit Korea under the arrangement of a protectorate.[60] But after the emperor sent secret emissaries to the Second Peace Conference at The Hague in 1907, the Japanese Resident-General forced the Korean emperor to abdicate and had the Korean cabinet disband the Self-Strengthening Society. Because the surviving portions of Yun's diary are missing entries between July 3, 1906, and January 1, 1916, it is difficult to know how exactly he encountered the changing Japanese policy during that period. But it is not difficult to discern that he worked to combine religious and nationalist education with hopes of making Korea self-governing as soon as possible. Indeed, years before Japan annexed Korea as a colony, Japanese officials in Korea warned each other that Yun's Anglo-Korean School was preparing young men to become nationalist leaders.[61]

Yun thus stood in Japan's way. His emulation of Washington in colonial Korea landed him in jail during the conspiracy case. Elsewhere in the world, Washington's industrial-education model, a frequent topic of discussion in the *Journal of Race Development*, was imported by German and British imperialists in Africa to instill industry and docility in their colonial subjects.[62] But the Japanese colonists in Korea preferred to institute their own system of education, which they proudly presented in each *Annual Report on Reforms and Progress*. A year after annexation, the colonial government announced an educational ordinance that explicitly aimed to create "loyal and good subjects" of the Japanese empire.[63]

Perhaps Yun should have learned upon returning to the United States in 1910 that Washington had failed to appease his oppressors as well. In 1906, the same year he opened the Anglo-Korean School, a mob of white supremacists murdered dozens of African Americans and destroyed many Black-owned businesses in Atlanta, while the police arrested hundreds of African Americans who took up arms to defend their families in the city's most prosperous Black community. The Atlanta riot symbolized the limits of Washington's vision, that African Americans would be left alone to achieve upward socioeconomic

Fig. 3.2 Education reformer R. C. Ogden, Secretary of War William Howard Taft, educator Booker T. Washington, and industrialist Andrew Carnegie gathered in April 1906 to celebrate the twenty-fifth anniversary of the Tuskegee Institute's founding. Photographer: Francis B. Johnston. Library of Congress Prints and Photographs Division, LC-J694-353A.

mobility in the South if they focused on accumulating capital and refrained from demanding racial equality from white Americans. The immediate causes of the riot were unsubstantiated newspaper accounts of sexual assaults of local white women by Black men. The stage was set, however, by the recently concluded gubernatorial election in which two candidates, including the eventual winner, Hoke Smith (the same man who would later present Yun's case to the Japanese minister in 1912), advocated disenfranchisement of all Black voters. After the riot Washington lost much support, and prominent critics of the "self-help" ideology including W. E. B. Du Bois gained momentum with their more aggressive approach to racial justice.[64]

The tragedy of Yun's educational project did not simply lie in the fact that he had emulated a model that had already proven ineffective in the United States. Black Americans were not immune to the narratives of progress. Ever since Japan won the Russo-Japanese War, various African American leaders with conflicting visions of Black uplift—from Du Bois to Washington—almost unanimously held up Japan as a potential leader of the nonwhite races around the world. The

Black leaders' interest in the Japanese people went far beyond the struggles of racialized immigrants in the American West, who they believed shared the suffering of white supremacy under the jurisdiction of the United States. While Yun remained incarcerated, Washington personally told a Japanese associate of his that "[t]he wonderful progress of the Japanese and their sudden rise to the position of the great nations of the world has nowhere been studied with greater interest or enthusiasm than by the Negroes of America." Just three months before his death, Washington demonstrated that he continued to hold Japan in high regard when he addressed the National Negro Business League, an organization he had founded at the turn of the century to promote economic growth. "It is seldom that it is ever so true that, in the space of one generation, that so many evidences [sic] of real progress in the fundamental things of life can be seen," he said, "Perhaps the changes in Japan are the nearest akin to it."[65]

When Yun was suddenly released from jail in 1915, six months before Washington made this remark, American elites and Japanese imperialists interpreted the Korean's release as a milestone in Japan's progress. The annual report spread the news that the very Japanese colonial governor whom Yun and others had plotted to assassinate took notice of "their sincere repentance" and asked for their release to the Japanese emperor, who in turn "magnanimously granted them a special pardon by reason of his great love and mercy." While Arthur Judson Brown and Warren Candler remained publicly silent, George Trumbull Ladd, writing in the *Journal of Race Development*, praised the colonial justice system for showing mercy to Yun, a man of "weak and shifty moral character" who eventually "professed penitence for his behavior in the past." Indeed, Yun's words played no small role in creating the impression that the Japanese emperor's grace was changing the Korean attitude toward their colonizers. Upon release, Yun declared through the colonial government's official Korean-language organ *Maeil Sinbo* that he would dedicate his energy to work toward the "harmony and happiness" of the Korean and Japanese peoples.[66]

Many Koreans clearly took this declaration with a grain of salt. Korean anticolonial activists remained quiet for several years following Yun's pardon, as the world remained occupied by World War I. Yet in early 1919, a few weeks after the declaration of armistice, Yun was approached by one of the organizing leaders of a new Korean independence movement, Shin Ik-hŭi. Shin asked the former diplomat if he'd like to go to the Paris Peace Conference and present Korea's case for independence. But Yun, who had been working as general secretary of the Seoul YMCA since 1916, declined the offer. He explained that nations that did not participate in the Great War, like Korea, would not come up for discussion at the peace conference. The leaders of the new independence movement disagreed. As Song Chin-u, another organizing leader, told Yun the next day, they believed the peace conference would grant the "small nations" of the world their right to "self-determination." If Korea would be denied its right to self-determine, Song explained to Yun, the United States might even declare war against Japan. After all, standing at the center of the peace conference was US president Woodrow Wilson, who had declared during the previous year that all people in the aftermath of the war may be "dominated and governed only by their own consent," by the principle of self-determination. Yun remained unconvinced. When Ch'oe Nam-sŏn, the author of the Korean declaration of independence, approached him on behalf of the organizing leaders, Yun again refused to join the anticolonial movement. He believed that it was "inconceivable" that the United States would go to war with Japan for Korea's independence.[67]

Yet on March 1, 1919, two days before a public funeral procession for the recently deceased Emperor Kojong was to take place, thousands of Koreans staged public protests in Seoul to draw Wilson's attention. The Korean demonstrators championed the principle of self-determination aloud, hoping that articulating their anticolonial aspirations in the same recognizable language would prompt the American president to deliver Korea from Japan's rule. Thus began the two-month-long struggle that came to be known as the March First Movement.[68]

The day after the protests began, Yun discouraged Koreans' petitions to Wilson by giving an interview to the colonial government's official Japanese-language organ, *Keijō Nippō*, and its official Korean-language organ, *Maeil Sinbo*. In the interview Yun merely articulated for the public what he had told the organizing leaders in private and added that the Korean demonstration would only arouse Japan's anger toward the "weak race" instead of winning its "good will."[69]

Far from discouraging the protestors, Yun's words enraged many Koreans. He received threatening notes, and a flyer denouncing Yun soon began to circulate in Seoul.[70] The news of his interview quickly spread from the Korean peninsula to the Korean American communities in the United States, where *Sinhan Minbo*, the official organ of the main Korean diasporic organization, the KNA, called him "treacherous." Unintentionally, Yun came to stand as the leading opponent of Wilson and the president's Korean champions across the Pacific Ocean.[71]

Yun never publicly justified his refusal to participate in the March First Movement by referring to the conspiracy case, but, just as many disappointed Koreans and Korean Americans assumed, the three-year-long incarceration anchored his decision. In June 1919, when he learned that Koreans in Shanghai were cursing him for refusing to help them establish the Korean Provisional Government (KPG) there, Yun defended his position by venting in his diary that "every public movement" he had participated in not only had been a "failure" but also had brought him "personal sufferings" that he did not have "the courage to face again."[72]

His continuing faith in the principle of self-help was partly responsible for his refusal to join the movement to appeal to Wilson as well. "Booker Washington said that freedom is a conquest and not a bequest," he criticized the organizers of the March First Movement in his diary after the movement failed to achieve its goal.[73] Yun's discouragement of petitions to Wilson did not mean that he believed the future of Koreans was lost. He contended in his diary that Japan would not be able to hold Korea as a colony forever, as "no nation has ever succeeded in keeping down the intellectual growth of another race." That intellectual growth, however, would require general acceptance of the principle of self-help. As "B. Washington insisted," Yun wrote in his diary in August 1919, "[the] Negro must attain economic equality before he can claim social equality[;] so the Koreans must reach economic equality before we may claim political equality." "First seek to improve your condition intellectual, and economical," then "equal treatment and equal opportunities . . . will be added unto you."[74] Once Koreans achieved social equality with the Japanese, Yun argued, they would be ready to achieve emancipation.

Such ideas did not find a receptive audience in 1919. Even those who had been personally familiar with Yun's ideas rejected the self-help ideology and engaged in the campaign to solicit Wilson's help. Kim Kyu-shik, an American-educated Christian who had lavishly praised Yun's Anglo-Korean School in 1910, traveled to Paris from Shanghai during the peace conference disguised as a Chinese delegate.[75] In the United States, the Korean nationalists led by Syngman Rhee (Yi Sŭng-man) and Philip Jaisohn (Sŏ Chae-p'il), two Christians who had personally known Yun in the final years of Korean sovereignty, attacked Yun's vision of "economic salvation." The idea was "the pitiful idealism of the slave," they derided. When the Japanese "control[led] finance" and "natural resources" in Korea, there was no freedom to "improve the economic life" of Koreans, as Yun advocated. The Koreans in the United States argued that Koreans had only one choice to make: between "national self-determination" and "racial suicide."[76]

Koreans in the United States were not as naive as Yun thought they were. In January 1919, before the March First Movement began, and before Kim arrived in Paris, the KNA's *Shinhan Minbo* published a revealing editorial on the subject of self-determination. The editorial admitted that there was a possibility that Koreans would not be able to determine their futures at this particular moment. But because the word "self-determination" entered into the vocabulary of subjugated people around the world, it reasoned, all imperial powers, including the Allied Powers, would have to confront the issue of self-determination sooner or later. In fact, Korean immigrants were encouraged to learn that African American journalist William Monroe Trotter—a longtime opponent of Booker T. Washington—was in Paris, uninvited, demanding the right to self-determination and equal rights of African Americans at home. In June, an editorial in *Shinhan Minbo* reporting on Trotter's efforts called African Americans "our black brothers."[77]

Yet as many Koreans would find out, championing the principle of self-determination had its own limits. The problem Koreans faced was not simply that they had not been the intended audience of Wilson's wartime speeches. The problem was that Wilson, like his predecessors in the White House, believed that not all races were deserving of self-government.

Woodrow Wilson and Colonial Empires in the Pacific

When he first became president in 1913, Woodrow Wilson was an unlikely figure to be perceived as the leader of various colonized people around the world. After all, he had reportedly told a friend that it would be an "irony of fate" if his administration had to chiefly engage in foreign affairs. Yet when the world war erupted in 1914 and the United States entered it in 1917, Wilson applied his religious faith to engage in what his biographer has called "missionary diplomacy," a mission to bring to the world the blessings of democracy and Christianity.[78] Like many missionaries of his time, however, Wilson's vision of the world was also shaped by prevalent ideas about race and self-government, which was why, in spite of his differences from his predecessors, Wilson did not bring an end to the imperial order in the Pacific.

The perception of Wilson as a champion of the colonized peoples around the world was an unintended consequence of the president's wartime speeches that were widely disseminated by the Allied propaganda as well as the globalized telegraph and news wire system.[79] In his famous Fourteen Points speech, delivered early in 1918 to the US Congress, Wilson demanded that the world be made safe for every "peace-loving nation" that, like the United States, wished to "live its own life, determine its own institutions, be assured of justice and fair dealing by the other peoples of the world as against force and selfish aggression." After using the first four points to declare open diplomacy, freedom of the seas, free trade, and reduction of armaments, Wilson spent most of the other points talking about territorial settlements for Russia, various small European nations, and the non-Turkish members of the Ottoman Empire, before reserving the final point to propose a "general association of nations" to guarantee political independence and territorial integrity to "great and small states alike." But point five of the speech, without a specific geographical reference, suggested something different. It declared there would be an "adjustment of *all* colonial claims" in the aftermath of the war.[80]

While Wilson's point five gave hope to various colonized people around the world, it made some of his allies nervous. On the eve of the armistice, Wilson's advisers were forced to clarify what the president had meant by the words "adjustment of all colonial claims." Further elaboration was necessary to get the British and the French on board with the proposed terms of the peace which, as the Germans had agreed, would be based on the Fourteen Points. In October 1918 Wilson's foreign policy adviser "Colonel" Edward House tasked Walter Lippmann, a young progressive journalist who had cofounded the *New Republic*, with writing a long report explaining the Fourteen Points, with the assistance of Frank Cobb, the editor of the *New York World*.[81] Lippmann was particularly suited to unpack the meaning of the Fourteen Points, since he had been the secretary of the Inquiry, a group of academics organized at the request of Wilson to prepare for the postwar peace settlement. He was one of the three coauthors of the Inquiry memorandum that served as a basis of Wilson's Fourteen Points.[82] In his report, Lippmann explained that point five applied only to those colonial claims "created by the war," more precisely, "the German colonies and any other colonies which may come under international consideration as a result of the war."[83] This meant that colonies ruled by the Allied powers—such as the Philippines, India, French Indochina, and Korea—would not be part of the discussion.

Yet as Lippmann explained, point five also manifested the general principle that colonial powers should act as "trustees" of the colonized people, not their "owners." He argued that the leaders gathered at the upcoming peace conference may even write a "code of colonial conduct" for all imperial powers, including Japan and Britain, which were poised to become two "chief heirs" of the German colonial empire. After all, as Lippmann pointed out, Wilson had argued in the Fourteen Points that the "interests of the populations" in the colonies should have "equitable weight" as the governments that ruled these colonial populations.[84]

Yet point five did not denote that the aspirations of the colonized people would be respected. It merely meant, according to Lippmann, that the world powers gathered as an international community would ensure that each colonized population's interests would be guaranteed in the following way:

> That they should not be militarized, that exploitation should be conducted on the principle of the "open door," and under the strictest regulation as to labor conditions, profits, and taxes, that a sanitary regime be maintained, that permanent improvements in the way of roads, etc., be made, that native organization and custom be respected, that the protecting authority be stable and experienced enough to thwart intrigue and corruption, that the [protecting] power have adequate resources in money and competent administrators to act successfully.[85]

This was far from the emancipation that Koreans and other colonized people around the world expected. In fact, the list conformed to what Roosevelt had aimed to accomplish in American colonies and was entirely consistent with what Roosevelt had praised after reading the *Annual Report on Reforms and Progress in Korea*. Protecting the colonized people from outright economic exploitation, improving sanitation, building infrastructure, maintaining order, and creating efficient bureaucracy—these were all markers of "reform" that distinguished "progressive" imperialism from older forms of imperialism. In some ways, the consistency was no coincidence. Among the nine scholars on the Inquiry committee tasked with researching the colonial question was George H. Blakeslee, the editor of the *Journal of Race Development*.[86]

When House cabled Lippmann's report on the Fourteen Points to Wilson, the president curtly replied that the interpretations were "satisfactory." The details of Lippmann's report, the president said, should be regarded as "merely illustrative suggestions" that could be taken up later at the peace conference. Perhaps because of such a mixed response by Wilson, not much attention has been paid to the so-called Lippmann-Cobb interpretation that House used as the basis of his discussion with the Allied powers prior to Wilson's arrival in Paris. In fact, because the Inquiry memorandum did not include any discussion of colonial issues, it has been assumed that the Inquiry had little influence on Wilson's approach to the colonial question.[87]

Yet disconnecting Wilson's point five from members of the Inquiry does little to clarify Wilson's position on the colonial question, which has been subject to conflicting interpretations. Those sympathetic to Wilson have argued that the president aimed to extend the anticolonial tradition of the United States (beginning with the American Revolution) to the world, as well as to build on the momentum of domestic progressivism to create a more democratic world order based on the consent of the governed.[88] Meanwhile, those more critical of Wilson have argued that the president addressed the colonial question in order to counter the Soviet challenge to the existing capitalist-imperialist world order that Americans had protected.[89]

The conflicting interpretation of Wilson's vision usually revolves around the words he used to articulate it. In February 1918, Wilson followed up his Fourteen Points address by declaring that, in the postwar world, all people may be "dominated and governed only by their own consent," by the principle of self-determination.[90] Given that Wilson had never used that term before, and that it was Soviet leaders Vladimir Lenin and Leon Trotsky who first called for a postwar settlement based on the principle of "national self-determination" in 1917, it is not so easy to dismiss the possibility that Wilson was, in fact, responding to the Soviet challenge.[91] Historians more sympathetic to Wilson, however, have pointed out that the president rarely used the term and argue that Wilson's postwar vision should be understood instead by focusing on a term he used far more often, self-government. They contend that Wilson believed in all people's capacity of self-government and that the United States would become a model of how other people around the world would govern themselves.[92]

Examining Wilson's use of self-government, however, confirms that the president subscribed to the same set of ideas that had been circulating in academic journals, including the *Journal of Race Development*: that certain races perceived to be not yet able to govern themselves required the tutelage of a stronger power that would provide much in the form of "reform" for the interests of the colonized people. In fact, before his presidency, Wilson had used the term to justify the prolonged colonial rule of the Philippines. As the president of Princeton University, Wilson had publicly declared in 1907 that Filipinos should not be given their right of self-government because it was not something that could be "given." It was a "form of character" that could only be developed after a "long apprenticeship of obedience" for those who lacked the "self-control of maturity."[93] His declaration aligned with his support for the Spanish-American War in 1898 and welcoming of the acquisition of Cuba and the Philippines.[94]

After Wilson won the presidency, he declared in his hometown of Staunton, Virginia, that he hoped to "deprive" the United States of the Philippines, but his Republican predecessors were eager to prove that Wilson would not do so.[95] When former president William Howard Taft appeared in front of the Senate Committee on the Philippines in 1914, he used Wilson's own extensive definition of the term self-government to argue against a House resolution that proposed to provide the Filipinos a "more autonomous government." After Wilson articulated his vision for the postwar order in 1918, Theodore Roosevelt argued that Wilson's use of the term self-determination was nothing more than "phrase-mongering." Not only did Wilson not decolonize any part of the American empire, but Wilson and his secretary of state William Jennings Bryan used the US military to invade Mexico, Honduras, Nicaragua, the Dominican Republic, and Haiti. When Argentina attempted to convene a conference of Pan-American neutral powers during World War I to protect Latin America from becoming entangled in the war by the United States, the Wilson administration thwarted this effort by pressuring various Latin American countries to turn down Argentina's invitation. Thus, Roosevelt publicly portrayed Wilson as a hypocrite who denied the people of these countries "the right of self-determination, and have made democracy within their limits not merely unsafe but nonexistent."[96]

For the Filipinos, however, there was a reason to believe that Wilson would live up to his words. He was a Democrat. Philippine independence had been a major plank of the Democratic Party ever since William Jennings Bryan challenged William McKinley in the presidential election of 1900, and Wilson followed his party's plans for the Philippines during his presidency. When Representative William Atkinson Jones, a fellow Democrat from Virginia, proposed a bill for "a more autonomous government" for the Philippines,

Wilson supported the legislation and signed it almost immediately after it passed both houses of Congress in 1916. The Jones Act, or the Philippine Autonomy Act, as it was called, reorganized the Philippine legislature into a bicameral body entirely composed of Filipinos. Furthermore, it promised that the United States would withdraw from the Philippines as soon as a "stable government" could be established. Under the governorship of Francis Burton Harrison, a Tammany Hall Democrat who served as Wilson's top administrator in the Philippines (1913–1921), the Philippines also saw a drastic rise in efforts to create a more self-sustaining economy.[97] By the end of the world war, Filipino nationalists believed they had showcased their own ability to establish a stable government by maintaining order at home while the United States was fighting the war in Europe. Harrison praised the Filipinos for demonstrating the "greatest self[-]restraint" and the "greatest respect for the American flag."[98]

The drive toward Filipino self-government reached a climax in April 1919, when Wilson penned a letter to Filipino nationalists declaring that the end of the American rule was "almost in sight." Yet the letter was part of Wilson's strategy to prevent the issue from coming up at the peace conference. The Philippine Independence Mission, led by the president of the Philippine Senate, Manuel Quezon, had grown nervous that the Republicans had taken control of Congress in the election of 1918 and wished to receive a definite promise of independence from Wilson. Wilson, who left for Paris before the mission arrived in Washington, devised a way to defer the decision on Philippine independence without causing any embarrassment. He had the secretary of war Newton D. Baker give the mission a warm welcome and deliver the promising letter.[99]

Nevertheless, Wilson's statement sustained the hopes of not only the Filipinos but also the Koreans, who believed that the two colonized peoples' fates were tied to each other. Given that many Republicans were arguing against Philippine independence by pointing to the islands' vulnerability to Japanese invasion, the Sinhan Minbo explained in an editorial about Wilson's letter, Japan stood as the enemy of both Korean and Filipino independence.[100]

Yet the parallel between the Philippines and Korea, as it had been since the end of the Russo-Japanese War, continued to be used by the colonizers to justify Japanese rule of Korea. In spring 1919, Baron Gotō Shinpei repeatedly deployed it as he traveled across the United States on his way to the Paris Peace Conference. One of Japan's most prominent officials, Gotō had served, over the previous two decades, as director of civilian affairs in the colonial government in Taiwan, director of the South Manchuria Railway Company, director of the Colonization Bureau (which oversaw Japan's overseas empire), home minister, and foreign minister. In Abraham Lincoln's hometown of Springfield, Illinois, Gotō delivered a speech declaring that Japan's actions in Taiwan and Korea did not differ from what the United States did in Puerto Rico and the

Philippines. Given that Koreans had never been told that the end of Japan's rule was "almost in sight," his argument rested on shaky grounds. Yet no American protested against Gotō when he stated upon arriving in New York that, although Koreans were not yet capable of self-government, Japan was "willing to grant Korea independence as the United States [was] to grant [the] Philippine[s] freedom."[101]

For Yun Ch'i-ho, however, comparing the Philippines and Korea only highlighted Japan's failure as a "progressive" colonial power. Even as he discouraged Korean petitions to Wilson, Yun criticized the Japanese colonial government by highlighting how the American governor of the Philippines, while his Japanese counterpart was busy suppressing the Korean anticolonial demonstrators, encouraged the colonizers and the colonized to collaborate in preparation for the Far Eastern Olympic Games to be held in Manila. The Japanese colonial government did not even allow Korean boys to play "inter-school sports in Seoul." In Yun's opinion, the March First demonstrations proved that Japan had "not only failed to win the good will of the Koreans, but also lost their confidence so that they dare not trust any promise she may make." After the demonstrations ended, Yun excoriated the "apologists" of the Japanese empire who compared Korea to the Philippines in their attempt to explain how "generous" Japan was towards its colonial subjects. He pointed out that the United States had promised to make the Philippines independent "as soon as practicable," something that Japan never did.[102]

But the situation in the Philippines was not as peaceful as Yun thought. To be sure, Gotō's argument that Japan's governance of Taiwan and Korea differed little from the Philippines was wide off the mark. The Japanese in Taiwan built a de facto police state to eliminate the old elites and force the colonized people into compliance, whereas the Americans in the Philippines built a hierarchical collaborative state that relied on educated elites (*ilustrados*) and the constabulary to convince the colonized people that the United States would eventually provide them self-government.[103] But the relationship between the colonizers and the colonized in the Philippines was hardly amicable. While the March First Movement was unfolding in Korea, workers of the Manila Electric Light & Railroad Company (Meralco) went on a four-month strike in response to food shortage, inflation, and rising rent. Simultaneously, the rising price of rice brewed Filipinos' discontent, and signs of social unrest began to appear in various regions producing agricultural commodities for mainland United States. In his annual report to Congress, Governor General Harrison downplayed these developments in 1919 by explaining that they were "well handled by the constabulary," but given that force's violent record it could be assumed that the colonial state's violence and the threat of violence are what kept the Philippines in order.[104]

As the unrest in the Philippines cast the United States in an unfavorable light, Americans preferred to compare the Japanese rule in Korea with the British rule in Egypt when they justified the US government's refusal to heed their calls for self-government. In spring 1919, as both Korea and Egypt were swept up by anticolonial movements strategically couched in the language of self-determination, the *New York Times* argued that enabling the native population to govern themselves again would only "buy a dubious moral satisfaction at the probable cost of most of the material prosperity of the country." More important, the US State Department instructed the American consulate in Seoul—under the supervision of the American embassy in Tokyo—to refrain from encouraging "any belief that the United States [would] assist the Korean nationalists in carrying out their plans," since that was "the attitude of the American Government in the Egyptian trouble." When Wilson left Paris in July without heeding Egyptians' or Koreans' appeals, the president confirmed what Yun predicted when he first learned about the parallel developments in March. "As long as the Peace Conf[erence] stands aloof from the Egyptian question," he wrote, "so long will they have nothing to do with the Korean problem."[105]

Yet many Korean protestors, especially immigrants and exiles in the United States, endeavored to prove that Koreans had a unique relationship with Americans. Unlike in Egypt, where American Protestant missionaries enjoyed a mutually beneficial relationship with the British colonial government against the resisting Muslim nationalists, American missionaries in Korea had been responsible for the Christian backgrounds of a significant number of the anticolonial demonstrators. Emphasizing the fact that sixteen of the thirty-three signers of the Korean declaration of independence were Protestants, the Korean Americans who gathered in Philadelphia in April 1919 attempted to gain American attention by characterizing their anticolonial protests as a Christian movement. To forge a strong publicity campaign, they also created the League of the Friends of Korea, a coalition of Korean Americans and white Americans that included several missionaries. Korean Americans had strong faith in the missionaries. After all, the only American who asked Roosevelt for American intervention against Japan in the final years of Korean sovereignty was missionary Homer Hulbert. Although Wilson did not respond to Koreans' appeals, both the publicity campaign and the missionary connections appeared to make headway in August 1919, when Senator Selden Spencer of Missouri quoted from Hulbert's letters to advocate on the Senate floor for an American investigation into the situation in Korea.[106]

On the other side of the Pacific Ocean, Yun argued that not even appeals to the Christian communities in the United States would help emancipate Korea. "It is often said that [a] Japanese is a Japanese first and then a Christian or something else. It is just as true to say that an American [is an American] first and then a Christian or something else," the general secretary of Seoul YMCA cynically commented in his diary a week after the League of the Friends of Korea was formed.[107] His own experience gave him little reason to believe that missionaries would help Koreans, any more than the president of the United States would. Unfortunately for Koreans, the missionaries proved him correct.

American Missionaries and the "Red Summer" in Korea

The American missionary response to the March First Movement in many ways resembled much of its earlier response to the Korean Conspiracy Case. Upon witnessing the brutality of the colonial police, American missionaries in Korea sent letters home that detailed how the Japanese were mistreating Korean Christians. The American missionary leaders in the United States again stopped short of asking for American intervention. Yet this time the missionary response to the Korean situation became even more complicated by the Black-white relations in the United States. In light of what NAACP Field Secretary James Weldon Johnson would call the "Red Summer"—a series of race riots across the United States that resulted in thousands of African Americans injured, hundreds killed, and seventy-seven lynched in 1919—the Japanese deployed stories of white-on-Black violence to undermine American missionaries' criticism of Japanese rule and to discourage Koreans from appealing to the United States.[108]

As in the conspiracy case, Arthur Judson Brown, the secretary of the Presbyterian Board of Missions, emerged as an unofficial spokesperson of missionary leaders in the United States. This time, however, Brown came into the spotlight by coincidence. Just as reports of Japanese colonial violence in Korea reached the United States in spring 1919, Brown's book *The Mastery of the Far East* was published. In it Brown described Japanese colonization in providential terms. "In the evolution of the race and the development of the plan of God," he wrote, "the time had come when it was for the best interests of the world and for the welfare of the Koreans themselves that Korea should come under the tutelage of Japan." To explain Japan's colonial project in familiar terms, Brown drew comparisons with American rule in the Philippines and white American relations with African Americans in Georgia, the latter reproduced verbatim from his 1912 report of the meeting on the Korean Conspiracy Case.[109]

Unlike the conspiracy case, however, Brown did not convene a meeting to devise a collective response of the various Protestant denominations to the March First Movement. That task fell to the ecumenical organization the Federal Council of Churches of Christ in America (FCC), in particular its Commission on Relations with the Orient, which was led by a returned missionary from Japan named Sidney Gulick. Originally named the Commission on Relations with Japan, the FCC commission was established in 1914 in response to the anti-Japanese immigration campaigns in California that had culminated in the passage of the Alien Land Law. As the commission expanded its scope to cover the greater "Orient," Gulick was forced to address other issues too. In response to public interest, Gulick published various missionaries' eyewitness accounts of Japanese colonial violence during the March First Movement under the title *The Korean Situation*, which was later entered into the *Congressional Record*.[110]

Yet the FCC by no means advocated Korean self-determination. To be sure, the report was intended to protect Koreans from further "inhumane treatment and injustice." Yet as Gulick and his coeditor of *The Korean Situation* explained, the publication of missionaries' accounts was necessary to generate American support for "the progressive, anti-militaristic forces in Japan" that would "secure justice and fair dealing" in colonial Korea.[111] What the FCC advocated was not the end of colonial rule but a more humane colonial rule.

Perhaps this should not have been surprising. During the Korean Conspiracy Case, Gulick, then still living in Japan, defended the arrest of Yun Ch'i-ho and other converts. He claimed that American newspapers falsely accused the Japanese of persecution based on "misrepresentation of facts." The Japanese co-lonial governor, he said, was working to prevent the church from being "per-verted from its true function and of being made a nursery of disloyalty and sedition." He argued that Japan protected religious freedom in the colony. As proof, he adduced a passage from the *Annual Report on Reforms and Progress*.[112]

In spite of Gulick's and the FCC's conciliatory posture toward Japanese rule of Korea, American missionaries became targets of the Japanese press. A week into the March First protests, US Chargé d'Affaires J. V. A. MacMurray warned Secretary of State Robert Lansing that, "as in the case of the previous Korean conspiracy," there may be "an attempt to involve and to compromise the American missionaries." The following week, the American consul in Seoul re-ceived a formal statement from the colonial governor declaring that missionaries were not complicit in the protests. But the declaration proved ineffective. The Japanese press, according to Roland Morris, the US Minister in Tokyo, made "scant mention of this fact" and blamed the missionaries for preaching to Koreans "the principle of self-determination."[113] By the end of the summer, news reached the United States that the Japanese press was attacking American missionaries, specifically by arguing that the missionaries should "prevent such a barbarous thing as lynching [of African Americans] in their own country before thinking of enlightening Koreans." While the violence of the Red Summer prompted the FCC to finally recognize its own shortcomings in addressing race relations and formulate a program to combat racism, it also offered the Japanese press with an opportunity to highlight American racism, which the Japanese delegation had directly experienced in Paris.[114]

That racism came in the form of Wilson's rejection of a proposal to add a racial nondiscrimination clause to the Covenant of the League of Nations. The Japanese delegation proposed this clause primarily to counteract anti-Japanese legislation in the United States and the British dominions that diminished Japan's status among the circle of great powers. But after Japan's proposal was approved by a majority vote in the League of Nations commission (11 out of 17), Wilson, the chairman of the commission, overturned the decision saying that it needed unanimous support. The American president feared that Britain and its dominions would refuse to join the League if the Covenant contained the clause that undermined various anti-immigration laws, especially after the Australian delegation (representing the White Australia policy that prohibited the immigration of Japanese and Chinese alike) refused to compromise with the Japanese delegation during the conversations leading up to the vote.[115]

Although they knew the nondiscrimination clause did not seek universal racial equality, Black American leaders saw in Japan's proposal a valiant effort to fight against white supremacy. Among the most vocal in their support was James Weldon Johnson, who became so excited by the proposal that he endorsed Japan's imperialist actions. Johnson, a former diplomat who had served as US consul in Venezuela and Nicaragua under Theodore Roosevelt and William Howard Taft, was well aware that Japan's claims to the former German concession in Shandong, China, violated the principle of "self-determination." But since the postwar settlement was likely to "degenerate into the old game" of land grabbing among imperial powers, Johnson rationalized his view in the *New York Age*, "we want to see Japan grab as much as she possibly can." "We should like to see Japan relatively as powerful in the Orient as the United States is in the western continent," he wrote, "We should like to see an Asiatic Monroe Doctrine with Japan as its interpreter and administrator."[116]

Perhaps because of such positive views of Japan, the majority of African American newspapers did not protest against the Japanese appropriation of American racial violence during the Red Summer. To be sure, later in 1921, Black socialists A. Philip Randolph and Chandler Owen argued that the Japanese press merely used the news of white-on-Black violence to prepare its own citizens for war against the United States.[117] But they were the exception. During the Red Summer, major African American newspapers, including the *New York Age*, the *Chicago Defender*, the *Philadelphia Tribune*, and *Baltimore Afro-American*, remained silent on the widely circulating news that Japan was using the news of anti-Black violence to undercut Wilson's rhetoric. Meanwhile, NAACP's *Crisis* reprinted in appreciation a passage from the *Nippu Jiji*, a Japanese American newspaper in Hawai'i: "Certain elements among the Americans, finding a capital opportunity in the Korean question, make it an excuse for anti-Japanese agitation. . . . But, who knows but that the United States, the symbol of democracy and liberty, is being confronted with the Negro question far more seriously than the Korean question."[118]

The Korean immigrants and exiles in the United States who learned about the proliferation of Black-Korean comparisons thought little of them, but Yun Ch'i-ho became furious when the colonial government began deploying the comparisons in Korea to discourage the colonized from looking up to the United States. Upon attending a conference at the main colonial government building in Seoul during the Red Summer, Yun encountered an official who "mentioned the horrible race discriminations of the Whites against the Blacks in America, and asked the people [in the audience] if the Japanese had ever treated the Korean[s] in a like manner." When he returned home, Yun ranted in his diary, exclaiming that the official "should have remembered that the difference between the

Fig. 3.3 A 1919 article on the Red Summer that appeared in the Japanese colonial government's Korean-language newspaper, *Maeil Sinbo*. The caption explains that a Japanese in the United States photographed this racially motivated murder of a Black man. The photographer was Jun Fujita (1888–1963). "Miin ŭi hŭgin taehaksal," *Maeil Sinbo*, December 15, 1919, 3. Taehanmin'guk Shinmun Ak'aibŭ, Kungnip Chungang Tosŏgwan, South Korea.

Jap[anese] and the Kor[ean] [was] not so fundamental and glaring as the difference between the White and the Black."[119]

The Japanese colonial government in Korea continued to deploy stories of white-on-Black violence after the Red Summer. Late in 1919 the *Maeil Sinbo* explained in detail "what Americans call 'lynching'" (transliterated to Korean as *rinch'i*). The article defined lynching as "an extrajudicial punishment" that had been prevalent in the American South but recently had begun to proliferate in cities such as Washington, DC, and Chicago. The article was accompanied by a photograph, taken by the Japanese immigrant photographer Jun Fujita during the Chicago race riot of 1919, of a white lynch mob murdering a Black man with a brick.[120]

As the Japanese spread the news of white-on-Black violence, it appears that Yun lost faith in the conviction that Koreans should emulate African Americans. "Many a Japanese writer points to the cruel discrimination of the Whites in America against the Negroes as a sort of excuse for the Japanese atrocities in Korea," he complained in October 1920. He then responded to the continued use of the Black-Korean comparisons by making a chart, in which he made side-by-side comparisons to differentiate the two peoples by describing African Americans with racist remarks that cannot be found anywhere else in the diary:

Negroes in U.S.	Koreans in Korea
1. The White people of America owe nothing to the Negro for their civilization.	1. Is there anything, in religion, science, art, literature, that Japan does not owe to Korea for their introduction?
2. The Negro, i[n] physical appearance and mental capacities, is inferior to the White.	2. In physical appearance and mental capacities the Korean is a perfect equal with the Japanese.
3. The Negro was brought to America as slaves to be employed as beasts [of] burden.	3. The Koreans for centuries maintained diplomatic relations with Japan on equal footing.
4. When the Whites bought the Negro slaves they did not promise them (Negroes) anything but bare means of existence in exchange of their labor.	4. When the annexation was forced into effect [...] the Japanese Emperor and the Government promised the Korean that he would be treated as kindly as the Japanese—the children of the same benevolent, fatherly Emperor.
5. The Negro never owned America.	5. The Koreans owned Korea.*

*October 9, 1920, *YCHI*, 8: 148.

This entry is striking not simply because Yun had praised Booker T. Washington as recently as January 1920. It is also shocking because he did not hesitate to use such racist language in his depiction of African Americans. Given that he would never mention Washington again, it appears that Yun, like many African American leaders, came to see the limits of the Tuskegee program. But there was an important difference in that the African Americans who criticized the shortcomings of Washington's approach after the Atlanta riot of 1906 never dismissed the entire Black population as Yun did after the Red Summer of 1919. The way he rejected the Black-Korean comparisons strongly suggested that, despite his three-decade-long engagement with African Americans, Yun cared about African Americans only to the extent that learning about their experiences would help him guide Koreans' "development." Once he decided that Washington's principle of "self-help" would be of no use to Koreans, he lost interest in all things African American. For the rest of his life, he never attempted to find another African American leader to follow or even read about, even though there were numerous others engaged in racial "uplift" projects. Instead, he searched for pathways for Koreans' upward socioeconomic mobility almost exclusively within the missionary network and the Japanese empire.

In the first two decades of the twentieth century, American and Japanese imperialists assessed each other's worth and defended their own colonial policies against critics by engaging in comparative exercises that brought disparate geographies into conversation. The comparisons heavily focused on the "subject races," but they revealed far more about the people making the comparisons than the people being compared. The American and Japanese imperialists who referred to the Philippines as a point of comparison for Korea cast themselves as members of "progressive" races who ruled their colonies by social "reform" and racial "tutelage." The lived realities of the Filipinos and Koreans did not match the lofty rhetoric of their oppressors, of course. Although there were signs of infrastructural and economic reform, the supposed end goal of self-government remained far out of sight. When American and Japanese imperialists needed to justify keeping Koreans under colonial rule, they conveniently pointed to the conditions in the American South, where Jim Crow laws and racial violence sustained racial inequality. Although the Black-Korean comparison for decades served as a source of inspiration for certain members of a "subject race" like Yun, it ultimately proved most effective in denying Koreans their right to self-government.

American missionary leaders' reactions to the Korean Conspiracy Case and the March First Movement revealed that even some of the white Americans most invested in the lives of Koreans were taken with ideas about "race development"

Fig. 3.4 Yun Ch'i-ho, dressed in a white, Korean-style overcoat, posed for this photo in 1926 with Emory University alumni in Seoul. Even as he denounced American racism, Yun continued to serve as a key liaison between Korean Protestants and American missionaries until World War II. Yun Ch'i-ho Papers, box 17, folder 5. Stuart A. Rose Manuscript, Archives, and Rare Book Library, Emory University.

that had gained currency among American academics, diplomats, and politicians. When missionaries witnessed Japan's violent acts against Koreans, they demanded the reform of Japan's colonial rule. They did not ask for the decolonization of Korea. It remains unclear as to how many Korean Christians knew this fact, but those who had insight into the missionary leaders, like Yun, remained unconvinced by various Korean nationalists' argument that missionaries, and the US president best known for his "missionary diplomacy," would help them bring an end to Japan's rule.

In the ensuing years, American missionaries remained concerned with the colonial government's treatment of Koreans but stopped short of supporting their anticolonial aspirations. The March First Movement proved to be a watershed moment in Korea's history, but not exactly the way Koreans had hoped. While the Korean Provisional Government in Shanghai persistently attempted to expose Japan's colonial violence on the world stage, the Japanese colonial government deflected foreign criticism by changing its method of colonial administration in the aftermath of widespread protests in 1919. The colonial administrators discarded the "military rule" in Korea and instituted what became known as the "cultural rule," incorporating moderate Korean nationalists into the colonial system through cultural hegemony rather than direct suppression.[121] They also converted the largely symbolic privy council (*chungch'uwŏn*) into a body of Korean advisers and instituting a new system of limited self-rule (*chach'ije*) that enabled Koreans to run city assemblies and local chambers of commerce.[122] Having noticed the changes in Japan's colonial administration in the 1920s, many Americans believed that the Japanese had reformed themselves to become better colonists. But most Americans had not seen the whole picture. Korea appeared relatively peaceful only because the colonists had pushed out anti-colonial guerrilla warfare out to Manchuria, where the Japanese Army from Korea joined forces with Japan's consular police to conduct "search-and-destroy" missions. When American missionaries in Korea criticized Japan's imperial violence in Manchuria, the colonial government and its defenders pushed back by deploying yet another comparison: they argued that Japan was simply engaged in its own version of the "Punitive Expedition" in Manchuria, akin to the American military operations in Northern Mexico during World War I, when the Wilson administration deployed troops across the border in search of the Mexican revolutionary Pancho Villa.[123]

Empires of Exclusion

The Abrogation of the Gentlemen's Agreement, 1919–1924

Like so many people around the world, Kiyoshi Karl Kawakami followed the Paris Peace Conference from afar with excitement and nervousness. When Japan's former foreign minister Baron Gotō Shinpei passed through the United States on his way to Paris, Kawakami accompanied him across the country from his office in San Francisco with the intention of attending the conference together. But Kawakami turned around in New York. As he explained to Sidney Gulick, an American missionary who stood as the single most important white ally of Japanese immigrants, California's anti-Japanese immigration sentiment was on the rise again.[1]

What made the postwar anti-Japanese campaigns so formidable, Kawakami told Gulick, was the emergence of V. S. McClatchy as the new leader of the exclusionist lobby. McClatchy was different from the working-class exclusionists who organized the Asiatic Exclusion League in San Francisco during the Russo-Japanese War. He was also different from the professional-class exclusionists who secured the Alien Land Act in 1913. One of the largest landowners in Northern California and the president of the *Sacramento Bee*, McClatchy was on a first name basis with some of the most powerful people in his state. Yet even money and connections were not what made him so dangerous. As Kawakami explained to Gulick, McClatchy had toured Japan, China, Korea, and the Philippines after the Great War and, upon returning to California, began using what he learned in Asia against Japanese immigrants in the United States.

McClatchy single-handedly changed the terms of the debates over Japanese immigration and immigrants by reframing them within the larger international context. By coincidence, he passed through Korea during the March First demonstrations, and he used the pages of the *Sacramento Bee* to expose the violence with which the Japanese colonial government suppressed Korean demonstrators.[2] Koreans in the United States immediately praised him as a

The Allure of Empire. Chris Suh, Oxford University Press. © Oxford University Press 2023.
DOI: 10.1093/oso/9780197631614.003.0005

champion of their anticolonial cause, but for McClatchy, exposing Japan's colonial violence was important for a different reason.[3] He declared in the *Bee*
that the most pressing question confronting Americans could be summarized
as "Shall this country of ours be held for our white descendants, or shall it
be turned over to the Japanese [so] that they may rule those descendants as
they rule in Korea to-day?"[4] Echoes of McClatchy's words could be heard in
the renewed anti-Japanese campaigns in California and various congressional
hearings on Japanese immigration. Japan's troubled relationship with other
parts of Asia came to shape the political debates regarding the future of Japanese
immigrants to the United States.

This chapter argues that such international framing of the Japanese immigration issue was crucial to the success of the California exclusionists' campaigns
for the restriction of alien land rights in 1920 and the end of Japanese immigration to the United States in 1924. By doing so, it reassesses the meaning of
Japanese exclusion to its contemporaries. As dominant works in immigration
history have argued, the Immigration Act of 1924, or the Johnson-Reed Act,
represented the culmination of Anglo-Saxon nativism that resurfaced during
the economic depression of 1920–1921. It also symbolized the convergence of
Progressive Era social science, demography, and law that codified the Japanese
"race" as "unassimilable" and "ineligible to citizenship."[5] Yet the domestic focus
of this scholarship has obscured one of the defining features of the post–World
War I anti-Japanese movement: its persistent effort to cast its desire for exclusion as a reaction to Japan's activities in Asia. Uncovering this feature allows for a
more precise understanding of how the interwar exclusionists succeeded where
their prewar counterparts had failed while simultaneously enabling a more ex-
pansive understanding of how US immigration restriction functioned as an instrument for Americans' exercise of global power.[6]

An act against Japanese immigrants was not just an expression of domestic
racism, but a geopolitical decision against an imperial partner in the Pacific.
What had been the case from the beginning of California's anti-Japanese movement in 1905 became even more obvious in the aftermath of World War I when
Woodrow Wilson rejected Japan's proposal to add a "racial equality clause" to
the Covenant of the League of Nations, a proposal that many white supremacists
interpreted as a challenge to the anti-Asian immigration policies of the United
States, Canada, Australia, and New Zealand.[7] McClatchy was aware of how
exclusionists in the British dominions similarly wished to keep their countries
"white."[8] Yet instead of expressing solidarity with them, he justified his demand
for Japanese exclusion as a response to Japan's imperial actions against what he
called "other nations of her own color."[9] He expediently downplayed his desire
for white supremacy by publicly positioning himself as a supporter of the Korean
and Chinese victims of Japan's imperial violence.

McClatchy's internationally framed arguments had two dimensions: one focused on what the Japanese empire did in its overseas possessions, and the other focused on what it did in its metropole. The first line of argument established the Japanese as a militant "race," inciting the fear that the Japanese could colonize the United States as they had done already in places like Korea. Although this argument built on the popular "Yellow Peril" literature warning of a coming Asian invasion, McClatchy gave his racist campaign a semblance of humanitarianism by making sympathetic gestures toward the Koreans who were suffering under Japan's rule.[10] The second line of argument established Japan as an exclusionary empire, insisting that Japan was in no position to criticize the American desire for exclusion since Japan practiced immigration restriction at home, against laborers from Korea and China. Although this argument ignored the fact that immigration restrictions practiced by the United States and Japan were drastically different in scale and method, McClatchy succeeded in presenting Japan as an exclusionary state that hypocritically demanded an open door for its emigrants abroad.

While both arguments shaped the political campaign for the 1920 Alien Land Law in California, the second argument proved particularly influential in the congressional decision to end Japanese immigration. After McClatchy convinced several key politicians to see Japan as an exclusionary state, the architects of the Johnson-Reed Act justified the provision for Japanese exclusion with the statement that "Japan herself, in the exercise of a similarly wise protection for her own people, excludes the Chinese and Koreans."[11]

Seen this way, the 1924 Immigration Act marks not only the culmination of post–World War I Anglo-Saxon nativism and the convergence of demography, economics, and law in the American racial codification of "unassailability," but also the end of an era when the United States held back on Japanese exclusion based on US policymakers' positive view of the Japanese empire.[12] As policymakers' perception of Japanese "civilizing" capacity took a negative turn after World War I, Japan's imperial activities in Asia became the very reason why Americans decided to no longer hold back a unilateral exclusion policy against Japan.

It is within this complex relationship between the changing American perceptions of the Japanese empire and the creation of a new US immigration policy that the actions of the Koreans and Japanese in the United States must be understood.[13] Despite McClatchy's obvious racist motives, Koreans in the United States, including the president of the Korean Provisional Government (KPG) Syngman Rhee, celebrated his coverage of the March First Movement. Although it was contradictory that an Asian immigrant group supported one of the most infamous anti-Asian immigration activists, many Koreans in the United States found it politically expedient to align themselves with McClatchy, especially as his campaign influenced several members of Congress to denounce Japan's colonial rule in Korea. Japanese immigrant elites in California likewise engaged with the exclusionists' arguments in surprising ways. While some, like Kanzaki Kiichi of the Japanese Association of America, attempted to disentangle the "domestic" issue of Japanese immigrants from the "foreign" issue of Japan's relationship with Korea and China, other Japanese immigrants, like Kiyoshi Karl Kawakami, defended Japan's actions in Asia. Meanwhile, a Japanese American scholar ostracized from the Japanese immigrant community, Yoshi S. Kuno, publicly conceded that Japan did take a contradictory posture toward immigration. Yet admitting Japan's own restrictive policy, as Kuno did, turned out to be dangerous. It served as evidence that the US exclusionists had a rational basis for demanding exclusion. For both Korean and Japanese immigrants, their political activities were shaped and limited by exclusionists who set the terms of the debates regarding US immigration restriction as well as the United States' broader relationship with Asia.

California Exclusionists and the Korean Independence Movement

Based on his family history, V. S. McClatchy was an unlikely man to take interest in events across the Pacific. He was born in 1857 to an Irish immigrant named James McClatchy, a former newspaper editor for the *New York Tribune* who had moved to California during the Gold Rush. The elder McClatchy failed to find gold but emerged as a leader of land squatters who successfully turned themselves into landowners, eventually becoming a large landowner himself in the Sutter Basin and the publisher of the *Sacramento Bee*.[14] His sons, V. S. (Valentine Stuart) and C. K. (Charles Kenny), inherited the land and the paper, causes to which they devoted much of their lives. While running the *Bee* together, V. S. served as the chair of the California State Reclamation Board (1911–1917), and C. K. vocally campaigned against Japanese immigrants' right to own agricultural land in California.[15] Although V. S. remained publicly silent on the Japanese immigrant issue until the end of World War I, his postwar rhetoric demonstrated that he was well versed in the predominant arguments for exclusion before the war.[16] In his newspaper articles and in congressional testimonies, V. S. McClatchy repeatedly argued that Japanese immigrants cheapened the value of American labor and prevented the white working class from becoming independent landowners. Like Chester Rowell, he pointed to the racial composition and labor conditions in Hawaiʻi as a warning sign for Californians. Following E. A. Ross and the

Asiatic Exclusion League, he cited the high birth rate of Japanese immigrants to arouse fear over their rapid population growth.[17]

McClatchy's emergence had much to do with the fact that previous leaders of California's anti-Japanese movements were no longer in any position to guide the state's nativists. After 1913 the Asiatic Exclusion League exercised minimal influence in politics. Olaf Tveitmoe followed, rather than led, the state's anti-Japanese movements.[18] Chester Rowell, the leader of the Lincoln-Roosevelt League, still remained active in politics, yet he was struck by a mysterious illness that bound him to bed for much of 1919.[19] Furthermore, Rowell's interactions with Japanese elites, not only local Isseis like Kiyoshi Karl Kawakami but also luminaries such as Japan's former foreign minister Gotō Shinpei, tempered his racism to the point that he appeared conciliatory toward the Japanese.[20] He and like-minded lawmakers in Sacramento successfully prevented the revision of the 1913 Alien Land Law to eliminate the three-year lease clause. Ironically, it was the relentless work of V. S. McClatchy, a wealthy landowner who had little to gain economically by prohibiting Japanese immigrants from leasing land, that delivered what the white working class demanded from the state's professional class.

McClatchy's appeal depended on his ability to recast these old arguments for exclusion within an international frame, which he developed during his tour of Asia in 1919. While he publicly stated that he took the trip on the advice of his physician who recommended time off from work to focus on his health, McClatchy's writings suggest that he went to Asia to confirm his hunch that the rise of a Japanese presence in California was but a local phase of a transpacific problem caused by the rise of the Japanese empire. In China he found much evidence to support the claim that Japan was the "Germany of Asia." Japan had taken advantage of the wartime chaos to occupy the former German concessions in Shandong, bribe Chinese officials to secure railroad rights, and then refuse to return these concessions to China after the war. In attempting to hide the infamous Twenty-One Demands from its allies in 1915, Japan had shown "the unparallel piece of bad faith" to the United States and Britain. Such actions, McClatchy argued, foreshadowed possible interference with American commercial interests in China, as well as a possible takeover of the Philippines upon its independence from the United States. Most important, McClatchy suggested that Japanese actions in Asia provided a preview of what could happen in California if Japan's imperial expansion was not restrained.[21]

McClatchy found the most visceral evidence of the dangers of Japanese expansion in Korea. Like many foreign visitors to Korea of his time, he was shown all the work that Japan had done for the "development" of the colony. He was impressed by the railroad network, public education system, reforestation campaigns, and sanitary improvements made in the capital. Yet because of the

Fig. 4.1 A rare photograph of V. S. McClatchy. John B. Wallace, "Waving the Yellow
Flag in California," *Dearborn Independent*, September 11, 1920, 6. Chronicling
America: Historic American Newspapers, Library of Congress.

timing of his visit, McClatchy also witnessed the violence that often accompanied
such reform projects. He reported how the Japanese "gendarmes" and "coolies"
violently suppressed the Koreans, who, in his words, displayed "wonderful" capacity in "self-control and organized passive resistance." McClatchy smuggled
out in his money belt what became the first full text of the Korean declaration
of independence to reach the United States, and upon return, he shared it with
various newspapers for dissemination. His personal account of the March First
Movement in the *Sacramento Bee* was also prominently featured on the front page
of William Randolph Hearst's anti-Asian paper, the *San Francisco Examiner*.[22]

Many Koreans in the United States welcomed McClatchy's actions.
Immediately after the text of the declaration became available, the Korean
National Association's organ, the *Sinhan Minbo*, published in San Francisco,
translated the English version back to Korean for its subscribers.[23] The *Sinhan
Minbo* also translated McClatchy's *Sacramento Bee* article and published it as an
uncensored account of the anticolonial movement.[24] Koreans on the East Coast

were even more enthusiastic. When Syngman Rhee learned about McClatchy's role in exposing Japanese colonial violence, he invited the Californian to join him at the First Korean Congress scheduled to be held in Philadelphia. "Your name is so closely related with the Independence Movement, and I am sure that every Korean would be delighted like my-self to receive any letter that bears your name," he wrote.[25] Although McClatchy did not attend, he mailed his copy of the declaration to Rhee and gave the organizers of the Korean Congress permission to reprint parts of *Germany of Asia*.[26] Soon McClatchy's article was entered into the *Congressional Record* along with various missionaries' reports on Japanese violence against Korean converts when the organizers' counselor submitted to the Senate Foreign Relations Committee a statement on behalf of the newly founded Korean Commission, which aimed to represent the Korean Provisional Government in the United States.[27] What is more, McClatchy reached out to a member of the House Foreign Affairs Committee, Representative William E. Mason of Illinois, asking that the US government offer a "kind word and, if it may, a helping hand to Korea." McClatchy highlighted Korea's situation with a comparison to that of the Philippines. While the United States was making "every effort" to "prepare the people for self[-]government" in its colony, he said, Japan was using "ruthless methods" to "destroy the national identity of the people."[28]

McClatchy, of course, had little interest in the aspirations of the Koreans. He simply found the story of Japan's repression of Koreans useful to stoke white Americans' fear of Japanese immigrants. Immediately after docking in San Francisco, McClatchy told the *Chronicle* that Korea's independence was "forever lost." In the *Sacramento Bee*, he noted that the organizers of the March First Movement were influenced by a "mistaken belief" that the principle of self-determination, as articulated by Woodrow Wilson, could be applied to Korea, a statement that the staff of the *Sinhan Minbo* certainly read but deliberately omitted in their translation of the text.[29] In December 1919, in an article written for the *Grizzly Bear*, the official organ of the nativist fraternal organization the Native Sons of the Golden West, McClatchy revealed his true intention of highlighting Japan's colonial violence in Korea. He said that his readers had to decide between preserving the American West for "our white descendants" and allowing the Japanese to take over and rule "those descendants as they rule in Korea."[30]

McClatchy's argument found a receptive audience in California. At the Los Angeles County Anti-Asiatic Association meeting, William I. Traeger, a grand trustee of the Native Sons, aroused the crowd by auguring that "what has happened in Corea will happen here if the Japanese got the upper hand."[31] In a statement to the House Immigration Committee, Albert Chappelle, a private investigator associated with the Los Angeles district attorney's office, argued that "Japanese robbery and butchery in Korea, done again in Shantung," showed what the Japanese were capable of when they remained "unrestrained by fear or by policy."[32] Elwood Mead, the chair of the California Land Settlement Board, maintained that the Japanese immigrants who bought land against the wishes of white Californians were motivated by the "same spirit" as their counterparts in Korea and China.[33]

Perhaps the most significant development in the convergence between the anti-Japanese movement and the Korean independence movement was US Senator James D. Phelan's decision to introduce a congressional resolution to express sympathy with the anticolonial aspirations of the Koreans.[34] Phelan, whose long record of involvement in anti-Japanese campaigns dated back to 1900, was running for reelection to the US Senate with the campaign slogan "Keep California White."[35] But ironically, Phelan's position on Japanese immigration was compatible with his position on the Korean independence movement. As a Democrat, he had no problem publicly stating that he supported Wilson's vision of the postwar order just as the organizing leaders of the March First Movement did. Phelan, so occupied with finding any damaging material against the Japanese, could make a sympathetic gesture toward Koreans without undermining Wilson. The resolution did not make any promises regarding the end of Japanese colonial rule in Korea.

Phelan's stance stood in stark contrast to his Republican counterpart, Senator Hiram Johnson. For the former governor of California, the events in East Asia only served as evidence that joining the League of Nations would be a terrible decision for the United States. It would mean, as he wrote C. K. McClatchy, that Americans would be "sending their sons into Europe, Asia, and Africa, to settle with their blood, every foreign quarrel which may rise." He also interpreted the League as an alliance of imperial powers and abhorred the idea of aligning the interests of the United States with Japan's. After reading V. S.'s article on Korea, Johnson wrote that, if the Koreans were to successfully stage a "real revolt" against Japan with China's support, the United States under the League of Nations could be "compelled to draft an army to fight [for] Japan, and to whip the aggression of China, and keep Korea in subjection."[36]

In Congress, where he similarly painted a dark future for the United States if it became a member of the League, Johnson was joined by other "irreconcilables" who also used Japan's treatment of Korea as an excuse to justify why the United States shouldn't join.[37] William Borah of Idaho argued that the League respected no "principle of self-determination or the rights of small nations except as the five great nations see fit to grant it as a benevolent despot." Since ratifying the Treaty of Versailles would make the United States an ally of the imperial powers that suppressed anticolonial demonstrations in Egypt, India, Ireland, and Korea, he said, American refusal to enter the League would not "break the heart" of

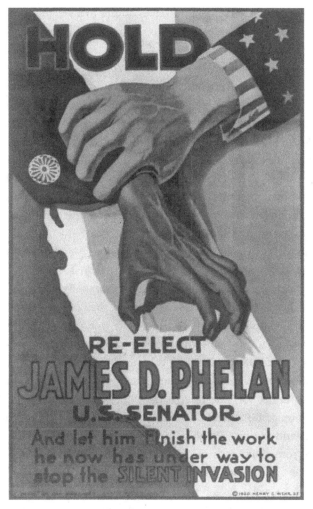

Fig. 4.2 Senator James D. Phelan, who introduced a congressional resolution to express sympathy with the anticolonial aspirations of the Koreans under Japanese rule, ran for re-election with the slogan "Keep California White." Phelan campaign poster 1920. Copyright Henry C. Wehr. Library of Congress Prints and Photographs Division, LC-USZ62-90410.

the world as Wilson claimed.[38] George W. Norris of Nebraska used the Japanese violence in Korea as a prelude to what would happen in China if the United States let its wartime ally do as it wished: Japan would be blotting out "the Christian religion and destroying the Christian churches."[39] Likewise, Robert La Follette Sr. of Wisconsin argued that the League's covenant was "so cunningly conceived that the first act of revolution in India, Korea, Egypt, or Ireland will be interpreted as a 'threat of war' and a disturbance of the 'peace of nations.'" "Can it be hoped that at Geneva, with the confidence of the world blasted in the stability of our purposes and ourselves bound to a covenant which pledges our support for the status quo, we shall be a powerful advocate for Korea, India, Egypt, and Ireland?" he asked.[40]

While Korean Americans enthusiastically supported Phelan's resolution and closely followed the "irreconcilable" senators' mentions of the Korean independence struggles in Congress, opponents of Japanese exclusion pointed out that these politicians only brought up the March First Movement to smear the Japanese government and Japanese Americans.[41] Sōga Yasutarō, the editor of the Honolulu newspaper *Nippu Jiji*, described Phelan's act as a scheme to create "dissensions" between Japan and the United States.[42] John P. Irish, one of the leading white opponents of the California Alien Land Law, went further by responding to Phelan's resolution in the Japanese colonial government's official English-language organ, the *Seoul Press*. In his article, which was also published in the San Francisco Japanese American newspaper the *Nichibei Shinbun*, Irish openly wondered whether American missionaries in Korea had "any right to criticize" the Japanese actions there, while Phelan was engaged in "a campaign of lies and a shameful agitation" against the "progressive Japanese in our midst."[43]

Yet the exclusionists' strategy worked, and it worked particularly well to undermine one of their most powerful opponents, Sidney Gulick. Gulick had been spearheading a campaign to counter anti-Japanese racism in the United States ever since the passage of the first Alien Land Act in 1913. In 1919 he organized the National Committee for Constructive Immigration Legislation (NCCIL) to introduce an immigration restriction plan that could potentially appease both the exclusionists and the Japanese. Unlike the existing restriction measures against immigrants from Asia, such as the Chinese Exclusion Law, the Gentlemen's Agreement, and the Asiatic Barred Zone Act, Gulick's "Percentage Plan" would not single out a specific nation or geographical area as a target of exclusion and instead would uniformly restrict immigration from all countries using a census-based quota system.[44] In June 1919 he received an opportunity to present his plan to the House Immigration Committee.[45] Yet the news of Japan's militant actions in Asia diminished his chance of receiving significant congressional or popular support. Robert Newton Lynch, the vice president of the San Francisco Chamber of Commerce, discouraged Gulick from campaigning for the Percentage Plan in California, as Japan's actions in Korea and China made it "somewhat difficult" to advocate for concessions regarding Japanese immigration. As Wallace R. Farrington, the editor of the *Honolulu Advertiser*, warned Gulick, American missionaries returning from Asia were confirming many of McClatchy's statements about Japanese militarism.[46] Gulick himself directly felt the pressure of the missionary reports. He was forced to take time off from his Percentage Plan campaign to help edit a collection of missionaries' accounts of the violence in Korea for the Federal Council of Churches of Christ in America (FCC).[47]

The Korean situation was more than just a distraction that stole the momentum of the Percentage Plan; it forced Gulick to abandon a key aspect of his argument, that immigration reform was necessary to maintain the missionary enterprise in Asia. Although he insisted in front of the House Immigration Committee that the anti-Japanese movement in California threatened the well-being of "Christian work" in Japan, Gulick was well aware that this argument had been weakened by the widespread perception that Japan was hostile toward Christianity—a stance demonstrated by its treatment of the Korean converts.[48] The publication of the FCC's report on Korea did little to change this perception of Japan or appease the Korean immigrants who believed that Gulick was "pro-Japanese."[49] It also did not stop the exclusionists from attacking him. While Phelan continued to call him an "agent" of Japan, McClatchy appeared in front of the House Immigration Committee to directly undercut his religious argument. McClatchy contended that Japan's relationship with Christianity had been "sufficiently indicated" through its suppression of the March First Movement, during which the Korean converts were "subjected to the greatest persecution and torture," on the "theory that their Christianity imbued them with liberal ideas more or less dangerous to the maintenance of Japan's power."[50]

In reality, McClatchy had little sympathy for Korean Christians—in fact, he directly told Gulick that he opposed the Percentage Plan in part because its provision to admit victims of religious persecution would enable "a considerable portion of the Korean nation" to legally immigrate to the United States.[51] Yet his strategic deployment of the news of Japanese violence in Korea, verified by various missionary accounts, proved useful in discouraging many American friends of Japan from taking action against the exclusionists.

The impact of his strategy became obvious when Harada Tasuku, a pastor and educator who had been commissioned by the Japanese business leader Shibusawa Eiichi to study the anti-Japanese movement in California, received responses to a questionnaire he sent out to prominent Americans on the eve of the 1920 election. In addition to Gulick, President Wallace Alexander of the San Francisco Chamber of Commerce, President Ozora Davis of the Chicago Theological Seminary, and well-known academics George Trumbull Ladd of Yale and Payson Treat of Stanford responded that the news of Japanese colonial violence in Seoul, along with Japan's refusal to return Shandong, made it difficult to gain American support for Japanese immigration. The collective feeling of the friends of Japan was summarized by H. B. Johnson, the superintendent of the Pacific Coast Japanese Mission of the Methodist Church who had long defended Japanese immigrant rights. He lamented that the "mixing of Far Eastern questions with purely domestic ones" contributed to the spreading of the anti-Japanese sentiment in California, where voters did not reelect Phelan but chose to strengthen the existing Alien Land Law.[52]

California Exclusionists and
Japan's Immigration Policy

Deploying the news of Japanese violence in Korea was only one of the two prongs of McClatchy's strategy. He also repeatedly told stories of Japan's refusal to admit Korean and Chinese migrant workers. Although he knew little about Japan's immigration policy, his incomplete knowledge did not prevent him from creating a strong impression on voters in California and members of the US Congress that Japan had an exclusionary policy.

McClatchy first learned about Japan's immigration restriction during his tour from an English-language newspaper published in Japan. According to the *Japan Chronicle*, some two hundred Chinese "coolies" had been repatriated from Hiroshima in early 1919 after their employer, an ironworks company, failed to gain work authorization for them from the local prefectural government.[53] When he returned to California, McClatchy expanded upon this story to argue that Japan restricted the immigration of the Chinese and Koreans for the same reason that the United States wanted to exclude the Japanese: that the low standards of living of the immigrants made economic competition impossible for their own people. McClatchy probably mentioned the Koreans as excluded subjects to capitalize on the plight of the colonized people already seen as victims of the Japanese empire. Yet the details of Japan's immigration policy mattered far less for him than the contention that Japan was an exclusionary state.

McClatchy pursued this line of argument not only in print but also in person when he appeared before the US House and Senate Immigration Committees. In a letter prepared for the House Committee in anticipation of the hearings on Gulick's Percentage Plan, McClatchy explained that Japan's pride should not be hurt by American exclusion, for it was in effect the same measure that Japan "enforces against Chinese and Koreans, and for precisely similar reasons." Just as the Japanese did to the Chinese and Koreans, McClatchy contended, Americans wished to prevent further immigration of the Japanese for "economic and not on racial grounds." When he appeared in person at the Percentage Plan hearings, McClatchy stated that Japan was "inconsistent" in its argument for racial equality, as it excluded the two Asian groups at home all the while protesting against Western exclusion of the Japanese abroad.[54] In his testimony to the Senate committee that same year, he argued that Japan "does not permit, and . . . never has permitted, the introduction into Japan of Chinese and Korean labor."[55]

Contrary to McClatchy's claim, there was a history of Chinese and Korean labor migration to Japan. A more accurate claim would have been that Japan had become more restrictive in recent years. During the Russo-Japanese War, Japanese industrialists addressed the labor shortage at home by admitting a record high number of Chinese laborers. Following the annexation of Korea, Japanese industrialists and the colonial government began recruiting Korean laborers from the colony. Tens of thousands of recruited Koreans migrated to Japan during World War I to support the manufacturing boom. It was not until the end of the war that Japan—out of fear that the end of the boom would cause labor struggles among the unemployed, and that participants of the March First Movement would cause problems in the metropole—began restricting the migration of Korean laborers.[56]

The Japanese restriction of Chinese and Korean laborers relied on different methods for each group. The Imperial Ordinance No. 352, which McClatchy repeatedly mentioned, was relevant only in the case of Chinese laborers. The ordinance, cited in the deportation case of the two hundred Chinese laborers in early 1919, was promulgated in 1899 in part to expand the rights of foreigners in Japan. It declared that foreigners who had been previously denied the freedom of residence except in foreign settlements could begin to reside and work outside those settlements to enter into "mixed residence" with the Japanese. The ordinance also proclaimed that "laborers" were not entitled to this freedom, unless they received permission from local authorities. The architects of this ordinance sought to prevent Chinese labor migration and competition with the Japanese working class. By the enforcement decree announced by the Ministry of Home Affairs—which defined "laborers" as manual workers engaged in agriculture, fishing, mining, construction, manufacturing, transportation, and stevedoring—foreigners specializing in these fields became legally prohibited from working in or being admitted to Japan without explicit permission.[57]

Still, Japan was home to a large number of foreign workers. In addition to the thousands of Chinese and Korean laborers working illegally in these fields without permits, there were countless Chinese and Koreans engaged in housekeeping, cooking, and domestic services who did not require a permit. In the case of Koreans, Japan did not need to rely on this ordinance to regulate their migration to Japan, especially after Koreans became Japan's colonial subjects. Even before they arrived in the metropole, Korean migration was restricted by the colonial government, which could refuse to issue passports. Once arriving in the metropole, the Koreans were under surveillance of the local police, who had the power to deport those working in Japan without police-issued passports.[58]

In either case, the Japanese restriction of Chinese and Korean laborers was different from the American restriction of Asian immigrants both in scale and method. Unlike the United States, Japan did not have a central, federal system that oversaw immigration regulation, such as the Bureau of Immigration, and instead left the matter in the hands of prefectural governments.[59] The Imperial Ordinance No. 352 was clearly aimed at the Chinese, of course. But it did not explicitly name a country, a geographical area, or a particular "race" as its target of exclusion as the Chinese Exclusion Acts and the Asiatic Barred Zone Act did in the United States.

Yet the knowledge that Japan did have a legal mechanism to prohibit the entry of foreign laborers proved useful to defend the existing American policy toward Japanese immigrants. Surprisingly, exclusionists were not the only Americans deploying this knowledge to explain the logic of existing policy. In the wake of the passage of the California Alien Land Law in 1913, Secretary of State William Jennings Bryan, who had unsuccessfully tried to dissuade Hiram Johnson from signing the act, explained to the Japanese minister in Washington that the recent anti-Japanese legislation was similar to Japan's Ordinance No. 352 in that they were both products of "economic conditions," rather than expressions of "political or racial antagonism." Upon investigating the State Department archives, Bryan learned that back in 1907, when the State Department was working with the Japanese Foreign Ministry on the Gentlemen's Agreement, Japan had deported several hundred Chinese laborers for their employers' violation of the ordinance. Bryan used this case to explain to the Japanese minister that Californians were merely trying to do what Japan had done.[60] Likewise, Stanford president David Starr Jordan invoked the ordinance as he defended the Gentlemen's Agreement against Gulick and McClatchy, both of whom wanted to replace the existing agreement with a comprehensive immigration law, but for different reasons. Jordan dismissed McClatchy's accusation that Japan had violated the terms of the agreement by insisting that the Asian empire, as demonstrated in its policy of "shutting out Chinese and Koreans," clearly understood the dangers of unrestricted immigration.[61]

John Dewey, one of the most prominent philosophers of his time, went one step further by characterizing Japan's criticism of the United States as hypocritical. When McClatchy passed through Japan, the pragmatist philosopher was there giving lectures at the invitation of his former students. He was impressed by the Japanese people, whom he described as a "patient race" whose "nobility of character" entitled them to racial equality in the League of Nations. Yet after reading about Japan's treatment of the Chinese and Koreans, Dewey vented his frustration at Japan's criticism of US immigration policy. Chinese and Korean immigration to Japan was "practically forbidden," he wrote, and the Japanese "discriminate[d] more against the Chinese than we do." Dewey spent the next two years in China, where he arrived just in time to witness the May Fourth Movement that shaped his view of post–World War I China as an emerging democracy that struggled against Japanese imperialism.[62]

Unlike Dewey and Jordan, McClatchy was not satisfied with penning criticism. He used the knowledge of Japan's immigration restriction to lobby for a prohibition of Japanese immigration to the United States. The success of McClatchy's continuous reference to Ordinance No. 352 became evident when several members of the House Immigration Committee held hearings on the Japanese immigration question. In 1919, Representative John E. Raker of California questioned whether Japan had its own laws excluding the Chinese and Koreans, to which one expert, economist Jeremiah Jenks of the US Immigration Commission, said yes. During the 1920 hearings, it became clear that Raker was not the only committee member who was taken by McClatchy's view. When Raker asked the same question during the testimony of A. Wesley Mell, the secretary of the Pacific Agency for the American Bible Society, two other members of the Immigration Committee, Representative Isaac Siegel of New York and Representative Albert Johnson of Washington, attempted to get a clear answer from Mell about Japan's immigration policy at home. When Mell replied that he did not understand the "purport" of such a question, Johnson, the chair of the Immigration Committee, declared that it was to acknowledge the fact that the Japanese had economic reasons for keeping the Korean laborers out of their country, much as the Americans did.[63]

In California politics, McClatchy's argument found fertile ground in the renewed anti-Japanese movement that was focused on the revision of the Alien Land Law. In the election of 1920, the exclusionists essentially aimed to realize what the Asiatic Exclusion League attempted to achieve after the passage of the 1913 Alien Land Law. Through the democratic process of a ballot initiative, the exclusionists aimed to close the loopholes in the 1913 law that enabled the Japanese to lease land for up to three years and purchase land under the name of their American-born Nisei (second-generation) children. Although the immigration policy and the land policy were different issues, Californians often treated the two issues as one and the same, and reference to Ordinance No. 352 became part of the anti-Japanese rhetoric in the campaign to strengthen the existing land law. After McClatchy wrote an article in the *Grizzly Bear* mentioning the Japanese ordinance against foreign laborers and the Japanese violence in Korea, two members of the Native Sons of the Golden West, William Traeger and George J. Burns, published articles essentially reiterating McClatchy's reasons why the Japanese should be prohibited from immigrating to the United States and owning land in California. McClatchy himself repeated his own internationally framed arguments for exclusion by reprinting the *Germany of Asia* and the text of his 1920 testimony to the House Immigration Committee as pamphlets to convince voters to support the proposed Alien Land Law.[64] Perhaps one of the most significant markers of McClatchy's influence could be found in the anti-Japanese rhetoric of J. M. Inman, a California state senator who led the campaign for the Alien Land Law in the California legislature. In an article in the *Grizzly Bear* declaring that the time had come to "eliminate the Japs as California landholders," Inman undermined the American friends of Japan's cry for "justice" and "brother-hood of man" by pointing out that they were "strangely silent" about the exist-ence of Ordinance No. 352.[65]

McClatchy, who wrote the official argument for the ballot initiative that was included in the voter information guide, added another dimension to the argument by insisting that Japan did not allow foreigners to own land. McClatchy's understanding of Japanese land laws was even less clear than his understanding of Ordinance No. 352. He did not appear to have learned about this during his 1919 tour, and it is possible, if not likely, that he did not even learn of their existence until the California State Board of Control, in its June 1920 report titled *California and the Oriental*, explicated Japan's land laws as part of its survey of foreign land ownership rights in various countries in the Pacific.[66] Yet ignorance of the details did not deter McClatchy from deploying the idea of Japanese land laws for the cause of the exclusionists. In the official pamphlet that was circulated among the California electorate for the election of 1920, he argued, "By what right does Japan object to California extending to her own citizens and lands the same protection given by Japan to the Japanese and their lands?"[67]

After the California electorate voted for the revision of the Alien Land Law in 1920, echoes of McClatchy's arguments could be heard from various Americans who wished to silence Japan's cries of injustice. "Japan herself will not permit aliens to own land," Elwood Mead argued in early 1921. "It will not permit Chinese or Korean coolies to settle in Japan as farm laborers, the reason being that it would lower the wages of the Japanese." On both counts, he said, Japan displayed "sound statesmanship," but it did not display sound judgment in protesting the similarly protective policies of the United States. That same year Lothrop Stoddard, the author of the postwar sensation *The Rising Tide of Color* (1920), defended the Alien Land Law and called for a stronger immi-gration policy regarding Japan. "[W]hen you hear a Japanese talking about the inherent and universal rules of justice," Stoddard recommended in a speech on Japanese immigration delivered at the Boston City Club, "just remember Imperial Ordinance No. 352."[68]

Although a few Japanese in the United States would respond to these charges by claiming that Japan did not exclude foreigners, they mostly remained silent on this issue, at least until the idea that Japan was an exclusionary regime became so influential to the point that it helped justify Japanese exclusion through the Johnson-Reed Act of 1924.[69] Their silence, however, was not simply due to their ignorance of the conditions in Japan. Rather, it was because they no longer could argue for inclusion in the United States based on the imperial achievements of their home country.

Issei Transnationalism and
Exclusionists' Attack on Japan

In an article published in the *Annals of the American Academy of Political and Social Science* shortly after the passage of the 1920 Alien Land Law, Kanzaki Kiichi, general secretary of the Japanese Association of America, lamented how the news of Japanese activities in Asia shaped the debates about the Japanese question in the United States. It was regrettable, he said, that the "anti-Japanese propagandists have deliberately intermingled the Far Eastern question with the domestic one." The Japanese immigrant issue was "entirely domestic," "wholly separate from and independent of the former." It was especially unfortunate, he said, for the Japanese in the United States had begun to develop a "social consciousness" that was "distinct from" that of the Japanese back in Asia.[70]

Kanzaki's article signaled the end of an era when arguments for Japanese immigrant inclusion could rely on the achievements of the Japanese empire. It also belied the extent to which Japanese immigrants, especially the first-generation Issei elites, had collaborated with the Japanese government in their struggle for inclusion. In addition to moral reform campaigns, Issei leaders and the Japanese consul in San Francisco collaborated on what they called the "campaign of education," an effort to create a positive image of Japan in the minds of white Americans. Under the directorship of Kiyoshi Karl Kawakami, the Pacific Press Bureau spent much of the war years defending Japan's imperial expansion into China and attempting to calm the American war scare against Japan in various articles written for mainstream American journals.[71] Kawakami's defense of Japan, of course, did not please all his readers. In the sensational bestseller *The Japanese Conquest of American Opinion* (1917), a popular public speaker named Montaville Flowers described Kawakami as a dangerous public figure "with whom the diplomats and peoples of other nations must reckon."[72]

Kawakami's defense of the Japanese empire continued after the war ended. While Chinese and Korean nationalists were protesting against the Japanese empire during the Paris Peace Conference, he accompanied Baron Gotō Shinpei across the United States in the summer of 1919 to influence American public opinion on Japan's activities in China and Korea.[73] After learning about McClatchy's rising influence, Kawakami returned to California, where he wrote several articles defending Japan. Regarding China, he insisted that it was imperative for Japan to secure its own economic interests in the country because mainland Japan was "congested" with a growing population and "devoid" of natural resources to sustain this growth, while the Japanese people remained "deprived" of their freedom to migrate to the United States and the British dominions.[74] Regarding Korea, Kawakami acknowledged the violence that crushed the March

Fig. 4.3 An undated photo of Kiyoshi Karl
Kawakami when he headed the Pacific
Press Bureau. Nippu Jiji Photograph
Archive, "Japanese" Collection; Copyright
holder: Hawaii Times Photo Archives
Foundation; Digitization: Densho; and
bilingual metadata: Hoover Institution
Library & Archives and National Museum of
Japanese History; https://ddr.densho.org/
ddr-njpa-4-677/.

First Movement, but he insisted that this should not be used as a synecdoche of
the colonial experience as the "misleading Korean propaganda" did. "After all has
been said and done about the Japanese atrocities and brutalities incident to the
recent uprisings in Korea," he argued, "we must not forget what Japan has done
for the benefit of the Korean people."[75]

Like many advocates for Japanese immigrants, Kawakami became alarmed by
McClatchy's rise in the anti-Japanese movement, and to fight against the exclu-
sionist he attempted to join forces with Sidney Gulick. In the summer of 1919,
Kawakami offered to bring Gulick out to California to counter the influence of
McClatchy who, in his words, "added strength to the agitation already started

by Phelan and Hearst" since returning from his trip to Asia. Even though Gulick declined the offer, explaining that he was unwilling to go unless American citizens funded the trip, Kawakami's letter ended up strengthening the exclusionists' case in an unexpected turn of events. Through questionable means, Phelan acquired the letter and published it as proof for his claim that Gulick was "a Japanese agent."[76]

With his plan to coordinate with Gulick aborted, Kawakami engaged in vigorous campaigns to counter the exclusionists himself, especially in the months leading up to the 1920 election. In a bold move, he appeared in front of the House Immigration Committee when it visited California that summer to hold hearings on the Japanese question. During his testimony, Kawakami frustrated the committee by refusing to give straightforward answers to questions about his basic personal information, such as his wife's birthday and the date of their wedding. He then claimed that Phelan's associates had been going through his wastepaper basket to steal letters and denied his connections to the Japanese government. Upon being asked whether he was "the propagandist of the western division of the Japanese Government," Kawakami replied that he did not "call it propaganda" but "publicity."[77]

Yet many white Americans refused to see the difference. Kawakami's bold advocacy for Japanese immigrants eventually caught the attention of the Bureau of Investigation (BOI), the predecessor of the FBI. Although the BOI was primarily concerned with identifying Communists during this period of the "Red Scare," it was particularly concerned that Kawakami was working to directly influence California voters by printing and distributing anti-exclusionist pamphlets. Two weeks before the election, a BOI agent in San Francisco reported that, according to the local company doing the printing for Kawakami, the director of the Pacific Press Bureau had already spent $40,000 there to date and had given orders for an additional 600,000 copies each of two key pamphlets, as well as an unidentified number of a third pamphlet, all arguing against the ballot initiative.[78] Although the revised Alien Land Law would ultimately pass by a three-to-one margin, Kawakami's actions raised major concerns. Had the election taken place shortly after the House Immigration Committee held hearings in California, the Los Angeles office of the BOI reported, there was "no doubt" the initiative "would have carried with an overwhelming majority." Yet because the Japanese in California had carried out an "intensive campaign of propaganda" with "a great amount of money," the Japanese immigrant elites proved to have "considerable influence on the election."[79]

In addition to pamphleteering, Kawakami publicly engaged with McClatchy to argue against the exclusionists' claim that Japan prohibited foreign ownership of land in Japan. He explained in the pages of McClatchy's *Sacramento Bee* that the Japanese government did permit foreigners to own land and submitted statistical proof for his argument. He conceded that the amount of land owned by foreigners was "very small," yet this was not the result of any legal prohibitions as McClatchy had claimed. The reason why American farmers could not purchase land in Japan was the same reason why they could not buy it in places like Monaco. In both cases, he argued, there wasn't land available to purchase in densely populated countries.[80]

Yet on the eve of the election, Kawakami's defense of Japan was undercut by the emergence of another Issei who portrayed the Japanese empire in a different light. Yoshi S. Kuno, a professor in the Oriental Studies Department at the University of California, Berkeley, and a contributor to the *Journal of Race Development*, had a personal reason to publicly undermine Kawakami and other Issei elites. He had come close to losing his job during the world war for refusing to participate in the "campaign for education."[81] When he refuted one of Kawakami's wartime articles, Issei elites strove to have him removed from the university by complaining to the administration that Kuno hailed from a lower-class family, could not speak "good Japanese," and therefore entirely lacked the "ability to impart a knowledge of the Japanese language to others."[82] In response, the university investigated Kuno's qualifications as an instructor. Meanwhile, the Japanese consulate in San Francisco convinced the Japanese Foreign Ministry to provide funds to establish a professorship in Japanese history at Stanford University. Stanford, in turn, appointed one of David Starr Jordan's favorite students, Yamato Ichihashi, to the position. According to Kuno, Ichihashi was his antithesis: the Stanford professor's "splendid command of English and his very superficial knowledge of conditions in Japan" made him a fitting "mouthpiece for Japanese promoters."[83]

In the days leading up to the election, Kuno exacted his revenge against the Issei elites with a series of articles on Japanese immigrants in the *Oakland Tribune*. To be sure, Kuno's articles contained many arguments against the exclusionists. Japanese Americans, he contended, were not pawns of the landed aristocracy. They were immigrants with "wonderful saving capacity" who became landowners through thrift and hard work. He explained that the rise in the Japanese population was caused by childbirth within the United States, not Japan's violation of the Gentlemen's Agreement. He maintained that law-abiding Japanese immigrants could not be deported and that, upon facing adversity, they would rebound like "rubber balls." Yet capturing most readers' attention were his criticisms of the Japanese immigrant community. He provocatively argued that the Japanese Association of America functioned as a "quasi-government" with recognition from the home government through the San Francisco and Los Angeles consulates. Most important, he explained that the Japanese born in the United States were claimed as subjects of the Japanese empire and contended that Japanese children had instilled into them "two codes of morality and two loyalties" by attending Japanese schools after regular school hours.[84] He thus unintentionally helped stir up the bugaboos about Japanese schools and dual citizenship that would plague the second-generation Nisei through World War II.

One of the most significant contributions Kuno made in the political debate was supporting McClatchy's claim that Japan had an exclusionary immigration policy toward foreign laborers. As much as Kawakami defended Japanese imperialism in China and Korea and Japan's land policy in the metropole, the head of the PPB remained remarkably silent about McClatchy's claims about Japan's own immigration policy. Kuno was different. In his essay, Kuno insisted that Japanese Americans must look at "home conditions in Japan" to understand the motivations behind California's exclusionist movement. In Japan, immigration restriction was necessary not only to protect Japanese laborers' standard of living but also to prevent Japanese violence against foreign laborers, as the recruitment of Chinese laborers sparked anti-Chinese "agitations" that eventually developed into "race prejudice." It was important to keep in mind that the Issei posed a greater economic threat to the white Californians than the Chinese did to the Japanese, Kuno contended. He claimed the Issei in California received "much better treatment" than Chinese immigrants in Japan.[85]

Kuno's essay immediately drew the attention of the leaders on both sides of the battle over the Alien Land Law. While Kanzaki Kiichi disputed the veracity of Kuno's claims, John P. Irish, the wealthy landowner who wrote the official argument against the ballot initiative in the voter information guide, composed a letter to the *Tribune* questioning Kuno's "ethics."[86] But Kuno's critics did not have much of a chance, as local newspapers drew in readers with reports that he was receiving death threats from the California Issei community.[87] Meanwhile, McClatchy seized the opportunity to prove that he had been correct the whole time by republishing parts of Kuno's essay in the *Sacramento Bee* under titles such as "Admits Japanese Maintain Tokyo Government Here" and "Japanese Exclude yet They Protest Exclusion Here."[88] As he gloated to David Starr Jordan after the election, McClatchy was pleased that Kuno had "corroborated some of the most serious charges" the exclusionist had made.[89]

Kuno's true purpose in revealing Japan's immigration policy, however, had little to do with supporting the exclusionists or exposing Japan's hypocrisy. Beyond the personal reasons for writing the articles, he was motivated by the idea that US-Japan relations could be improved by changing the attitude of the Issei masses and the Japanese government. He believed that Japanese immigrant communities had been misled by the Issei elites and the Japanese government in their limited understanding of the American desire for exclusion. As he directly told McClatchy, Kuno wished to "make it known that a number of laws and regulations in Japan are framed for the interest of Japan, without regard to the interest of other nations," so that the Japanese immigrants could better understand that Americans and Japanese actually had more in common in their protection of their native-born populations. Furthermore, Kuno hoped that the Japanese would become "accustom[ed]" to listening "with profit to the criticisms of others," for self-awareness would be key to improved international relations.[90]

Indeed, back in Japan Kuno's attitude was consistent with that of the prominent journalist Ishibashi Tanzan. In February 1919, when Japan proposed the racial equality clause to be included in the League of Nations Covenant, Ishibashi criticized his countrymen for demanding the right of immigration to Western countries while their own government restricted the migration of the Chinese, Koreans, and Taiwanese to Japan. He warned then that demanding racial equality at the Paris Peace Conference would earn "only a derisive smile" directed toward the Japanese, who were "unaware of their own failings." Ishibashi, best known for his advocacy for a "small Japan policy" in the interwar period, stood against the expansionists who argued that settling Japanese migrants abroad, including the United States, would directly contribute to Japan's economy and its international standing. As for the 1920 Alien Land Act, Ishibashi attempted to calm his readers' anger toward white Californians and explain the logic of the law by asking them to imagine a scenario where eighty to ninety thousand US laborers migrated to Hokkaido, Taiwan, and Korea, cultivated the land, and laid down their roots.[91]

That Ishibashi emerged as a major liberal voice in Japan while Kuno became ostracized from California's Japanese community revealed the difference between the two worlds. The political climate in California left little room for Japanese Americans to be publicly self-critical, as exclusionists under McClatchy's leadership constantly searched for material to damage the reputation of Japanese Americans and justify their anti-Japanese campaigns. In fact, as Kuno would find out, the situation would get even worse for Japanese Americans very quickly. The exclusionists used his description of Japanese Americans and the Japanese government in front of the US Congress as they lobbied in Washington, DC, for Japanese exclusion.

Japan's Immigration Policy in the Making of the Johnson-Reed Act

After the election of 1920, McClatchy became emboldened to use the same strategy he used in California to advocate for the federal exclusion of Japanese immigrants. The exclusionists in Congress followed his example and placed the Japanese immigration issue within the larger context of geopolitics. But they initially faced a difficult road ahead. In contrast to the California phase of exclusionist politics, the main opponent of the exclusionists on the national level was the US State Department, which was committed to continue regulating Japanese immigration through the bilateral Gentlemen's Agreement. But the Johnson-Reed Act became possible in spring 1924 as the exclusionists in Congress took advantage of the embattled executive branch headed by Calvin Coolidge, who faced serious challenges from his own party ahead of the presidential election later that fall. With the president unable to take a strong stance against Congress, the exclusionists were able to outmaneuver the State Department, and they used the existence of Japan's restrictive immigration policy toward Chinese and Korean labors as a pretext for unilaterally stopping Japanese immigration to the United States.

In the interwar years, the State Department continued to believe that the bilateral framework could hold up to stop both Japanese immigration and American nativist campaigns. There was a good reason to believe that this framework would continue to work. In response to white American hostility toward the growing Japanese immigrant population, the Japanese Foreign Ministry agreed to stop issuing passports to "picture brides" as of March 1, 1920, making it more difficult for Issei bachelors to get married and have children in the age of anti-miscegenation laws.[92] In January 1921, before the new Republican administration led by Warren Harding entered the White House, the State Department and the Foreign Ministry settled on a draft of an agreement—called the Morris-Shidehara agreement—that they hoped to add to the 1911 Treaty of Commerce and Navigation. It proposed all Japanese subjects "lawfully" residing in US states and territories be accorded the "same rights without discrimination" as the citizens of other countries, including the right to acquire property.[93]

When McClatchy learned about this proposed agreement, he traveled to Washington and mobilized US senators and representatives from California to voice opposition. McClatchy's conversations with the secretary of state, the American ambassador to Japan, and the State Department's leading Asia expert were all unproductive, as the State Department continued to advocate for the Morris-Shidehara agreement.[94] Yet the Californians on Capitol Hill helped him submit a report explaining his case for Japanese exclusion, both to the State Department and to Congress. Entitled *Japanese Immigration and Colonization*, McClatchy's brief in essence reiterated all the arguments he had deployed since his Asia tour in 1919. He rehashed all the claims from *Germany of Asia*, and he used portions of Yoshi Kuno's articles—repackaged under the title "Japan's Secret Policy"—to legitimate his own argument that Japan had an exclusionist policy at home. McClatchy's brief received endorsement from every single member of Congress representing California in both houses, including Hiram Johnson, who had replaced James D. Phelan on the Senate Immigration Committee. Using McClatchy's brief as their collective statement, the California politicians claimed that their desire for exclusion contained "no spirit of animosity, or hostility, or race prejudice," and that exclusion was only necessary for the "protection and preservation" of the United States.[95]

The Morris-Shidehara agreement never received serious consideration from the Harding administration, whose priority in the Pacific was not maintaining the bilateral immigration agreement with Japan but adopting a multilateralist approach to maintain peace without joining the League of Nations. In November 1921, Washington hosted delegations from seven countries that had fought together as allies during World War I (Japan, China, France, Britain, Italy, Belgium, and Portugal), as well as one neutral country that had a large colonial empire in the Pacific (the Netherlands). The Washington Naval Conference, as it was called, hoped to prevent large-scale military conflicts in the future and became responsible for three interrelated treaties that aimed to guarantee peace in different ways. The Four-Power Treaty, signed by the United States, Britain, France, and Japan, agreed to maintain the status quo in the Pacific by promising to refrain from expanding their colonial empires in the region. The Five-Power Treaty, signed by the four powers plus Italy, agreed to curb the naval arms race by limiting the maximum tonnage of naval vessels allowed to be maintained by the United States, Britain, Japan, France, and Italy at the ratio of 5: 5: 3: 1.75: 1.75, respectively. The Nine-Power Treaty, signed by the five powers plus China, Portugal, Belgium, and the Netherlands, reaffirmed the Open Door policy in China and promised to guarantee China's territorial integrity. In addition, the Japanese delegation led by Admiral Katō Tomosaburō agreed to return Shandong to China, ending one of the most important unresolved controversies from the Paris Peace Conference.[96] Although the US delegation to the Washington Naval Conference had prepared extensively to talk about the immigration issue between the United States and Japan, the conference concluded in February 1922 without touching on it.[97]

Following the Washington Naval Conference, the California exclusionists' path to securing Japanese exclusion was cleared by the US Supreme Court. Headed by former US president William Howard Taft, the court defended various legal actions taken against people of Japanese ancestry. In its 1922 decision on the citizenship case of Takao Ozawa—an Issei who, like Yoshi Kuno, grew up in San Francisco and attended the University of California, Berkeley—the court declared in a unanimous decision that a person of Japanese descent was "ineligible to citizenship." Ozawa hoped to claim his citizenship by claiming whiteness, but the court denied him by ruling that a "white person" was synonymous with the words "a person of the Caucasian race."[98] In 1923 the Supreme Court also ruled against the test cases challenging the California Alien Land Law, coordinated by the Issei elite and two white landowners named J. J. O'Brien and W. L. Porterfield, giving the Californians legal support at the federal level.[99]

The California exclusionists also secured a strong ally in Congress, the chair of the House Committee on Immigration and Naturalization, Albert Johnson of Washington. Johnson, a former newspaper editor who had participated in anti-South Asian riots in his home state before entering national politics as a member of the Republican Party, became familiar with McClatchy's arguments during the 1919 and 1920 committee hearings.[100] In 1921, Johnson successfully introduced in Congress the Emergency Immigration Act, which, in striking resemblance to Sidney Gulick's Percentage Plan proposal, used the 1910 census to create a national quota system that would admit a number equivalent to 3 percent of all foreign-born Americans living in the United States that year.[101] The 1921 act did not have a provision excluding the Japanese, but it was scheduled to expire on June 30, 1924. As he directly explained to McClatchy, Johnson sought to use this occasion to establish a permanent, comprehensive immigration law that would not only further restrict immigration (by using the 1890 census and dropping the percentage of welcome immigrants to 2 percent of all foreign-born), but also prohibit Japanese immigration by declaring all aliens "ineligible to citizenship," as the Supreme Court defined them, ineligible for admission.[102] Johnson, who was the co-sponsor of the joint immigration bill that would later be known as the Johnson-Reed Act, did not forget to deploy the internationally framed argument for exclusion that McClatchy had popularized. In its report to Congress, the House Committee on Immigration justified the exclusionary provision against all "persons ineligible to citizenship" by arguing that "Japan herself, in the exercise of a similarly wise protection for her own people, excludes the Chinese and Koreans."[103]

Upon reading this House committee report, the Japanese minister in Washington, Hanihara Masanao, protested to the US secretary of state, Charles Evans Hughes, that Japan practiced "no such discrimination as was charged" against "people of her own color."[104] But the idea that Japan had an exclusionist policy continued to be influential in Congress, as McClatchy and other Californians appeared in front of the Senate Committee on Immigration and Naturalization to argue for Japanese exclusion. In the hearings before the Senate committee regarding the Japanese exclusion provision in the Johnson bill, McClatchy repeated all of the charges against the Japanese he so effectively deployed a few years earlier, explaining that the United States was trying to exclude the Japanese "precisely" on the same grounds upon which Japan excluded the Chinese and Koreans. McClatchy demonstrated that his view was supported by the California department of the American Legion, the California branch of the American Federation of Labor, the California State Grange, and the Native Sons of the Golden West, whose joint statement argued that Japan was hypocritical to protest American exclusion of the Japanese since Japan was "discriminating against her own color." Passing the bill with a special provision protecting the Japanese, McClatchy contended, would be unfair. If the United States were to "except Japan" from the immigration act, it "would be a gross discrimination in favor of Japan against all other races who under our law are ineligible to citizenship."[105]

Joining McClatchy at the hearings was James D. Phelan, who had lost his re-election campaign but remained politically active on the Japanese immigration issue. Not only did he repeat after McClatchy but he also used the knowledge acquired from his 1921 visit to Japan and Korea to impugn the integrity of the representatives of the FCC, especially Sidney Gulick, who testified in front of the Senate committee with hopes of preventing Japanese exclusion. "I believe the Christian missionaries when I was in Korea protested bitterly against the brutal methods of the Japanese Government in that stricken and subject country of Korea," he proclaimed, "and the missionaries are here pleading for the Japanese!"[106]

Against the wishes of the California exclusionists and the House immigration committee, the Senate immigration committee chaired by LeBaron Colt of Rhode Island introduced an amendment that would preserve the Gentlemen's Agreement. As Colt explained on behalf of the committee, the amendment sought to leave the Japanese immigration issue "exactly in its present condition, excepted out of the quota law." While it would not provide Japan an immigration quota as the State Department wished, it also would not exclude Japanese immigrants by an act of Congress as the House Committee proposed.[107] The Senate debate ensued without Hiram Johnson, who was campaigning in the Midwest with hopes of becoming the Republican Party's nominee for the presidential election in November.[108] But the California exclusionists had another strong advocate of their cause in Samuel Shortridge, the Republican who had defeated Phelan in the election of 1920. Shortridge demanded the Senate reject the committee's amendment and tried his best to convert his colleagues to the California exclusionists' position by reiterating McClatchy's main talking points over and over again.[109] "Japan excludes the Chinese from Japan" and it "does not permit the Korean laborer to come and permanently reside in Japan and for economic if not political reasons." Therefore, he contended, "it does not become her statesmen to complain of us when we are doing exactly what she has done, and is doing, in respect of immigration."[110] When the Senate still seemed unconvinced, Shortridge vented his frustration by reminding them that "I said yesterday and beg to repeat that Japan excludes Chinese from Japan, excludes Koreans from Japan, and for economic and political reasons." "Nobody questions the wisdom of her legislation," Shortridge argued, and no one should question the wisdom of the proposed American legislation.[111]

In the end, however, Shortridge turned out to be not so dependable, and McClatchy and Phelan took matters into their own hands. Shortridge repeated himself too much during congressional hearings, but much more important, the first-term senator had made many enemies in Congress. As racist as he was against the Japanese, Shortridge proved to be a strong defender of African Americans, and this greatly angered the Southern Democrats. He had been corresponding and meeting with NAACP executive secretary James Weldon Johnson about the Dyer Anti-Lynching bill, which had passed the House but was sitting in the Senate due to Democrats' filibuster. Shortridge was the sole member of the Senate Committee on the Judiciary who did not believe the anti-lynching bill was unconstitutional.[112] And in March 1924, he played an instrumental role in the confirmation of Walter L. Cohen, a Black American, as the collector of customs of the Port of New Orleans. Even though Democrats blocked Cohen's nomination the previous year with the help of ten Republicans, Shortridge ended up providing the crucial vote in Cohen's confirmation, which was approved by a single vote.[113] This did not bode well for the exclusionists. Since Shortridge had "forced a negro on them," the Senate Democrats told Phelan that they would "force the Japanese on him" by voting for the Senate committee's amendment.[114]

Upon Phelan's intervention—explaining to the Southern Democrats that such an action would only punish the Pacific Coast and the country, and revealing that Shortridge had promised not to bring up the anti-lynching bill again—the Democrats agreed to vote against the amendment. Meanwhile, Albert Johnson worked behind the scenes to convince the Senate Republicans to vote against the amendment. When McClatchy, Phelan, Johnson, and Shortridge gathered the day before the vote, according to Phelan, they learned from the tally that they had secured over fifty votes, with 90 percent of the Democrats, "enough to win."[115]

On the day of the vote, the California group received an unexpected boost on behalf of their cause when the Senate became unified in rage over a letter from the Japanese ambassador. The letter, written several days earlier to Secretary of State Hughes, insinuated that Japanese exclusion as recommended by the House committee would have "grave consequences." The letter received the briefest mention in the Senate two days earlier, when Claude A. Swanson of Virginia read aloud Phelan's response to it.[116] On the day of the vote, however, the letter changed the terms of the immigration debate, as Henry Cabot Lodge of Massachusetts suddenly gave the letter a new meaning. Speaking immediately after Shortridge (who reminded the Senate yet again that Japan exercised the right of exclusion "against Chosen and China"), Lodge argued that the ambassador's letter contained "a veiled threat" to the United States' "sovereign rights." He insisted that a country that caved in to such threats was not a "sovereign country" but "a subject country."[117] This interpretation of Hanihara's letter

even convinced David Reed of Pennsylvania—a key member of the Senate immigration committee whose name, along with Albert Johnson's, would be associated forever with the landmark Immigration Act of 1924—to vote against
his own committee's amendment "on account of that veiled threat." The Senate
defeated the amendment seventy-six to two, with eighteen absent. LeBaron Colt
represented one of the two votes cast for preserving the Gentlemen's Agreement.
As the House committee had recommended, Japanese immigrants would not be
considered separately from other aliens ineligible to citizenship, and the stage
was set for the passage of the Johnson-Reed bill, which received approval from
both houses a month later.[118]

Because the controversy over the Hanihara letter overshadowed all other
arguments for exclusion on the day of the vote, the dominant historical
interpretations of the Johnson-Reed Act have pointed to the letter as a key
reason for Congress's decision to exclude the Japanese.[119] Yet as Albert Johnson
declared in a public statement, this was a "misunderstanding." Even before the
letter appeared the House had already voted "four to one" to exclude Japanese
immigrants, he said, and the day before the Senate vote he was told that "at least
54" votes had been secured to defeat the Senate committee amendment. The
Hanihara letter's contribution was making the Senate vote a "practical unanimous action."[120]

The significance of the internationally framed argument for exclusion was
not lost on Hanihara himself, who continued to voice his protest to Hughes.
Hanihara argued that the House committee's statement about Japan's immigration policy toward the Chinese and Koreans represented Americans' "misappre-
hension" of the Imperial Ordinance No. 352. The ordinance, the ambassador
explained, had been promulgated "to reduce the restriction that had previously
been maintained as to settlements and residents of foreigners rather than the
reverse." The comparison between Japan's existing immigration policies and the
United States' proposed exclusion, he insisted, was misleading.[121]

The ambassador's last hope was President Calvin Coolidge. Coolidge believed
that further restriction of Japanese immigrants could be accomplished without
abandoning the bilateral framework that Theodore Roosevelt had established
with the Gentlemen's Agreement. In the wake of the immigration bill's passage,
he even considered vetoing it. But to do so would be taking a political risk. He became president because Warren Harding unexpectedly died. Worse, in response
to the public outrage over the corruption of Harding's cabinet, he announced in
January 1924 a special counsel to investigate the Teapot Dome Scandal, in which
Secretary of the Interior Albert B. Fall took bribes from private oil companies in
exchange for leasing them the navy's oil reserves. The public's faith in the executive branch had reached a low point and, with the presidential primaries already
under way, Coolidge worried that Hiram Johnson, Robert La Follette, and other

popular politicians might succeed in challenging him to receive his party's nomination at the Republican National Convention in June.[122]

Coolidge discussed the possibility of a veto with Republican leaders in Congress but was ultimately dissuaded from getting in the way of the Johnson-Reed Act. Although some Republicans in the House, including the majority leader Nicholas Longworth, would have sided with the president, the sentiment in Congress against Japan, as Hughes communicated to the Japanese minister, was so strong that the bill would have passed over the president's veto.[123] Coolidge then met with both Senate and House immigration committee members to propose alternatives. He first asked them for a two-year delay before the act went into effect so that the State Department could work with the Japanese Foreign Ministry to arrange a separate immigration agreement. When the committees said no, he asked for one year, to which they also said no. In his final attempt, he asked for a deferment of the law's implementation date until March 1, 1925. Yet Congress had no interest in negotiating with the president.[124] In a public speech delivered after he signed the Johnson-Reed Act, which took effect on July 1, Coolidge made little effort to hide his discontent with Congress. The enactment of the Japanese exclusion provision, he said, "does not imply any change in our sentiment of admiration and cordial friendship for the Japanese people." The president explained that the law "rather expresses the determination of the Congress to exercise its prerogative in defining by legislation the control of immigration instead of leaving it to international arrangements." The Johnson-Reed Act, in this sense, marked the end of not only the bilateral Gentlemen's Agreement but also the two-decades-long supremacy of the executive branch in shaping American immigration law as an instrument of global power.

Aftermath of Exclusion

As expected, news of the Johnson-Reed Act sparked nationwide outrage in Japan. Japanese demonstrators in Tokyo, Kyoto, Osaka, Nagoya, Hiroshima, Kobe, and many other cities gathered to stage mass protests denouncing the immigration act. The press declared July 1, the day that it went into effect, National Humiliation Day. Some even committed suicide. Before disemboweling himself, one man wrote a letter to the US minister in Tokyo explaining that he would rather die than live resenting the United States. Longtime Japanese friends of the United States, including Nitobe Inazō, whose book *Bushido* had greatly shaped Theodore Roosevelt's view of Japanese culture, vowed he would refrain from visiting the United States again until it repealed Japanese exclusion.[125]

To many, Japanese exclusion was particularly painful because US-Japan relations recently appeared to be healing from Wilson's rejection of the racial equality proposal in Paris. The Washington Conference hosted by Warren Harding and Charles Evans Hughes inaugurated a new era of disarmament, and the spirit of interwar pacifism reached a symbolic milestone when Jane Addams, the renowned social reformer at Hull-House and the founding president of the Women's International League for Peace and Freedom (WILPF), visited Japan during her world tour of 1923 and was greeted by ecstatic crowds of Japanese people wherever she went.[126] Then when the Kantō earthquake unexpectedly destroyed much of the greater Tokyo area in fall 1923, Calvin Coolidge directed the US Red Cross to collect donations, and the United States raised $12 million in relief for Japan, more than any other country in the world. At the end of the year, Prime Minister Yamamoto Gonnohyōe sent a personal note of appreciation to Coolidge through the Japanese minister in Washington.[127]

Some Japanese were not at all surprised that the United States cut off Japanese immigration. Ishibashi Tanzan, the liberal journalist who criticized Japan's proposal of a racial nondiscrimination clause at the Paris Peace Conference as a hypocritical act, responded to the Johnson-Reed Act by telling his readers that Japan made a critical mistake in the late nineteenth century when it sent lower-class Japanese to settle in the United States. Just as the Chinese peddlers who migrated to Japan in the late nineteenth century created long-standing anti-Chinese prejudice among the Japanese people, he said, the early Issei settlers (whom he described as the "vulgar class") created a negative image of Japan from which Americans could not be disabused.[128] Other Japanese intellectuals compared the US and Japanese immigration restrictions to understand the logic behind American exclusion. Takahashi Seigo, a professor of political science at Waseda University who had studied under historian Charles Beard at Columbia University, lamented that American animosity was partly due to the fact that most of the Japanese immigrants were of the "lower classes" like the Koreans in Japan. Likewise, Asari Junshiro, a future director of the International Labor Office in Tokyo, pointed out that Japanese laborers' low standard of living threatened American laborers just as the Koreans had in Japan.[129]

In fact, by the time Congress was debating the Johnson-Reed Act, Japan was addressing its own issue regarding migrant laborers from Korea and China. Even though the recruitment of Korean laborers declined from over 28,000 at the peak in 1917 to a mere 600 in 1923, nativists in Japan perceived Korean laborers as an economic threat, and tensions eventually evolved into a massacre in the fall of 1923, in the aftermath of the Kantō earthquake.[130] Responding to rumors that Koreans were poisoning wells, committing arson, and robbing the Japanese people, Japanese vigilantism against Koreans continued for three weeks. The Japanese government reported at the time that violent mobs killed 231 Koreans during this period, but later estimates were of somewhere between 3,781 and 5,781 Koreans murdered. The experiences of the Chinese were not too dissimilar, though newspapers paid far more attention to the anti-Korean violence to the point that few people at the time knew about the episodes of anti-Chinese violence. Thousands of Chinese migrants had been working in Japan without permit when they were also attacked by mobs in the aftermath of the Kantō earthquake. While the exact number of victims also remains uncertain, it has been widely accepted that Japanese vigilantes murdered 380 Chinese workers in Tokyo's Ōshima district alone.[131]

Although the news of Japanese violence against Chinese and Korean laborers could not portray Japan in any positive light, Kiyoshi Karl Kawakami decided to use it anyway to argue that Americans who had supported the Johnson-Reed Act were mistaken about Japan's immigration policy. After years of silence on Japan's policy toward Korean and Chinese migrants, Kawakami, who had moved to Washington, DC, after the Pacific Press Bureau (PPB) closed after the election of 1920, contended that Japan had "no exclusion law against Chinese and Korean laborers" as American exclusionists claimed and that, because of the lack of an exclusionist policy, Japanese laborers came into stiff competition with foreigners. The violence committed against foreigners by the "riffraff elements of the Japanese" in the wake of the Kantō earthquake, Kawakami explained in *Current History*, was "undoubtedly partly due to the ill feeling created by this competition." The violent episode also served as proof that Imperial Ordinance No. 352 had been "misinterpreted by uninformed foreigners."[132]

Here, Kawakami was contradicting himself. A few months earlier, he had a different take on anti-Korean violence in Japan. In the very same magazine, Kawakami explained that Koreans took advantage of the chaos created by the earthquake and committed "incendiarism," "looting," and acts of violence upon "defenseless Japanese." This was why the "nerve-shattered Japanese, enraged by these inhuman acts, were inclined to take the law in their own hands."[133] Kawakami had essentially condoned lynching.

Koreans in the United States, who received information about anti-Korean violence through US missionaries and newspapers, retaliated against Kawakami. A Korean student named An Sun-nam at the University of Missouri wrote directly to *Current History* to complain that Kawakami's article did the victims a "grave injustice." An used testimonies of white Americans who fled Tokyo to argue that the widespread stories of Korean "looting and arson" had been fabricated by nativists in Japan to justify their own violent acts. The KNA's *Sinhan Minbo*, which filled its front page one issue after another with news of the murdered Koreans in Japan, applauded the Korean student as he attacked Kawakami.[134] With few exceptions (such as a student named Hyun Chŏl who implored his countrymen to see the Johnson-Reed Act as the culmination of American xenophobia against all "yellow people," including Koreans), Korean Americans remained far more concerned with Japan's colonial violence in Asia than they were with the Johnson-Reed Act, which they usually referred to as the "Japanese exclusion act." This was especially ironic since the new US immigration law also excluded Koreans as "aliens ineligible to citizenship."[135]

If Kawakami's decision to suddenly address Japan's own struggle with Korean laborers spoke volumes about the way this journalist used the plight of Koreans as rhetorical ammunition against American exclusionists, so did V. S. McClatchy's remarkable silence about the massacred Koreans. Although the Koreans in Japan were victims of colonial violence, much like the participants in the March First Movement, and although the news of this violence reached the United States through missionary channels, McClatchy, who organized the California Joint Immigration Committee (CJIC) in the aftermath of the Johnson-Reed Act, did not mention the Kantō massacre once in his writings. Instead, he continued to reference Japanese regulation of foreign laborers, even writing a whole pamphlet on Japan's treatment of foreigners in 1925 against American missionaries and business leaders' efforts to grant Japan its immigration quota.[136] It was clear that McClatchy cared about the events across the Pacific only to the extent that they could help him secure his own goals at home.

From the 1920 Alien Land Act to the 1924 Johnson-Reed Act, internationally framed arguments for Japanese exclusion played a crucial role in securing the California exclusionists' victory. As American perception of the Japanese empire took a negative turn, McClatchy and his followers exploited the news of Japanese violence against other Asian peoples and Japanese restriction of Asian laborers to convince the California electorate and the US Congress that they should deprive the Japanese of the right to own land and prohibit further Japanese immigration. By appearing sympathetic to the Asian victims of the Japanese empire, and by arguing that Japan's own immigration restriction was a rational policy based on economic factors, the exclusionists came to reject Japan's request for racial inclusion based on its own actions against Asian immigrants, thereby making the American motivation for Japanese exclusion appear as anti-imperial and race-neutral. Against this strategy, the American friends of Japan such as Sidney Gulick were often left helpless. Gulick's report on Japanese colonial violence did little to change the American perception of Japan, and by the time he began to counter McClatchy's claims about Japan's immigration policy, belatedly in 1925, the Johnson-Reed Act had already gone into effect.[137] The exclusionists also set the terms of the transnational politics of Japanese and Korean immigrants. While Korean immigrants mostly sided with the exclusionists, Japanese immigrants, with few exceptions, were forced to defend their own case against the exclusionists, by defending the actions of Japan or insisting that they had few ties to the Asian empire.

Faith in Facts

The Institute of Pacific Relations and
the Quest for International Peace, 1925–1933

In October 1929, sixty-five-year-old Yun Ch'i-ho arrived in Kyoto, Japan. As the most prominent Korean in the international missionary community, he had been invited to attend a conference convened by the Institute of Pacific Relations (IPR), an international nongovernmental organization that worked to address, as the title of its biennial conferences indicated, the "problems of the Pacific." This was the first time the organization held its conference outside Hawai'i. Various American missionaries, business leaders, and academics had launched the organization there four years earlier with hopes of repairing transpacific relationships in the aftermath of the Johnson-Reed Act. The Kyoto conference was also the first time Koreans were invited. Yun Ch'i-ho, though, was acutely aware that this organization had little interest in the aspirations of colonized peoples. The Kyoto conference also included a delegation from the Philippines, but conversations were dominated by delegates from the United States, Japan, China, Britain, and the British dominions of Canada, Australia, and New Zealand. After attending several sessions at the conference, Yun felt "so out of place." The IPR appeared to be a "mutual admiration society" among the sovereign powers.[1]

Given the history of Asian exclusion from the British dominions and the United States, however, the cordiality of the interracial exchanges was remarkable, especially between Japanese and US delegates. Indeed, Japanese hospitality greatly impressed NAACP executive secretary James Weldon Johnson, the sole Black American at the conference. Upon arriving back in the United States from Kyoto, Johnson spoke at the San Francisco Chamber of Commerce and characterized the IPR as a haven of racial harmony. At the conference he saw "men and women of almost every race in the world coming together, talking

The Allure of Empire. Chris Suh, Oxford University Press. © Oxford University Press 2023.
DOI: 10.1093/oso/9780197631614.003.0006

Fig. 5.1 Yun Ch'i-ho and other members of the Korean delegation to the 3rd IPR conference held in Kyoto, Japan, 1929. Yun, as the head of the delegation, is standing at the center. The female member of the Korean delegation in the photo is Kim Hwal-lan, a cofounder of the Korea YWCA (1922–) who taught at Ewha Women's College after studying at Ohio Wesleyan University and Boston University. Kim Yŏng-hŭi, ed., *Chwaong Yun Ch'i-ho sŏnsaeng yakchŏn* (Kyŏngsŏng: Kidokkyo Chosŏn Kamnihoe Ch'ongniwŏn, 1934). Robert W. Woodruff Library, Emory University.

together, learning to know each other and therefore developing out of that a mutual respect for each other."[2]

Yet Johnson was primarily thinking of the color line, the relations between the white and nonwhite delegates. Inter-Asian relations were not as harmonious. The IPR's Japan and China Councils openly clashed in Kyoto over the three northeastern provinces of China, commonly known as Manchuria. While the Chinese delegation affirmed China's sovereignty over Manchuria, the Japanese delegation argued that, since Japan had done extensive work to "develop" the region, it had a special right to claim Manchuria's natural resources. Even for Americans who did not speak a word of Japanese or Chinese, the clash was difficult to ignore. Both sides presented their cases in English, presumably to make their arguments legible to the Anglophone attendees. That Johnson refused to mention this in San Francisco said a lot more about him than the Kyoto conference. After all, during the Washington Conference in 1921, Johnson had publicly sided with Kiyoshi Karl Kawakami, who claimed that China's "nagging attitude" toward Japan provided the main cause of conflicts in post–World War I Asia.[3]

When Johnson published his autobiography *Along This Way* in 1933, how-ever, he made sure to include a scene of an argument between the IPR's Japan and China Councils.[4] The difference between Johnson's 1929 speech and his 1933 autobiography reflected changes in international relations during the intervening years. In 1931, Japan's army in the Kwangtung Leased Territory advanced further into Manchuria and set up the puppet state of Manchukuo, sparking an interna-tional crisis that drew in various empires, including the United States, to wrestle with the question of who deserved to claim sovereignty over that region. This pivotal event changed many IPR members' perception of the organization, in-cluding Yun Ch'i-ho's. The IPR, he observed two years after the Kyoto conference, "degenerated into a sort of private League of Nations where the representatives of suzerain states meet to air their mutual grievances and to study how best they can hold on to the privileges and prestige which they (the states) have obtained over weaker nations."[5] This was a cynical interpretation characteristic of Yun. But it was undeniable that the most powerful members of the IPR—representing the United States, Japan, and China—relied on the institute to find ways to pursue their national interests rather than international cooperation.

This chapter examines the IPR's efforts to improve transpacific relations in the aftermath of Japanese exclusion and explains how those efforts came to be derailed by the Manchurian Crisis (1931–1933), which culminated in Japan's departure from the League of Nations in 1933 and the Japan Council's from the IPR in 1936. It begins by explaining how the IPR grew out of YMCA affiliates' concern with the negative effects of the Johnson-Reed Act and uncovers how IPR members, especially in the first years of the organization's existence, debated whether human migration was a "natural right." It then tracks how IPR members came to embrace the idea that Japan must solve its "overpopulation" problem not by emigration and imperial expansion, but by increasing the productivity of its people and its land. When Japan's army acted independently of Tokyo and invaded Manchuria, some IPR members worried that this would make the end of the nongovernmental organization. The organization, however, only became more prominent after, in effect, splitting into two. While the majority of the IPR, led by the US and China Councils, continued to argue that im-perial expansion would do little to solve Japan's "overpopulation" problem, the Japan Council provided intellectual legitimacy to the Japanese imperialists' argument, that Japan needed the entirety of Manchuria to feed the people in the metropole and pos-sibly to serve as an outlet for Japan's "surplus" population.

Because there was no institutionalized Asian studies at this time, several IPR researchers provided much-needed expertise to the League of Nations when it investigated the legitimacy of Japan's claims. In the end, the IPR's research on Japan, China, and, to a surprising degree, Korea contributed to the League of Nations' conclusion that Japan's invasion of Manchuria was not an acceptable response to a population crisis, a conclusion that the US government came to support.

In hindsight, it is easy to interpret the IPR's significance solely based on what it did during the Manchurian Crisis. But it is important to take the organization's optimism in its initial years seriously. Until the Manchurian crisis, many IPR members, especially the Americans, genuinely believed that it represented a new hope for the future of transpacific relations.

The most important source of this optimism was the organization's research program. The IPR's purpose was not simply bringing prominent figures like Yun and Johnson together but bringing them to discuss pathbreaking research that the organization had funded to better understand what it called the "problems of the Pacific." This is what distinguished the IPR from the large number of contemporary internationalist organizations.[6] Discovering new facts and sharing them with the public, the IPR believed, would create mutual understanding across the Pacific and ensure a lasting peace.[7] The IPR held the faith that its research program would rescue facts from the stream of sensational literature and empirically document, verify, and substantiate various arguments that Pacific Rim countries made to justify their foreign and immigration policies.

The IPR invested heavily in quantitative social science research, especially in the fields of demography and agricultural economics. This was not simply a reflection of the changes in US social science.[8] Nor was this just a parallel effort to the postwar transatlantic scholarly exchanges, focused heavily on rural reconstruction.[9] The IPR's research was also a reaction to the postwar hysteria over neo-Malthusianism, the idea that a country, and even the world, could collapse to bare subsistence conditions if its population growth outpaced its agricultural production. The urgency of this research became further justified by the Japanese government's declaration on the world stage that it was heading toward this dystopia if it did not find a solution fast enough.[10]

If the IPR didn't ultimately contribute to the preservation of peace across the Pacific, it was because their research was based on the enduring ideas about race and progress that had shaped US policymaking during the previous two and a half decades. This is not surprising. As historian Jeremy Adelman has explained, the modern social sciences were born contemporaneously with nation-states, and thus social scientists' "positionality" began as "servants of the nation working on international peace and security for the nation."[11] Even after the catastrophe of World War I made many intellectuals rethink the nature of interdependent relationships, between the colonizers and the colonized, and among the imperial powers, social scientists who gathered at the IPR could not shed their racialized assumptions quickly enough to challenge the long-standing imperial order. That the IPR, the nongovernmental organization that historian Akira Iriye has famously described as "one of the most influential expressions of postwar internationalism," rested on these problematic assumptions about race demonstrates why the inter-imperial order was able to last so long after the end of World War I.[12]

Founding the Institute of Pacific Relations

The IPR was originally conceived as an international meeting of YMCA affiliates working in the Pacific Rim countries. The Honolulu YMCA first proposed it in 1921, and with the YMCA leader John R. Mott's support, it planned for a meeting to take place in 1925. Much of the organization of the meeting, as well as the roster of American participants of the inaugural conference, was entrusted to J. Merle Davis. Davis had spent sixteen years as head of the YMCA in Tokyo before returning to the United States in 1920, and because of him, US-Japan relations, especially the issue of Japanese exclusion, came to dominate discussions in the first years of the IPR's history.[13]

To the IPR, Pacific relations were synonymous with race relations. In fact, many of the organizing leaders of the IPR on the American side, including Davis, had first worked together on a sociological study called the Survey of Race Relations (SRR) conducted out of Stanford University. Although the most famous member of this study was sociologist Robert E. Park of the University of Chicago, who served as its research director, the core members were returned missionaries from Japan. George Gleason, who attended the inaugural IPR conference in 1925 along with Davis and Park, had spent two decades working as the head of the Osaka YMCA before coming up with the idea of the survey. Missionaries were not the only ones connecting the SRR to the IPR. Ray Lyman Wilbur, president of Stanford University, first served as the chair of the SRR and then chair of the inaugural IPR conference as well as the Pacific Council, the executive body of the IPR.[14]

But the IPR was by no means an extension of the SRR. The SRR's conception of race relations was domestically focused and modeled after European immigrants' experience. Park believed that all immigrant groups experienced the same "race relations cycle"—a linear progression from contact, competition, accommodation, to assimilation. But Asians, or "Orientals," as Park called them, could not even get past the first stage of contact because of white American prejudice. "Like the Negro," Park wrote in a 1924 article explaining the purpose of the SRR, the "Oriental" wore a "racial uniform which he cannot lay aside." As white Americans refused to see beneath the uniform, Park argued, white public opinion of the "Oriental" prevented him from achieving assimilation, the final stage where a person was "accepted simply on his merits, as an individual." Park's arguments implied that the path to Asian and Black assimilation depended less on the minority populations' demonstration of their own capacity and more on white Americans' change in attitude. Until white Americans saw beyond the "racial uniform," they would remain blind to Asian and Black capacity for assimilation.[15] Furthermore, Park differentiated among different Asian groups with unmistakable condescension, stating that, while the Chinese population was "willing to accept an inferior status," the Japanese population was willing to make themselves "irritating to the American rather than to acknowledge an inferior status."[16]

The IPR also could not follow the SRR's model for research if it wished to receive funding. Although the survey amassed an impressive collection of interviews documenting Asian immigrants' struggles of achieving assimilation in the American West, the results of the study greatly disappointed, if not infuriated, the SRR's financial sponsors. In 1925 the SRR's *Tentative Findings* report concluded that, since the enactment of "the land laws and the federal exclusion law," the Pacific coast had shown a "kindlier feeling" toward its Japanese American residents. It even uncritically reported that McClatchy's exclusionist lobby, the California Joint Immigration Committee (CJIC), had expressed that it was ready to see the Japanese already in the United States receive "fair and friendly treatment insofar as this involves no modification of existing laws."[17] This was a naive, if not insensitive, statement suggesting that exclusion had brought peace. In response to the *Tentative Findings* report, the Institute of Social and Religious Research, which had been founded by John D. Rockefeller Jr., refused to give more money to the SRR until Park produced a monograph based on the surveys, which he never did.[18]

The transformation of the IPR from a YMCA meeting to a research institute had much to do with satisfying the demands of its core financial source, the Rockefeller Foundation. After the end of the SRR, trustees of the Rockefeller Foundation refused to fund the IPR until academics, journalists, and businessmen outnumbered YMCA officials on the advisory board. The foundation wanted to make sure that the IPR would be an institute of scientific research rather than an international gathering of YMCA leaders. It also hoped that the IPR's research would meet the scientific standards of the academic community.[19] As the IPR officially explained, by the time the first conference was organized in 1925, the missionaries let go of their control and allowed the institute to become a "self-governing body." "Any idea of Christian propaganda, which was somewhat prominent in the earlier stages of the evolution of the Institute," it reported on its very first conference, "was wholly dropped."[20] Although J. Merle Davis would serve as its executive secretary, the IPR was to become a nonreligious organization.

While the IPR's transformation alienated the Federal Council of Churches (FCC), the main ecumenical body representing missionaries like Sidney Gulick, it proved effective in attracting several noted exclusionists to IPR conferences.[21] Labor leader Paul Scharrenberg, who had refused to support the SRR because there were "too many preachers running the thing," attended every single IPR conference through 1936 as a representative of McClatchy's CJIC.[22] McClatchy himself was more skeptical of the IPR, and he became hostile to the organization during the 1930s. Yet in 1928 the IPR leadership even considered inviting him to an IPR conference, scheduled to be held in Japan the following year, because they believed he was "no worse than Scharrenberg."[23]

Few Americans' enthusiasm for the IPR matched that of Chester Rowell. Rowell had achieved quite a transformation since he first sounded the alarm on Japanese immigration to California at the turn of the century. As he helped prepare San Francisco for the Panama-Pacific International Exposition in 1915, Rowell had become more interested in international cooperation. After sitting out from the postwar anti-Japanese movement led by McClatchy, he spent much of his time combating what he believed was American isolationism. As he declared at the inaugural meeting of the IPR in Honolulu, he was excited by the opportunity to "educat[e] our own people in the international mind."[24]

Rowell's embrace of the IPR in the postwar era was not a foregone conclusion, especially since the organization was so clearly tied to business leaders of Hawai'i, a place that he had repeatedly pointed to as an example of what California would become if its politicians did not prohibit Asian immigration. In the summer of 1920, Rowell toured the islands and reported on how the "Paradise of the Pacific," as the islands' boosters called it, had hardened into a society of "capitalistic feudalism." Because of the unstrained political power of the "Big Five" sugar companies, he said, the islands had become not only "Orientalized" but also ripe for class conflict. The Oahu sugar strike of 1920, sustained for six months by thousands of Japanese and Filipino plantation workers demanding higher wages, brought into focus the deeply entrenched problem of social and economic inequality. For Rowell, the sugar oligarchy's greatest crime was what it had done to white families. Hawai'i's political system, he said, prevented the growth of "a middle class of individual farmers," "with American standards for themselves and American opportunities for their children." In concluding his report on the 1920 trip, Rowell lamented how Theodore Roosevelt's dream of turning Hawai'i into a haven for small-scale landowning white families, "even at the cost of not raising cheap sugar," had clearly failed to materialize.[25]

But revisiting Hawai'i for the inaugural IPR conference in 1925 clearly changed Rowell's outlook. Writing in the *Survey* magazine, a clearinghouse for social reformers on the East Coast, Rowell boasted that "this island laboratory of races and civilizations, situated east of the East and west of the West, embodying in small all the problems of the Pacific, offered the ideal atmosphere" for the IPR conference. It brought together delegates from the United States, Canada, Australia, New Zealand, Japan, China, Korea, and the Philippines to discuss various problems that affected Pacific Rim countries, from immigration restriction in white countries to industrial development in Asia. Rowell's endorsement was all the more surprising given that the conference was heavily funded by Frank C. Atherton, vice president and general manager of Castle & Cooke, an embodiment of the Hawai'ian sugar oligarchy. Yet far from reiterating the usual diatribe against special interests, Rowell became so enamored with IPR that he echoed the local boosters' description of Hawai'i as the "cross-roads of the Pacific."[26] In fact, he returned there in 1927 to attend the second IPR conference and, until 1939, traveled to every single one of the nongovernmental organization's biennial conferences.

What most excited Rowell about the IPR was its mission to bring social scientific expertise to discuss problems that had contributed to political tensions in the Pacific. In the wake of the infamous Scopes Trial in July 1925, when a science teacher in Tennessee was found guilty of violating a state law that banned the teaching of human evolution, this faith in science and expertise seemed all the more important. Rowell excoriated the "antiscience" crusade of some of his contemporaries, such as former populist leader and secretary of state William Jennings Bryan, by describing it as the "cancer of ignorance" that threatened the "commonwealth" of American society.[27]

The IPR provided opportunities for journalists like Rowell to collaborate with prominent social scientists including George Blakeslee, who had edited the *Journal of Race Development* from 1910 to 1919, and Robert E. Park. But neither Blakeslee nor Park exerted the most significant influence on the organization's research program. To be sure, both of them attended the inaugural conference, as well as the third conference held in Kyoto. The IPR published several volumes written by Park's students that relied heavily on the findings of the SRR, including Roderick D. McKenzie's *Oriental Exclusion* (1927) and Eliot G. Mears's *Resident Orientals on the American Pacific Coast* (1928).[28] But if the IPR's report on its international research program serves as a window into the organization's priorities, the Chicago school's qualitative studies fell far below quantitative studies. According to the report, studies of food supply, population growth, and land utilization in Asia served as the "foundation of IPR research work" in the institution's first decade.[29]

On the surface the two subjects seem unrelated: the qualitative studies of immigrant populations focused on the United States and the quantitative studies of food supply, population growth, and land utilization focused on Asia. To the IPR, however, it was logical to see the two issues within a single frame of analysis. After all, Asian immigration to the American West was but a local phase of the larger human movement across the Pacific.

The IPR's mission to study the conditions in Asia to better understand the lives of Asian immigrants in the United States was indicative of its international vision but as well as its desire to counter the popular "Yellow Peril" narrative. There already existed sensational writers such as Lothrop Stoddard, who held no academic position but enjoyed the immense commercial popularity of his book

The Rising Tide of Color (1920). Because of him, many Americans feared that the "white world" would soon be flooded by the "outward thrust of surplus colored men from overcrowded colored homelands" across the Pacific.[30] Yet far more dangerous were works published by well-established scholars with academic authority, such as E. A. Ross of the University of Wisconsin, whose work Stoddard repeatedly cited in *The Rising Tide of Color*. Ross, who had earlier lost his faculty position at Stanford, only became a more powerful voice against Asian migration ever since he traveled to China in 1910. His reputation reached new heights after he served as president of the American Sociological Society from 1914 to 1915 and cofounded the American Association of University Professors in 1915. Writing in the wake of the Johnson-Reed Act, which he characterized as "a triumph of the common people and far-sighted idealists against the alliance of employers and sentimentalists," Ross brought the Malthusian ideas to the fore, reviving the old fear that if population growth outpaced food production, the standard of living would decline across the world. In his book *Standing Room Only?* (1927), Ross identified Japan as the primary threat to the world. With an "uncurbed prolificacy of her people," Ross warned, Japan felt the urgency to find "more room" for its "cramped" population. But with white countries bordering the Pacific refusing to accept "Japan's overflow," he explained, Japan was eager to find an alternative. The problem was, Ross observed, imperial expansion by use of force appeared to be the "best way" for Japan to secure more room for its surplus population.[31]

Although Stoddard's and Ross's arguments had little factual basis, the IPR found it difficult to lay the concept of "Yellow Peril" to rest. As the Japan Council of the IPR implored at the organization's conferences, the fear of Japan's population problem was not simply a discursive construct of fear-mongering racists. By the time Ross's book was published in 1927, many Japanese had already accepted the idea that there was a population crisis in existence and a world conflict looming in the future. They believed something had to be done to change Japan's trajectory.

Debating the "Natural Right" of Immigration

When J. Merle Davis returned to Japan in 1926 to help prepare for the first IPR conference to be held in an Asian country, he was struck by how many newspaper articles he read and conversations he had focused on "the peril of the nation due to over-population."[32] During his absence from Japan, the mood of the country had significantly changed. After the Japanese government conducted its very first census in 1920, the whole country appeared to have accepted the idea that Japan would soon run out of room and resources to support all of its citizens. Although advocates of birth control in Japan began vigorous public campaigns to educate Japanese women about the practice following Margaret Sanger's visit in 1922, Davis saw that birth control wasn't becoming popular fast enough to be considered a viable solution.[33] In his meetings with Japanese bureaucrats, Davis learned of two alternatives. One group believed that Japan could solve the population problem with land development projects that would "double its yield" of necessary resources to feed the people. Another group insisted that Japan could solve it by engineering mass outmigration of its "surplus" subjects to Manchuria, Korea, Siberia, and Latin America.[34]

The latter proposal greatly concerned Davis. Ultranationalists like Uchida Ryōhei, the leader of the Black Dragon Society (which Davis described as "the Fascist organization of Japan"), took advantage of the widely spread panic to aggressively push forward their own agenda. In their minds, Davis explained, Japan could kill two birds with one stone. By sending the Japanese abroad, Japan could solve its overpopulation problem at home and expand the boundaries of its empire through the strategic settlement of Japanese emigrants.[35]

Yet this was not necessarily a fascist idea. After the United States passed the Johnson-Reed Act in 1924, liberal Japanese bureaucrats identified Brazil as the primary destination for its emigrants precisely with this logic. Although the Japanese government and private emigration companies had been collaborating to recruit, transport, and manage land for Japanese agricultural settlers in Brazil well before 1924, the success stories of Japanese farmers in Brazil (some of whom were former residents of the United States) gave the Japanese policymakers and intellectuals the confidence to embrace outmigration as a solution to the domestic problem and so much more. In Kobe, the Ministry of Home Affairs established in 1924 the Migrant Accommodation Center where Brazil-bound Japanese emigrants could learn Portuguese and information about their future home.[36]

In fact, those who attended the 1927 conference in Honolulu heard this proposal directly from a well-known Japanese liberal. Sawayanagi Masatarō, a member of the Japanese House of Peers who had visited the United States multiple times to examine the American education system, initially explained at the inaugural conference in 1925 that Japan did not intend to claim "the right of free entry into the territory of another country." What it objected to, the representative of the Japan Council said, was "discrimination on account of race." Yet at the 1927 conference, he changed his position. "The only satisfactory method of solving the problem of immigration," he argued, "is through the recognition by the nations bordering on the Pacific ocean, of the natural right of immigration." Humankind, he contended, had the natural right to "share the resources of [the] world on some equitable basis and to enjoy the freedom of movement and residence." Speaking on behalf of the Japan Council, Sawayanagi declared that "thinking leaders of all progressive lands" must recognize this right, for it is only then the Pacific Rim countries could honestly say that they embraced "justice and fair play as fundamental principles of international and interracial relations."[37]

Predictably, this argument for the natural right of immigration and resource sharing drew hostile responses from certain American IPR members. No matter how enamored Scharrenberg became with the IPR, he believed that Americans could not "afford to accept Dr. Sawayanagi's suggestion for mankind's freedom of movement and residence." Echoing E. A. Ross and Lothrop Stoddard, Scharrenberg argued, "To do so would be suicidal to the white race. The Asiatics would slowly but surely crowd the white race off the earth."[38] Even Chester Rowell found this outlook troubling. Although Rowell distanced himself from Scharrenberg and even supported the proposal to grant Japan its token annual immigration quota, he could not accept the idea that all nations were entitled to send their people abroad out of some natural right. "If we were to accept the doctrine that any people, merely by maintaining a huge birthrate, thereby obtained the inalienable right of overflow on their neighbors either by immigration or by conquest, we should be thereby establishing the principle that the earth shall belong to the prolific," he explained to V. S. McClatchy, who had been monitoring the IPR from afar.[39]

Sawayanagi's argument had an American precedent. Espousing a strikingly similar outlook was Robert E. Park. Upon returning from the 1925 IPR meeting, he argued in the *Survey* magazine that the world had "a general tendency to re-dress the economic balance and to restore the equilibrium between population and food supply, labor and capital, in a world economy." The "racial barriers" the United States erected in the form of exclusionary immigration laws, he explained, were only temporary stop gaps conceived by myopic legislators who did not un-derstand that the world was destined to head toward achieving that equilibrium. Reminding the readers of *Survey* that Asian migration to the United States began only after the United States attempted to enter Asian markets, Park contended that it was only "natural enough" that Asian people living in overcrowded coun-tries with limited resources, such as Japan, sought to "seek their fortunes, either permanently or temporarily, in the new countries of undeveloped resources."[40]

Even amid the spirit of internationalism, few Americans at the 1927 meeting were willing to entertain Sawayanagi's argument. Some of Park's own students admitted that it was too idealistic to believe that nations around the world would suddenly come to the consensus that a nation with high population density had a right to use another nation as a pressure valve for its "surplus" population. In a study prepared for the 1927 IPR conference, Roderick McKenzie of the University of Washington argued that human migration "must be controlled." Allowing people to "migrate at will from one part of the world to another," he warned, would "invite waste" and "precipitate conflict." A more realistic solution, according to McKenzie, was instituting "a sound and rational immigration policy acceptable to all nations concerned," a policy that would, instead of "guarding national boundary lines," engineer human migration in a way that would ensure maximum efficiency and a minimum of conflict.[41]

This clash over the natural right of immigration quickly faded after 1927, as it gave way to a new debate about a different proposal to solve Japan's population problem. In fact, it was one of the three proposals that J. Merle Davis encountered when he visited Japan in 1926. Under the auspices of the IPR's research program, social scientists had been investigating how Japan could possibly increase the productivity of its land and its people. By the time the IPR convened in 1929 in Kyoto, various IPR members grew enthusiastic about this possibility, though it, too, would elicit hostile responses from several IPR members.

Surveying the Land

In 1927, the Japanese cabinet established the Population and Food Problems Investigation Committee (Jinkō Shokuryō Mondai Chōsakai). For the IPR this was a welcome development. Japan's overpopulation and food shortage were serious problems on their own. But to the IPR, especially members of the American Council, they held additional importance in their effect on international relations. As Carl Alsberg, a cofounder of Stanford's Food Research Institute and the director of the IPR's land utilization surveys, explained, the IPR considered agricultural policy both as one of the "determinants" of a nation's foreign policy, as well as one of the products of foreign policy. Directly quoting University of Wisconsin economist Richard T. Ely, Alsberg declared that a nation's land policy must, in addition to dedicating itself to ensuring "the greatest possible general welfare," aim to maintain international peace by developing "a conscious program of social control with respect to the acquisition, ownership, conservation, and uses of the land of the country," and with respect to the "human relations arising out of use and ownership."[42]

Yet before the Japanese government could devise such a program of social control, someone had to turn its land into measurable units. Within the IPR, the task of making Japan's land problem legible to Japanese policymakers fell to two people who carried out separate but related projects: Ernest Francis Penrose, a British economist at Nagoya College of Commerce, and Nasu Shiroshi, a professor of agricultural economics at Tokyo Imperial University. Penrose, who would complete a Stanford doctoral dissertation that argued against the Malthusian prediction of Japan's future, was tasked by the IPR with amassing statistical data on Japan's food supply and production of foodstuffs, industrial crops, and minerals.[43] Nasu, who had served as an adviser to the Japanese delegation to the League of Nations Labor Conference in Geneva, was a member of the Population and Food Problems Investigation Committee appointed by the Japanese cabinet. The land utilization survey he directed was one of the IPR's largest and most expensive projects, and his speeches delivered at various IPR conferences captured the attention of not only the Japanese in Japan but also their counterparts in Hawai'i and California as well as non-Japanese members of the IPR.[44]

Nasu was openly critical of anti-Asian immigration laws in the United States and the British dominions, but he refused to believe that reopening immigration to these countries would solve Japan's population problem. To be sure, Nasu declared at the 1927 IPR meeting that the West's "extreme selfishness, unwarranted international suspicion, conceited nationalism and unscrupulous monopolization of huge wealth and resources" prevented Japan from securing international parity. But rather than prying open these countries' doors to Japanese immigration, Nasu believed that Japan "should work in unison" with them to contribute toward the "progress of the world." Emigration did little to slow down population growth in Japan anyway. Over the span of fifty years, Nasu calculated, a little over 1.4 million people had emigrated from Japan. Meanwhile, Japan's population was increasing by almost one million every year. A more realistic solution for Japan, Nasu projected, was using the state to develop the "productive power of the land and people" to their maximum potential and feed all people in Japan.[45]

Underlying Nasu's projection was his belief that Japan suffered from an incomplete transition to a modern, capitalist society. First of all, he explained, Japan's industrial development had been slow compared to the West's. Even after the wartime industrial boom, the farming population comprised more than one-half of total households. Second, he noted, Japanese farmers did not use "modern" methods to till the land. With the exception of government-owned pasturages and farms in Hokkaido, Japanese farms were cultivated by mostly manual human labor that was "sometimes assisted by horses or cows" but rarely aided by "motor-driven machines." Hence, Nasu believed it was apt to describe Japanese agriculture as "'not yet capitalized'—a special feature worth recording."[46]

The most important factor that prevented Japan from completing its capitalist transformation, in Nasu's view, was the traditional habits of the Japanese people. He believed their disinclination to leave behind their "feudal" traditions was holding them back from becoming autonomous individuals who were free to compete in a capitalist society. "On the ruins of feudalism," Nasu argued, Japanese agriculture still retained its "old form." No "fundamental change" had taken place in the system of farm labor since the Meiji Restoration. Tenant farmers continued to depend on unpaid family labor to meet the demands of their landlords instead of becoming capitalist entrepreneurs with "a desire for profit." Nasu recognized the structural problems confronting these tenant farmers. The high price of arable land prevented them from becoming independent landowners. To this end, Nasu recommended that the Japanese government find a way to drive down the price of land so that tenant farmers could achieve upward social mobility. But he also believed that the government should reshape the mindset and the behavior of these tenant farmers to solve the problem of Japan's overpopulation and its lack of integration into the world market.[47]

With his unshakable confidence in technology's ability to solve social problems, Nasu challenged the Malthusian prophecy and Western fear of Japanese invasion. "As a rule the population of a country is not restricted by its food supplying power," he contended. Thomas Malthus's own Great Britain, with its rapid industrial development in the nineteenth century, proved this point. Through its "complicated combination of agriculture, manufacturing and commercial development," he explained, Britain had disproved Malthus's prophecy. If Britain could do it, why not Japan? To Nasu, it was therefore "impossible to foretell" how many people Japan could support with its limited arable land once the country finished its capitalist transformation.[48]

Yet what Nasu took for granted was that a modern, capitalist Japan would have to more aggressively extract resources abroad to support population growth and maintain a high standard of living at home. Even if Japan did not use its overseas possessions to settle its surplus population, it still needed those possessions for natural resources. In addition to extolling the Campaign to Increase Rice Production (Sanmai zōshōku keikaku), which had turned Korea into a rice-producing colony, Nasu praised how the Japanese South Manchuria Railway (SMR) Company made Chinese workers produce soybean cakes to fertilize Japan's soil and mine iron and coal to increase Japan's industrialization. For him, imperial exploitation was Japan's logical path to full integration into the modern, capitalist world. After all, that was precisely the path Great Britain had charted by colonizing various parts around the world, many times without using them as outlets for its surplus population.[49]

It is no wonder that a radical organization excoriated the IPR, insisting that its acronym should stand for the "Institute of Pirates and Robbers." Although American politicians in the 1940s would later accuse the IPR of being pro-Communist, the organization was anything but radical in its initial years of operation. Its acceptance of imperialism as a given fact of life stood in stark contrast to the disposition of contemporary international organizations affiliated with the Communist International (Comintern). After World War I, the Comintern and its regional affiliates created opportunities for various radicals across the Pacific— including the Chinese, Filipinos, Indians, Japanese, Koreans, Australians, and Americans—to forge solidarities against empires of all color by attending the Congress of the Peoples of the East, taking classes at the Communist University of the Toilers of the East (KUTV), and participating in international meetings organized by the League against Imperialism (LIA) and the Pan-Pacific Trade Union Secretariat (PPTUS). Due to state repression of radical activities in the United States and Japan, as well as in their colonies in the Philippines and Korea, radical activists had little opportunity to pose serious challenges to the IPR.

Nevertheless, the IPR paid close attention to what they thought about the organization. Following the 1929 conference in Kyoto, the IPR printed an excerpt from the *Pan-Pacific Worker*, the official organ of the PPTUS's Australian bureau, that described the IPR as an institution "organized to further develop imperialist aggression [and] deepen the exploitation of colonial peoples . . . against the growing enlightenment of colonial or semi-colonial peoples."[50]

But there was no consensus within the IPR when it came to the proposed imperialist solutions to Japan's population growth and land utilization problems. In fact, the cordial spirit of the first two IPR conferences dissipated at the 1929 Kyoto conference as the China Council, whose membership mostly consisted of YMCA leaders and American-educated academics who supported Chiang Kai-shek's Nationalist Party, clashed with the Japan Council over Manchuria.

The conflict arose, in part, from the fact that Manchuria had descended into chaos the previous year. From 1916 to 1928, Manchuria had been ruled by the warlord Zhang Zuolin. For decades Zhang had collaborated with the SMR, which developed agriculture and industry along the railway lines it controlled in the Kwantung Leased Territory, a small tip of a peninsula that Japan took from Russia at the end of the Russo-Japanese War. But in 1928 the Kwantung Army, a branch of the Japanese Imperial Army in charge of protecting the Kwantung Leased Territory and the South Manchurian Railway Zone, decided to end its partnership with Zhang. The Kwantung Army was furious that the warlord had failed to stop Chiang Kai-shek's forces, which had recently massacred thousands of Chinese Communist Party (CCP) members and suspected supporters in Shanghai, from completing the Northern Expedition, an ambitious military campaign that sought to unify all of China under Nationalist leadership. The Kwantung Army assassinated Zhang, but it backfired. The warlord's son, Zhang Xueliang, responded by siding with Chiang and constructing extensive railway lines to compete against the SMR. By the time the IPR gathered in Kyoto, the sovereignty question in Manchuria had become even more complicated by the fact that the Soviets had begun to re-establish their presence in the railroad business.[51]

At the 1929 IPR conference, Yenching University professor Shuhsi Hsu (Xu Shuxi) spoke on behalf of the China Council and asserted that China needed Manchuria for its own survival. Manchuria was the "only outlet" left for China's "surplus population," which threatened to turn China into its own Malthusian dystopia. Speaking in a tone that Americans would have understood well, Hsu, who had received his PhD from Columbia University a few years earlier, described the plight of the Chinese "masses" with unmistakable condescension and genuine concern. Until the Chinese people could be "brought up to the level where they will know how to adjust their number to material circumstances," Hsu said in English, China could not allow other powers to use the region as a solution for their own problems.[52]

Representing the Japanese side at the conference was Matsuoka Yōsuke, a former vice president of the SMR. Matsuoka spent his teenage years in Portland, Oregon, and Oakland, California, before attending the University of Oregon law school, and at the Kyoto conference he directly rebutted Hsu in English. Were it not for the security and economic opportunities provided by the SMR, he argued, Chinese laborers would not have migrated in such large numbers in recent years to a region that they had neglected for centuries. What is more, he aggressively argued, since China had not contributed a "cent" to the "development of Manchuria and Eastern Inner Mongolia," what Japan gained from Manchuria was "not from China" but from Japan's "own investment and by her own efforts."[53]

Amid the high tension between the Japan and China councils, the Korea council voiced its own concerns about Manchuria, specifically about the lives of Korean migrant farmers who constituted the majority of Japan's imperial subjects in Manchuria. Leading the Korea Council at the Kyoto conference was Yun Ch'i-ho. After the Korean protestors had failed to get their appeals heard by the world leaders gathered at the Paris Peace Conference, Yun remained pessimistic about what an organization like the IPR could do for the colonized people. He privately expressed his irritation when he received the Japan Council's invitation to the 1929 meeting. Yet given his hostility to the rising influence of communism in Korea, it is quite possible that he believed that Koreans could benefit from working with the IPR, which still had many YMCA affiliates on its roster.[54] At the Kyoto conference, he publicly denounced Korean communists in Manchuria as "undesirables," and he pleaded with Chinese IPR members to help Korean migrant workers, who were in Manchuria "simply to seek rice," receive "fair protection of life and property." Between the Japanese consular police and the Chinese migrant workers, he said, the Koreans were "made to suffer."[55]

Most Americans, however, did not initially seem concerned about this tension over the Manchuria question. Even as the Japan and China Councils openly clashed, most American attendees held the faith that the IPR's research projects would help secure international peace. Furthermore, there was little indication that Japan would take aggressive action to secure its resources in Manchuria at this time. Japan had consistently abided by the Nine-Power Treaty, which had been signed during the Washington Conference in 1922 to respect the sovereignty and territorial integrity of China. In 1928, it joined the United States, France, and several other Western powers in signing the Kellogg-Briand Pact, which promised that signatory states would not use war to resolve international conflict. Based on Japan's actions in the early years of the Great Depression, there was little indication that it would resort to violence as it searched for economic security. Only months before the stock market crash in 1929, former vice minister of finance Hamaguchi Osachi replaced the army general Tanaka Giichi as prime minister of Japan. Hamaguchi responded to the Great Depression by implementing several austerity measures that included the downsizing of the Imperial Japanese Navy. In April 1930, Japan agreed to stop the naval arms race by signing the London Naval Treaty with the United States, Britain, France, and Italy, a move that signaled to the world that Japan's liberal politicians were ably steering the country out of harm's way. Hamaguchi resigned in April 1931, unable to fully recover from an assassination attempt by a right-wing extremist who was discontent with the London treaty. But Japan stayed on course. The next prime minister was Wakatsuki Reijirō, who had represented Japan at the London Naval Conference and returned home to unprecedented fanfare.[56]

Then things fell apart in September 1931. Just as IPR members were arriving in China for their biennial conference scheduled to be held in Shanghai, Japan's Kwantung Army staged an explosion of SMR tracks near Mukden and used it as an excuse to launch a full-scale invasion of Manchuria in defiance of Wakatsuki's foreign policy. Some members of the IPR, such as Chester Rowell, initially worried that it would put an end to the IPR's research program. But this international crisis instead created an opportunity to showcase the political importance of the program.[57] As the Manchurian question evolved from a subject of academic debate to a cause of military conflict, the IPR's research came to assist the League of Nations and the US government in making sense of the Manchurian Crisis.

Making Sense of the Manchurian Crisis

When the Kwantung Army invaded Manchuria, it appeared as if the IPR research program had been preparing for this moment. Although the military strike did not take place until September, it was widely regarded by the international community that the Japanese military invaded Manchuria in response to two incidents from the previous summer, both of which highlighted the importance of land utilization and population control in shaping international relations.

The first incident was a widely publicized Sino-Korean conflict in the small village of Wanpaoshan in the summer of 1931. It began when Korean settlers, who had subleased land in the area for rice cultivation, dug an irrigation ditch to make their land suitable for paddy cultivation. The ditch, however, cut across lands cultivated by Chinese settlers, and after the local Chinese authorities failed to resolve the dispute through a joint investigation with the local Japanese consulate (which was in charge of protecting the Koreans), some four hundred frustrated Chinese farmers, armed with various agricultural tools, took the matter into their own hands. They drove the Koreans away and filled in the ditch, until the Japanese police opened fire and returned the Koreans to the subleased land. The Wanpaoshan Incident itself resulted in no casualties, but the sensational coverage of the incident in Korea resulted in anti-Chinese riots that killed 127

Chinese residents in Japan's colony, wounded another 393, and destroyed count-less Chinese-owned properties. The anti-Chinese riots in Korea, in turn, sparked not only incidents of anti-Korean violence in China but also an anti-Japanese boycott in Shanghai, the latter of which the Kwantung Army perceived as a threat to the economic interests of the SMR and Japan.[58]

The second event was not directly related to the issue of land utilization but nonetheless highlighted the high stakes of conducting land surveys. Captain Nakamura Shintarō, an intelligence officer in the Kwantung Army, was on a reconnaissance mission on the Russia-Manchuria border under the guise of an "agricultural expert" when Zhang Xueliang's troops arrested him on suspi-cion of being a spy. After Zhang's troops found narcotics, maps, and surveying instruments in Nakamura's belongings, they executed him and his translator. Coming on the heels of the Wanpaoshan Incident and the subsequent anti-Japanese boycott in Shanghai, the story enflamed Japanese soldiers' anger and led them to stage an explosion on the railroad tracks near Mukden before using it as a pretext to launch a full-scale invasion.[59]

The Kwantung Army's actions, carried out independently of Tokyo, caused a major political crisis at the metropole. Unable to control the Kwangtung Army, Wakatsuki resigned in December 1931. Then, after the Kwantung Army created the puppet state of Manchukuo to give it a semblance of a nation-state that self-determined to become free from China, Wakatsuki's successor, Inukai Tsuyoshi, was assassinated in the prime minister's residence in May 1932 by young naval officers who resented his refusal to recognize Manchukuo as a sovereign state. It was only after former Minister of Navy and Governor General of Korea Saitō Makoto became prime minister that the foreign ministry, led by Uchida Kōsai, finally recognized Manchukuo and established diplomatic relations with the puppet state.[60] By then, the idea that Japan could achieve prosperity through co-operative diplomacy abroad and broadening popular rights at home, an idea that had sustained Japan's growth from the Russo-Japanese War to the early years of the Great Depression, lost its popular appeal, thus allowing the military officers and civilian bureaucrats to replace parliamentarians as leaders of Japan.[61]

In its official report submitted to the League of Nations in 1932, Japan's new for-eign ministry defended the Kwantung Army by taking advantage of Western per-ception of Japan as an overpopulated country short on natural resources. Uchida's foreign ministry stated that the "most pressing question" confronting Japan was population growth, and that because the exclusion of Japanese emigrants from all "suitable" lands in Western countries forced Japan to find alternative solutions, it needed to develop new industries in Japan with raw materials extracted from Manchuria and export manufactured goods to China. "Japan's fate hangs upon the realisation or non-realisation of this project," the foreign ministry explained, and China presented a "serious obstacle in the way of Japan's very existence, more especially as her claims for racial equality and for the liberty of emigration are denied her." From this perspective the Kwantung Army had merely attempted to provide Japan with what it needed to overcome the population problem.[62]

Most League of Nations member states rejected this line of argument. In February 1933, forty-two of the forty-four nations gathered in Geneva voted to adopt the report submitted by the League of Nations' Commission of Enquiry, commonly known as the Lytton Commission after its leader, Victor Bulwer-Lytton. The Lytton Commission (consisting of five men hailing from not only Britain, France, and Italy but also Germany, a former Axis power, and the United States, a non-member of the League) spent six weeks in Manchuria investigating the vast region. In October 1932, it released a report that identified Manchukuo as a puppet state and concluded that Japan had overplayed Manchuria's importance for its own survival. As the "most competent authorities on this subject" agreed, the Lytton Commission argued, Manchuria served as an outlet for China's surplus population, not Japan's. The Commission also dismissed Japan's claim that natural resources from Manchuria were essential to support Japan's population growth at home. While it was true that Japan's agricultural industry relied on soybean products from Manchuria for human consumption and land fertilization in Japan, the report predicted that Manchurian bean cakes would "likely" decline in importance since chemical fertilizers manufactured in Japan improved the productivity of soil within Japan.[63]

To arrive at this conclusion, the Lytton Commission relied on a small group of experts, one of whom was American IPR researcher C. Walter Young.[64] Thus it was no coincidence that the Lytton Commission's report bore a striking resemblance to Young's previous work as well as various IPR research he cited. At the 1929 Kyoto Conference, Young presented a paper titled "Chinese Colonization in Manchuria." He argued that, in contrast to Japan, China addressed its own problems of "overpopulation and inadequate land utilization" in Shandong and Hebei provinces by encouraging millions of Chinese to migrate to Manchuria.[65] Young corroborated his argument with quantitative data produced by John Lossing Buck and Franklin Ho (He Lian). Buck, an American agricultural economist researching at Nanjing University, received IPR funding to conduct the Chinese counterpart to Nasu's study of land utilization in Japan.[66] Ho, a Yale-educated economist at the Nankai Institute of Economics, produced for the IPR a detailed statistical analysis of Chinese migrants, many of whom were driven by famine and the civil war to become farmhands, tenant farmers, or industrial workers in the factories and mines owned by the SMR.[67]

In his 1930 article published in the *Annales of the American Academy of Political and Social Science*, Young directly challenged Nasu Shiroshi's thesis. The American questioned the extent to which the natural resources in Manchuria were actually essential to Japan's mission to solve its population problems. With quantitative data, Young contradicted Nasu's argument that Japan's agriculture depended heavily on soybean cakes from Manchuria to fertilize, and thereby increase the productivity of, Japanese soil. Whereas Nasu compared the total tonnage of Manchurian soybean cakes to the tonnage of chemical fertilizers produced in Japan, Young contended that the chemical fertilizers, with their "superior concentration" and "scientific usefulness," actually had already been making Japan less dependent on imported bean cakes. "If a prediction may be hazarded as to Japan's dependence on Manchuria for fertilizers," Young argued, "it must be that this dependence will have a declining importance."[68] This was what the Lytton Commission concluded in their report as well.

The most significant, direct contribution that Young and the IPR made to the Lytton Commission's report was on the status of 800,000 Koreans, to whom the commission gave "special attention" because of the Wanpaoshan Incident. Although the Lytton Commission gathered Japanese, Chinese, and Korean accounts of the incident during its investigation trip, much of its conclusion was actually based on Young's study, "Korean Problems in Manchuria as Factor in the Sino-Japanese Dispute," which was submitted to the League of Nations as a supplementary document to the commission's report. In it Young explained that, contrary to Chinese claims, Koreans could "hardly be considered a vanguard of Japanese advance into the zones of colonization in Manchuria." While there were a few "pro-Japanese among them" working for the SMR, Young argued that the majority of Koreans were farmers who had escaped poverty in their native land.[69] The Lytton Commission accordingly determined that, aside from a few "undesirable Koreans" in Manchuria, the "great majority of Koreans only wanted to be left alone to earn their livelihood."[70]

Prominently cited in Young's footnotes were papers written by a little-known Korean agricultural economist named Hoon K. Lee (Yi Hun-gu), who was in charge of conducting a land utilization survey of Korea for the IPR. The stakes of Yi's work were clear to the Americans because he was trained to make it legible. Yi studied first at Tokyo Imperial University from 1921 to 1924 under the direction of Nasu Shiroshi. Following two years of teaching at a secondary school in rural Korea, he studied at Kansas State Agricultural College and the University of Wisconsin's College of Agriculture.[71] Thus Yi joined the two generations of international students from Asia and Latin America who arrived in the Midwest, the "heartland" of the United States, to study social politics and agronomy, both of which were colored by prevalent ideas about race and Malthusianism.[72] In 1930, Yi was further educated by another key agricultural economist when he spent a postgraduate year at Nanjing University working for John Lossing Buck, who was in charge of the IPR's land utilization survey in China.[73]

Perhaps more than any other monograph that came out of IPR research projects, Yi's work highlighted the volatile relationship among land policy, social engineering, and international conflict. According to Yi, the Korean migration to Manchuria had little to do with Japanese settler colonialism in Korea and much to do with the failed land policies of the Japanese colonial government. As Yi explained in his book *Land Utilization and Rural Economy in Korea*, which was completed in 1932 but not published until 1936, the reason why so many Koreans had settled in Manchuria was that the integration of Korea into the world market had made many Koreans unable to sustain their standards of living at home. After the colonial government launched the Campaign to Increase Rice Production in 1920 to support population growth in Japan, the increased production of agriculture—with chemical fertilizers and improved irrigation technology—initially brought profit to many Koreans, especially to large landlords who did not work the land themselves. But when the Japanese banking industry faced a crisis in 1927 and the world market collapsed in 1929, Korean farmers also bore the burden. For the small landowning farmers, the depressed cost of rice made the return on their investments much lower than what they put in, forcing them to sell the land, often to the Japanese. Far from decreasing the rate of tenancy in Korea, then, Korea's integration into the world market turned many small landowners into tenant farmers. Moreover, because the "consumption side" of Koreans' lives was "becoming rapidly modern," more and more "middle-class" Koreans were going into debt, "heavy farm debts" that served as "the last d[i]ke to support anything like the accustomed standard of living." The dikes, of course, collapsed when the international financial market collapsed, and many left for Manchuria in search of new opportunities.[74]

The Sino-Korean conflict that served as a spark to the Manchurian Crisis, in this regard, was an unexpected result of an attempt to prevent conflict through agricultural development. The idea that increasing the productivity of a nation's soil and encouraging farmers to become more capitalistic would solve the problem of overpopulation, emigration, and international conflict proved to be impotent to prevent conflict. The failure of that idea was embodied by the transformation of Yi's teacher Shiroshi Nasu who, in 1932, emerged as the leading proponent of Japanese mass emigration to Manchuria.[75]

When the League of Nations voted to adopt the findings of the Lytton Commission in February 1933, it in effect endorsed the position long held by various non-Japanese IPR members. Indeed, given how fiercely the Japan Council of the IPR had clashed with other councils at previous conferences, it was not difficult to anticipate how the nongovernmental organization's Japanese members would respond to the League's decision. Heading the Japanese delegation in Geneva was none other than Matsuoka Yōsuke, the former vice president of the SMR, who had argued at the 1929 IPR meeting that Japan had transformed Manchuria from a barren region into a place of economic opportunity. As the press cameras flashed on, Matsuoka responded to the League's decision by dramatically walking his delegation out of the meeting hall to signal Japan's withdrawal from the League of Nations, which became formalized the next month.

The US government, as a nonmember of the League of Nations, refrained from making any official statements about the Lytton Report when it was released.[76] But the position of the US government was not difficult to discern. After declaring in January 1932 that the United States would not recognize Japan's territorial claims enacted by force, a declaration that would become known as the Stimson Doctrine, Secretary of State Henry Stimson privately welcomed the report as a "magnificent achievement."[77]

But this did not prove to be the IPR's undoing. The organization continued to hold conferences after the Manchurian Crisis, and the Japan Council did not withdraw, at least not immediately. During and after the Manchurian Crisis, the head of the Japan Council, Nitobe Inazō, personally attempted to convince Americans that, once they looked at the "facts," they would come to understand why Japan needed Manchuria. Nitobe's two visits to North America, in 1932 and 1933, represented the continuing faith in social scientific research that had inspired optimism during the first years of the IPR's existence. As he learned during his visits, however, presenting the results of social scientific research had its limits, especially when Japanese IPR members believed in "facts" that had been disputed by their US and Chinese counterparts.

Japan against the World?

In May 1932, while the League of Nations was still waiting to receive the Lytton Report, Nitobe arrived in California to begin his tour. He was moved by a sense of urgency. Back in 1924, Nitobe, who studied economics and political science at Johns Hopkins University under Richard T. Ely, had been so infuriated by the Johnson-Reed Act that he vowed not to return to the United States until the end of Japanese exclusion. Yet long before exclusion was repealed, Nitobe undertook a nine-month American tour, during which he tried, in vain, to convince Americans that Japan needed Manchuria to survive.

Nitobe was known as Japan's foremost expert of "colonization studies" as well as a lifelong advocate of international peace. Few people noted the irony during his lifetime. After all, many American and Japanese liberals genuinely believed that colonization would bring peace. Over his long career, Nitobe taught at Sapporo Agricultural College in Hokkaido, worked as director of agriculture in Taiwan, visited the Philippines several times to observe the US colonization project, and then finished his academic career a professor of agriculture and colonial administration at the most prestigious universities in the metropole. An admirer and former classmate of Woodrow Wilson, Nitobe became an undersecretary general of the League of Nations after World War I and lived in Geneva until retirement in 1926.[78] From the perspective of various Western powers, Nitobe embodied the cooperative spirit of Japan's liberal imperialists. Even as late as 1931, he openly dismissed emigration as a solution to Japan's overpopulation problem. Emigration, he argued, "has rarely been a remedy for the evils of saturate population." Against the "strange fear" among the world's leaders that "over-population in Japan may turn out to be a source of world menace," he explained, the Japanese were approaching this issue "coolly and calmly in the spirit of science."[79]

Yet after the Kwantung Army invaded Manchuria, Nitobe reversed his position and changed his tone. Though he acted as a private citizen, Nitobe's intention of representing the foreign ministry's views was clear. In Washington, he met with President Herbert Hoover and Secretary of State Henry Stimson, the latter of whom lectured the Japanese visitor on the Nine-Power Treaty signed a decade earlier to affirm the sovereignty and territorial integrity of China.[80]

Fig. 5.2 An undated photograph of Niobe Inazō, the author of *Bushido: The Soul of Japan* (1899). Before heading the IPR's Japan Council, Niobe served as Under-Secretary General of the League of Nations in Geneva from 1919 to 1926. Publisher: Bain News Service. Library of Congress Prints and Photographs Division, LC-DIG-ggbain-06329.

Although Nitobe was sure that when the "facts are before the people of the United States" they would see that Japan had acted for self-preservation, his audience remained unconvinced.[81] At the Williamstown Institute of Politics, he clashed with well-known Chinese YMCA leader T. Z. Koo (Gu Ziren) by repeating the Japanese foreign ministry's official position that Manchukuo had been established by the Manchus living in Manchuria in the spirit of "self-determination."[82]

After the Lytton Commission's report became public in October, Nitobe became more aggressive in his defense of Japan's imperial expansion. Japan, he argued at the Pacific Institute of International Relations in Riverside, had "very little coal, scarcely any oil, . . . very little iron or any other metal." Exacerbating Japan's dire situation, of course, was that the United States and the British dominions had denied entrance to Japanese emigrants and barred the selling of Japanese products with tariffs. Yet when Japan, accepting the racial barriers erected by the Western countries, turned to a "sparsely populated and undeveloped land" near its border and wished to "develop" it, he continued, the "whole world" rose to impede Japan. "Now, is that fair?" he asked. If the world "really wants peace," and if it "sincerely desires to form a family," he contended, nations could not tell a "hungry sister or shivering brother" to "Go in peace." If the League Assembly adopted the Lytton Commission's report, Nitobe argued in Malthusian terms, the "only thing" for Japan was to "starve."[83]

The League of Nations Assembly, of course, adopted the conclusions of the Lytton Commission in February 1933. With the mission to gather support in the United States for Japan clearly failed, Nitobe left the United States in March for Japan. He remained committed to the Foreign Ministry's narrative that Japan had acted for its self-preservation. Before he left, he told a crowd of second-generation Japanese immigrants that Japan was "entitled to a just and proper access to the natural wealth of Manchuria." In defiance of the League and American IPR reports, Nitobe reminded them that it was necessary for the "subsistence of the Japanese people."[84]

Japanese immigrants did not need this reminder. Numerous Japanese Americans had already moved from California to Manchuria following the passage of the 1920 Alien Land Act. Some Japanese in California had been recruited by Matsuoka Yōsuke to work for the SMR in the Kwantung Leased Territory to oversee rice cultivation and land reclamation. After years of experiencing racism in the American West, these immigrants chose to live as overlords of Korean and Chinese workers under the protection of the Kwangtung Army rather than as racialized subjects under US jurisdiction. The migration of Japanese from California to Manchuria would continue long after Nitobe's speech. In the late 1930s, as US-Japan relations became worse, Matsuoka used the success stories of earlier California transplants to entice more people from California to Manchukuo, where the immigrants would make their lives anew as settler colonialists.[85]

It is worth noting that Japanese elites did not immediately give up on the dream of maintaining cordial US-Japan relations in the aftermath of the Manchurian Crisis. The case of Matsuoka is illustrative. After walking out of the League of Nations meeting in 1933, Matsuoka passed through the United States where he met the new president of the United States Franklin D. Roosevelt in Washington and Henry Ford in Detroit. Then he stopped by Portland to dedicate a headstone to the grave of his "American mother," Isabelle Dunbar Beveridge, who had housed and taught him English when he was a young Methodist convert from Japan peddling coffee door to door.[86] Before he sailed for Japan from San Francisco in April, only weeks after Nitobe's departure, Matsuoka traveled to Palo Alto to visit former president Herbert Hoover at his home and delivered a speech in San Francisco where he urged the American-born Nisei to become the "bridge of friendship and understanding between Japan and America."[87]

Nitobe, too, did not give up on this dream. Later in 1933, he returned again to North America, this time to attend the IPR conference in Banff, Canada. Nitobe was still the chair of the Japan Council, which had sent only a small delegation that included agronomist Nasu Shiroshi who, like Nitobe, abandoned the position he held in the 1920s and began to advocate for Japanese migration to Manchuria as a solution to Japan's population problems.[88] After leaving the conference with abdominal pain, Nitobe rested in Victoria to recuperate before his scheduled tour of the United States. There he contracted pneumonia and died.[89] The man who embodied the spirit of postwar internationalism died a defender of Japan's new military leadership. Three years later the Japan Council attended its final IPR conference until after World War II.[90]

The history of the IPR from its founding to the Manchurian Crisis demonstrated the continuing importance of the Asian migration issue in transpacific relations. Although the Johnson-Reed Act closed the gates to Japanese immigrants in 1924, it did not close the debates on Asian migration, in the United States or in Japan. As the Japanese government announced that its population growth was outpacing its food production, various people on both sides of the Pacific were compelled to research Japan's population problem. The maintenance of international peace, they believed, depended on finding a solution to this problem, which had been exacerbated by the United States and British dominions' exclusion of Japanese immigrants.

The IPR's approach to Japan's population problem bespoke the enduring appeal of progressive imperialism on both sides of the Pacific. In contrast to the radical activists aligned with the Comintern, white and nonwhite IPR members supported the social engineering projects that facilitated the extraction of labor and resources from abroad in order to support those at the metropole, as long as these projects also enabled the laborers abroad to achieve upward socioeconomic mobility. This was not just in the cases of Americans and the Japanese. Chinese Nationalists in the IPR treated Manchuria as their own area for capitalist expansion, and American-educated Chinese social scientists did not hide their enthusiasm for technocratic rule and social engineering projects, even as they excoriated their Japanese counterparts.

Before the IPR could reach a solution to the overpopulation problem, the Kwangtung Army sparked the most serious international conflict in Asia since the end of World War I. Instead of contributing to international peace, the nongovernmental organization's research ended up assisting the League of Nations, and indirectly the United States, in invalidating Japan's claims of necessary territorial expansion. The fact that this was the IPR's most significant contribution disappointed many of its founding members, including J. Merle Davis who had resigned after the 1929 meeting. Later in his autobiography, Davis explained that he left the organization because of the "growing political interpretation of the Institute's function and program which had overshadowed its economic, cultural and inter-racial emphasis."[91]

The Manchurian Crisis marked the last time the IPR made significant contributions to US relations with Asia until World War II.[92] What the world hungered for during the Great Depression was not quantitative data to better understand the "problems of the Pacific" but a new set of US policies that would finally undo what Theodore Roosevelt's generation had set up three decades earlier.

Toward a New Order

*The End of the Inter-Imperial Relationship
across the Color Line, 1933–1941*

In November 1932, just as the League of Nations Council in Geneva was preparing to deliberate on Japan's invasion of Manchuria, *Asia* magazine in New York published an excerpt from Count Kaneko Kentarō's memoir. In 1904, the Japanese government had sent Kaneko as its special envoy to the United States during the Russo-Japanese War, and, thanks in part to Theodore Roosevelt's obsession with *jūjutsu*, the Japanese diplomat met with the US president multiple times. In the portion of the memoir published nearly three decades later, Kaneko recalled that the president, during their final meeting in 1905 at his summer home in Oyster Bay, New York, recommended that Japan should declare its own Monroe Doctrine in Asia because it was the "only nation in Asia" that understood the "principles and methods of Western civilization."[1]

The timing of this publication was not coincidental. Various American-educated Japanese elites, including Nitobe Inazō, who was on an American tour at this time, hoped to convince the American public that what Japan had done in Manchuria was consistent with what Roosevelt had endorsed during his presidency. While there is no document in the Theodore Roosevelt papers proving that the president used the words Monroe Doctrine to describe his vision for Japan's future in Asia, there is plenty of evidence that the Rough Rider recommended to Japanese diplomats that they use the US policy in the Western Hemisphere as a model to establish a hegemonic relationship with countries in East Asia.

By the time *Asia* published Kaneko's memoir, however, few Americans remembered that US imperialists of Roosevelt's generation had eagerly embraced Japan as a partner across the Pacific. While Roosevelt's secretary of state Elihu Root, approaching ninety, told Herbert Hoover's secretary of state Henry Stimson that

The Allure of Empire. Chris Suh, Oxford University Press. © Oxford University Press 2023.
DOI: 10.1093/oso/9780197631614.003.0007

China's three provinces occupied "the same relation" to Japan that Cuba did to the United States, Americans were generally hostile to the idea that Japan's imperial expansion reflected its emulation of the United States. Academic experts had openly expressed their irritation at what one called Japan's "Imitation Monroe Doctrine" during World War I. By the 1930s, this irritation evolved into a source of antagonism.[2]

Americans could easily reject Japan's suggestions of the two powers' similarities because the United States in the 1930s was a different empire than the one built by Theodore Roosevelt's generation. In November 1932, the same month *Asia* magazine published Kaneko's words, Franklin D. Roosevelt became the first Democrat to win the presidential election since Woodrow Wilson. At his inauguration in March 1933, Roosevelt promised not only a series of economic reforms that would be known as the New Deal but also a new foreign policy based on the idea of a "good neighbor." In Latin America the Good Neighbor policy would soon replace the Roosevelt Corollary. Most notably, in 1934, the United States repealed most of the provisions of the Platt Amendment, which had given the United States the right to intervene in Cuba's internal affairs for three decades.[3] The retraction of the US empire was not limited to the Caribbean. Two months before the United States restored Cuba's full sovereignty, Roosevelt signed a bill to make the Philippines independent after a period of ten years. The United States, as a distant cousin named Nicholas Roosevelt put it, was "laying down the White Man's Burden."[4]

This chapter assesses this shift in US policy during the Great Depression by addressing a deceptively simple question: what was so "new" about the New Deal–era US policy, especially toward the Pacific? Roosevelt faced an unprecedented global economic crisis. But the preponderance of economic considerations was just one feature among many that distinguished his administration from its predecessors. Just as important, in an era that witnessed the rise of fascism around the world, the Roosevelt administration rejected the vision of a collaborative imperial rule of the Pacific that had sustained US-Japan relations since the Russo-Japanese War.

The appeal of inter-imperial collaboration with Japan faded along with the mode of racial thinking that had dominated the Progressive Era. When the United States set the timetable for Philippine independence to prevent Filipino laborers and agribusinesses from competing with their counterparts in the continental United States, few Americans lamented the fact that their government was "laying down the White Man's Burden." Once they abandoned the imperial project to "uplift" the "subject races," most Americans stopped paying attention to Japan's imperial "reform" projects in East Asia, including in Korea and Manchukuo. After the Sino-Japanese War began in 1937, the widespread images of Japanese violence against Chinese civilians stamped out much of the remaining belief that Japan was a harbinger of progress.

But the dominant racial thinking of the Progressive Era did not disappear overnight. It was not until 1939, two years into the Sino-Japanese War, that the Roosevelt administration decided to terminate the 1911 Treaty of Commerce and Navigation with Japan. The ideas born out of imperial expansion during the Progressive Era were challenged, revised, and finally subsumed over the course of almost a decade, from the time Japan invaded Manchuria in September 1931 to the time Japan bombed the Philippines and Hawai'i in December 1941. During those ten years, various Americans who first came to think of the United States as a Pacific power during Theodore Roosevelt's presidency, including Chester Rowell, E. A. Ross, and Henry Stimson, changed their long-held ideas about Asian peoples. Others held on to ideas from the past and stood against the changes Franklin Roosevelt sought to make. These included Senator Hiram Johnson, nativist lobbyist V. S. McClatchy, African American critic W. E. B. Du Bois, Japanese immigrant journalist Kiyoshi Karl Kawakami, and US-educated Korean Christian leader Yun Ch'i-ho. To them, Franklin Roosevelt's presidency was an extended epilogue to the Progressive Era.

"Laying Down the White Man's Burden"

In spring 1933 Theodore Roosevelt's eldest son, Theodore Roosevelt Jr., resigned as governor general of the Philippines and returned home. Ted, as his family called him, had followed his father's path as far as he could. He studied at Harvard, fought in a war, began his political career in the New York State Assembly, and entered national politics as assistant secretary of the navy. Had he won the New York State gubernatorial election in 1924 against Al Smith, his career trajectory might have risen as high as his father's. After traveling to Asia with his brother Kermit to hunt various exotic animals, Ted returned to politics when Herbert Hoover appointed him governor general of Puerto Rico (1929–1932) and later the Philippines (1932–1933).[5]

To those who watched the United States rise as a Pacific power since the turn of the twentieth century, Ted represented the last of his kind. As his father had envisioned for US colonial administrators, Ted used his time in the overseas possessions to showcase the American capacity for reform. In Puerto Rico he worked to improve infrastructure, sanitation, finance, education, and bureaucracy, all of which he proudly presented in his annual reports to Congress. When Hoover visited Puerto Rico during his Caribbean tour in 1931, Republicans began rumors that Ted would enter the White House by becoming Hoover's running mate in the upcoming re-election campaign.[6] But to "every one's surprise," the *Outlook and Independent* reported, Ted refused the offer of the vice presidential nomination. Instead he accepted the position of governor general of the Philippines when it became vacant. In the US colony, he became known as the "poor man's governor." Instead of working exclusively with Filipino elites, he appealed directly to the Filipino people as he worked to develop America's colonial possession in the Pacific, a goal that he proudly announced in his annual report to Congress.[7]

Ted's career in colonial administration ended when Franklin D. Roosevelt, a distant cousin, defeated Hoover in the election of 1932. Many Republican appointees expected their terms to end when the Democratic administration entered the White House, but for Ted, partisan politics was not the reason why his career in colonial administration ended. Even before the presidential election of 1932, a great number of House and Senate Republicans had voted for the Hare-Hawes-Cutting bill to make the Philippines independent from the United States.[8]

Republican champions of this act in the Senate included Hiram Johnson and Samuel Shortridge, two Californians who had campaigned to convince Congress to prohibit Japanese immigration with the Johnson-Reed Act in 1924. Indeed, to longtime supporters of California's anti-Asian immigration movements, the passage of the Philippines independence bill represented a momentous victory in the continuing efforts to prohibit Asian immigration. V. S. McClatchy lobbied for a bill to prohibit Filipino migrants. As in the case of its successful campaign to stop Japanese immigration, McClatchy's California Joint Immigration Committee (CJIC) found eager sponsors for anti-Filipino migration bills at both the state and national level: Representative Richard Welch of California and Representative Albert Johnson of Washington. The CJIC's anti-Filipino migration campaign, however, stalled in 1930, as representatives from the Philippines legislature and the American sugar industry, which depended heavily on Filipino labor, blocked Welch's exclusion bill.[9]

As the Wall Street Crash of 1929 morphed into the Great Depression, the California nativist lobby found a new opportunity to achieve its goal. In fact, McClatchy and the CJIC succeeded in 1933 precisely because they attached themselves to the US sugar and dairy industries, which aimed to make the Philippines independent to ease their competition with products from the Pacific. Leading charge were Senator Harry Hawes of Missouri (who represented a state with a robust dairy industry), Senator Bronson Cutting of New Mexico (who believed in the Democratic Party's promise of Philippine independence made during the Wilson administration), and the chair of the House Committee on Insular Affairs, Butler Hare of South Carolina (who represented a state heavily influenced by the cotton industry). The fruit of agribusiness's efforts was the Hare-Hawes-Cutting Act, which promised Philippine independence in ten years in exchange for subjecting the Philippines' agricultural products to tariff restriction. Due to Richard Welch and Hiram Johnson's efforts, it also included a provision to stop Filipino labor migration.[10] Although this was presented as a bill to decolonize the Philippines, it was easy to see that it was a measure to help big businesses and white workers. The Anti-Imperialist League of the United States, a Communist International (Comintern) organization, declared that the Filipinos who supported this act were "traitors to the cause of independence" and lackeys of "Wall St." This bill, they argued, stood against "immediate and unconditional independence" that "revolutionary workers and peasants in the Philippines" demanded.[11]

Hoover hated Communists, but he also opposed this act. Progressive imperialism had not yet died. In his veto message, Hoover repeatedly emphasized Americans' responsibility to the Philippines. As a direct result of the Hare-Hawes-Cutting Act, he argued, the Philippines would be thrown into "economic and social chaos." The islands would remain unprotected by the US military, and the act would endanger not only Filipino security but also American interests in the Pacific. Taking these risks for the "presumed relief to certain American agricultural industries from competition by Philippine products," he contended, was inconsistent with what the United States had stood for over the past three decades.[12]

In January 1933, Congress passed the Hare-Hawes-Cutting Act over Hoover's veto, but the act failed to make the Philippines independent because the Philippine Senate rejected the terms of independence. In a report submitted to Roosevelt later that year, the Philippine Senate laid out four reasons for its rejection. First, the proposed trade deal would "seriously imperil" the economy of the Philippines; second, the immigration restriction was "objectionable and offensive"; third, the powers of the proposed commissioner for the islands were "too indefinite"; and fourth, the idea that US army and naval bases would remain in the Philippines after the ten-year period was inconsistent with the meaning of "true independence."[13]

Unmentioned in this report was the actual reason for the act's rejection: the president of the Philippine Senate, Manuel Quezon, was engaged in a power struggle at home, and he convinced his own Senate that he could negotiate better terms of independence with the new administration led by Franklin D. Roosevelt. When Quezon returned to Washington, Congress promptly introduced another bill, the Tydings-McDuffie Act, which differed little from what the Philippine Senate had rejected. The only significant difference was that the United States promised to simultaneously relinquish its army bases and the islands after ten years while tabling the question of the US naval base in the Philippines. Quezon's strategy was successful. On March 24, 1934, Roosevelt signed the bill with the Filipino politician looking over his shoulder. Quezon then became the president of the Commonwealth of the Philippines, which was to become an independent nation after a long transition period that would symbolically end on the Fourth of July following the Commonwealth's tenth anniversary.[14]

The naval base question was not a trivial issue. The refusal to settle it upon signing the bill was indicative of the president's greater concerns about the state of the US Navy in the Pacific. By early 1934, top navy officials considered retreating the US defensive line back to the Alaska-Hawai'i-Panama line to make defense more manageable while updating the outmoded naval vessels.[15] Roosevelt, who had served as assistant secretary of the navy under Woodrow Wilson, did not desire a military retreat. In 1934, just three days after Roosevelt signed the Tydings-McDuffie Act, Congress passed a bill to increase naval spending. Sponsored by Representative Carl Vinson of Georgia and Senator Park Trammell of Florida, the bill attempted to address two problems at once. By allowing $238 million in emergency public works funds to be used to build thirty-two warships over the next three years, the bill allowed the navy to update its fleet and created jobs at shipyards to ease unemployment.[16]

Not all members of Congress agreed with this strategy. The Vinson-Trammell Act was poised to build up what Republican Senator Gerald P. Nye of North Dakota and his colleagues on the Special Committee on Investigation of the Munitions Industry, informally known as the Nye Committee, called the "industrial-military complex." Although there was little direct evidence demonstrating that Wilson had led the country into World War I to uphold an "unhealthy alliance" between the military and the business community, the Nye Committee received support from various influential figures. Dorothy Detzer, the executive secretary of the Women's International League for Peace and Freedom (WILPF), had first approached Nye to investigate the munitions industry. Oswald Garrison Villard, the publisher of the Nation, publicly argued that J. P. Morgan & Company had forced the United States into war in order to retrieve the billions loaned to Britain and France during the war. Charles A. Beard, the progressive historian, later used the transcripts of the Nye Committee hearings as evidence to argue, in his book The Devil Theory of War (1936), that the American people must prevent the banking industry from shaping foreign policy.[17]

During Roosevelt's first term, however, it was not the munitions or banking industries but the sugar industry that exercised great influence on US foreign policy. Banks, of course, were heavily invested in American sugar as well, but the strongest political lobby in Washington that shaped the policy debates around where the boundaries of American power should end in the Pacific was the work of the sugar interests. This would become even more apparent when, only a few months after the United States set the timetable for the decolonization of one territory in the Pacific, Congress would take up the question of possible statehood of another, in Hawai'i.[18]

But just as things appeared to be going in the way of the business interests, the race question popped up again to prevent Hawai'i's statehood. The debates over Hawai'i during the Great Depression demonstrated how much American ideas about race and progress had changed since the dawn of the twentieth century, while revealing how they continued to limit the extent to which business interests could shape American life.

Forgetting "Race Suicide"

In July 1934, Roosevelt became the first sitting president to visit Hawai'i. He decided to take a long detour on his way back to Washington from his tour of the Virgin Islands, Panama, and Haiti, where he attempted to personify the Good Neighbor policy he had proclaimed on his inauguration day. After arriving from Panama, Roosevelt delivered a glowing speech touting all the "progress" Hawai'i had made since annexation. He was impressed by the "efficiency" of the army and navy that were stationed some 2,336 miles west of San Francisco for the purpose of national defense, not "imperialistic aims." Yet what impressed him most was the fact that Hawai'i's residents had exceeded the expectations of an earlier generation of mainlanders: they had improved their standards of living, raised their economic and educational levels to be higher than many parts of continental America, and showcased the "excellent appearance of neatness and cleanliness in the homes." Hawai'i, the president said, deserved "emulation" in every part of the nation.[19]

That a sitting president could say these words in public without controversy proved how much had changed since the turn of the century. When Theodore Roosevelt was president, it was unthinkable that anyone would point to Hawai'i as a place worthy of emulation. The Rough Rider had called it a prime example of "race suicide," a place where the white race would die. He was concerned by the rapidly rising Asian population in the islands, and in 1903 he confessed to his secretary of agriculture that he would like to preserve Hawai'i "for the small, white land-owners" and "discourage by every method the race suicide" caused by the Hawai'ian Sugar Planters' Association, which was "bringing every kind of Asiatic to help them to make fortunes for a moment and insure the extinguishment of their blood in the future."[20] Indeed, prominent reformers in California had campaigned for Japanese exclusion by warning that further Japanese immigration to the continental United States would lead to the "Hawaiianization" of the American West. By the Great Depression, that fear had noticeably subsided.

But Hawai'i's elite did not welcome Roosevelt with open arms. The president had recently signed the Jones-Costigan Amendment to the Agricultural Adjustment Act (AAA), also known as the Sugar Act of 1934, which sought to protect sugar beet and sugarcane producers in continental United States by stabilizing sugar production in Hawai'i, Puerto Rico, Cuba, and the Philippines.

The production quotas the AAA had set for the sugar-producing territories placed Hawaiʻi, whose sugar exports to the mainland accounted for more than 70 percent of all its exports, at a significant disadvantage in comparison to sugar-producing states in the continent.[21]

Outraged Hawaiʻian sugar interests initially took the case to the US Court of Appeals for the District of Columbia, and when the court ruled against them, they launched a campaign for Hawaiʻi statehood. If Hawaiʻi became a state, they reasoned, its sugar would have to be treated as a domestic product. In June 1935, Hawaiʻi's delegate to the House of Representatives, Samuel Wilder King, introduced the first statehood bill to receive serious consideration from Congress. The House Committee on Territories appointed a six-member sub-committee who traveled to Hawaiʻi that fall and held hearings on Hawaiʻi's qualifications for statehood.[22]

Yet the influence of the Hawaiʻian sugar companies was not solely responsible for Congress's unprecedented move to consider statehood. Just as important was the fact that, by 1935, many mainlanders shared the president's rosy view of the islands. In fact, beginning in the 1920s, American social scientists presented Hawaiʻi as a "racial laboratory." Led by Robert E. Park's student Romanzo Colfax Adams at the University of Hawaiʻi, sociologists produced numerous studies challenging earlier generations' perceptions of the islands.[23]

The impact of these studies on racial thinking was evident in the transformation of sociologist E. A. Ross, the man who had coined the term "race suicide." After visiting Hawaiʻi as part of his world tour in 1928 and 1929, Ross drew on Adams's study of Hawaiʻi to conclude that, because white Americans in Hawaiʻi were "superior to the common run," nonwhite youths who grew up in Hawaiʻi lived without much experience of racism and experienced "painful disillusionment" about American society upon visiting the mainland.[24] This does not mean that hostility toward Hawaiʻi disappeared. After Congress limited Filipino migration to the United States in 1934, V. S. McClatchy's CJIC began campaigning against Hawaiʻi statehood.[25] Yet as the statehood hearings revealed, few people thought of Hawaiʻi the way that McClatchy and his generation of xenophobic reformers did.

In fact, influential Hawaiʻian politicians spoke of the Asian labor issue as a thing of the past. When a joint committee of twelve senators and twelve representatives arrived in 1937 to conduct another set of hearings on the possibility of statehood, particularly powerful testimony was provided by John H. Wilson, former mayor of Honolulu who was then serving as postmaster of Hawaiʻi. Wilson had studied at Stanford in the same class with Herbert Hoover until the overthrow of the Hawaiʻian monarchy cut his education short, and he was acutely aware of how mainlanders perceived Hawaiʻi since his student days. He told the joint commission that the "bugaboo" about "Asiatic labor" spread around by American labor unions and the California reformers during the previous decades, encapsulated by the title of the AFL's pamphlet *Meat vs. Rice: American Manhood against Asiatic Coolieism, Which Shall Survive?* (1901), rested on false assumptions. The widespread idea that "Asiatics" subsisting on rice would undermine white workers, who needed to consume meat to survive, had no factual basis. The "Asiatics" in Hawai'i were living with better food than their counterparts in Japan or China, Wilson argued. The younger generation of Asians growing up in the islands ate "beefsteak and onions, and they g[o]t their orange juice and ham and eggs for breakfast."[26]

Fear of a changing racial hierarchy, however, continued to haunt some white Americans. According to Romanzo Adams, who testified as an expert witness at the hearings, Hawai'i was majority Asian. Japanese residents constituted over 38.1 percent of the population in 1937, while "other Asiatic" residents including Filipinos, Koreans, and Chinese accounted for an additional 22 percent. While Adams did not see this as a problem, certain members of the joint committee worried that, if granted statehood, Hawai'i would send an Asian, probably a Japanese American, to Congress. The committee asked multiple witnesses about their feelings about electing an Asian representative.[27] While many answered that they would not object to it, the tone of the hearings was set on the first day when a white navy veteran argued that Hawai'i's statehood would lead to the election of a Japanese American governor and, as in the American South, the Ku Klux Klan would rise in the islands "for the white man to get justice."[28]

Many locals were outraged by the Southern comparison. They believed this was part of a political stratagem devised by a southern member of the congressional committee, Representative John E. Rankin of Mississippi, who had been despised by the local community long before he set foot on the islands. In 1933 he proposed a bill to waive the residency requirement for Hawai'ian governorship and allow a mainlander to enter local politics at the highest level. Ironically, the local press called the Rankin bill a plan to install a "carpetbag" government, in reference to the Northern occupation of the South after the Civil War. After passing the House, the Rankin bill was defeated by a Senate filibuster. But locals did not forget. In 1937 they continued to refer to Rankin as the congressman who attempted to install "carpetbag governors" in the territory.[29]

Because of the overwhelming support for statehood among witnesses who spoke at the hearings, residents of Hawai'i were disappointed to learn that the committee, upon returning to Washington, recommended that the US government refrain from taking any action at that time. Listed on the committee report were many reasons, including the committee's argument that the exact proportion of Hawai'i's population desiring statehood was inconclusive without a plebiscite. Yet race emerged as the most important deciding factor. The committee explained that the "present disturbed condition of international affairs" required "further study and consideration" of the statehood question.[30]

This deliberately vague phrase referred to the undeclared Sino-Japanese War, which had begun when the Imperial Japanese Army and China's National Revolutionary Army clashed at the Marco Polo Bridge near Beijing in July 1937. The war was fought between Japan and China, not between Japanese and Chinese Americans. But congressional committee members could not suppress the thought that the immigrant population in Hawai'i would participate in the struggle and, worse, get the United States involved.

What is interesting, however, is that the questions about immigrants' loyalty were either directed at or in reference to the state's Japanese population only.[31] Like Roosevelt, the committee was concerned about the possibility of the United States fighting a war with Japan, not China. As much as the president was impressed by what he saw during his visit to the islands, he believed that Japan's relationship with Hawai'i's Japanese population was a cause for worry. In 1936 the president drafted a memo stating that Japanese naval personnel visiting Hawai'i were engaged in activities "deliberately calculated to advance Japanese nationalism and to cement bonds of loyalty" among the immigrant population.[32]

The statehood hearings revealed that, even as the business interests exerted tremendous influence in politics during the Great Depression, fear of racial conflict and US involvement in a war between two nonwhite peoples prevailed to determine American policy. "Race suicide" no longer held sway in American politics, but many policymakers were wary of, if not opposed to, the possibility that Asian Americans might end up holding some of the highest offices in government. It was one thing to have a territory with a large Asian American population, another to have a state governed and represented by Asian American politicians. The Sino-Japanese War provided a timely excuse for American policymakers to express their anxieties about the rising power of Japanese Americans, the largest group of Asian Americans in Hawai'i and the continental United States, without making explicit their broader concerns about the coming challenges to the long-entrenched racial hierarchy.

The Sino-Japanese War had a broad impact on American politics far beyond the question of Hawai'i statehood. It provided an opportunity for the administration, as well as various diplomats who had been working at the margins of national politics, to revive the idea that Americans had a responsibility to the international society. Almost two decades after Woodrow Wilson's political opponents in Congress prevented the United States from joining the League of Nations, Roosevelt and his allies steered the country toward a more active international engagement, against the wishes of noninterventionists who shaped much of the foreign policy since the end of World War I.

Reviving Wilson

On October 5, 1937, a day before the joint commission began its hearings on the possibility of Hawai'i statehood, Roosevelt shocked the nation by suddenly delivering what would become known as the "Quarantine" speech. Speaking in Chicago, where he arrived to dedicate a new bridge, he argued that "peace-loving nations" must make a concerted effort to contain belligerent nations that created "international anarchy and instability," much in the same way that a communally oriented society must quarantine sick patients to protect itself from a "contagion."[33]

Japan was not once mentioned in the speech, yet in the context of the Sino-Japanese War, the president's words signaled to his supporters and opponents alike that Washington was poised to take a more active role in shaping the world. This was a radical departure from the policies of his first term. Up to this moment, his administration had operated in accordance with the Neutrality Acts, which had been passed annually by Congress since 1935 to prevent American entanglement in foreign wars. The Neutrality Acts took various forms, but most importantly they prohibited the American manufacturing and shipping industry from exporting and transporting arms and ammunitions to belligerents. When Italy invaded Ethiopia in 1935, Roosevelt invoked the Neutrality Act to disengage the United States from war. He did the same regarding the Spanish Civil War. Yet in the summer of 1937, when Japan and China came into conflict, Roosevelt refused to invoke the Neutrality Act, most recently passed in January of that year. Given that Japan and China were not formally at war (neither side made an official declaration), he technically did not have to invoke the act. But by indicating that the United States would mobilize itself to address "international anarchy and instability," he appeared to suggest that his administration would soon intervene in the conflict.[34]

Some of Roosevelt's political opponents claimed that the president was attempting to shift the public's attention to the outside world from the troubled home front. Since his re-election in November 1936, Roosevelt's New Deal appeared impotent to stave off a severe recession in 1937. Furthermore, after his failed attempt to increase the number of Supreme Court justices who would decide favorably on cases related to his programs (popularly known as his "Court-packing" plan), Roosevelt was embroiled in another political quagmire just before he delivered the Quarantine speech. A few weeks after the Marco Polo Bridge incident, Roosevelt nominated for a vacant Supreme Court seat Hugo Black, a senator from Alabama who had supported every piece of New Deal legislation. Black's staunch support was not the main issue. Black had been rumored to have been a member of the Ku Klux Klan in Alabama, and he was confirmed by the Senate because no evidence of his Klan affiliation appeared at the time of his confirmation hearings. But Black's Klan membership, which lasted until 1925, was confirmed the following year when journalist Ray Sprigle exposed Black's past and won the Pulitzer Prize for his reporting.[35]

But as Chester Rowell, a personal friend of Hoover's who regularly excoriated Roosevelt in his daily column of the *San Francisco Chronicle*, explained, the "Quarantine" speech was not a smokescreen. It had little to do with "Hugo Black or the Ku Klux Klan."[36] Rather, as Rowell observed, it was a sign that Roosevelt would recommit the country to the Wilsonian vision of collective international security, a vision that he had endorsed as Wilson's assistant secretary of the navy and a vice president candidate in the election of 1920.[37]

In fact, when Roosevelt received congressional approval for a drastic increase in naval expenditure in 1938, it marked an important victory over several of the same "irreconcilables" in Congress who defeated Wilson and prevented the United States from joining the League of Nations. In his message to Congress on January 28, 1938, Roosevelt argued that the US government's previous attempts to engage in an international agreement on arms reduction had fallen short of guaranteeing American national security. In response to this speech, Representative Carl Vinson of Georgia, who had already cosponsored a naval expansion bill in 1934, proposed another bill that would allow the United States to build 105,000 tons of battleships, 68,754 tons of cruisers, 40,000 tons of aircraft carriers, 38,000 tons of destroyers, and 13,658 tons of submarines.[38] Although Senator Henry Cabot Lodge Jr. of Massachusetts, the son of Wilson's main nemesis in Congress, voted for the measure, Senators William Borah of Idaho, George W. Norris of Nebraska, and Robert M. La Follette Jr. of Wisconsin voted against the measure, while Hiram Johnson abstained.[39]

Yet the administration remained cautious, as illustrated by its response to the *Panay* incident. On December 12, 1937, Japanese aircraft flying over the Yangzi River near Nanjing, then the capital of China, bombed and sank the USS *Panay* and three American oil tankers that belonged to Stanvac (Standard-Vacuum Oil Company). The gunboat *Panay*, which had been carrying members of the US embassy evacuating from Nanjing in the midst of Japan's attack on the city, quickly emerged in the American public's eyes as a symbol of Japanese treachery when photographs and film footage of the attack reached millions of Americans. Yet the sinking of an American naval vessel did not lead the United States into war in 1937, as it had in 1898, when the United States had declared war against Spain after the USS *Maine* sank in Havana's harbor. Roosevelt initially tinkered with the possibility of responding to the attack with economic sanctions and an embargo, but he gauged the low level of the American public's desire for intervention and accepted Japan's apology on Christmas Day.[40]

The *Panay* incident provided an opportunity for Senator Hiram Johnson, the longtime anti-Japanese politician who had played a significant role in preventing the United States from joining the League of Nations, to attack the administration. Theodore Roosevelt's old running mate, now in his seventies, had an extensive experience with public standoffs with a Democratic president. As governor of California, he had triumphed over Woodrow Wilson who tried to dissuade him from signing the Alien Land Act of 1913. As US Senator, he had again defeated Wilson when the president tried to convince Congress to ratify the Treaty of Paris. But this time it was different. Johnson, who detested Herbert Hoover's connections to the big business and the utility interests, supported Roosevelt and the New Deal in his first term. The senator then had a severe cerebral vascular stroke in 1936, after which he mostly stayed in the peripheries of congressional debates on the Court-packing controversy, confirmation of Hugo Black, and the Neutrality Act of 1937. Johnson grew distrustful of the president, whose actions in his second term signaled that he was willing to ignore the long-established checks and balances of government. Just as important, much in the way that political historians would critique FDR's second term many decades later, Johnson saw the administration's response to the 1937 recession as the end of genuine economic reform and the beginning of a business-friendly policy premised on the idea that the economy could be saved by encouraging people's consumption. When the president refused to do much in response to the *Panay* incident, Johnson found his moment to vent his pent-up frustration. After threatening to "quarantine" belligerent nations, the senator said, Roosevelt had embarrassed the country by "not carrying that threat into effect." He claimed that the president put the country in a "pusillanimous position" for the whole world to see by failing to take a stronger stand against Japan.[41]

What Johnson refused to acknowledge, however, was how difficult it was for any president to change the country's long-standing foreign policy. The State Department was full of career diplomats who still considered Japan as an important partner, or at the very least a major power that would prevent East Asia from falling into chaos, just as Theodore Roosevelt did. The agent of chaos, according to their view, was not Japan but China. After World War I, the United States under President Warren G. Harding and Secretary of State Charles Evans Hughes had improved US-China relations by hosting the Washington Conference and convincing its attendees to respect China's territorial integrity and promise no interference by signing the Nine-Power Treaty (1922). The "Open Door," in this sense, was upheld as the guiding policy for the purpose not only of supporting US economic interests but also of maintaining a balance of power among the involved empires. Yet many US policymakers remained unconvinced of China's ability to maintain internal stability. Sun Yat-sen's entry into a cooperative agreement with the Soviet Union in 1923, antiforeign demonstrations and riots that immobilized Shanghai in 1925, and the rise of the Red Army in 1927 against Chiang Kai-shek's attempt to unite the country following Sun Yat-sen's death convinced many American diplomats that China was perpetually unstable.[42]

The most vocal among these diplomats was J. V. A. MacMurray, a former chief of the Division of Far Eastern Affairs who served as US minister to Lithuania, Latvia, Estonia, and Turkey, as well as the head of the Joint Committee on Philippines Affairs, under Roosevelt. MacMurray, a Princetonian who entered foreign service in 1907 with a letter from Wilson, served as US minister to China during the tumultuous years following Sun Yat-sen's death. Upon request of his eventual successor in the Division of Far Eastern Affairs, Stanley K. Hornbeck, MacMurray produced a long report for the State Department titled "Developments Affecting American Policy in the Far East" in 1935. The report severely disappointed Hornbeck who, as a member of the US delegation to the Paris Peace Conference back in 1919, had disagreed with Wilson's decision to allow Japan to retain Shandong. But other US diplomats liked what they read. Both the US ambassador in Tokyo, Joseph Grew, and Secretary of State Cordell Hull expressed appreciation of MacMurray's analysis when they read it at the beginning of the Sino-Japanese War. Grew wished "every officer, from the President down" could study the report, for it would "relieve" Americans of the "generally accepted theory that Japan has always been the big bully and China the downtrodden innocent."[43] Indeed, a week after the Marco Polo Bridge Incident, Roosevelt met with MacMurray at the White House. While we do not know what they discussed, it is not difficult to imagine what MacMurray would have said based on his 1935 report.[44] "If we were to 'save' China from Japan," MacMurray predicted in a paragraph that would influence a young diplomat named George F. Kennan, it would only help the Soviet Union, which would simply replace Japan in China and achieve its "mastery of the Far East."[45]

Perhaps the most controversial statement MacMurray made in his report was his argument that Japan was more valuable to American interests than China:

> Our actual trade with Japan has long been far greater than with China; and our political relations with Japan have had such additional importance as is consequent upon the fact that she might prove to be a contestant with us, economically or even militarily. China, by contrast, was a mere congeries of human beings, primitive in its political and economic organization, difficult and often troublesome to deal with in either aspect, and by its weakness constantly inviting aggressions that threatened such interests as we might have or hope for.[46]

In addition to emphasizing the fact that American trade with Japan had always been far more profitable than American trade with China (which could be

Fig. 6.1 J. V. A. MacMurray (right) and Norman Davis (left) at the White House for a meeting with Franklin D. Roosevelt on July 15, 1937, eight days after the Marco Polo Bridge Incident sparked the Sino-Japanese War. MacMurray was the US ambassador to Turkey at this time, but he had previously served as the head of the State Department's Far East Division. Davis was the US ambassador-at-large to Europe. Photographer: Harris & Ewing. Harris & Ewing Collection, Library of Congress Prints and Photographs Division, LC-DIG-hec-23033.

corroborated by many contemporary quantitative studies), the bifurcated vision of Japan and China, representing two different ways of being, demonstrated the continuing influence of ideas about race that emerged during the Progressive Era.[47] The "weakness" of Chinese "inviting" foreign intervention; China's "primitive" economy and society; and, most insulting, the statement that China was "a mere congeries" of people—these were all reminiscent of what previous generations of Americans had said about China since the Eight-Nation Alliance defeated the Boxer Rebellion in 1901. The idea that weak nations invited foreign intervention was at the core of Theodore Roosevelt's vision of the world order in which "strong" nations such as the United States and Japan should establish their spheres of influence to maintain stability.

Not everyone shared this view, of course, but one of the most surprising dissenters was Theodore Roosevelt Jr. Coincidentally, Ted's wife and their son were visiting Shanghai when the city became a battlefield of the Sino-Japanese War.[48] In July 1938, after they returned to the United States, Ted joined his wife at a "Bowl of Rice" party held in New York City's Chinatown to raise funds to benefit Chinese civilians in the Sino-Japanese conflict. Eventually, he became the chairman of the United Council for Civilian Relief in China.[49]

If Theodore Roosevelt Jr. represented the fading generation of progressive imperialists during his time as governor general of the Philippines, by the Sino-Japanese War he represented the new of generation of Americans who saw China anew. But it was not just the news of Japan's violence that changed American perception of China. As Americans found out during the Sino-Japanese War, the China that was fighting against Japan was not the same nation that Roosevelt and Wilson had known, nor was it the China that MacMurray described in his report to the State Department.

Seeing China Anew

The "new" China Americans encountered during the Sino-Japanese War was a product of deliberate efforts by Americans who wished to present a country worthy of respect and sympathy. The most influential voices were children of China missionaries. In addition to novelist Pearl S. Buck, who followed the success of *The Good Earth* (1931) by publishing almost a book a year about China, Henry Luce played an indispensable role in shaping the American view of "new" China as the publisher of *Time* and *Life* magazines.[50]

Encapsulating Luce's vision was a *March of Time* newsreel released in American theaters in September 1937. Entitled "War in China," the newsreel argued that Chiang Kai-shek, "counseled by his American educated wife," had laid the foundation of a "modern nation": infrastructural development led to new bridges and railroad tracks, social politics provided housing to China's "under-privileged," and educational reform taught "coolies" how to use the very machines that had "made the West the master of the East." If China appeared short of being progressive and united in American eyes, the source of that short-coming was not the Chinese people. Just as China's "transition to a progressive reorganized nation [was] in full swing," the newsreel argued, Japan invaded the country to keep it from completing its "modernization."[51]

The success of the missionary argument depended heavily on American perceptions of Chinese converts, and none was more important to Luce than Mei-ling Soong, better known as Madame Chiang Kai-shek.[52] Having been educated at Piedmont Academy and Wesleyan College in Georgia before receiving her undergraduate degree at Wellesley College, Soong was painfully aware of the fact that Americans had long held Japan and China in dichotomous terms, the former "progressive" and the latter "backward." When Theodore Roosevelt Jr. decided to publish her husband's diary in 1937, Soong used this as an opportunity to include her own essay and directly address this perception. The reason why China was still playing "catch up," she argued, was not the inability of the Chinese people. Rather, it was the scale of economic, social, and political development required to transform a large nation like China. To express disappointment at China because it had not yet achieved total transformation at the same pace as Japan, she wrote, was to deploy a "metaphorical carpetbag." American "travelers" and "political or economic experts" in China, Soong suggested, imposed their view of modernity and prevented a true reconstruction on its own terms.[53]

There were numerous Americans whose interpretation of China said far more about themselves than about the place they described, but perhaps the most surprising among them was W. E. B. Du Bois, the author of *The Black Reconstruction* (1935). In this book, Du Bois situated the struggles of emancipated African Americans within the context of global capitalism that subjugated various nonwhite peoples around the world anew. But when he visited China in 1936 as part of his world tour that also included the Soviet Union, Germany, Japan, and Manchukuo, he did not see the Chinese proletariat the same way he saw their Black American counterparts. "Everywhere one sees men doing what machines do in Europe and America: pile-driving, pumping water, acting like beasts of burden, crowding in great masses begging to delve and dig and carry for a pittance," he wrote in his weekly column in the *Pittsburgh Courier* upon return.[54] In October 1937, as the Sino-Japanese War raged on, Du Bois expressed in the same column that the war should be understood not as a war between two countries but as a war between an Asian power and an Asian pawn of Europe. China, he said, was "licking the European boots that kicked her and fawning on the West." When Japan showed China a way out of Western subjugation, he continued, "China preferred to be a coolie for England" rather than accept Japan's leadership of Asia. "Thus the straight road to world dominance of the yellow race was ruined by the same spirit that animates the 'white folks' nigger,'" he wrote in a sentence that his contemporaries would have understood as a reference to the perceived servility and self-hatred of Black Americans denounced as "Uncle Toms." "Negroes must think straight in this crisis," he argued; Japan was fighting China to "save China from Europe" and wading in "blood" toward "Asiatic freedom."[55]

Du Bois's negative view of China rested heavily on his fondness for Japan, which reached its peak after his world tour. Standing at Port Arthur, Manchukuo, where Japan had fired the first shots of the Russo-Japanese War, he relived the moment when he first became fascinated with Japan. Ever since its victory over Russia, he explained in his *Pittsburgh Courier* column in 1937, Japan had

Fig. 6.2 W. E. B. Du Bois with Japanese professors in Tokyo, 1936. W. E. B. Du Bois Papers, Robert S. Cox Special Collections and University Archives Research Center, UMass Amherst Libraries.

valiantly struggled against white empires. After meeting with Matsuoka Yōsuke, the diplomat who had walked Japan out of the League of Nations, Du Bois defended Japan against the League, which he believed was influenced by Britain, France, and the United States. To him, the hypocrisy of these three powers was undeniable. "[G]orged with the loot of the world," he said, they "suddenly became highly moral on the subject of annexing other people's land" when a nonwhite power competed with their interests. But Du Bois wasn't just taken by the idea that Japan was fighting on the nonwhite side of the color line. He was also captivated by Japan's progressive imperialism. In addition to explaining how the Japanese in Manchukuo had established various social services for the society's most vulnerable population, Du Bois portrayed the puppet state as a paradise even for the colonized people. The people appeared "happy," there was "no unemployment," and a "lynching" in Manchukuo was "unthinkable." Instead of arguing against empire, Du Bois concluded that Japan's actions in Manchukuo proved that "no nation should rule a colony whose people they cannot conceive as Equals."[56]

While Du Bois attempted to reconcile his fondness for the Asian empire and the Comintern by accepting Matsuoka's claim that "in some ways Japan was the most communistic of modern states," his views were hardly representative of the Black American left.[57] To be sure, there were Black Americans associated with the paramilitary organization the Pacific Movement of the Eastern World who held Japan as the champion of nonwhite peoples, as well as working-class Black women like Pearl D. Sherrod, who raised funds for Japan during the Sino-Japanese War through her Detroit-based organization, the Development of Our Own.[58] But prominent members of the Black American left tended to see Japan as an empire first and a nonwhite nation second. The Negro Commission of the National Committee of the Communist Party, U.S.A. published a pamphlet titled *Is Japan the Champion of the Colored Races?* (1938), to which it answered no.[59] Labor leader A. Philip Randolph urged Black Americans to boycott Japanese goods to stop supporting the Japanese "War Machine."[60] Singer and activist Paul Robeson, a well-known Soviet sympathizer, learned Chinese during the Sino-Japanese War in order to sing the Chinese national anthem at the China Defense Committee's fundraising event in London.[61] Poet Langston Hughes, who visited Japan, Korea, and China during the Depression, denounced Japan's "savage treatment of Koreans and Chinese" alongside Hitler's "tyranny over the Jews" and Mussolini's "slaughter in Ethiopia" when he spoke at the Second International Congress of Writers for the Defense of Culture in 1937.[62] Journalist George Padmore, who contributed to NAACP's organ *Crisis*, placed Japan alongside Germany and Italy as imperial powers that used the "overpopulation" thesis to demand "a re-division of the colonial world."[63] It is not clear if James Weldon Johnson, who died after a car accident in 1938, shared Du Bois's view of Japan, but if so he certainly did not express it in public during the Sino-Japanese War.

In the end, it was the images of women and children, murdered by invading Japanese troops, that did the most to convince many Americans to denounce Japan and voice support for China. The images became so widely accepted that Americans became used to the phrase the "rape of Nanking."[64] Here again, children of US missionaries played an important role in shaping the American view of China. Pearl S. Buck had grown up in Zhenjiang, not far from Nanjing, and then lived on the campus of the University of Nanjing from 1920 to 1933. During the Sino-Japanese War, she used the *Asia* magazine, published by her second husband Richard Walsh, to excoriate Japanese militarists. Meanwhile, in the same issue of *Life* magazine that presented Japan's attack on USS *Panay*, Henry Luce's editors presented photos of Chinese victims and described Japan's attack as "quite possibly the worst holocaust in modern history."[65]

Yet as many perceptive critics of the US policy pointed out, Americans' emotional support for Chinese war victims was undercut by American economic support for Japan. In 1938 the United States provided Japan with about 56 percent of all its essential materiel for the war. Over 90 percent of Japan's copper and scrap metal imports, essential to the production of guns, bullets, and bayonets, came from the United States. This contradiction was most succinctly expressed by former secretary of state Henry Stimson who, in the *Washington Post*, declared that "China's principal need is not that something should be done by outside nations to help her but that outside nations should stop helping her enemy."[66]

At this juncture, Stimson, who first entered public service three decades earlier as a trust-busting US Attorney for the Southern District of New York during Theodore Roosevelt's presidency, reemerged in national politics as the symbolic leader of the American Committee for Non-Participation in Japanese Aggression (ACNPJA). The ACNPJA, created by Southern Presbyterian missionary sons Harry B. Price and Frank W. Price, had no interest in subtlety. In August 1938 the ACNPJA published *America's Share in Japan's War Guilt*, a pamphlet that condemned Japan's "rape" of China and attempted to mobilize American public support for a boycott of Japanese imports and an embargo of exports that could aid the Japanese war effort.[67]

The ACNPJA's political influence became most visible when Congress debated another Neutrality Act in 1939. Although the debate primarily focused on the arms embargo that had been preventing Roosevelt from providing Britain and France full support in Europe, Roosevelt's concerns over Japan's advances in China also shaped the terms of the debate. Particularly important was the testimony of Geraldine T. Fitch, who represented the ACNPJA at the Senate hearings. Fitch's husband, George, a missionary and head of the YMCA in Nanjing, had already played an important role as one of the few eyewitnesses of the atrocities in that city, and during the hearings, she depicted the horrors of Japanese violence against Chinese women and children with photographs and letters that he had sent her.[68]

Fitch did more than reiterate the mission statement of the ACNPJA. She also tapped into the long-standing American dream of the China market for American exports, a dream best captured by the title of Carl Crowe's book, *Four Hundred Million Customers* (1937). As seen in the cases of Korea and Manchukuo, Fitch said, Japan did not leave an "open door" for American businesses. But in the case of China, Japanese occupation would affect far more than American access to the China market. According to Fitch, Japan would turn China into an export economy and engage in direct competition with American agribusiness, especially the cotton industry.[69]

The US cotton industry, however, was less worried about Japanese competition than the decline of exports due to war. Even before the Sino-Japanese War, American cotton traders established independent relationships with the Japanese textile industry to ensure continued export of American cotton to Japan regardless of the changing geopolitics.[70] Perhaps because of their proactiveness, Japan remained the number one importer of US cotton even during the Sino-Japanese War.[71] The US government helped as well. In 1939, two years into

Fig. 6.3 American Committee for Non-Participation in
Japanese Aggression (ACNPJA)'s pamphlet *America's
Share in Japan's War Guilt* (1938). Philip J. Jaffe Papers,
box 27, folder 13, Stuart A. Rose Manuscript, Archives,
and Rare Book Library, Emory University.

the war, the US government implemented a new export subsidy policy, which
enabled foreign countries, including Japan, to purchase surplus American cotton
at a low price, with the US government paying the difference between domestic
quotations and foreign sales price.[72]

Unlike in the case of the Philippines, economic concerns did not ultimately
shape US policy toward Japan and China. "The question of interference with
American nationals and American interests, while highly important, is not as
significant as is the paramount issue raised by the apparent Japanese intention
to dominate and hold a large area of the world, by unilateral action based on
force, for Japan's sole advantage," wrote Secretary of State Cordell Hull to the
American embassy in Tokyo in July 1939. Trade was one of the central pillars of
human life that ensured "civilization and security," he admitted. Yet what really
threatened the civilization and security, in his view, was Japan's commitment to
unilateralism in an international society.[73]

But wasn't unilateralism exactly what the United States had been pursuing under the guise of international commitment to foreign aid and racial "uplift" abroad all these years? This was the question that the Roosevelt administration was forced to answer as various Americans, including Japanese Americans, raised skepticism of its disavowal of its past.

Between Two Empires

On July 26, 1939, a few weeks after Hull warned about Japan's intention to "dominate and hold a large area of the world," the administration notified the Japanese government that it would be abrogating the Treaty of Commerce and Navigation (1911) in six months. As *Foreign Affairs* noted, this announcement came "suddenly and dramatically."[74] But the Roosevelt administration had little difficulty convincing the American people that this was the right move. Public-opinion polls had been showing that an overwhelming majority in the United States sided with China in the ongoing war, and in Congress both sides of the aisle agreed that something had to be done to stop Japan's violence. The ACNPJA could not be more pleased. Proposed by Republican senator Arthur Vanderburg, abrogation was an attractive strategy that even got the White House to agree. This way, instead of singling out Japan as a target of the US embargo, the United States could let the commercial treaty expire, take Japan off the list of "most favored nations," and withhold from Japan exports that were reserved for the United States' allies.[75]

The Treaty of Commerce and Navigation primarily concerned trade relations, but in Japanese American communities, uncertainty over what the abrogation would bring generated countless articles in their local newspapers. As racial minorities in the United States, Japanese Americans, many of whom were Japanese citizens, worried about how the end of the treaty and Japan's status as a "most favored nation" would change their lives.[76]

While some in the Japanese American community called their fellow immigrants to sever their relationship with Japan to show loyalty to the United States, others openly criticized US foreign policy.[77] The United States has developed a "psychosis," an editorial in San Francisco's *Shin Sekai Asahi Shinbun* declared. It sees a "wolf every time Japan makes a continental move for self-preservation." This "psychopathic attitude," it continued, only demonstrated Americans' lack of self-awareness. The United States had held up "the open door, like the Monroe doctrine," solely for its own advantage. Why should Japan be criticized for trying to do the same?[78]

The author of this editorial was none other than Kiyoshi Karl Kawakami, the Japan-born journalist who had headed the Pacific Press Bureau in the San

Francisco consulate during World War I. The trajectory of his life showed how one of the most dedicated students of American Progressivism had abandoned the idea that Japan's emulation of the US empire would solidify Japan's status as a great world power. After his failed attempt to convince the California electorate to vote against the expansion of the Alien Land Law in 1920, Kawakami worked as a Washington correspondent for a number of Japanese newspapers.[79] His work, however, was not entirely uncontroversial. In 1937, a few months before Japan invaded China, Kawakami traveled to Austria, Germany, and Italy, where he interviewed Benito Mussolini for the *New York Times*. As the news of the Sino-Japanese conflict turned American opinion against Japan, Kawakami went on the defensive, even publishing a book titled *Japan in China, Her Motives and Aims* (1938). The book's foreword was written by Viscount Ishii Kikujirō, a career diplomat who had represented Japan in Korea, China, France, and the United States before serving as a foreign minister and a member of the emperor's Privy Council.[80]

Like Kawakami, many Japanese American journalists aligned themselves with the Japanese Foreign Ministry. While Japanese American newspapers in Hawai'i and California often reiterated the Foreign Ministry's official statements, others went above and beyond to convince readers to support Japan.[81] The most notorious among the Issei was Sei Fujii, editor of *Kashū Mainichi Shinbun*. Like Kawakami, Fujii's experience of racism as a young man forever colored his view of the United States. Fujii graduated from the University of Southern California law school but was never admitted to the state bar because of his "alien" status. He then took his talents to the editorial page of *Kashū Mainichi Shinbun*, where "Uncle Fujii" defended Japan's "right" to dominate China.[82] Fujii's Nisei counterpart was Kazumaro "Buddy" Uno, a journalist for the Los Angeles–based *Rafu Shimpō* who traveled to the battlefront in China to report on the valiance of the Japanese army to the Japanese American community.[83] These journalists' support of Japan became convenient ammunition against the Japanese American community in the hands of V. S. McClatchy, who campaigned against them until his death in 1938. "Japan controls Issei thoughts and action and the Issei naturally see only the Japanese side of these questions," McClatchy wrote to the *Shinsekai Asahi Shinbun* and the IPR's New York office only months before his death, "Partly because of these influences two-thirds of the Nisei retain Japanese citizenship involving control by Japan."[84]

But of course, Japanese Americans did not all think alike. Japanese American leftists vehemently denounced immigrants' support of Japanese imperialism, and many of them expressed solidarity with Chinese, Filipino, and Korean radical activists who shared their antipathy to empires of all color. Yet to voice their criticism, these radicals had to find alternate venues. One of the most important antiwar Issei intellectuals, Ayako Ishigaki, left her job writing a column for women readers at *Rafu Shimpō* in the fall of 1937 and dedicated herself to criticizing Japanese and American imperialism in the pages of radical East Coast newspapers and magazines, such as the *Daily Worker* and *China Today*.[85] Nisei activists began publishing a pro-labor, anti-imperialist newspaper named *Dōhō* in Los Angeles. In *Dōhō*, left-leaning Japanese Americans such as John Kitahara bravely took on what he called the "fire-eating pro-militarist" newspapermen in the Japanese American community who attempted to silence anyone speaking out against the war[86]

As various Japanese American newspapers pointed out, however, agreeing with the Japanese Foreign Ministry's position was not necessary espousing a pro-Japanese view. There were plenty of prominent white Americans who took the same position as the Foreign Ministry, and Japanese American community newspapers leaned on these men to deflect accusations of their "disloyalty" to the United States.[87]

Most important among such figures was William R. Castle Jr., who had served as Hoover's undersecretary of state during the Manchurian Crisis. Castle was a scion of one of Hawai'i's Big Five sugar tycoons. Following an administrative career as an assistant dean at Harvard, his alma mater, he joined the State Department in 1919, rising through the ranks quickly to serve as assistant secretary of state under Coolidge and as US ambassador to Japan (1930) and undersecretary of state (1931–1933) under Hoover. Writing in the *Atlantic Monthly* in October 1940, Castle argued that a "Japanese Monroe Doctrine" was no different from declaring that the "Americas was for Americans." If the United States could declare that it had a right to secure a dominant position in its surrounding areas for its own security purposes, Castle argued, so could Japan. Americans' objection to Japan's assertion, he contended, was an undeniable sign of Americans' double standard.[88]

Castle directly contradicted the Roosevelt administration's position, which was explained to the American people by its own undersecretary of state, Sumner Welles. Welles was in a special position to assess Japan's claims of a Monroe Doctrine in Asia. After beginning his diplomatic career as secretary of the US embassy in Tokyo, he spent almost two decades in various roles representing the United States in Latin America until Roosevelt appointed him assistant secretary of state in 1933 and then undersecretary of state in 1936. Japan's claim to its own Monroe Doctrine, he explained on the radio in February 1941, was "grimly humorous." It demonstrated not only its devious attempt to mask an imperial expansion but also its poor understanding of American activities in the Western Hemisphere. The Monroe Doctrine, he said, had always been "a policy of defense, and not a policy of aggression."[89]

There existed plenty of historic examples that showed the US Monroe Doctrine had been a policy of aggression, but at this moment, Welles was confident that he had a good case. After Roosevelt declared the Good Neighbor policy at his first inauguration, the United States withdrew troops from Nicaragua, which had been occupied since William Howard Taft's intervention in 1912, and from Haiti, which had been occupied since Woodrow Wilson's in 1915.[90] Two months after signing the Tydings-McDuffie Act in 1934, the Roosevelt administration terminated the Platt Amendment, which had given the United States the right to military intervention in Cuba. Like the decision to decolonize the Philippines, the decision to withdraw US troops from the Caribbean was not motivated by anti-imperialism. US military intervention, Welles wrote Roosevelt and Hull, would only prove to Cubans "once more" that they do not have to be responsible for "their own lack of patriotism or lack of vision" and that the United States would be there to "repair the damage" Cubans had done.[91]

Regardless of the reason behind the withdrawal of US troops, it was easy for people like Welles to convince the American public that the United States and Japan were taking different paths because the Japanese empire was expanding. This difference became even more easily discernable after Japan declared its mission to form the Greater East Asia Co-Prosperity Sphere. Scholars have provided various interpretations of this concept, which Japan's foreign minister, Matsuoka Yōsuke, publicly named in a radio speech in August 1940. On the one hand, it was a declaration aimed at Europeans. After Nazi Germany defeated the Netherlands in May and France in June, Dutch and French colonies in Asia (referred to as the Dutch East Indies and French Indochina at this time) became vulnerable to not only anticolonial nationalist movements from within but also conquest by other imperial powers, including Germany. The two colonies in Southeast Asia were crucial to Japan's success in the prolonged Sino-Japanese War. The Dutch East Indies were home to rich oilfields, rubber plantations, and mineral mines, all of which were important to Japan's war industry. French Indochina, alongside British Burma, provided a major route through which Chiang Kai-shek's forces acquired foreign supplies.[92]

On the other hand, the Co-Prosperity Sphere was the latest iteration of Japan's attempt to convince other Asians that Japan's expansion did not aim to colonize them. In the preceding years, Japanese academics and government officials had considered various descriptive labels for Japan's ambitions for a new order, including the East Asian Federation (Tōa Renmei, 1936), the East Asia Cooperative Body (Tōa Kyōdōtai, 1939), and the Greater East Asia Co-Existence Sphere (Dai Tōa Kyōeiken, 1940) before the Foreign Ministry chose the concept of co-prosperity as its selling point.[93] By August 1940 many Asians were already sold. In March Chiang Kai-shek's former rival within the Kuomintang, Wang Jingwei, was selected by the Japanese as the head of the new collaborationist government in Nanjing, just as Puyi, the deposed last emperor of the Qing dynasty, had been selected the emperor of Manchukuo in 1934.[94]

Japan's pan-Asianist campaign attracted not just Chinese elites but also Chinese Americans who had moved to China in search of a better life.[95] Japan's efforts to recruit other Asians into its expansionist campaign were not limited to new territorial possessions. While the Japanese colonial government in Taiwan under Kobayashi Seizō (1936–1940) incorporated the islanders into the empire through the kōminka (imperialization) movement, the Japanese colonial government in Korea under Minami Jirō (1936–1942) emphasized the concepts of naisen ittai (Japanese-Korean unity) and senman ittai (Korean-Manchurian unity) to assimilate Koreans into the Japanese empire.[96]

Surprisingly, one of the most prominent Korean champions of the co-prosperity sphere was Yun Ch'i-ho. The former diplomat's long-standing resentment toward the Japanese empire began to soften during the Manchurian Crisis, when he became taken with the idea that Japan's occupation of China's three eastern provinces would allow a "million" Korean settlers to secure "life and property throughout that vast territory." But Yun wasn't concerned about poverty simply for its own sake. The Great Depression, he observed, created a ripe condition for the Korean communists to convince the Korean working class and students that the Comintern would provide them a way out of economic repression as well as Japanese colonialism. Yun was well aware that the Japanese government had been actively monitoring and repressing radical activists, and he sought to use the colonial government as a bulwark against communism. "Seeing that the Korean has to choose between the Japanese regime and the Russian Bolshevism I for one prefer the former to the latter," he confessed in his diary. Furthermore, he was irritated that the United States, after condoning Japan's rule over Korea for two and half decades, aligned itself with the League of Nations to stand against Japan's expansion into Manchuria. "In so far as international justice is concerned," he expressed his view with a biblical reference, "America which swallowed a camel in the case of Korea needn't strain at [a] gnat in the matter of Manchuria." Never mind that he had spent decades criticizing Japan for emulating American and European empires. Yun came to tolerate Japan's imperial violence as long as it would allow Koreans to escape poverty and help stop the spread of communism.[97]

Still, Yun's relationship with the colonial government remained unstable. He continued to interact with well-known anti-colonial activists of his generation, including An Ch'ang-ho, the founder of the Korean National Association in the United States. An traveled back and forth between the United States and China after the Provisional Korean Government was established in Shanghai during the March First Movement in 1919. In 1932, during the Manchurian Crisis, An was arrested in Shanghai by the invading Japanese forces and taken to Korea to be tried and incarcerated. Yun went to see An multiple times in jail, both during An's initial term that ended in 1935 on a bail and during his final term that ended in 1938 when An was transported to a hospital, where Yun found his friend "reduced to a mere skeleton" due to failing health. Two weeks before An passed, Yun rejected the colonial government's invitation to join the Privy Council (*Chungch'uwŏn*) that brought prominent Koreans to serve in an advisory role.[98] Then a few months later, the seventy-three-year-old Yun was summoned by the colonial police and asked about his connections with Korean anti-colonial leaders in the United States. Yun walked free after reminding the man, who he only identified as the "inquisitor" in his diary, that he had publicly discouraged Koreans from participating in the March First Movement. But clearly, this incident had an effect on him. In December 1938, Yun met with Governor General Minami to discuss ways to make Japanese-Korean unity a reality. The next summer, just four days before the Roosevelt administration gave notice to Japan about the abrogation of the 1911 treaty, Yun delivered a speech denouncing Western imperialism at a massive rally held in Seoul. Then the following summer, in a move to set an example for Koreans, Yun officially changed his family name to a Japanese one, Ito, an act that would solidify his infamy in postcolonial Korean historiography.[99]

Far more concerning for Americans was the effect of Japan's Pan-Asianist campaign within the boundaries of the US empire. Filipinos' warming relationship with the Japanese Empire was symbolized by the establishment of the Philippine Society of Japan (Hirippin kyōkai) in Tokyo and the Philippine Japan Society (Nippi kyōkai) in Manila, in 1935 and 1936 respectively. Members of the Philippine Society included Pio Duran, a prominent professor of law at the University of the Philippines whose firm represented various Japanese businesses in the Philippines. But more alarming to the US were Filipino politicians. The founding president of the Philippine Japan Society was Maximo Kalaw, a US-educated political scientist who represented the Philippines at the 1929 IPR conference in Kyoto. After the Tydings-McDuffie Act, Kalaw was elected to the Philippines Commonwealth Assembly, and in November 1939, as the Chinese forces launched the Winter Offensive against Japan, he visited Japan, where he was feted at the Philippine Society.[100] And then there was the President of the Commonwealth, Manuel Quezon. In 1938, Quezon took a three-week trip to Japan after which he publicly asked the Filipino people to adopt their own "Bushido." In response, Henry Luce's *Time* magazine revealed its true colors by calling Quezon a "little brown cricket" who acted like "royalty."[101]

In the continental United States, both the US state and the culture industry scrutinized Asian immigrants for signs of subversion. The FBI kept tabs on Chinese, Filipino, and Japanese radicals who were expressing solidarity with their non-Asian counterparts in the United States.[102] But, as in the case of the Hawai'i statehood question, the people most suspected of fifth-column activities were Japanese Americans who supported Japan during the Sino-Japanese War.

In addition to Japanese intelligence officers posing as students in US universities, Japanese Americans with high visibility became subjects of government surveillance and public attack. The case of Kiyoshi Karl Kawakami is illustrative. The FBI, which had been tracking Kawakami for decades, interviewed the journalist in person when he returned from his latest trip to Japan in the summer of 1939.[103] In August 1940, soon after the Alien Registration Act (Smith Act) went into effect to streamline the deportation process for foreigners accused of sedition and required all adult alien residents to register with the federal government, the *Saturday Evening Post* published an article titled "Alien Poison." It presented a photo of Kawakami, with his white American wife Mildred, alongside well-known Nazi propagandists in the United States.[104]

Kawakami was able to push back against this accusation of sedition because he had recently begun denouncing Japan's foreign policy. In fact, this is precisely what later allowed him to walk free after the FBI arrested him the day after the Pearl Harbor attack in December 1941.[105] Just weeks before he and his wife were named "alien poison," Kawakami publicly excoriated Japan's foreign minister, Matsuoka Yōsuke, in the *Washington Post*. This was a remarkable development. As the FBI well knew, the two men maintained a cordial relationship when Matsuoka attended the Paris Peace Conference in 1919. When Matsuoka walked Japan out of the League of Nations in 1933, Kawakami publicly defended him.[106] Yet when Matsuoka became foreign minister in 1940, Kawakami described him as an "untamable savage" on a "one-man campaign against all the great parties of Japan." A month later, when Matsuoka entered Japan into the Tripartite Pact with Germany and Italy, Kawakami argued that this decision was "proof that Japan today is devoid of a forceful leadership such as was exercised by Emperor Meiji, assisted by Prince Ito and other far-seeing statesmen, up to three decades ago."[107]

Kawakami's description of Japan revealed as much about the author, now sixty-seven years old, as it did about the country. Most of the elder statesmen who had brought Japan into the circle of empires during the late Meiji era had passed away. Since the Russo-Japanese War, Japan's leaders embraced parliamentary rule that simultaneously supported overseas imperial expansion and democratic reform at home. But as the Great Depression deepened, Japan's leaders embraced a more authoritarian rule, though it remained clear that authoritarianism did not bring stability. Since the beginning of the Sino-Japanese War, Japan had four different prime ministers, a cycle of chaos that only stopped when Konoe Fumimaro, the first of the four, returned to the position by request of the Army in July 1940. Military officers were not the only ones responsible for this change. A new generation of technocrats, especially those who got to test their vision of an alternate model of economic planning and governance in Manchukuo, proved particularly influential. In addition to future prime minister

Tōjō Hideki (Kwantung Army Chief of Staff), Manchukuo produced Hoshino Naoki (the puppet state's vice minister of financial affairs) and Kishi Nobusuke (its vice minister of industry), both of whom would go onto play important roles in the Tōjō cabinet (1941–1944) during the Pacific War.[108] Meanwhile, the aging Baron Kaneko Kentarō, the man who popularized the idea that Theodore Roosevelt recommended Japan's own Monroe Doctrine, remained sidelined. By the time Japan signed the Tripartite Pact, Kaneko was eighty-seven years old, and his health was too fragile to fight it.[109]

Franklin Roosevelt himself came to adopt such a view of Japan through his longtime minister in Tokyo, Joseph Grew, who told him the country was no longer "the Japan we have known and loved." Grew's ambassadorship to Japan, which began during Herbert Hoover's presidency, was made possible by his friendship with William R. Castle Jr. Yet unlike Castle, Grew was concerned about Japan's leadership.[110] In December 1940, the ambassador wrote to Roosevelt that, unless Americans were prepared to withdraw from the "entire sphere of 'Greater East Asia including South Seas' (which God forbid)," the United States was bound to clash with Japan. There no longer was a politician powerful enough in Japan to reverse the course of its aggressive foreign policy set by Matsuoka, Grew told Roosevelt, and the only way for the United States to stop Japan was by taking the matter into its own hands.[111]

Grew's letter arrived in Washington just as the United States was heading into a new direction. In the preceding months, Britain survived Germany's aerial bombings and Hitler gave up on his plan of land invasion. After the Battle of Britain, public-opinion polls in the United States began to show that the American people, for the first time since the beginning of the war, would rather support Britain than avoid the war.[112] Then, Roosevelt was re-elected for an unprecedented third term. The country was ready to engage more aggressively with affairs outside the Western Hemisphere and leave behind the collaborative, multipolar imperial order that had been based on the idea that Japan would maintain peace and order on the opposite side of the Pacific.

No Separate Spheres

In July and August 1941, the US government froze Japan's financial assets within its jurisdiction and placed an embargo on petroleum exports. The immediate precipitant for this action was the signing of a protocol between Japan and the French Vichy government for a joint defense and military cooperation, which enabled Japan to use airfields and naval bases in the French colony as well as station seventy-five thousand troops in Cam Ranh Bay, in southern Indochina, within striking distances of British bases in Malaya, Singapore, and Burma.[113] To many Americans, the US government's reaction was the latest example of how the administration was rapidly preparing the nation for war since the election of 1940. Until 1941, the administration had been cautious about any action that could potentially provoke Japan. It did not even push for Congress to fund the fortification of Guam when it was recommended by the Navy's defense review board.[114] Yet in March 1941, Congress responded to Roosevelt's request to turn the country into an "arsenal of democracy" by approving the Lend-Lease Act. The act empowered the president to supply his allies, especially Britain, with not only food and oil but also tanks, planes, and ships, as long as this aid would contribute to US national security. When Japan moved closer to British bases in Southeast Asia, the Roosevelt administration further assisted its ally by cutting off Japan's financial and natural resources. A few weeks after it placed the oil embargo, Roosevelt secretly traveled to Newfoundland to meet Churchill and sign the Atlantic Charter.[115]

But why should the United States react to Japan's threat to the British Empire? This was the question that the noninterventionist group America First Committee (AFC) wanted the American people to ask themselves. Because of the outsized shadow cast by AFC's most infamous member, aviator Charles Lindbergh, it has been easy to lose sight of the fact that the organization attracted a wide range of Americans across the political spectrum. Before various members and supporters quit the organization because of Lindbergh— who, in September 1941, publicly accused not only Churchill and Roosevelt but also what he called the "Jewish race" of drawing the country into war—the AFC enjoyed a close relationship with several key politicians on both sides of the aisle. Republican Senator Robert Taft, the twenty-seventh president's son, and his wife formed the Cincinnati chapter of the AFC. William Castle Jr. and Miriam Marsh Clark, the wife of the Democratic senator from Missouri who served on the Nye Committee, formed the Washington, DC, chapter. The AFC received support from the American left as well. Kathryn Lewis, the daughter of CIO leader John L. Lewis, was a member of the national committee, as was minister Norman Thomas, who had run for the US presidency as a candidate of the Socialist Party. And there were the old Progressives—Theodore Roosevelt's daughter Alice Roosevelt Longworth and his running mate in the 1912 election, Senator Hiram Johnson. Johnson, in spite of his failing health, appeared on the radio in June 1941, under the auspices of the AFC, to attack the lend-lease program and the president.[116]

Because the AFC was founded during the Battle of Britain in 1940 to counter the political influence of the Committee to Defend America by Aiding the Allies (CDAAA), the AFC's primary focus was Europe. But having William Castle Jr. on the organization's roster also led the AFC to resurrect the idea the United States should leave Japan to establish its hegemony in Asia. In a July

1941 pamphlet titled "Nobody Knows the Trouble We're In," the AFC asked Americans to look at a map of the Pacific and see the "absurdity" of the fear that Japan could attack the Western Hemisphere from "Saigon or Cam-Ranh [*sic*] Bay." The closest US base was in Manila, but Congress and the president had already agreed that the Philippines was no longer worth American investment. In August 1941 the New York chapter of the AFC claimed that Southeast Asia lay within Japan's sphere of influence. American interference there, it hypothetically argued, was comparable to Japan's prevention of American "acquisition of bases in Brazil."[117] This was a comparison that many Americans would have understood. The previous year, the US government had responded to increasing German activities in Brazil, a country with large German, Italian, and Japanese immigrant populations, by negotiating a contract with the Pan American Airports Corporation to build airbases throughout Latin America under the auspices of the Airport Development Program (ADP). Brazil was at this time a neutral country, but Pan American Airways, a private company, could use its Brazilian subsidiary to build airbases that were ostensibly for commercial purposes but could easily be converted for military purposes.[118] From the AFC's perspective, it made little sense to stop Japan from acquiring bases in French Indochina when the United States had already done so in Brazil.

From Roosevelt's perspective, the main problem with Japan was that, along with other Axis powers, it insisted on dividing the world into separate spheres of influence. Unlike many of his predecessors, Roosevelt had little faith in a multipolar imperial order. His vision of a world order headed by the United States was clearly presented in the State of the Union in January 1941. In what has been dubbed the "Four Freedoms" speech, he outlined a "new order" founded upon "four essential human freedoms": freedom of speech, freedom of worship, freedom from want, and freedom from fear. Together, these four freedoms would secure the American way of life at home against the rising tide of fascism. What is more, Roosevelt argued, this new order would ensure "supremacy of human rights everywhere," not just in the Western Hemisphere.[119]

In defense of this envisioned world order, Roosevelt publicly took on one of his strongest critics, Senator Burton K. Wheeler of Montana. Wheeler, a key supporter of the AFC, was a Democrat who first rose to national prominence in 1923 for holding the Warren G. Harding administration accountable for refusing to prosecute corrupt officials implicated in the Teapot Dome scandal. He then became Robert La Follette Sr.'s running mate on the Progressive Party's ticket for the presidential election of 1924 and, like Hiram Johnson, supported FDR's New Deal until the Court-packing controversy. Wheeler's progressive reputation continued to grow as Frank Capra's film *Mr. Smith Goes to Washington* (1939), a movie about a novice senator fighting against government corruption, was loosely based on Wheeler's experiences. During Roosevelt's third term,

Wheeler positioned himself as carrying the torch of La Follette Sr., who had stood against Wilson's entry into World War I. He criticized the lend-lease program by claiming that it was part of the president's plan to "plow under every fourth American boy" by sending them to war.[120] In retaliation, Roosevelt seized onto a diary entry, mysteriously leaked to the press, that had been written by his recently deceased ambassador to Germany, William Dodd. Dodd had recorded a dinner conversation at the house of Rexford G. Tugwell, among the president's closest advisers collectively known as the Brain Trust. At the dinner, the diary entry said, a US senator proposed "German domination of all Europe, our domination of the Americas and Japanese domination of the Far East." Upon being asked about this entry at a press conference, Roosevelt revealed that Dodd had personally told him this senator was Wheeler and replied that anyone who saw Nazi domination of Europe as "inevitable," as Wheeler did, "in effect" favored it.[121]

Regarding Japanese domination of Asia, however, Roosevelt and his advisers still faced an uphill battle to convince the American people that it was a major concern. Even in 1941, much of the national attention remained on the war in Europe, where Germany broke the non-aggression pact with the Soviet Union and began its eastward invasion. To draw the American people's attention to the Pacific, the Roosevelt administration turned to an economic argument to explain that what happened in Southeast Asia would inevitably affect the US domestic economy. Japan's advances in Southeast Asia, acting Secretary of State Sumner Welles publicly argued only days before Japan and the French Vichy government signed the protocol for a joint defense and military cooperation in July 1941, jeopardized American access to rubber and tin, both of which were "essential defense material."[122]

The AFC quickly countered Welles by presenting its own economic argument to the public. It pointed out that the creation of synthetic rubber made large quantities of rubber imports unnecessary, and the import of tin from Bolivia would sufficiently meet the demand at home.[123] Wheeler, still leading the noninterventionists against Roosevelt in Congress, took charge of attacking Welles in public. Reminiscent of J. V. A. MacMurray's memo to the State Department, Wheeler explained that Japan was "one of our best customers for cotton and petroleum and we are one of her best customers, and there is no reason why we should not live in peace with her." Meanwhile, Castle repeatedly argued in public that, since Japan was one of the largest purchasers of US raw cotton, the administration's move to antagonize Japan indicated that "we are far less interested in the sufferings of our own people in the South than we are in China."[124]

Whatever momentum the AFC had in 1941 was destroyed when Lindbergh delivered his infamous anti-Semitic speech in September. While Wheeler got eggs thrown at him during public appearances, Castle retreated to Hot Springs, Virginia, for convalescence. But the Republican could not avoid scrutiny, either, as the journalist John L. Spivak of the leftist magazine *New Masses* tracked him down at his resort. Castle was noticeably ill, Spivak observed, and he appeared acutely aware of the irreparable damage Lindbergh's speech had done to the AFC. Castle was most embarrassed, however, by the discovery of a letter he himself had written to Merwin K. Hart, a well-known anti–New Dealer. In it, the former undersecretary expressed concerns about newspaper editor Verne Marshall, whose anti-interventionism he admired but whose public campaign against the war distressed him. Marshall "is so violent on the subject of Jews and the New Deal that he is likely badly to overstep the mark," Castle wrote Hart. But his seeming discomfort with an anti-Semite disappeared in the next line. "God knows, I have no particular affection for such people," Castle wrote, "but I should much prefer to express it in private to you than in a public advertisement." According to Spivak, Castle frantically tried to do damage control by stating that some of his "best friends" were Jewish. But the *New Masses* printed a copy of the letter, which was undeniable proof that he lacked sympathy for the Jewish people fleeing Nazi Germany.[125]

Yet Castle did not end his campaign for separate spheres diplomacy here. After Cordell Hull, in a note delivered to the Japanese minister in Washington Nomura Kichisaburō and Japanese special envoy Kurusu Saburō on November 26, 1941, demanded that Japan withdraw its military from Indochina and China to retract its empire to the size it had been before the Manchurian crisis, Castle tried one last time to convince the American public that the United States should not interfere with Japan's activities in Asia.[126] On December 1, he wrote a letter to the *New York Herald Tribune* recommending that the United States avoid war with Japan at all costs. Castle argued that Japan, for its own sake, could not pull out of China without risking "complete collapse and revolution at home." Furthermore, he predicted that, if the United States entered the war against Japan in the Pacific, it would divert vital resources from the Atlantic, where the war against Germany was difficult as it is. Fight Japan, he said, and the United States plays into Hitler's hands.[127]

For an unknown reason, the *New York Herald Tribune* delayed publishing Castle's letter until December 7. Readers who picked up this newspaper, on Sunday morning, might have entertained the idea for a few hours. But just before 1:00 P.M. Eastern time, the Japanese Navy bombed Pearl Harbor, located in Castle's birth place of Hawai'i. Americans on the mainland soon heard the news by radio, but they largely remained uninformed about the exact scale of Japanese attacks. Hours before the Pearl Harbor attack, Japan had begun bombing British bases in Malaya and had landed troops in Thailand. The bombing of Hawai'i was followed, on the same day, by attacks on Singapore, Guam, Wake Island, Hong

Kong, and the Philippines. The day after Japan's coordinated attacks on US and British overseas possessions, Roosevelt delivered a speech calling December 7 "a date which will live in infamy."[128] It was a date of a tragedy of many sorts, including the thousands of lives lost during the attacks, but for Castle it was also a date of embarrassment.

The same day Roosevelt gave this speech, Castle wrote the *New York Herald Tribune* again, lamenting how his words, which were "factually and psychologically true" at the time of his writing, became irrelevant after the "dastardly attack." Yet instead of spending time justifying his views, Castle wanted to move on. Now Americans' "only duty" was winning the war, he said. "It is useless to dwell on the past."[129]

The long decade between Japan's invasion of Manchuria in 1931 and its attack on American and British bases in 1941 witnessed the gradual collapse of the inter-imperial framework for transpacific governance established by Theodore Roosevelt's generation. There was no single factor or event that caused its demise. The American desire for economic recovery, manifested by its decision to place the Philippines on a path to independence in exchange for restricting Filipino labor migration and reducing the flow of agricultural products to the continental United States, set the stage for various policy changes that culminated in the end of the bilateral relationship. The shifting American views of China, exhibited by the widespread sympathy for the Chinese during the Sino-Japanese War, enabled the Franklin D. Roosevelt administration to gradually prepare the nation to take a more active stance against Japan's expansion in Asia, despite the efforts of non-interventionists in Congress and the America First Committee.

But the disintegration of the amicable US-Japan relationship also had much to do with the declining American interest in their own overseas colonial projects and, by extension, the end of the long-standing practice that used America's imperial record in Cuba and the Philippines as a measuring stick to assess Japan's "racial capacity." Ever since the Russo-Japanese War, Americans had perceived the Japanese as trustworthy collaborators in large part because the Asian empire appeared to be contributing to the "development" of the "subject races." This perception took a negative turn after Japan suppressed the March First Movement in Korea and refused to return Shandong to the Republic of China during the Paris Peace Conference. But it was not until the United States set the timetable for Philippine independence and ended Cuba's protectorate status, that American policymakers stopped seeing Japan as a comparable empire. Japan's claim, that it was doing in East Asia what the United States was doing in the Caribbean, fell on deaf ears. By the time the congressional committee considered the possibility of Hawai'i statehood during the Sino-Japanese

War, few Americans believed in Japan's promise to bring peace and order on the opposite side of the Pacific. After the United States abrogated the 1911 Treaty of Commerce and Navigation, the administration received little pushback outside Japanese American communities and the America First Committee. Although many Americans were shocked by the events of December 7, the end of the two empires' relationship seemed abrupt only to those few who continued to believe that the world had not fundamentally changed.

On the eve of US entry into World War II, William R. Castle Jr. remained one of the few Americans who held out the hope that US-Japan relations could continue on as it had in the preceding decades. Most of the politicians and policymakers who had helped Theodore Roosevelt establish and implement the inter-imperial framework were deceased by this time, and his former allies who remained politically active, such as Hiram Johnson and Henry Stimson, had little interest in working with Japan. After the Sino-Japanese War began, even Theodore Roosevelt Jr. abandoned the idea that collaborating with Japan would be beneficial to US interests.

Likewise, on the eve of the war, few people in Asia believed that US-Japan relations would remain peaceful. Most of Japan's elder statesmen who had worked with Theodore Roosevelt's generation to set up and maintain the inter-imperial framework had passed away, and those still living, such as Count Kaneko Kentarō, were marginalized by the new generation of policymakers. Meanwhile, many of Japan's colonial subjects, including Yun Ch'i-ho, latched on to Japan's mission to create the Greater East Asia Co-Prosperity Sphere. They hoped to overcome the economic Depression and drive out American and British empires from Asia by aligning themselves with the Japanese empire. The idea that the vast region stretching across the Pacific Ocean could be governed by a collaborative, multipolar imperial order that cut across the color line had already faded away before Japan and the United States went to war.

Epilogue:
The World Empires Made

Like many nonwhite people around the world, Yun Ch'i-ho greeted the news of Japan's attack on Pearl Harbor as the dawn of a new era. The new era had not arrived suddenly. For the preceding four years, East Asia had been in a state of total war, and colonial newspapers kept Koreans updated on British actions against Japanese expansion in China. In 1939, Yun helped organize the Anti-British Association (Paeyŏng tongjihoe) and served as its founding president. As late as August 1941, when Japan's military advanced into French Indochina, Yun continued to perceive Britain as the primary threat to world peace. He claimed that British leaders were using "crafty diplomacy" to lure various countries, especially the United States, into a war that it could not win alone.[1]

After the US government placed an embargo in response to Japan's advancement in Southeast Asia, Yun shifted the blame to Franklin D. Roosevelt, who, as so many leaders of the Japanese empire claimed, put Japan in a difficult situation. On the day the Japanese military bombed US and British bases across the Pacific, Yun wrote in his diary that Japan had begun the "greatest war in the history of mankind," a war that would deliver the "the colored races" from the domination of "white races in general and the Anglo-Saxons in particular." The following day he spoke at an event sponsored by the Korean League for National Mobilization (Kungmin ch'ongnyŏk chosŏn yŏnmaeng), an organization established to generate Korean support for Japan's expansion. In his speech Yun described the Pacific theater as a site of a "holy war" (sŏngjŏn) and that Japan would deliver Asian people from the oppression of white supremacy.[2]

The origin of this holy war, Yun argued, traced back to the Russo-Japanese War. That war had tested Japan's "might and honor" on the world stage, he explained, and its victory enabled Japan to join the ranks of the great powers and take on the role of the leader of "new Asia." Yun contended that Japan had spent

The Allure of Empire. Chris Suh, Oxford University Press. © Oxford University Press 2023.
DOI: 10.1093/oso/9780197631614.003.0008

three and a half decades incorporating Koreans into the Japanese empire, and that, with the advent of the Pacific War, the time had finally come for Koreans to prove to the Japanese that the colonial project had been worth the effort.[3]

This was, of course, the exact opposite of Yun's own view during the Russo-Japanese War. Back then, as a Korean diplomat who witnessed Japan's emergence as a great power accompanied by Japan's subjugation of Korea, he refused to believe that Japan represented the interests of anyone but itself. Yet in 1941, the seventy-six-year-old Yun expressed no qualms about the Japanese empire. Ignoring the violence that Japanese soldiers committed against Chinese civilians, he greeted the news of Japan's seizure of Hong Kong from Britain on Christmas Day by expressing in his diary that "Japan deserves the undying gratitude of all colored races for having broken the spell of white domination in the East."[4] Yun had come to champion Japan as a leader of the so-called darker races, as many nonwhite intellectuals around the world had done since the Russo-Japanese War.

If Yun's 1941 speech represented a drastic shift in his position, W. E. B. Du Bois's writings before and after Pearl Harbor represented a persistent pattern in his worldview. While many other Black intellectuals ceased to hold Japan as a champion of the "darker races" after learning about Japan's violent war with China and its alliance with Nazi Germany, Du Bois, three years younger than Yun, continued to hold Japan in high regard long after his tour of Japan, China, and Manchukuo. During the Sino-Japanese War, he turned down an opportunity to join the American Committee for Non-Participation in Japanese Aggression (ACNPJA). Du Bois's controversial view did not go unnoticed. In February 1942, the FBI began investigating him not because of his romantic view of the Soviet Union, but because of his public defense of Japan.[5]

Du Bois's faith in Japan rested on a particular view of history that interpreted the previous four decades as a period defined by the "color line," a struggle of the darker races against the lighter ones. In *Phylon*, an academic journal he founded upon returning to teach at Atlanta University in 1940, Du Bois explained that Japan had continuously tried to "stand in alliance with England and America" and only came to "embrace the Axis" after enduring British and American racism for decades. This racism manifested itself most obviously in their immigration policies. After Australia and New Zealand prohibited Asian immigration, the United States negotiated the Gentlemen's Agreement with Japan from 1907 to 1908 to prohibit the entry of Japan's working class and allowed its Pacific Coast states to pass alien land laws. But racism did not end there. At the Paris Peace Conference in 1919, the United States rejected Japan's proposal to add a racial equality clause to the League of Nations Covenant. In 1924 the United States passed, signed, and implemented the Johnson-Reed Act, which, as Du Bois reminded his readers in 1941, was made possible by "a deal between Western and Southern senators through which the Western senators opposed the anti-lynching bill and the Southern senators supported Japanese exclusion."[6] From his perspective it was the United States, not Japan, that had sown the seeds of war.

Today, Yun Ch'i-ho and W. E. B. Du Bois occupy vastly different places in historical memory. While Yun has been dismissed as an unconscionable traitor in postcolonial South Korea, Du Bois has been praised in the United States as a trenchant critic whose words and ideas continue to hold a singular influence on discussions about race and empire.[7] But at the dawn of the Pacific War, Yun and Du Bois held compatible, if not overlapping, views of race, empire, Japan, and the United States, even as they held polar opposite perspectives on Russia. Both emphasized the color line, and both rallied against white empires by aligning themselves with the Japanese empire.

During World War II, Yun and Du Bois named the imperialism that American leaders attempted to hide. In his speech asking Congress to declare war against Japan, Franklin D. Roosevelt explained the "United States of America" was attacked by the "Empire of Japan," even though Pearl Harbor was located in an overseas territory acquired by US imperial expansion at the end of the nineteenth century. He also deleted from his final draft any mention of Japan's attack on the Philippines, which took place only ten hours after that on Hawai'i.[8] Having set the timetable for Philippine independence, he wrote empire out of his version of the story of US-Japan conflict, which he detailed in a document titled "Summary of Past Policy and of More Immediate Events, in Relation to the Pacific Area," submitted to Congress a week after Japan's attacks. Without once mentioning the Spanish-American War or the Philippine-American War, Roosevelt claimed that the sovereignty of the Philippines "passed" from Spain to the United States at the end of the nineteenth century. He then reduced the four-decade history of US colonial rule in the Philippines to two sentences, one explaining that the United States had pledged itself to a policy to "equip" Filipinos to become a "free and independent nation," and the other claiming that the United States had "consistently carried out" this pledge and policy throughout its rule.[9] There was no mention of the fact that the United States had repeatedly denied Filipinos' request for self-government in the first three decades of the twentieth century, or the fact that the United States decided to make the Philippines independent because US agribusiness and nativists claimed that competition with products and workers from the Philippines could be stopped by turning the colony into an independent, foreign nation.

By erasing this history of US empire, Roosevelt erased the long history of US inter-imperial collaboration with Japan. After all, there could be no inter-imperial collaboration if there was only one empire, the Empire of Japan. In the same document submitted to Congress, he minimized the history of the first three decades of the twentieth century by claiming that the "course of events which have led directly to the present crisis" began only a decade earlier, during Japan's "barbaric aggression" in Manchuria. When he discussed the preceding decades, he drew a straight line from the end of the nineteenth century to the Manchurian Crisis, a narrative that made the United States appear as a consistent defender of China against Japan's repeated attempts to violate China's territorial integrity. After a brief explanation of the Open Door policy, he mentioned the 1908 Root-Takahira Agreement and the 1921 Nine-Power Treaty to illustrate how the United States had gotten Japan to reaffirm this policy, one that Japan violated when it invaded Manchuria. Nowhere in Roosevelt's narrative was there any mention of the Russo-Japanese War, the Gentlemen's Agreement, the Panama-Pacific Exposition, or the Paris Peace Conference, where Wilson had acknowledged Japan's rights to Shandong, China.[10] All that his predecessors, especially his cousin Theodore, had done to establish and maintain a cordial relationship with Japan was missing in FDR's version of history.

Yet Yun and Du Bois, too, deliberately omitted crucial aspects of the history of US-Pacific relations. In their description of the US empire in the 1940s, they also erased the long history of US-Japan collaboration across the color line. They made no mention of how, after Japan defeated Russia, the United States tentatively included Japan in the circle of "civilized" powers with the expectation that Japan would "develop" its neighbors with its own "civilizing missions" in East Asia. Neither of them mentioned the fact that the United States supported Japan's decades-long colonial rule over various parts of Asia, including Korea, as part of the United States' policy to cooperate with nonwhite people who had reformed themselves to Western standards of "civilization."

In fact, Yun and Du Bois underestimated the ability of the US government to continue working with nonwhite peoples even after the allure of progressive empire faded in the United States. While US involvement in the Pacific has been characterized as a "race war," and while the forced removal and incarceration of Japanese Americans during World War II stand as indisputable evidence of racism and state violence, the US government was able to mobilize various nonwhite peoples for the United States against Japan.[11] To be sure, a number of Black Americans refused to register for the military draft, and some were even arrested for sedition. But the *Pittsburgh Courier*, the same newspaper that published Du Bois's article on Japanese colonialism, supported the war effort with the "Double V" campaign that encouraged Black Americans to see the war as an opportunity to achieve victory over foreign enemies as well as domestic racism. The NAACP, which endorsed the "Double V" campaign, experienced unprecedented growth in membership during the war.[12] Likewise, while many Koreans in Japan's empire fought on their colonizer's side, Koreans in the United States contributed funds to the US war efforts, and some even enlisted to fight in the US military. Immigrant leaders who organized the United Korean Committee of

North America lobbied the US government with hopes of gaining US recognition of the Korean Provisional Government in China.[13] In the Philippines, the US Armed Forces in the Far East (USAFFE), which had brought together the US Army, the Philippines Army, and the Philippines Scouts on the eve of war, fought against the invading Japanese army. And the United States disavowed its racism by enabling second-generation Japanese Americans to enlist in the military to fight for the United States, even if their families remained interned at home.[14] This is not to say, as World War II–era US propaganda did, that the United States achieved racial harmony in the military. Japanese American and African American soldiers served in segregated units and endured daily doses of racism at every stage of their service.[15] But the United States did succeed in making itself appear as an antithesis of the fascist states of Germany, Italy, and Japan, especially to its nonwhite allies. Japan's wartime atrocities, including its brutal massacres of civilians in Burma, China, Indonesia, Malaysia, the Philippines, Singapore, and Vietnam, made it difficult for millions of Asians to see the war as a conflict between the two sides of the color line.

In the Pacific theater, no group of nonwhite people received more US support than the Chinese. Although China had been long dismissed by Theodore Roosevelt's generation as a nation that could not protect itself, the experience of the 1930s, especially as China held its ground against Japan even after many years of the violent war, solidified American support for China. US-China relations were anything but smooth. General Joseph Stilwell, the US military adviser to China, openly complained about the difficulty of working with Chiang Kai-shek. But Roosevelt insisted on including China, more specifically, Chiang's Kuomintang, as one of the world's "great powers," against the wishes of Winston Churchill. The president wished to include China as one of the "Four Policemen" who would keep the postwar world in order. In November 1943, Roosevelt met with Chiang and Churchill in Cairo, Egypt, for a conference to affirm their postwar plans to dismantle Japan's colonial empire. Secretary of State Cordell Hull almost sounded like Theodore Roosevelt when he expressed concerns about Franklin Roosevelt's Four Policemen proposal: while the United States had shown "self-restraint" in its treatment of Latin America, he wrote in his memoir, another "great power" might abuse smaller nations "in another region."[16] Nevertheless, the Franklin Roosevelt administration remained committed to having China as one of the "Big Four."

To be sure, the inclusion of China among the great powers was not on equal terms, as Du Bois was quick to point out. In *Color and Democracy: Colonies and Peace* (1945), a book he finished in the wake of the Dumbarton Oaks conference that brought representatives from the Soviet Union, Britain, and China to Washington, DC, in the fall of 1944 to prepare a new international order, Du Bois raised some important questions about this landmark meeting. China was brought in for the final six days of the conference that had lasted six weeks. It was as if China was called in to perform a "review" of proposals that the three white powers had already agreed upon, he said. More important, the three white powers "suppressed" China's proposal of an "international declaration on racial equality." This, of course, eerily resembled what had happened to Japan during the Paris Peace Conference in 1919. It was after the United States rejected Japan's proposal of a racial nondiscrimination clause in the League of Nations Covenant, Du Bois said, that Japan "gradually turned and began to work toward the hegemony of Asia." In the case of China's aborted attempt to add the racial equality declaration, Du Bois placed the blame on not only the three white powers but also the Chinese themselves. Recalling his 1936 trip to Asia, Du Bois commented in 1945 that, while he could understand China's "bitterness and determined opposition to the substitution of Asiatic for an European imperialism" by Japan, he could not understand the "seemingly placid attitude of the Chinese toward Britain."[17] In 1943, Du Bois criticized Chiang Kai-shek and Mei-ling Soong in the *Phylon*, the husband for his cooperation with Europeans and the wife for her silence on "the plight of minority peoples" and "the continued discrimination against Chinese in the United States."[18]

But the United States did not always act as Du Bois predicted. In December 1943, following an immensely popular tour of the United States by Mei-ling Soong (during which she did remain silent on racism in the United States), the US government did something that was unthinkable only a decade earlier: it ended Chinese exclusion and made the non-US born Chinese eligible for American citizenship.[19]

While the mass removal and incarceration of over 120,000 Japanese Americans in 1942 demonstrated the convergence of the US federal government and West Coast exclusionists' views, the end of Chinese exclusion the following year evidenced how the US government continued to use its immigration policy as an instrument of geopolitics against nativists' wishes. Years after V. S. McClatchy's death, the California Joint Immigration Commission (CJIC) worked to oppose the repeal of Chinese exclusion. Spearheading this effort was V. S.'s son, H. J. McClatchy. The Magnuson Act (1943), which repealed Chinese exclusion and granted the Chinese right to naturalize as US citizens, gave the Asian ally only a symbolic immigration quota of 105 people per year. But it was enough to anger California's exclusionists and convince many Chinese and Chinese Americans to see the US empire as a champion of their cause.[20]

Because the surviving entries of Yun Ch'i-ho's diary do not date beyond past October 1943, two years before his death, it is difficult to know how he took in the news of the Cairo Conference, the end of Chinese Exclusion, and the Dumbarton Oaks Conference. But it is clear that Yun, like Du Bois, missed much more than the symbolic importance of the repeal of Chinese exclusion during World War II. The color line metaphor came up short in describing the world US imperialists created. This was the result of a deliberate, sustained effort by US policymakers who knew that imperial rule could be made more stable by including select groups of nonwhite people in the governance of the world as well as in the US body politic. And this strategy did not end with China. As the United States prepared for the postwar order, it searched for Asian collaborators in areas where it planned to occupy and govern, including Korea.

In fact, Yun Ch'i-ho's name often appeared on the short list of possible Korean collaborators with the United States. Although he had been "forced to collaborate with Japanese in some of his activities," the War Department's Military Intelligence Service (MIS) noted in 1944, Yun was "undoubtedly loyal to Korea; his prestige in Korea was high in 1941, and he would no doubt be a valuable collaborator in Allied activities in Korea."[21] On June 23, 1945, only six weeks before the United States dropped atomic bombs on Japan, the Office of Strategic Services (OSS) agreed that Yun was "strongly anti-Japanese and would aid the Allied cause if the opportunity arose."[22] The positive evaluation of Yun continued even after US troops landed in Korea in September 1945. In its first report, the US Army's Counter Intelligence Corps (CIC) identified Yun as "one of the three Korean key man [sic]" with "an unusual command of the English language and understanding of the American mind," although it observed that he was "too old to accept any great responsibilities."[23] This image US intelligence created of Yun is all the more surprising given that, as the British Ministry of Information reported based on its reading of Japanese newspapers, Yun led a six-person Korean delegation to Tokyo in February 1945, to express appreciation to the Japanese imperial government for its consideration of giving Koreans their political representation in the Diet. During that trip, Yun became one of the first Koreans to become members of Japan's House of Peers.[24]

When Japan's colonial rule of Korea ended in August 1945, so did Yun's time as a public figure. Immediately before the US troops landed in Korea, members of the Provisional Korean Commission went aboard the US command ship *Catoctin* on the shores of the Korean peninsula and submitted a list of Koreans who had collaborated with the Japanese. They were particularly "emphatic in their denunciation" of four people, including Yun.[25]

The eighty-year-old Yun Ch'i-ho was acutely aware that he was running out of time. In October 1945, two months before his death, he wrote a lengthy note laying out his vision for the future of his country. With Japan's defeat, he could no longer dream of a Pan-Asian empire headed by Japan. But the note, which did not reach the public during his lifetime, only demonstrated that Yun continued to be seized with the idea that imperial rule would prepare Koreans for self-government. "To hear the Koreans talk about running a democratic government sounds to me very much like hearing a child of six talking about driving an

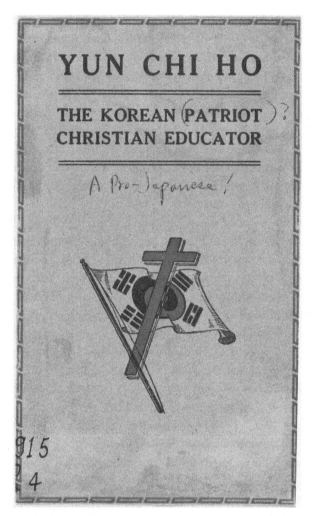

Fig E.1 An unknown reader, presumably after World War
II, expressed disbelief upon encountering this pamphlet that
described Yun Ch'i-ho as a "Korean patriot." The reader wrote
emphatically that Yun was a "pro-Japanese." The pamphlet
was published by the Methodist Episcopal Church, South in
1914, when Yun remained incarcerated during the Korean
Conspiracy Case. Emory University Library processed the
pamphlet in 1942. C. F. Reid, *Yun Chi Ho, the Korean Patriot
and Christian Educator* (Nashville, TN: Publishing House
of the Methodist Episcopal Church, South, 1914). Stuart
A. Rose Manuscript, Archives, and Rare Book Library, Emory
University.

automobile or piloting an airplane," he said; "what Korea needs today, and for many years to come, is a benevolent Paternalism. I wish some strongman would arise who could, with a firm hand and unselfish devotion, keep the demagogue[s] and communists from imposing, in the uneducated and undisciplined masses of Korea, the mere forms and slogans of democracy, on [the] one hand; and on the other, the atrocities and absurdities of communism."[26] Even at the dawn of global decolonization, Yun could not decolonize his mind.[27] Having lived eight decades that witnessed the European partition of Africa, the US annexation and colonization of former Spanish colonies in the Pacific and the Caribbean, and the Japanese annexation and colonization of various parts of Asia, Yun could not imagine an alternative to empire.

In 1945, Yun was out of sync with most his countrymen as well as various people around the world. His view no longer complemented that of W. E. B. Du Bois, who finally ceased to hold Japan as the leader of colored races. In *Color and Democracy*, Du Bois revised some of the ideas he had developed during World War I. In the "African Roots of the War" (1915), he had traced the origin of that war to the European rivalries over Africa and openly wished that Japan would not "join heart and soul with the whites" against the "rest of the yellows, browns, and blacks." World War II confirmed that "the new determination of Japan to exploit Asia for herself" caused not only the Sino-Japanese War but also the Pacific War with European and US empires, which, in his opinion, were fighting to prevent Japan from monopolizing the "Asiatic cheap labor" and "Asiatic raw materials." "Thus it is evident that imperialism is a twofold cause of war," he said. It caused war between the colonizers and the colonized, and it also caused war among the imperial powers who competed for these colonies.[28] Here ended Du Bois's long fascination with Japan. In the immediate aftermath of the war, he left for Manchester, England, for the Fifth Pan-African Conference held in October 1945. There, he championed decolonization alongside future Ghana president Kwame Nkrumah and Trinidadian Pan-Africanist George Padmore.[29] Asia continued to hold a place in his mind. After returning to the United States, Du Bois closely followed India and Burma's independence from Britain in 1947 and 1948, respectively, as well as Indonesia's successful resistance against the Netherlands, which attempted to reclaim its former colony that had been occupied by Japan during the war. "Asia is disappearing as a colonial area," he declared in 1948. And of course, the most exciting development in Asia for Du Bois was the communist revolution led by Mao Zedong against the Kuomintang in the Chinese Civil War (1946–1949). Although he decried wars in general, Du Bois could not hide his enthusiasm when he said that Mao was finally "beating Chiang Kai-shek, puppet of the West, to his knees."[30]

Korea did not interest Du Bois until it became a site of another civil war in 1950, but Koreans' struggles to reclaim their full sovereignty began soon after

World War II. In December 1945, a few weeks after Yun's death, South Korea witnessed widespread protests against the Moscow Agreement reached by three major powers—the Soviet Union, Great Britain, and the United States—to establish a four-way trusteeship of the Korean peninsula among the three of them and China. General Douglas MacArthur, Supreme Commander for the Allied Powers in Japan, had warned Washington that imposing trusteeship on Korea might lead the Korean people to "physically revolt." But the US delegation in Moscow led by Secretary of State James Byrnes, a Wilsonian Democrat from South Carolina, disregarded this warning. The US delegation instead insisted on the joint trusteeship to carry out what it believed to be the most appropriate plan for people whom MacArthur described as, by "occidental standards," "not ready for self-government."[31]

In the age of decolonization, the idea of trusteeship was unacceptable to most Koreans, but many US policymakers, including Byrnes and MacArthur, shared Yun Ch'i-ho's idea that Korea, and many other parts of the decolonizing world, could not be left alone to determine their own futures. The US policymakers tasked with creating a postwar order cast off the most obvious manifestations of empire, especially colonization. But they made sure to maintain the United States' hierarchical relationship with nonwhite peoples that had been long established by empire.[32] This unequal power relationship was reinvented, if not rebranded, in the age of decolonization under various names, including "development," "modernization," and "nation-building," all of which consisted of a strikingly similar set of infrastructural and social reforms characteristic of various colonial projects during the Progressive Era that were allegedly aimed at preparing the colonized people for self-government. The United States paved roads, built schools, improved sanitation, increased commerce, and imposed order in various nonwhite countries without directly ruling them.[33] The assumption behind these postwar projects was most succinctly encapsulated by an infamous public statement made by MacArthur. Upon returning to the United States in 1951, he addressed a joint congressional committee and argued that, in contrast to Germans, whom he described as "a mature race," the Japanese needed the instruction of the United States. "Measured by the standards of modern civilization," he said, "they would be like a boy of twelve as compared with our development of forty-five years."[34]

Although MacArthur said these words after President Harry S. Truman relieved him of duty, MacArthur's ideas continue to resonate with various policymakers who would steer the United States to invest in the economic development and military armament of several places in Asia that became allies against communism, including Japan, South Korea, the Philippines, Taiwan, India, and Indonesia. Ironically, in anti-communist Asia, postcolonial nation-building depended heavily on collaboration with and assistance from the US empire.[35] To gain its Asian allies' trust, the United States also reshaped its immigration policy. After ending Chinese exclusion in 1943, the United States granted the Philippines independence, reopened immigration from India in 1946, and replaced the "Asiatic Barred Zone" with the "Asia-Pacific Triangle" in 1952 to resume immigration from various countries in Asia, including Japan and South Korea. While the Immigration Act of 1952 empowered the US government to exclude, deport, and detain any non-US citizens whom it deemed subversive and potentially subversive, it also eliminated the race-based restrictions in the naturalization statute and made Asians eligible for US citizenship.[36] Before the Bandung Conference of 1955 convened to mark the rise of postcolonial Africa and Asia, the United States had found a way to maintain its influence over various parts in Asia by convincing many Asian elites that they could secure their own interests within a world led by the United States.

In this sense, the postwar world did not witness a clean break from the first four decades of the twentieth century, even after the rupture of World War II. As in the Progressive Era, the United States during the Cold War maintained a transpacific order by deploying its military to engage in violent counterinsurgency campaigns as well as forging strategic partnerships across the color line and selectively admitting nonwhite immigrants from its geopolitical partners. This strategy did not work on the millions of Asian radicals who refused to forget the violence with which the US and European empires had extracted labor and capital from colonial Asia. But when these radicals sought to create the world anew, they faced opposition from not only Americans but also Americans' Asian allies. Racial solidary against white supremacy remained elusive. In the age of decolonization, the problem of empire's allure remained unresolved.

NOTE ON SOURCES AND ABBREVIATIONS

The following abbreviations are used for archives and primary source collections that appear multiple times in the notes. A full list of archives consulted for this book is available in the Bibliography section.

For Yun Ch'i-ho's diary, I have cross-checked the original version, available at the Stuart A. Rose Manuscript, Archives, and Rare Book Library at Emory University, with the edited volumes published by Kuksa P'yŏnch'an Wiwŏnhoe (the National Institute of Korean History). Because the edited volumes are more easily accessible to readers, I have cited the original only when there was a discrepancy between the two versions.

BOICF	Investigative Case Files of the Bureau of Investigation, 1908–1922, National Archives and Records Administration, 955 reels
BTWP	Louis R. Harlan and Raymond W. Smock ed., *Booker T. Washington Papers*, University of Illinois Press, 14 vols.
CHRP	Chester H. Rowell Papers, Bancroft Library, University of California, Berkeley
CIKK	*Chuhan ilbon kongsagwan kirok* [Records of the Japanese Legation in Korea], Kuksa P'yŏnch'an Wiwŏnhoe, 26 vols.
DS-DMK	Records of the Department of State, Despatches from U.S. Ministers to Korea, 1883–1905, National Archives and Records Administration, 22 reels
DS-IAK	Records of the Department of State Relating to Internal Affairs of Korea (Chosun), 1910–1929, National Archives and Records Administration, 9 reels
DSJP	David Starr Jordan Papers, Hoover Institution Library and Archives
FDRPLM	Franklin D. Roosevelt Presidential Library and Museum

GFP	Gulick Family Papers, Houghton Library, Harvard University
GKP	George Kennan Papers, Library of Congress
HJP	Hiram Johnson Papers, Bancroft Library, University of California, Berkeley
HNAP	Horace Newton Allen Papers, New York Public Library, 10 reels
HTUC	*Hanminjok tongnip undongsa charyojip* [Documents of the Korean Independence Movement], Kuksa P'yŏnch'an Wiwŏnhoe, 20 vols.
IPRR	Institute of Pacific Relations Records, Rare Book & Manuscript Library, Columbia University
JARPC	Japanese American Research Project Collection, Library Special Collections, Charles E. Young Research Library, University of California, Los Angeles
JDPP	James D. Phelan Papers, Bancroft Library, University of California, Berkeley
JFP	Josephine Fowler Papers, Library Special Collections, Charles E. Young Research Library, University of California, Los Angeles
JUSPC	Japanese in the United States Pamphlet Collection, Hoover Institution Library
JWJ&GNJP	James Weldon Johnson and Grace Nail Johnson Papers, Beinecke Rare Book and Manuscript Library, Yale University
KS	*Kojong Sillok* [Royal Records of Emperor Kojong], Kuksa P'yŏnch'an Wiwŏnhoe, 48 vols.
LTR	*Letters of Theodore Roosevelt*, Harvard University Press, 8 vols.
MLP	Meyer Lissner Papers, Special Collections, Green Library, Stanford University
PHS-KM	United Presbyterian Church in the U.S.A. Commission on Ecumenical Mission and Relations Secretaries' Files: Korea Mission, Presbyterian Historical Society
PPIER	Panama-Pacific International Exposition Records, Bancroft Library, University of California, Berkeley
PWW	Papers of Woodrow Wilson, Princeton University Press, 69 vols.
SMRCE	*The Syngman Rhee Correspondence in English, 1904–1948.* Institute for Modern Korean Studies, Yonsei University, 8 vols.
SRRR	Survey of Race Relations Records, Hoover Institution Library and Archives

TM	*Tongambu munsŏ* [Records of the Resident General of Korea], Kuksa P'yŏnch'an Wiwŏnhoe, 10 vols.
TRP	Theodore Roosevelt Papers, Library of Congress, 485 reels
WCP	Warren A. Candler Papers, Stuart A. Rose Manuscript, Archives, and Rare Book Library, Emory University
WDSP	Willard Dickerman Strait Papers, Division of Rare and Manuscript Collections, Cornell University, 12 reels
WEBDBP	W. E. B. Du Bois Papers, Special Collections and University Archives, University of Massachusetts Amherst Libraries
WHTP	William Howard Taft Papers, Library of Congress, 658 reels
YCHI	*Yun Ch'i-ho Ilgi* [Yun Ch'i-ho's Dairy], Kuksa P'yŏnch'an Wiwŏnhoe, 11 vols.
YCHP	Yun Ch'i-ho Papers, Stuart A. Rose Manuscript, Archives, and Rare Book Library, Emory University
YCHS	*Yun Ch'i-ho Sŏhanjip* [Yun Ch'i-ho's Letters], Kuksa P'yŏnch'an Wiwŏnhoe
YIP	Yuji Ichioka Papers, Library Special Collections, Charles E. Young Research Library, University of California, Los Angeles
YKP	Yoshi Saburo Kuno Papers, Bancroft Library, University of California, Berkeley

NOTES

Introduction

1. Du Bois, *The Souls of Black Folk*, ed. Brent Hayes Edwards (New York: Oxford University Press, 2007), 15.

2. Du Bois, "Atlanta University" (1905), in *Writings by W. E. B. Du Bois in Non-Periodical Literature*, ed. Herbert Aptheker (Millwood, NY: Kraus-Thomson, 1982), 59. For context, see Reginald Kearney, *African American Views of the Japanese: Solidarity or Sedition?* (Albany: State University of New York Press, 1998), 19, 37–38; C. L. Stebbins to W. E. B. Du Bois, May 16, 1905, Series 1A. General Correspondence, 1877–1965, WEBDBP.

3. Du Bois, "Atlanta University," 59; Michael Keevak, *Becoming Yellow: A Short History of Racial Thinking* (Princeton, NJ: Princeton University Press, 2011).

4. June 2, 1905, *YCHI*, 6: 112–113.

5. Kwŏn T'ae-ŏk, "1904–1910 nyŏn ilche ŭi han'guk ch'imnyak kusang kwa shijŏnggaesŏn," *Han'guksaron* 31 (1994): 213–260; Yi T'ae-jin, *Ilbon ŭi Han'guk pyŏnghap kangje yŏn'gu: choyak kangje wa chŏhang ŭi yŏksa* (Kyŏnggi-do P'aju-si: Chisik Sanopsa, 2016), 135–161.

6. Chŏn Bok-hee, "19 segi mal chinbojŏk chishigin ŭi injongjuŭijŏk t'ŭksŏng: tongnipshinmun kwa Yun ch'i-ho rŭl chungshim ŭro," *Han'guk chŏngch'i hakhoe po* 29, no. 1 (October 1995): 125–145.

7. Yun Ch'i-ho's Diary, October 3, 1905, box 11, folder 10, YCHP.

8. On Asian settler colonialism, see Candace Fujikane, "Asian Settler Colonialism in the U.S. Colony of Hawai'i," in *Asian Settler Colonialism: From Local Governance to the Habits of Everyday Life in Hawai'i*, ed. Candace Fujikane and Jonathan Y. Okamura (Honolulu: University of Hawai'i Press, 2008), 1–42; Dean Itsuji Saranillio, "Why Asian Settler Colonialism Matters: A Thought Piece on Critiques, Debates, and Indigenous Difference," *Settler Colonial Studies* 3, no. 4 (2013): 280–294.

9. Yun Ch'i-ho's Diary, October 16, 1905, box 11, folder 10, YCHP; Ratification of the Treaty of Peace signed at Portsmouth August 23, 1905, enclosure to George Meyer to Elihu Root, December 13, 1905, no. 341, *FRUS 1905*, 825.

10. Elihu Root to Edwin Morgan, November 24, 1905, *FRUS 1905*, 631.

11. David Fort Godshalk, *Veiled Visions: The 1906 Atlanta Race Riot and the Reshaping of American Race Relations* (Chapel Hill: University of North Carolina Press, 2005).

12. *The American National Red Cross Bulletin No. 3* (Washington, DC: Office of the Corporation, 1906), 18–19; U.S. Congress, *Japanese in the City of San Francisco, Cal.: Message from the President of the United States, Transmitting the Final Report of Secretary Metcalf on the Situation Affecting the Japanese in the City of San Francisco* (Washington, DC: US Government Printing Office, 1907).

13. Du Bois, "The Color Line Belts the World" (1906), republished in Bill V. Mullen and Cathryn Watson eds., *W. E. B. Du Bois on Asia: Crossing the World Color Line* (Jackson: University

Press of Mississippi, 2005), 33–34. Although Du Bois made no comment on the contrasting responses of the Roosevelt administration, various African American newspapers complained that the US government cared more about Japanese immigrants than about African Americans. See Kearney, *African American Views of the Japanese*, 44–47.

14. Thomas A. Guglielmo, *White on Arrival: Italians, Race, Color, and Power in Chicago, 1890–1945* (New York: Oxford University Press, 2003).

15. Joseph M. Henning, *Outposts of Civilization: Race, Religion, and the Formative Years of American-Japanese Relations* (New York: New York University Press, 2000). US policymakers during this period understood the majority of people living in the Russian empire as "white." See *Reports of the Immigration Commission: Dictionary of Races or Peoples* (Washington, DC: Government Printing Office, 1911), 111–116.

16. For the most prominent examples, see Bruce Cumings, *Dominion from Sea to Sea: Pacific Ascendancy and American Power* (New Haven, CT: Yale University Press, 2009); Daniel Immerwahr, *How to Hide an Empire: A History of the Greater United States* (New York: Farrar, Straus & Giroux, 2019).

17. Jane Burbank and Frederik Cooper, *Empires in World History: Power and the Politics of Difference* (Princeton, NJ: Princeton University Press, 2010), 8–17.

18. For exemplary works that explain the importance of immigration restriction in US-Asia relations, see Charles E. Neu, *An Uncertain Friendship: Theodore Roosevelt and Japan, 1906–1909* (Cambridge, MA: Harvard University Press, 1967); Akira Iriye, *Pacific Estrangement: Japanese and American Expansion, 1897–1911* (Cambridge, MA: Harvard University Press, 1972); Paul A. Kramer, *The Blood of Government: Race, Empire, the United States, and the Philippines* (Chapel Hill: University of North Carolina Press, 2006); Andrea Geiger, *Subverting Exclusion: Transpacific Encounters with Race, Caste, and Borders, 1885–1928* (New Haven, CT: Yale University Press, 2011).

19. Kei Tanaka, "Japanese Picture Marriage in 1900–1924 California: Construction of Japanese Race and Gender" (PhD diss., Rutgers, the State University of New Jersey, 2002); Cecilia Tsu, *Garden of the World: Asian Immigrants and the Making of Agriculture in California's Santa Clara Valley* (New York: Oxford University Press, 2013), 107–138. In contrast to Japanese "picture brides" married to foreign-born Japanese working-class men, adult Chinese women could enter only if they were US citizens or wives of merchants and US citizens. See Sucheng Chan, "The Exclusion of Chinese Women, 1870–1943," in her *Entry Denied: Exclusion and the Chinese Community in America, 1882–1943* (Philadelphia: Temple University Press, 1991), 94–146.

20. For calls to bring these fields together, see Gordon H. Chang, "Asian Immigrants and American Foreign Relations," in *Pacific Passage: The Study of American–East Asian Relations on the Eve of the Twenty-First Century*, ed. Warren I. Cohen (New York: Columbia University Press, 1996), 103–118; Donna R. Gabaccia, *Foreign Relations: American Immigration in Global Perspective* (Princeton, NJ: Princeton University Press, 2012); Paul A. Kramer, "The Geopolitics of Mobility: Immigration Policy and American Global Power in the Long Twentieth Century," *American Historical Review* 123, no. 2 (April 2018): 393–438.

21. The best synthesis focusing on the color line remains Matthew Frye Jacobson, *Barbarian Virtues: The United States Encounters Foreign Peoples at Home and Abroad, 1876–1917* (New York: Hill & Wang, 2000).

22. Gerald Horne, "Race from Power: U.S. Foreign Policy and the General Crisis of 'White Supremacy,'" *Diplomatic History* 23, no. 3 (Summer 1999): 437–461; Noenoe K. Silva, *Aloha Betrayed: Native Hawaiian Resistance to American Colonialism* (Durham, NC: Duke University Press, 2004); Dean Itsuji Saranillio, *Unsustainable Empire: Alternative Histories of Hawai'i Statehood* (Durham, NC: Duke University Press, 2018).

23. Ian Haney Lopez, *White by Law: The Legal Construction of Race* (New York: NYU Press, 1996); Erika Lee, *At America's Gates: Chinese Immigration during the Exclusion Era, 1882–1943* (Chapel Hill: University of North Carolina Press, 2003); Mae M. Ngai, *Impossible Subjects: Illegal Aliens and the Making of Modern America* (Princeton, NJ: Princeton University Press, 2004).

24. Marilyn Lake and Henry Reynolds, *Drawing the Global Colour Line: White Men's Countries and the International Challenge of Racial Equality* (Cambridge: Cambridge University

Press, 2008); Kornel S. Chang, *Pacific Connections: The Making of the U.S.-Canadian Borderlands* (Berkeley: University of California Press, 2012); Seema Sohi, *Echoes of Mutiny: Race, Surveillance, and Indian Anticolonialism in North America* (New York: Oxford University Press, 2014); Marilyn Lake, *Progressive New World: How Settler Colonialism and Transpacific Exchange Shaped American Reform* (Cambridge, MA: Harvard University Press, 2019).

25. Vicente L. Rafael, *White Love and Other Events in Filipino History* (Durham, NC: Duke University Press, 2000), 103–121; Gerald Horne, *Race War! White Supremacy and the Japanese Attack on the British Empire* (New York: NYU Press, 2005); Cemil Aydin, *The Politics of Anti-Westernism in Asia: Visions of World Order in Pan-Islamism and Pan-Asian Thought* (New York: Columbia University Press, 2007); Nico Slate, *Colored Cosmopolitanism: The Shared Struggle for Freedom in the United States and India* (Cambridge, MA: Harvard University Press, 2012); Moon-Ho Jung, *Menace to Empire: Anticolonial Solidarities and the Transpacific Origins of the US Security State* (Oakland: University of California Press, 2022).

26. Eiichiro Azuma, *Between Two Empires: Race, History, and Transnationalism in Japanese America* (New York: Oxford University Press, 2005); Richard S. Kim, *The Quest for Sovereignty: Korean Immigration Nationalism and U.S. Sovereignty, 1905–1945* (New York: Oxford University Press, 2011).

27. Duncan Bell, *Dreamworlds of Race: Empire and the Utopian Destiny of Anglo-America* (Princeton, NJ: Princeton University Press, 2020); David C. Atkinson, *The Burden of White Supremacy: Containing Asian Migration in the British Empire and the United States* (Chapel Hill: University of North Carolina Press, 2016).

28. In this sense, US-Japan relations during the Progressive Era presented a preview of what would happen in the mid-twentieth century when, as Thomas Borstelmann has explained, Americans shed some older notions of human hierarchy out of geopolitical necessity. See Thomas Borstelmann, *Just Like Us: The American Struggle to Understand Foreigners* (New York: Columbia University Press, 2020).

29. Daniel T. Rodgers, *Atlantic Crossings: Social Politics in a Progressive Age* (Cambridge, MA: Belknap Press of Harvard University Press, 1998); Thomas Bender, *A Nation among Nations: America's Place in World History* (New York: Hill & Wang, 2006), 246–295.

30. The literature on imperial reform of American colonies is vast. For representative examples focusing on the Philippines, see Glenn Anthony May, *Social Engineering in the Philippines: The Aims, Execution, and Impact of American Colonial Policy 1900–1913* (Westport, CT: Greenwood Press, 1980); Catherine Ceniza Choy, *Empire of Care: Nursing and Migration in Filipino American History* (Durham, NC: Duke University Press, 2003); Emily S. Rosenberg, *Financial Missionaries to the World: The Politics and Culture of Dollar Diplomacy, 1900–1930* (Durham, NC: Duke University, 2004); Michael Adas, *Dominance by Design: Technological Imperatives and America's Civilizing Mission* (Cambridge, MA: Belknap Press of Harvard University Press, 2006), 129–182; Ian Tyrrell, *Reforming the World: The Creation of America's Moral Empire* (Princeton, NJ: Princeton University Press, 2010), 123–145; Sarah Steinbock-Pratt, *Educating the Empire: American Teachers and Contested Colonization in the Philippines* (Cambridge: Cambridge University Press, 2019).

31. Alice L. Conklin, *A Mission to Civilize: The Republican Idea of Empire in France and West Africa, 1895–1930* (Stanford, CA: Stanford University Press, 1997); Sebastian Conrad, *Globalisation and the Nation in Imperial Germany*, trans. Sorcha O'Hagan (Cambridge: Cambridge University Press, 2010). On how the United States followed the British model of overseas imperialism, see A. G. Hopkins, *American Empire: A Global History* (Princeton, NJ: Princeton University Press, 2017).

32. Dean Clay, "Transatlantic Dimensions of the Congo Reform Movement, 1904–1908," *English Studies in Africa* 59, no. 1 (2016): 18–28; Charlie Laderman, *Sharing the Burden: The Armenian Question, Humanitarian Intervention, and Anglo-American Visions of Global Order* (New York: Oxford University Press, 2019); "Petition of Jews Is Going to Czar," *Chicago Daily Tribune*, June 26, 1903, 1.

33. "Negroes Seek Friendship in Czar," *Chicago Daily Tribune*, June 30, 1903, 1.

34. Joel Williamson, *The Crucible of Race: Black-White Relations in the American South since Emancipation* (New York: Oxford University Press, 1984).

35. William D. Carrigan and Clive Webb, *Forgotten Dead: Mob Violence Against Mexicans in the United States, 1848–1928* (New York: Oxford University Press, 2013); Beth Lew-Williams, "'Chinamen' and 'Delinquent Girls': Intimacy, Exclusion, and a Search for California's Color Line," *Journal of American History* 104, no. 3 (December 2017): 632–655. On policing in Chinatown, see Nayan Shah, *Contagious Divides: Epidemics and Race in San Francisco's Chinatown* (Berkeley: University of California Press, 2001); Mary Ting Yi Lui, *The Chinatown Trunk Mystery: Murder, Miscegenation, and Other Dangerous Encounters in Turn-of-the-Century New York City* (Princeton, NJ: Princeton University Press, 2004).

36. Lee, *At America's Gates*; Erika Lee and Judy Yung, *Angel Island: Immigrant Gateway to America* (New York: Oxford University Press, 2010).

37. Frederick E. Hoxie, *A Final Promise: The Campaign to Assimilate the Indians, 1880–1920* (Lincoln: University of Nebraska Press, 1984); Brenda Child, *Boarding School Seasons: American Indian Families, 1900–1940* (Lincoln: University of Nebraska Press, 1998); Stefan Aune, "Indian Fighters in the Philippines: Imperial Culture and Military Violence in the Philippine-American War," *Pacific Historical Review* 90, no. 4 (Fall 2021): 419–447.

38. Kristin Hoganson, *Fighting for American Manhood: How Gender Politics Provoked the Spanish-American and Philippine-American Wars* (New Haven, CT: Yale University Press, 1998), 180–199.

39. Howard Gillette, "The Military Occupation of Cuba, 1899–1902: Workshop for American Progressivism," *American Quarterly* 25, no. 4 (October 1973): 410–425; Lars Schoultz, *In Their Own Best Interest: A History of the U.S. Effort to Improve Latin Americans* (Cambridge, MA: Harvard University Press, 2020), 28–33, 52–54.

40. William Jennings Bryan, "Judge Parker on Imperialism" and "Independence Not a 'Scuttle' Policy," in *The Commoner Condensed* (Lincoln, NE: Woodruff-Collins Printing Co., 1905), 4: 367–369, 386–387. On Bryan's anti-imperialist campaign in 1900, see Michael Patrick Cullinane, *Liberty and American Anti-Imperialism, 1898–1909* (New York: Palgrave Macmillan, 2012), 51–73; Ian Tyrrell and Jay Sexton, "Introduction," *Empire's Twin: U.S. Anti-imperialism from the Founding Era to the Age of Terrorism* (Ithaca, NY: Cornell University Press, 2015), 1–18.

41. "Bryan's Experiences in the Hermit Kingdom," *Washington Post*, March 4, 1906, SM8; *The Commoner Condensed* (Chicago: Henneberry, 1907), 6: 78.

42. Martti Koskenniemi, *The Gentle Civilizer of Nations: The Rise and Fall of International Law 1870–1960* (Cambridge: Cambridge University Press, 2001); Alexis Dudden, *Japan's Colonization of Korea: Discourse and Power* (Honolulu: University of Hawaii Press, 2005); Benjamin Allen Coates, *Legalist Empire: International Law and American Foreign Relations in the Early Twentieth Century* (New York: Oxford University Press, 2016).

43. John L. Hennessey, "Contextualizing Colonial Connections: Reevaluating Takekoshi Yosaburō's *Japanese Rule in Formosa,*" *Japan Review* 35 (2020): 141–164; Andre Schmid, "Japanese Propaganda in the United States from 1905," and Daeyeol Ku, "The British and American Perceptions of Korea during the Colonial Period," both in *International Impact of Colonial Rule in Korea, 1910–1945,* ed. Yong-Chool Ha (Seattle: University of Washington Press, 2019), 73–102, 179–217.

44. Du Bois, "The African Roots of War," *Atlantic Monthly* 115 (May 1915): 710.

45. Frederick R. Dickinson, *War and National Reinvention: Japan in the Great War, 1914–1919* (Cambridge: Cambridge University Press, 1999), 84–116.

46. Frank Baldwin, "The March First Movement: Korean Challenge and Japanese Response" (PhD diss., Columbia University, 1969); Erez Manela, *The Wilsonian Moment: Self-Determination and the International Origins of Anticolonial Nationalism* (New York: Oxford University Press 2007), 119–135, 117–196.

47. Sin Chu-baek, "Ilje ŭi saeroun singminji chibaebangsik kwa chaejoilbonin mit 'chach'i' seryŏk ŭi taeŭng (1919–22)," *Yŏksa wa hyŏnsil* 39 (2001): 35–68; Kim Tong-myŏng, "Singminji sidae ŭi chibang 'chach'i': pu(hyŏbŭi)hoe ŭi chŏngch'ijŏk chŏn'gae," *Hanil kwan'gyesa yŏn'gu* 17 (2002): 161–197.

48. On the rise of international NGOs, see Akira Iriye, *Cultural Internationalism and World Order* (Baltimore: Johns Hopkins University Press, 1997).

49. Jesse Tarbert, *When Good Government Meant Big Government: The Quest to Extend Federal Power, 1913-1933* (New York: Columbia University Press, 2022), 128-139.

50. Jun Uchida, *Brokers of Empire: Japanese Settler Colonialism in Korea, 1876-1945* (Cambridge, MA: Harvard University Asia Center, 2011); Emer O'Dwyer, *Significant Soil: Settler Colonialism and Japan's Urban Empire in Manchuria* (Cambridge, MA: Harvard University Press, 2015).

51. Brazil and Peru eventually instituted immigration laws that prohibited and severely restricted Japanese immigration in 1934 and 1936, respectively. But it is important to note that neither country stopped Japanese immigration until the Great Depression. In Mexico, where the federal government did not have strong power over local leaders, Japanese immigrants largely avoided the state-level anti-Asian racism directed at the Chinese during and after the Mexican Revolution. See Jeffrey Lesser, *Negotiating National Identity: Immigrants, Minorities, and the Struggle for Ethnicity in Brazil* (Durham, NC: Duke University Press, 1999); Erika Lee, "The 'Yellow Peril' in the United States and Peru," in *Transnational Crossroads: Remapping the Americas and the Pacific*, ed. Camilla Fojas and Rudy P. Guevera Jr. (Lincoln: University of Nebraska Press, 2012), 315-358; Jerry García, *Looking Like the Enemy: Japanese Mexicans, the Mexican State, and U.S. Hegemony 1897-1945* (Tucson: University of Arizona Press, 2014).

52. Izumi Hirobe, *Japanese Pride, American Prejudice: Modifying the Exclusion Clause of the 1924 Immigration Act* (Stanford, CA: Stanford University Press, 2002); Rick Baldoz, *The Third Asiatic Invasion: Empire and Migration in Filipino America, 1898-1946* (New York: NYU Press, 2011).

53. Andrew Gordon, *Labor and Imperial Democracy in Prewar Japan* (Berkeley: University of California Press, 1991).

54. Eri Hotta, *Pan-Asianism and Japan's War, 1931-1945* (New York: Palgrave Macmillan, 2007); Sven Saaler and J. Victor Koschmann, eds., *Pan-Asianism in Modern Japanese History Colonialism, Regionalism and Borders* (New York: Routledge, 2007); Jeremy A. Yellen, *The Greater East Asia Co-Prosperity Sphere: When Total Empire Met Total War* (Ithaca, NY: Cornell University Press, 2019).

55. August 12, 1920; September 23, 1920; November 1, 1929, *YCHI*, 8: 119, 140, 9: 244. On Yun's activities during the 1920s, see Koen De Ceuster, "From Modernization to Collaboration: The Dilemma of Korean Cultural Nationalism: The Case of Yun Ch'i-ho (1865-1945)" (PhD diss., Katholieke Universiteit Leuven, 1994), 362-378.

56. Yun Ch'i-ho's Diary, November 10, 1934, box 15, folder 3, YCHP.

57. Mark Caprio, "Loyal Patriot? Traitorous Collaborator? The Yun Ch'iho Diaries and the Question of National Loyalty," *Journal of Colonialism and Colonial History* 7, no. 3 (2006): n.p.; *Ch'inil inmyŏng sajŏn* (Seoul: Minjok Munje Yŏn'guso, 2009), 697-702.

58. Kearney, *African American Views of the Japanese*; Marc Gallicchio, *The African American Encounter with Japan and China: Black Internationalism in Asia, 1895-1945* (Chapel Hill: University of North Carolina Press, 2000); Gerald Horne, *Facing the Rising Sun: African Americans, Japan, and the Rise of Afro-Asian Solidarity* (New York: NYU Press, 2018).

59. Jung, *Menace to Empire*; Josephine Fowler, *Japanese and Chinese Immigrant Activists: Organizing in American and International Communist Movements, 1919-1933* (New Brunswick, NJ: Rutgers University Press, 2007).

60. Du Bois, "Forum of Fact and Opinion," *Pittsburgh Courier*, February 13, 1937, 7. A few scholars have noted this passage: see Kearney, *African American Views of the Japanese*, 88; Yuichiro Onishi, *Transpacific Antiracism: Afro-Asian Solidarity in Twentieth-Century Black America, Japan, and Okinawa* (New York: NYU Press, 2013), 83-84.

61. Du Bois's view of Japan parallels his view of Liberia, where the descendants of African American settlers dispossessed the lands and exploited the labor of the indigenous Kru and Grebo people. Based on his writings about Liberia, Cedric Robinson argues that Du Bois was "blinded by the elitism characteristic of his class's prerogative" and that he "fell prey to American colonialism." See Robinson, "Du Bois and Black Sovereignty: The Case of Liberia," in *Imagining Home: Class, Culture and Nationalism in the African Diaspora*, ed. Sidney J. Lemelle and Robin D. G. Kelley (New York: Verso, 1994), 145.

62. On anarchism in East Asia during this period, see Thomas A. Stanley, *Ōsugi Sakae: Anarchist in Taishō Japan. The Creativity of the Ego* (Cambridge, MA: Harvard University Press, 1982);

Arif Dirlik, *Anarchism in the Chinese Revolution* (Berkeley: University of California Press, 1991). On Asian revolutionaries aligned with the Comintern, see Sabine Dullin, Étienne Forestier-Peyrat, Yuexin Rachel Lin, and Naoko Shimazu, eds., *The Russian Revolution in Asia: From Baku to Batavia* (London: Routledge, 2021).

63. Colleen Woods, "Seditious Crimes and Rebellious Conspiracies: Anti-Communism and US Empire in the Philippines," *Journal of Contemporary History* 53, no. 1 (January 2018): 61–88.

64. John K. Thornton, *Africa and Africans in the Making of the Atlantic World, 1400–1680* (New York: Cambridge University Press, 1992); C. A. Bayly, *Empire and Information: Intelligence Gathering and Social Communication in India, 1780–1870* (New York: Cambridge University Press, 1996); Yanna Yannakakis, *The Art of Being In-Between: Native Intermediaries, Indian Identity, and Local Rule in Colonial Oaxaca* (Durham, NC: Duke University Press, 2008).

65. John W. Dower, *War without Mercy: Race and Power in the Pacific War* (New York: Pantheon, 1986); Greg Robinson, *A Tragedy of Democracy: Japanese Confinement in North America* (New York: Columbia University Press, 2009); Lee, "The 'Yellow Peril' in the United States and Peru," 343–344.

66. Dirk Bönker, *Militarism in a Global Age: Naval Ambitions in Germany and the United States before World War I* (Ithaca, NY: Cornell University Press, 2012).

67. Simeon Man, *Soldiering through Empire: Race and the Making of the Decolonizing Pacific* (Oakland: University of California Press, 2018).

Chapter 1

1. Roosevelt to Cecil Spring Rice, June 13, 1904, *LTR*, 4: 830. Kaneko Kentarō met with Roosevelt again in July 1905 and reported to Tokyo that Roosevelt expressed his wish to see Japan establish its own "Monroe Doctrine in Asia." See Masayoshi Matsumura, *Baron Kaneko and the Russo-Japanese War (1904–05): A Study in the Public Diplomacy of Japan*, trans. Ian Ruxton (Morrisville, NC: Lulu Press, 2009), 385.

2. Roosevelt to Spring Rice, June 13, 1904, *LTR*, 4: 830.

3. Ibid., 4: 830–831; Suematsu Kenchō to Komura Juntarō, March 15, 1904, in Masayoshi Matsumura, *Baron Suematsu in Europe during the Russo-Japanese War (1904–5): His Battle with Yellow Peril*, trans. Ian Ruxton (Morrisville, NC: Lulu Press, 2011), 36.

4. Roosevelt to Theodore Elijah Burton, February 23, 1904, *LTR*, 4: 736.

5. Louis Perez Jr., *Cuba under the Platt Amendment, 1902–1934* (Pittsburgh: University of Pittsburgh Press, 1986).

6. John J. O'Brien to William Loeb, June 2, 1902; Roosevelt to Kermit Roosevelt, March 3, 1904; Roosevelt to Yoshiaki Yamashita, April 23, 1904, TRP, reels 44, 330, and 334.

7. Inazo Inazō, *Bushido: The Soul of Japan* (Philadelphia: The Leeds & Biddle Co., 1900), 3; Joseph M. Henning, *Outposts of Civilization: Race, Religion, and the Formative Years of American-Japanese Relations* (New York: New York University Press, 2000), 144.

8. Roosevelt's biographical sketch adapted from Edmund Morris, *The Rise of Theodore Roosevelt* (New York: Coward, McCann & Geoghegan, 1979); Gail Bederman, *Manliness & Civilization: A Cultural History of Gender and Race in the United States, 1880–1917* (Chicago: University of Chicago Press, 1995), 170–216.

9. Roosevelt to William McKinley, April 22, 1897; Roosevelt to Alfred Thayer Mahan, May 3, 1897, *LTR*, 1: 601, 607–608.

10. Roosevelt to Cecil Spring Rice, November 19, 1900, and Roosevelt to Hermann Speck von Sternburg, November 19, 1900, quoted in Thomas G. Dyer, *Theodore Roosevelt and the Idea of Race* (Baton Rouge: Louisiana State University Press, 1980), 136.

11. Kristin Hoganson, *Fighting for American Manhood: How Gender Politics Provoked the Spanish-American and Philippine-American Wars* (New Haven, CT: Yale University Press, 1998), 180–199; Jim Zwick, "'Prodigally Endowed with Sympathy for the Cause': Mark Twain's Involvement with the Anti-Imperialist League," in *Confronting Imperialism Essays on Mark Twain and the Anti-Imperialist League* (West Conshohocken: Infinity Publishing, 2007), 109–140; Michael Patrick Cullinane, *Liberty and American Anti-Imperialism, 1898–1909* (New York: Palgrave Macmillan, 2012), 115–147.

12. Christopher Capozzola, *Bound by War: How the United States and the Philippines Built America's First Pacific Century* (New York: Basic Books, 2020), 48–64.

13. Theodore Roosevelt, "Address at Mechanic's Pavilion, San Francisco, California, May 13, 1903," in *California Addresses by President Roosevelt* (San Francisco: The California Promotion Committee, 1903), 97–101.

14. John M. Thompson, *Great Power Rising: Theodore Roosevelt and the Politics of U.S. Foreign Policy* (New York: Oxford University Press, 2019), 51–76.

15. Roosevelt to Theodore Roosevelt Jr., February 10, 1904; Roosevelt to Spring Rice, March 19, 1904, *LTR*, 4: 724, 760–761.

16. Kaneko Kentarō, "Japan and the United States: A Proposed Economic Alliance," *International Quarterly* 3, no. 2 (December–March 1904): 403–404; Roosevelt to Kaneko Kentarō, April 23, 1904, *LTR*, 4: 777–778; Kaneko to Roosevelt, March 31, 1904; April 20, 1904, TRP, reel 43.

17. Roosevelt to Spring Rice, June 13, 1904, *LTR*, 4: 830.

18. David H. Burton, *Theodore Roosevelt: Confident Imperialist* (Philadelphia: University of Pennsylvania Press, 1969), 101–131; Thompson, *Great Power Rising*, 34–92.

19. Roosevelt to Elihu Root, May 20, 1904, *LTR*, 4: 801.

20. Roosevelt to Root, May 20, 1904, *LTR*, 4: 801; Serge Ricard, "The Roosevelt Corollary," *Presidential Studies Quarterly* 36, no. 1 (March 2006): 17–26. Leonard Wood, quoted in Louis Perez Jr., "Incurring a Debt of Gratitude: 1898 and the Moral Sources of United States Hegemony in Cuba," *American Historical Review* 104, no. 2 (April 1999): 375.

21. Howard Gillette, "The Military Occupation of Cuba, 1899–1902: Workshop for American Progressivism," *American Quarterly* 25, no. 4 (October 1973): 410–425.

22. Carl Schurz to Erving Winslow, July 29, 1904, *Speeches, Correspondence and Political Papers of Carl Schurz* (New York: G. P. Putnam's Sons, 1913), 6: 353; William Jennings Bryan, "Judge Parker on Imperialism," in *The Commoner Condensed* (Lincoln: Woodruff-Collins Printing Co., 1905), 4: 367.

23. Griffis, "The Russo-Japanese War," *Outlook* 79 (December 24, 1904): 1038–1040; *Bushido, the Soul of Japan; An Exposition of Japanese Thought, by Inazo Nitobé with an Introduction by William Elliot Griffis* (New York: G. P. Putnam's Sons, 1905); Kaneko, "The Magna Charta of Japan," *Century Magazine* 68, no. 3 (July 1904): 484–487; Kaneko, "The Yellow Peril Is the Golden Opportunity for Japan," *North American Review* 179, no. 576 (November 1904): 641–648.

24. Roosevelt to Spring Rice, December 27, 1904; Roosevelt to George von Lengerke Meyer, December 26, 1904, *LTR*, 4: 1085, 1087, 1079.

25. Richard Harding Davis to Roosevelt, May 26, 1904, TRP, reel 44; Davis, "The Passing of San Juan Hill," *Scribner's Magazine* 38, no. 2 (August 1905): 142–153; Fox, "The Trail of the Saxon," *Scribner's Magazine* 35, no. 6 (June 1904): 661; Fox, "The Backward Trail of the Saxon," *Scribner's Magazine* 37, no. 3 (March 1905): 280.

26. Kennan, "The Story of Port Arthur, VI," quoted in Collen Lye, *America's Asia: Racial Form and American Literature, 1893–1945* (Princeton, NJ: Princeton University Press, 2005), 25; Kennan, "A Visit to a Certain Place," *Outlook* 78 (September 17, 1904), 178–179.

27. Kennan, "Land of the Morning Calm," *Outlook* 78 (October 8, 1904): 366; Kennan, "George Kennan's Story of the War, XII," *Outlook* 59 (August 27, 1898): 1013; Kennan, "Cuban Character," *Outlook* 63 (December 23, 1899): 964; Kennan, "Cuban Character," *Outlook* 63 (December 30, 1899): 1022.

28. Kennan, "Land of the Morning Calm," 366.

29. Ibid., 364; Kennan, "The Capital of Korea," *Outlook* 78 (October 22, 1904): 469. On the reception, see Kennan Diary no. 2, June 24, 1904, box 22, 230–235, GKP.

30. Richard Berry to Kennan, February 21, 1905; Kennan to Roosevelt, March 29, 1905, box 7, folder 1905–1907, GKP.

31. William H. Taft to Elihu Root, July 29, 1905, reprinted in John Gilbert Reid, "Taft's Telegram to Root, July 29, 1905," *Pacific Historical Review* 9, no. 1 (March 1940): 69–70; Roosevelt to Taft, July 31, 1905, *LTR*, 4: 1293.

32. For key works that treat this document as a treaty, see Tyler Dennett, "President Roosevelt's Secret Pact with Japan," *Current History* 21, no. 1 (October 1924): 15–21; Yi Ki-baek, *A*

New History of Korea, trans. Edward W. Wagner with Edward J. Shultz (Seoul: Ilchogak, 1984), 309; Jongsuk Chay, Diplomacy of Asymmetry: Korean-American Relations to 1910 (Honolulu: University of Hawai'i Press, 1990), 143–144; Walter LaFeber, The Clash: A History of U.S.-Japan Relations (New York: W. W. Norton, 1997), 86; Bruce Cumings, Korea's Place in the Sun: A Modern History (New York: W. W. Norton, 2005), 142; Seung-young Kim, American Diplomacy and Strategy toward Korea and Northeast Asia, 1882–1950 and After: Perception of Polarity and US Commitment to a Periphery (New York: Palgrave Macmillan), 51–57.

33. Roosevelt to Taft, October 5, 1905; Roosevelt to Taft, October 7, 1905, LTR, 5: 46, 49; Esthus, Theodore Roosevelt and Japan, 104–105.

34. Roosevelt to Eliot, April 4, 1904, LTR, 4: 769–770; Perez Jr., Cuba under the Platt Amendment, 49–50.

35. Kennan, "Korea: A Degenerate State," Outlook 81 (October 7, 1905): 308, 315. For Kennan's problematic depiction of the Korean people, see Cumings, Korea's Place in the Sun, 129–130.

36. Kennan, "Korea: A Degenerate State," 314–315; W. W. Rockhill to Kennan, November 21, 1905, box 3, folder 1905, GKP. On muckrakers, see Richard Hofstadter, The Age of Reform: From Bryan to F.D.R. (New York: Vintage, 1955), 186–198.

37. Allen to Stevens, November 29, 1905; Stevens to Allen, January 10, 1906; Allen to Stevens, April 8, 1906, HNAP, reel 1.

38. Allen to Min Young-hwan, November 30, 1905; Allen to Yun Ch'i-ho, November 30, 1905, HNAP, reel 1. Although Fred Harvey Harrington pointed out that Allen recommended the Japanese takeover of Korea in 1904, scholars relying on Harrington's book have mistakenly believed that Allen had been punished for standing up for Korea. See Beale, Theodore Roosevelt, 321; Yi, A New History of Korea 309; Cumings, Korea's Place in the Sun, 142.

39. Fred Harvey Harrington, God, Mammon, and the Japanese: Dr. Horace N. Allen and Korean-American Relations, 1884–1905 (Madison: University of Wisconsin Press, 1944), 314–318.

40. Allen to Rockhill, January 4, 1904, HNAP, reel 4.

41. Harrington, God, Mammon, and the Japanese, 11–33.

42. Ibid., 41–67, 145, 164. Allen's title was US Minister Resident and Consul General from 1897 to 1901 and Envoy Extraordinary and Minister Plenipotentiary from 1901 to 1905.

43. Ibid., 128–130, 144–156, 186–192, 288–290. On concession imperialism, see Peter Duus, The Abacus and the Sword: The Japanese Penetration of Korea, 1895–1910 (Berkeley: University of California Press, 1998), 11.

44. Wayne Patterson, The Korean Frontier in America: Immigration to Hawai'i, 1896–1910 (Honolulu: University of Hawai'i Press, 1988).

45. Allen to Rockhill, April 19, 1904, HNAP, reel 4.

46. On the Japanese and American attempts to open Ŭiju, see Hayashi Gonsuke to Komura Juntarō, December 6, 1903, no. 440, CIKK, vol. 21; Allen to Hay, December 6, 1903, no. 628, DS-DMK, reel 20.

47. Allen to Rockhill, April 19, 1904, HNAP, reel 4; Rockhill to Allen, February 20, 1904, quoted in Harrington, God, Mammon, and the Japanese, 323–324.

48. Allen to Hay, February 24, 1904, DS-DMK, no. 676, reel 20.

49. "Telegram Received by the Japanese Minister from His Government on the 25th, February 6, 1904," FRUS 1904, 437. The exact word used in the February 1904 protocol is kaesŏn, which many Americans translated as "improvement."

50. Root to Min Young-chan, December 19, 1905, FRUS 1905, 629–630. For text of the treaty, see Takahira to Root, no. 79 B, FRUS 1905, 612–613.

51. Lloyd Griscom to John Hay, September 1, 1904, no. 115, FRUS 1904, 439. On Megata, see Michael Schiltz, The Money Doctors from Japan: Finance, Imperialism, and the Building of the Yen Bloc, 1895–1937 (Cambridge, MA: Harvard University Press, 2012), 90–117.

52. Allen to Rockhill, August 25, 1904; Stevens to Allen, March 20, 1905, HNAP, reel 1; Allen to James Morse, February 27, 1904, HNAP, reel 4. On Stevens, see Andrew C. Nahm, "Durham White Stevens and the Japanese Annexation of Korea," in The United States and Korea, ed. A. C. Nahm (Kalamazoo: Western Michigan University, 1979), 110–136.

53. Kennan Diary, "Japan No. 3," July 24, 1905, 150, 154, box 22, GKP; Kennan, "Korea," 308–310; Stevens to Kennan, November 2, 1905, box 3, folder 1905, GKP.

54. Allen to Yun, November 30, 1905, HNAP, reel 1; Yun to Allen, February 1, 1906, quoted in Address at the Naval War College, June 1906, HNAP, reel 5.
55. June 15, 1906, *YCHI*, 6: 231.
56. Donald Clark, "Yun Ch'i-ho (1864–1945): Portrait of a Korean Intellectual in an Era of Transition," *Occasional Papers on Korea* 4 (September 1975): 37–39; Hyung-chan Kim, *Letters in Exile: The Life and Times of Yun Ch'i-ho* (Oxford: Oxford Historical Shrine Society, 1980), 4–11.
57. December 10, 1889; December 24, 1889; May 12, 1891, *YCHI*, 1: 408, 415; 2: 191–192.
58. February 14, 1890, *YCHI*, 2: 18–19.
59. February 14, 1890, *YCHI*, 2: 19; Yun to Young John Allen, April 1, 1890, quoted in Andrew Urban, "Yun Ch'i-ho's Alienation by Way of Inclusion: A Korean International Student and Christian Reform in the 'New' South, 1888–1893," *Journal of Asian American Studies* 17 (October 2014): 307.
60. August 3, 1894; December 14, 1900, *YCHI*, 3: 351, 5:252.
61. December 9, 1889; November 23, 1890; January 16, 1891; March 11, 1891; May 2, 1891; May 10, 1891; March 13, 1892; May 21, 1892; July 12, 1892; January 1, 1893; April 16, 1893; and July 5, 1893; July 7, 1893, *YCHI*, 1: 408, 2: 122, 145–146, 160–161, 186, 190–191, 321, 348, 3: 1, 60, 115–116.
62. October 14, 1893, *YCHI*, 3: 187–188; Frederick E. Hoxie, *A Final Promise: The Campaign to Assimilate the Indians, 1880–1920* (Lincoln: University of Nebraska Press, 1984).
63. October 14, 1892; April 8, 1893, *YCHI*, 2: 388–389, 3: 55.
64. *KS*, vol. 33, May 10, 1895, art. 6; May 20, 1895, art. 2. On the establishment of the Korean cabinet, see Yu Yŏng-ik, *Kabo kyŏngjang yŏn'gu* (Seoul: Ilchogak, 1990); Sin Yong-ha, *Kabo kaehyŏk kwa Tongnip Hyŏphoe undong ŭi sahoesa* (Seoul: Sŏul Taehakkyo Ch'ulp'anbu, 2002), 21–31.
65. On Yun's activities in the Privy Council on behalf of the Independence Club, see *KS*, vol. 37, July 9, 1898, art. 2; vol. 38, October 7, 1898, art. 1; October 23, 1898, art. 7; November 2, 1898, art. 2.
66. Yun to Young J. Allen, March 28, 1902, in Kim, *YCHS*, 138–141. Yun served as the *kamni* of Tŏkwon, Wŏnsan, and Samwha and later *kunsu* of Ch'ŏnan, Chiksan, and Muan. For Yun's appointment as vice minister of foreign affairs, see *KS*, vol. 44, March 12, 1904, art. 1.
67. April 26, 1904, *YCHI*, 6: 20–22; *KS*, vol. 44, February 10, 1904, art. 2.
68. Allen to Hay, June 28, 1904, no. 763, DS-DMK, reel 21; April 26, 1904, *YCHI*, 6: 22; Edwin H. Grager, *Landownership under Colonial Rule: Korea's Japanese Experience, 1900–1935* (Honolulu: University of Hawai'i Press, 1994), 55–62.
69. May 27, 1904, *YCHI*, 6: 31; unnamed document written by Yun, circa August 1904, p. 9, box 17, folder 7, YCHP.
70. August 21, 1904, *YCHI*, 6: 56. For Yun's struggle with the August 1904 protocol, see also August 15, 1904; August 22, 1904, *YCHI*, 6: 53, 58–59; *KS*, vol. 44, August 22, 1904, art. 1. For the text of the protocol, see Takahira Kogorō to Alvey A. Adee, August 30, 1904, no. 79, *FRUS 1904*, 439.
71. December 23, 1904; May 10, 1905; June 14, 1905, *YCHI*, 6: 76, 110, 115.
72. D. W. Stevens, "Report of Audience of June 14th," *CIKK*, vol. 26; *KS*, vol. 46, July 10, 1905, art. 1. Yun's wife was a Chinese Methodist, and her death was mourned by the MECS missionary community. See C. F. Reid, *The Touch of Christ: A Tale of Missions* (Nashville, TN: Board of Missions, Methodist Episcopal Church, South, 1910). He remarried and had a Korean wife until her death in 1943.
73. August 30, 1905, *YCHI*, 6: 142–143; Patterson, *Korean Frontier in America*, 149–162. On Koreans in Mexico, see Kim Kwi-ok, "1905 nyŏn mekshik'o imin hanin nodongja yŏn'gu— hawai imin kwa pigyohamyŏnsŏ," *Chaeoe hanin yŏn'gu* 5 (1995): 162–195.
74. September 18, 1905; October 3, 1905, *YCHI*, 6: 153, 167; Eiichiro Azuma, *Between Two Empires: Race, History, and Transnationalism in Japanese America* (New York: Oxford University Press, 2005), 35–60.
75. October 14, 1905, *YCHI*, 6: 171. On Bryan's tour, see Daniel Scroop, "William Jennings Bryan's 1905–1906 World Tour," *Historical Journal* 56, no. 2 (June 2013): 459–486.
76. November 15, 1905, *YCHI*, 6: 193; "Bryan's Experiences in the Hermit Kingdom," *Washington Post*, March 4, 1906, SM8.

77. May 12, 1891, *YCHI*, 2: 191–192; October 16, 1905, *YCHI*, 6: 173–174.

78. Andre Schmid, *Korea between Empires, 1895–1919* (New York: Columbia University Press, 2002), 92–97.

79. November 29, 1905, *YCHI*, 6: 202.

80. "Coreans Send Unofficial Representative," *New York Sun*, July 26, 1905, 2.

81. P. K. Yoon and Syngman Rhee, "Petition from the Koreans of Hawai'i to President Roosevelt," July 12, 1905, reprinted in Henry Chung, *The Oriental Policy of the United States* (New York: Fleming H. Revell Co., 1919), 241–245; "Plea for Help for Korea," *Washington Post*, August 18, 1905, 3.

82. "Korea Repudiates Treaty," *New York Times*, December 13, 1905, 1.

83. Kennan, "Korea," 307; Abbott to Kennan, August 8, 1905, box 3, folder 1905, GKP.

84. Kennan, "The Japanese in Korea," *Outlook* 81 (November 11, 1905): 610, 612.

85. Kennan, "What Japan Has Done in Korea," *Outlook* 81 (November 18, 1905): 670; On Yi Chi-yong's appointments, see *KS*, vol. 44, February 11, 1904, art. 2; March 21, 1904, art. 1; vol. 45, February 13, 1905, art. 1; May 20, 1905, art. 1; vol. 46, September 9, 1905, art. 2. Yi also received 20,000 yen from the Japanese Foreign Ministry for signing the protocol of February 23, 1904. See Hayashi to Komura, January 11, 1904; January 16, 1904; January 21, 1904, CIKK, vol. 18, no. 16; no. 17; no. 28; Hayashi to Komura February 13, 1904, CIKK, vol. 23, no. 132.

86. Kennan, "The Japanese in Korea," 611.

87. Kennan, "The Japanese in Korea," 613–614. It was not until the annexation of Korea in 1910 that the Japanese government began to control its settlers there. Jun Uchida, *Brokers of Empire: Japanese Settler Colonialism in Korea, 1876–1946* (Cambridge, MA: Harvard University Press, 2011), 35–139.

88. "Editorial Comment," *Korea Review* 5, no. 1 (January 1905): 29; Kennan Diary No. 3, July 15, 1905, 122–128.

89. "Baron Kaneko's Mission in America," *Japan Weekly Chronicle*, October 12, 1905, 472; Hulbert, "Japan as a Colonizer," *Korea Review* 5, no. 9 (September 1, 1905): 361–362. On American teachers in the Philippines, see Sarah Steinbock-Pratt, *Educating the Empire: American Teachers and Contested Colonization in the Philippines* (Cambridge: Cambridge University Press, 2019).

90. Willard Straight Diary, March 16, 1904, p. 52, WDSP, reel 11; "Japan in Korea," December 20, 1904, pp. 7–9, WDSP, reel 9.

91. Straight to Henry Schoelkopf, September 17, 1905, WDSP, reel 1.

92. Morgan to Root, October 19, 1905, no. 23; Morgan to Root, November 20, 1905, no. 35, DS–DMK, reel 22. On Ilchinhoe, see Yumi Moon, *Populist Collaborators: The Ilchinhoe and the Japanese Colonization of Korea, 1896–1910* (Ithaca, NY: Cornell University Press, 2013).

93. Griscom to Roosevelt, October 12, 1905, TRP, reel 60.

94. Roosevelt to Griscom, October 31, 1905, TRP, reel 339.

95. Tosh Minohara, "The Russo-Japanese War and the Transformation of US-Japan Relations: Examining the Geopolitical Ramifications," *Japanese Journal of American Studies* 27 (2016): 45–68; Rotem Kowner, *Historical Dictionary of the Russo-Japanese War* (Lanham, MD: Rowman & Littlefield, 2017), 100.

96. Andrew Gordon, *Labor and Imperial Democracy in Prewar Japan* (Berkeley: University of California Press, 2001), 26–62.

97. Roosevelt to Abbott, October 16, 1905, *LTR*, 5: 698.

98. Katsura Tarō to Hayashi Gonsuke, November 6, 1905, CIKK, vol. 24, no. 14; Hayashi to Katsura, October 13, 1905, CIKK, vol. 26. no. 298.

99. Robert Thomas Tierney, *Monster of the Twentieth Century: Kōtoku Shūsui and Japan's First Anti-Imperialist Movement* (Oakland: University of California Press, 2015), 72–79.

100. Morgan to Root, November 22, 1905, no. 36, DS-DMK, reel 22; "Good Future for Korea," *Washington Post*, January 28, 1906, E1.

101. Katsura to Hayashi, November 6, 1905, CIKK, vol. 24, no. 14.

102. Stevens to Kennan, October 3, 1905, box 3, folder 1905, GKP; Kennan, "Japanese in Korea," 613.

103. Kennan, "What Japan Has Done in Korea," 672.

Chapter 2

1. Theodore Roosevelt to George Kennan, May 6, 1905, *LTR*, 4: 1168. For the text of the resolution, see *Journal of the Assembly during the Thirty-sixth Session of the Legislature of the State of California* (Sacramento: Superintendent State Printing, 1905), 1468–1469. Why Roosevelt took two months to respond to the California resolution is not clear.

2. For interpretations that present Roosevelt as a practical politician who compromised with nativists to prevent conflict with Japan, see Thomas A. Bailey, *Theodore Roosevelt and the Japanese-American Crises* (Stanford, CA: Stanford University Press, 1934), 327–328; Charles E. Neu, *An Uncertain Friendship: Theodore Roosevelt and Japan, 1906–1909* (Cambridge, MA: Harvard University Press, 1967), 49–50, 311–312; Lon Kurashige, *Two Faces of Exclusion: The Untold History of Anti-Asian Racism in the United States* (Chapel Hill: University of North Carolina Press, 2016), 94. For interpretations that present Roosevelt as an imperialist who focused on keeping East Asian markets open to US businesses and avoiding military conflict with Japan, see Akira Iriye, *Pacific Estrangement: Japanese and American Expansion, 1897–1911* (Cambridge, MA: Harvard University Press, 1972), 151–152; Walter LaFeber, *The Clash: A History of U.S.-Japan Relations* (New York: W. W. Norton, 1997), 89; Masuda Hajimu, "Rumors of War: Immigration Disputes and the Social Construction of American-Japanese Relations," *Diplomatic History* 33, no. 1 (January 2009): 1–37; John M. Thompson, *Great Power Rising: Theodore Roosevelt and the Politics of U.S. Foreign Policy* (New York: Oxford University Press, 2019), 121–134.

3. Gary Gerstle, *American Crucible: Race and Nation in the Twentieth Century* (Princeton, NJ: Princeton University Press, 2001), 55–56; George E. Paulsen, "The Abrogation of the Gresham-Yang Treaty," *Pacific Historical Review* 40, no. 4 (November 1971): 457–477; Katherine Benton-Cohen, *Inventing the Immigration Problem: The Dillingham Commission and Its Legacy* (Cambridge, MA: Harvard University Press, 2018).

4. For an influential narrative that draws a straight line between these two events, see Roger Daniels, *The Politics of Prejudice: The Anti-Japanese Movement in California and the Struggle for Japanese Exclusion* (Berkeley: University of California Press, 1962).

5. On the Lincoln-Roosevelt League, see Spencer Olin, *California's Prodigal Sons: Hiram Johnson and the Progressives, 1911–1917* (Berkeley: University of California Press, 1968).

6. On social politics, see Richard Hofstadter, *The Age of Reform: From Bryan to FDR* (New York: Vintage, 1955), 174–271; Daniel T. Rodgers, *Atlantic Crossings: Social Politics in a Progressive Age* (Cambridge, MA: Belknap Press of Harvard University Press, 1998), 20–32; Thomas Bender, *A Nation among Nations: America's Place in World History* (New York: Hill and Wang, 2006), 246–295.

7. Roosevelt to Henry Cabot Lodge, May 15, 1905; Roosevelt to John Hay, September 2, 1904, *LTR*, 4: 1180, 917.

8. Delber McKee, *Chinese Exclusion Versus the Open Door Policy, 1900–1906: Clashes over China Policy in the Roosevelt Era* (Detroit: Wayne State University Press, 1977), 176–177.

9. William R. Braisted, "The United States and the American China Development Company," *Far Eastern Quarterly* 11, no. 2 (February 1952): 147–165; Guanhua Wang, *In Search of Justice: The 1905–1906 Chinese Anti-American Boycott* (Cambridge, MA: Harvard University Press, 2001).

10. Theodore Roosevelt, Speech at Piedmont Park, Atlanta, Georgia, October 20, 1905, quoted in "The President on Chinese Immigration," *Journal of the American Asiatic Association* 5, no. 10 (November 1905): 299; Thompson, *Great Power Rising*, 102–119.

11. Theodore Roosevelt, State of the Union, December 5, 1905, quoted in Paul Kramer, "Imperial Openings: Civilization, Exemption, and the Geopolitics of Mobility in the History of Chinese Exclusion, 1868–1910," *Journal of the Gilded Age and Progressive Era* 14, no. 3 (July 2015): 337.

12. Wang, *In Search of Justice*, 178–191; Delber L. McKee, "The Chinese Boycott of 1905–1906 Reconsidered: The Role of Chinese Americans," *Pacific Historical Review* 55, no. 2 (May 1986): 165–191.

13. U.S. Congress, *Japanese in the City of San Francisco, Cal.: Message from the President of the United States, Transmitting the Final Report of Secretary Metcalf on the Situation Affecting the Japanese in the City of San Francisco* (Washington, DC: US Government Printing Office, 1907), 3;

Mae Ngai, *The Lucky Ones: One Family and the Extraordinary Invention of Chinese America* (New York: Houghton Mifflin, 2010), 49–57; "Hakkyo munjae," *Kongnip Sinbo*, December 22, 1906, 2.

14. "California's Protest against the Mongolian Invasion," *Organized Labor*, December 29, 1906, 1.

15. Theodore Roosevelt, State of the Union, December 3, 1906, *FRUS 1906*, xli–xliii.

16. "Roosevelt's Message," *Organized Labor*, December 8, 1906, 1.

17. Kennan, "Japanese in the San Francisco Schools," *Outlook* 86 (June 1, 1907): 246–252; Kennan, "Fight for Reform in San Francisco," *McClure's* 29 (September 1907): 547–560; "The Japanese Question," *Outlook* 84 (December 29, 1906): 1051; "The Japanese in America," *Outlook* 84 (December 29, 1906): 1086; "Would Divert Emigration," *New York Times*, September 30, 1905, 5; Kennan to Roosevelt, April 1, 1905, box 7, folder 1905–1907, GKP; "Japanese Citizenship," *Independent* 61, no. 3027 (December 6, 1906): 1363.

18. Neu, *Uncertain Friendship*, 54–57, 64–65, 59–60; Roosevelt to Victor Metcalf, November 27, 1906; Roosevelt to Edward Grey, December 18, 1906, *LTR*, 5: 510, 528.

19. Jordan to Roosevelt, December 1, 1905, TRP, reel 61; Christopher Lasch, "The Anti-Imperialists, the Philippines, and the Inequality of Man," *Journal of Southern History* 24, no. 3 (August 1958): 319–331.

20. Jordan, "The Sequel in Japan," *Pacific Monthly* 15, no. 1 (January 1906): 16–17; Jordan, *The Days of a Man: 1900–1922* (Yonkers-on-Hudson, NY: World Book Company, 1922), 58–59.

21. Jordan, "Japanese Exclusion," *Independent* 61, no. 3028 (December 13, 1906): 1426; Jordan to Roosevelt, January 3, 1907, box 77, folder Roosevelt, Theodore, 1901–1917, DSJP.

22. Roosevelt to Jordan, January 9, 1907, box 77, folder Roosevelt, Theodore, 1901–1917, DSJP.

23. Neu, *Uncertain Friendship*, 69–79, 163–180; Paul Kramer, "The Geopolitics of Mobility: Immigration Policy and American Global Power in the Long Twentieth Century," *American Historical Review* 123, no. 2 (April 2018): 417. The series of notes constituting the Gentlemen's Agreement are printed in *FRUS 1924*, 2: 339–369.

24. Geiger, *Subverting Exclusion*, 36–71; Iriye, *Pacific Estrangement*, 134–135.

25. Hyung Gu Lynn, "Malthusian Dreams, Colonial Imaginary: The Oriental Development Company and Emigration to Korea," in *Settler Colonialism in the Twentieth Century: Projects, Practices, Legacies*, ed. Caroline Elkins and Susan Pedersen (London: Routledge, 2005), 25–40.

26. "For California's Rights and Interests of Her People," *Organized Labor*, February 16, 1907, 1; *Proceedings of the Asiatic Exclusion League, September 1912* (San Francisco: Asiatic Exclusion League, 1912), 252–253. On the Canadian-Japanese Gentlemen's Agreement, see David Atkinson, *The Burden of White Supremacy: Containing Asian Migration in the British Empire and the United States* (Chapel Hill: University of North Carolina Press, 2016), 111–120.

27. Roosevelt to William Kent, February 4, 1909, *LTR*, 6: 1503–1504.

28. Kiyoshi Kawakami, "The Anti-Japanese Agitation in America (2)," *Taiyō* 17, no. 10 (July 1911): 12.

29. "Japanese and Corean Exclusion League Completes Organization and Adopts Strong Resolutions," *Organized Labor*, May 20, 1905, 4. The organization initially spelled *Korea* with a C but later changed its spelling.

30. Joan M. Jensen, *Passage from India: Asian Indian Immigrants in North America* (New Haven, CT: Yale University Press, 1988), 42–56; Erika Lee, "The 'Yellow Peril' and Asian Exclusion in the Americas," *Pacific Historical Review* 76, no. 4 (November 2007): 550–553; Seema Sohi, *Echoes of Mutiny: Race, Surveillance, and Indian Anticolonialism in North America* (New York: Oxford University Press, 2014), 25–28; Atkinson, *Burden of White Supremacy*, 97–103. For an explanation of the league's change in name to encompass "Hindoos," see *Proceedings of the Asiatic Exclusion League*, February 1908 (San Francisco: Asiatic Exclusion League, 1908), 8.

31. *Report of Proceedings of the Twenty-Eighth Annual Convention of the American Federation of Labor* (Washington, DC: National Tribune Co., 1908), 109.

32. Olaf Tveitmoe, "A Representative and Patriotic Convention," *Organized Labor*, May 13, 1905, 2–3; Tveitmoe, "The Anti-Japanese Convention," *Organized Labor*, May 6, 1905, 1.

33. Tveitmoe, "Trachomatous Japanese," *Organized Labor*, December 29, 1907, 4; Tveitmoe, "The Patriotism of Exclusion," *Organized Labor*, August 1, 1908, 2.

NOTES TO PAGES 65–70

34. Ross, "Japanese Competition," *Organized Labor,* May 19, 1900, 1. On the rally, see Daniels, *Politics of Prejudice,* 21–22; Kurashige, *Two Faces of Exclusion,* 79–80.
35. Ross, "Japanese Competition," 1.
36. Ross, "Causes of Race Superiority," *Annals of the American Academy of Political and Social Science* 18 (July 1901): 88–89. On "race suicide," see Gail Bederman, *Manliness and Civilization: A Cultural History of Gender and Race in the United States, 1880–1917* (Chicago: University of Chicago Press, 1995), 200–206; Nell Irvin Painter, *The History of White People* (New York: W. W. Norton, 2010), 245–255.
37. Jane Stanford to David Starr Jordan, May 9, 1900, box 1, folder 4, E. A. Ross Papers, Special Collections, Green Library, Stanford University; Alexander Saxton, *Indispensable Enemy: Labor and the Anti-Chinese Movement in California* (Berkeley: University of California Press, 1971), 113–121, 141–153; Beth Lew-Williams, *The Chinese Must Go: Violence, Exclusion, and the Making of the Alien in America* (Cambridge, MA: Harvard University Press, 2018), 40–43.
38. "Dr. Edward A. Ross Forced Out of Stanford University," *San Francisco Chronicle,* November 14, 1900, 1.
39. "Would Let Japan Enact Her Own Exclusion," *San Francisco Call,* January 14, 1907, 12; "Jordan Talks Rot, Asserts Tveitmoe," *Santa Cruz Sentinel,* January 17, 1907, 7; *Harper's Magazine* 101, no. 2637 (July 6, 1907): front cover; Olaf Tveitmoe to E. A. Ross, November 14, 1900, *Edward A. Ross Papers, 1859–1969* (Madison: Wisconsin Historical Society, 1982), reel 3.
40. Jordan, "With No Mark or Brand," *Addresses at the Annual Commencement* (Palo Alto, CA: Times Publishing Co., 1907), 19–21; Jordan to Roosevelt, January 3, 1907; Ross, "Value Rank of the American People," *Independent* 57 (November 1904): 1063.
41. John R. Jenswold, "Leaving the Door Ajar: Politics and Prejudices in the Making of the 1907 Immigration Law," *Mid-America: An Historical Review* 67, no. 1 (January 1985): 3–21.
42. Philip C. Jessup, *Elihu Root* (New York: Dodd, Mead & Co., 1938), 2: 15–18.
43. *Congressional Record—Senate,* 59th Cong., 2nd sess., February 14, 1907; February 15, 1907, 2951, 3036, 3028.
44. "Passing of the Tveitmoe," *Oakland Tribune,* November 23, 1907, 14; "Convicted Men Will Appeal Case," *San Francisco Call,* December 29, 1912, 21; Walton Bean, *Boss Ruef's San Francisco: The Story of the Union Labor Party, Big Business, and the Graft Prosecution* (Berkeley: University of California Press, 1952).
45. "Tveitmoe and Clancy Return This Saturday Night—Arrive at the Ferry Depot at 8 o' Clock," *Organized Labor,* March 8, 1913, 1; "Eight Years' Agitation Bearing Fruit," *Organized Labor,* May 3, 1913, 1.
46. Prescott F. Cogswell's speech in the transcript of the debate in the California legislature, April 29, 1913, p. 105, part II, box 41, unnamed folder, HJP.
47. See letters in part II, box 33, folder Tveitmoe, Olaf A., HJP; Olin, *California's Prodigal Sons,* 9–11.
48. Rowell, "Orientophobia," *Collier's* 42, no. 20 (February 3, 1909): 29; George Mowry, *The California Progressives* (Berkeley: University of California Press, 1951); Olin, *California's Prodigal Sons,* 11–22. For the names of founding members of the Lincoln-Roosevelt League, see *The Lincoln-Roosevelt League* (n.p.: 1908), http://digital.library.ucla.edu/campaign/librarian?VIEWPDF=1908_001_001_a.
49. "Meat v. Rice," *Organized Labor,* June 6, 1908, 2.
50. Rowell, "A New Race Problem," *Fresno Republican,* September 26, 1900, carton 2, folder 1900; Rowell, "Two Views of Japan," April 28, 1905, carton 2, folder 1905, CHRP. On Rowell, see Frank W. Van Nuys, "A Progressive Confronts the Race Question: Chester Rowell, the California Alien Land Act of 1913, and the Contradictions of Early Twentieth-Century Racial Thought," *California History* 73, no. 1 (Spring 1994): 2–13; Kurashige, *Two Faces of Exclusion,* 95–97, 100–101.
51. Roosevelt to Rowell, February 11, 1909, TRP, reel 354; Roosevelt to James Wilson, February 3, 1903, *LTR,* 3:416; Roosevelt to William Kent, February 4, 1909, *LTR,* 6: 1504.
52. Roosevelt to Philander Knox, February 8, 1909, *LTR,* 6: 1510–1514.

53. Roosevelt to Philip A. Stanton, February 8, 1909, *LTR*, 6: 1510; Neu, *Uncertain Friendship*, 292–305.

54. Philander Knox to Hiram Johnson, January 14, 1911, part II, box 34, folder U.S. Department of State, January 1911–December 1914, HJP.

55. Theodore Roosevelt to William H. Taft, December 22, 1910, *LTR*, 7: 190–191; Taft to Roosevelt, December 24, 1910, WHTP, reel 504. On the China consortium and Knox's "neutralization" plan, see Michael H. Hunt, *Frontier Defense and the Open Door: Manchuria in Chinese-American Relations, 1895–1911* (New Haven, CT: Yale University Press, 1973); Louisa Erickson Kilgroe, "The Iron Circle: J. P. Morgan and the International Banking Consortium for China, 1909–1922" (PhD diss., University of North Carolina, Chapel Hill, 1989).

56. Baker, "Wonderful Hawaii," *American Magazine* 73, no. 1 (November 1911): 28–38.

57. Roosevelt to Baker, October 27, 1911, *LTR*, 7: 425–426.

58. Christopher Capozzola, *Bound by War: How the United States and the Philippines Built America's First Pacific Century* (New York: Basic Books, 2020), 72–79; Atkinson, *The Burden of White Supremacy*, 114–130. On Mahan, see David Milne, *Worldmaking: The Art and Science of American Diplomacy* (New York: Farrar, Straus & Giroux, 2015), 21–68.

59. Sadao Asada, *From Mahan to Pearl Harbor: The Imperial Japanese Navy and the United States* (Annapolis, MD: Naval Institute Press, 2006), 18–20, 47–51.

60. Roosevelt to Taft, March 14, 1911, TRP, reel 365. On the Magdalena episode, see Eiichiro Azuma, *In Search of Our Frontier: Japanese America and Settler Colonialism in the Construction of Japan's Borderless Empire* (Oakland: University of California Press, 2019), 114–124.

61. Robert E. Hennings, "James D. Phelan and the Woodrow Wilson Anti-Oriental Statement of May 3, 1912," *California Historical Society Quarterly* 42, no. 4 (December 1963): 291–300.

62. Rowell to Johnson, January 6, 1913, part II, box 29, folder January–December 1913; Roosevelt to Johnson, June 30, 1913, part II, box 28, folder Theodore Roosevelt, 1910–1919, HJP.

63. Rowell, "The Japanese in California," *World's Work* 26, no. 2 (June 1913): 198.

64. Baker, "Wonderful Hawaii," 28; Rowell, "Orientophobia," 13; "Japanese Are Men," *The Guardian*, June 7, 1913, 2, box 1, Guardian of Boston / William Monroe Collection, Howard Gotlieb Archival Research Center, Boston University.

65. Rowell, "Orientophobia," 13. On Rowell and the post-Reconstruction South, see Kurashige, "Transpacific Accommodation and the Defense of Asian Immigrants," 309.

66. Jordan, "Relations of Japan and the United States," 119–120. On Jordan's racist view of Black Americans, see Jordan, *War and Waste* (Garden City, NY: Doubleday, Page & Company, 1913), 268–272.

67. Rowell, "A New Race Problem," *Fresno Republican*, September 26, 1900, carton 2, folder 1900, CHRP.

68. "No Discrimination for Japs," *The Liberator*, November 1, 1906, 4; "Shall It Be Justice—Or War?," *The Liberator*, April 25, 1913, 3; "Southern Negroes Ask President Wilson to Give Negroes Square Deal," *The Liberator*, August 8, 1913, 1.

69. Du Bois, "Colored California," *The Crisis* 6, no. 4 (August 1913), 194; "Race Upholds Japs on Coast Declares Du Bois," *Chicago Defender*, May, 24, 1913, 1.

70. Washington to the Editor of *New York Age*, March 14, 1913, *BTWP*, 12: 143; "Japanese Arrange Tuskegee Scholarship," *Chicago Defender*, March 29, 1913, 1. On the Tuskegee Institute, see Robert J. Norrell, *Up from Slavery: The Life of Booker T. Washington* (Cambridge, MA: Belknap Press of Harvard University Press, 2009), 61–74, 364–371.

71. Washington, quoted in Reginald Kearney, *African American Views of the Japanese: Solidarity or Sedition?* (Albany: State University of New York Press, 1998), 69; Netti J. Asburry to Washington, September 15, 1913, *BTWP*, 12: 279.

72. *Proceedings of the Asiatic Exclusion League, San Francisco, February 1913* (San Francisco: n.p., 1913), 294; Billy Kent to Bryan, April 7, 1913, *PWW*, 27: 265–266; Phelan, "The Japanese Question from a Californian Standpoint," *Independent* 74, no. 3369 (June 26, 1913): 1440.

73. Tillman to William Kent, May 16, 1913, quoted in Jun Furuya, "Gentlemen's Disagreement: The Controversy between the United States and Japan over the California Alien Land Law of 1913" (PhD diss., Princeton University, 1989), 229–230; Clarence Poe, "Rural Land Segregation between Whites and Negroes: A Reply to Mr. Stephenson," *South Atlantic Quarterly* 13, no. 3 (July 1914): 210–211.

74. Rowell, "While It Is Small," *Fresno Republican*, May 6, 1913, carton 2, folder Editorials, 1913, CHRP.

75. Rowell, "The Japanese in California," *World's Work* 26, no. 2 (June 1913): 199, 197.

76. Ibid., 199; A. Anderson to Hiram Johnson, May 14, 1913, part II, box 37, folder Anderson, A., HJP.

77. "Finding a Fortune in California Potatoes," *San Francisco Call*, March 10, 1912, 6.

78. "Proceedings of the Asiatic Exclusion League (5/18)," *Organized Labor*, May 24, 1913, 3; "Asiatic Exclusion League to Appeal to the People," *Organized Labor*, May 24, 1913, 4-5.

79. Rowell to Bryan, May 8, 1913, box 1, folder 1913, May-June, CHRP; "Signs Webb Bill," *San Francisco Bulletin*, May 19, 1913, 1.

80. W. C. Wall, quoted in the transcript of the California State Assembly, April 29, 1913, p. 99, part II, box 41, unnamed folder, HJP.

81. Rowell to Shima, September 15, 1913, box 1, folder 1913, September-October, CHRP. Rowell explains the real estate transaction in his letter to Kiyoshi Karl Kawakami, December 11, 1914, box 2, folder 1914, November-December, CHRP.

82. Eiichiro Azuma, *Between Two Empires: Race, History, and Transnationalism in Japanese America* (New York: Oxford University Press, 2005), 35-60, Shima quote from 47; Nayan Shah, *Contagious Divides: Epidemics and Race in San Francisco's Chinatown* (Berkeley: University of California Press, 2001), 23-24.

83. Geiger, *Subverting Exclusion*, 82-90; Rumi Yasutake, *Transnational Women's Activism: The United States, Japan, and Japanese Immigrant Communities in California, 1859-1920* (New York: NYU Press, 2004), 111-116.

84. A. E. Yoell to D. J. Keefe, January 7, 1913; Keefe to Yoell, January 18, 1913, *Records of the Immigration and Naturalization Service, Series A: Subject Correspondence Files, Part 1: Asian Immigration and Exclusion, 1906-1913* (Bethesda, MD: University Publications of America, 1993), reel 23.

85. Juichi Soeda and Tadao Kamiya, *A Survey of the Japanese Question in California* (San Francisco: n.p., 1913), 9; "Bryan Receives Tokyo Delegates," *San Francisco Call*, June 19, 1913, 1; Azuma, *Between Two Empires*, 52-53; Furuya, "Gentlemen's Disagreement," 131-143. On the Taishō political crisis, see Danny Orbach, *Curse on This Country: The Rebellious Army of Imperial Japan* (Ithaca, NY: Cornell University Press, 2017), 129-158.

86. "Han'guk kwan'gye migugin yŏnsŏl e kwanhan kŏn," April 20, 1909, no. 1, *CIKK*, vol. 10; Richard S. Kim, *Quest for Statehood*, 4-7; "70 wŏn paesanggŭm," *Sinhan Minbo*, July 4, 1913, 2. On Numano's power over Japanese American socialists, see Yuji Ichioka, *Issei: The World of the First Generation Japanese Immigrants, 1885-1924* (New York: Free Press, 1988), 134-136.

87. Pacific Press Bureau pamphlet, attached to Kawakami to C. C. Moore, April 23, 1914, carton 5, folder: K, 1911-1915, PPIEP; Shelley Sang-Hee Lee, *Claiming the Oriental Gateway: Prewar Seattle and Japanese America* (Philadelphia: Temple University Press, 2011), 51-63; Eiichiro Azuma, "Dancing with the Rising Sun: Strategic Alliance between Japanese Immigrants and Their 'Home' Government," in *The Transnational Politics of Asian Americans*, ed. Christian Collet and Pei-te Lien (Philadelphia: Temple University Press, 2009), 27-28.

88. Kawakami, "Socialism in Japan," *International Socialist Review* 2, no. 8 (February 1902): 562; Kawakami to Richard T. Ely, May 14, 1902, *Richard T. Ely Papers, 1812-1963* (Madison: Wisconsin Historical Society, 1982), reel 22.

89. *Iowa Alumnus* (Iowa City: State University of Iowa, 1904), 93; "Some of the People Who Will Welcome Envoys upon Their Arrival at Portsmouth Tomorrow," *Boston Globe*, August 6, 1905, 20; Kawakami, *Japan in World Politics* (New York: Macmillan, 1917), ix; Kawakami, "A Defense of Japanese Rule in Korea," *Pacific Monthly* 22, no. 3 (September 1909): 296.

90. Rowell to Kawakami, December 11, 1914, box 2, folder 1914, November-December, CHRP; Kawakami, "The Japanese on Our Farms," *Forum* 50 (July 1913): 89-90; "A Called-for Protest," *San Francisco Chronicle*, February 15, 1914, attached to Kawakami to Rowell, February 14, 1914, box 18, folder Kawakami, CHRP.

91. Rowell, "Japanese Agitation," *California Outlook* 17, no. 22 (November 28, 1914): 9. For Japanese American support of Rowell, see "California Press on California Situation," *Nichibei Shinbun*, December 20, 1914, 12. On China's participation, see Kin-Yee Ian Shin, "Making 'Chinese' Art: Knowledge and Authority in the Transpacific Progressive Era" (PhD diss., Columbia University, 2016), 202-272.

92. Rowell, "Japanese Agitation," 9. Franklin Hichborn, *Story of the Session of the California Legislature of 1915* (San Francisco: Press of the James H. Barry Co., 1916), 230–232.

93. Abigail M. Markwyn, *Empress San Francisco: The Pacific Rim, the Great West, and California at the Panama-Pacific International Exposition* (Lincoln: University of Nebraska Press, 2014), 162–171.

94. "Taft Is Japan Day Orator," *New York Times*, September 1, 1915, 9; Kawakami, "Baron Shibusawa," *Nichibei Shinbun*, November 21, 1915, 12.

95. Frederick Dickinson, *War and National Reinvention: Japan in the Great War, 1914–1919* (Cambridge, MA: Harvard University Press, 1999), 84–116.

96. Kawakami, "Japan in the European War," *Sunset Magazine* 33, no. 4 (October 1914): 665; "The Chinese Policy of Japan," *Sunset Magazine* 34, no. 5 (May 1915): 922.

97. Paul Reinsch, "Japan and Asiatic Leadership," *North American Review* 180, no. 578 (January 1905): 180, 578; Noel H. Pugach, *Paul S. Reinsch, Open Door Diplomat in Action* (Millwood, NY: KTO Press, 1979), 143–157.

98. Theodore Roosevelt, "American Preparedness," *New York Times Current History, A Monthly Magazine* (August 15, 1915): 841; Benjamin A. Coates, *Legalist Empire: International Law and American Foreign Relations in the Early Twentieth Century* (New York: Oxford University Press, 2016), 52–58; Thompson, *Great Power Rising*, 51–76.

99. Roosevelt, "American Preparedness," 841; Lloyd E. Ambrosius, "The Great War, Americanism Revisited, and the Anti-Wilson Crusade," in *Woodrow Wilson and American Internationalism* (Cambridge: Cambridge University Press, 2017), 114–127.

100. Kawakami, "Shall America Prepare against Japan?," *North American Review* 203, no. 726 (May 1916): 675–676. Kawakami is quoting from Theodore Roosevelt, "The Japanese Question," *Outlook Editorials* (New York: The Outlook Company, 1909), 78.

101. Jensen, *Passage from India*, 159–161.

102. A Bill to Regulate the Immigration of Aliens to, and the Residence of Aliens in, the United States, H.R., 10384, 64th Cong., 1st Sess., January 29, 1916, 7; "Japan Objects to the Burnett Bill," *The Immigration Journal* 1, no. 3 (May 1916): 41.

103. *Congressional Record—Senate*, 64th Cong. 2nd Sess., December 12, 1916, 221; *Congressional Record—House*, 64th Cong. 2nd Sess., January 16, 1917, 1494–1495.

104. From 1900 to 1939, the volume of US trade with Japan was considerably larger than that of US trade with China. See the "Merchandise Exported and Imported" section of 1910 and 1920 US census, and the "Foreign Commerce" section of the 1930 and 1940 US census.

Chapter 3

1. "Kŭngnak e hwansaenghan yugin," *Maeil Shinbo*, February 16, 1915, 3.

2. "Hanin ŭl kot'onghage ham," *Sinhan Minbo*, March 18, 1912, 3; "Miil kukche ŭi changnae," *Sinhan Minbo*, June 24, 1912, 1.

3. Yamato Ichihashi, "American Missions in Korea," *Nichibei Shinbun*, December 1, 1912, 4 (English section); Kiyoshi K. Kawakami, *American-Japanese Relations: An Inside View of Japan's Policies and Purposes* (New York: Fleming H. Revell Co., 1912), 266–284; George Kennan, "Is Japan Persecuting Christians in Korea?," *Outlook* 102 (December 14, 1912): 804–810.

4. On US-Japan competition and conflict, see Akira Iriye, *Pacific Estrangement: Japanese and American Expansion, 1891–1911* (Cambridge, MA: Harvard University Press, 1972); Walter LaFeber, *The Clash: A History of U.S.-Japan Relations* (New York: W. W. Norton, 1997).

5. Arthur S. Link, *Woodrow Wilson and the Progressive Era, 1910–1917* (New York: Harper Torch, 1954), 81–106. On the importance of Wilson's faith in his foreign policy, see Andrew Preston, *Sword of the Spirit, Shield of Faith: Religion in American War and Diplomacy* (New York: Alfred A. Knopf, 2012), 275–290.

6. Frank Prentiss Baldwin Jr., "The March First Movement: Korean Challenge and Japanese Response" (PhD diss., Columbia University, 1969), 14–77; Erez Manela, *The Wilsonian Moment: Self-Determination and the International Origins of Anticolonial Nationalism* (New York: Oxford University Press 2007).

7. Lawrence Abbott to Kennan, August 8, 1905, box 3, folder 1905, GKP.

8. Homer Hulbert, *The Passing of Korea* (New York: Doubleday, Page), 462; Frederick A. McKenzie, *The Colonial Policy of Japan in Korea* (London: Central Asian Society, 1906), 8; Thomas F. Millard, *The New Far East* (New York: Charles Scribner's Sons, 1906), 121; Millard, "Japanese Immigration into Korea," *Annals of the American Academy of Political and Social Science* 34, no. 2 (September 1909): 189.

9. William T. Ellis, "A Yankee Tilt for an Empire," *Harper's Weekly* 51, no. 2637 (July 6, 1907): 1159; Koen De Ceuster, "1907 nyŏn heigŭ t'ŭksa ŭi sŏnggong gwa chwajŏl," *Han'guksa hakpo* 30 (February 2008): 324–339. On Stead, see Duncan Bell, *Dreamworlds of Race: Empire and the Utopian Destiny of Anglo-America* (Princeton, NJ: Princeton University Press, 2020), 100–151.

10. "The Crisis in Korea," *Outlook* 86 (July 27, 1907): 626. On the abdication, see Peter Duus, *The Abacus and the Sword: The Japanese Penetration of Korea, 1895-1910* (Berkeley and Los Angeles: University of California Press, 1995), 207–211.

11. H. Percival Dodge to Elihu Root, September 19, 1907, no. 417, *FRUS 1907*, 2: 774.

12. Hayashi Gonsuke to Itō Hirobumi, November 16, 1907, no. 179; Itō to Hayashi, November 18, 1907, no. 150, both in *TM*, Vol. 4.

13. "Japan's Control a Benefit to Corea," *San Francisco Chronicle*, March 28, 1908, 1; Richard S. Kim, *Quest for Statehood: Korean Immigrant Nationalism and U.S. Sovereignty, 1905-1945* (New York: Oxford University Press, 2011), 26–45.

14. "Two Americans in the Japanese Service," *Outlook* 88 (April 4, 1908): 762.

15. Duus, *Abacus and the Sword*, 206–209, 223–228.

16. Takahira Kogorō, "Durham White Stevens," *North American Review* 188, no. 632 (July 1908): 13–14.

17. Charles E. Neu, *An Uncertain Friendship: Theodore Roosevelt and Japan, 1906-1909* (Cambridge, MA: Harvard University Press, 1967), 275–282.

18. Lydia N. Yu-Jose, *Japan View the Philippines, 1900-1941* (Manila: Anteneo de Manila University Press, 1992), 20–28.

19. Roosevelt, "Message of the President," December 8, 1908, *FRUS 1908*, xlvi–xlvii; Paul A. Kramer, *The Blood of Government: Race, Empire, the United States, and the Philippines* (Chapel Hill: University of North Carolina Press, 2006), 300–301.

20. Roosevelt, *Theodore Roosevelt: An Autobiography* (New York: Macmillan, 1913), 545.

21. Roosevelt, "The Japanese in Korea," reprinted in *Fear God and Take Your Own Part* (New York: George H. Doran Co., 1916), 294. Originally published in *Metropolitan* 41, no. 5 (March 1915): 12b, 76.

22. His Imperial Japanese Majesty's Residency General, *Annual Report for 1907 on Reforms and Progress in Korea* (Seoul, 1907), 1. The Japanese colonial government submitted annual reports to the US consul in Seoul, who in turn sent them to the State Department in Washington. See Consul General to Assistant Secretary of State, June 5, 1911, 895.00/543; Consul General to Secretary of State, June 9, 1914, 895.00/557, DS-IAK, reel 2

23. Roosevelt, "The Japanese in Korea," 293; Roosevelt to Terauchi, January 4, 1915, TRP, reel 357; Roosevelt to Kaneko, February 13, 1915, TRP, reel 358.

24. George H. Blakeslee, "Introduction," *Journal of Race Development* 1, no. 1 (July 1910): 1.

25. Robert Vitalis, *White World Order, Black Power Politics: The Birth of American International Relations* (Ithaca, NY: Cornell University Press, 2015), 17–19, 45–47, 71–72.

26. Blakeslee, "Introduction," 1; Nitobe Inazo, "Japan as a Colonizer," *Journal of Race Development* 2, no. 4 (April 1912): 347–361; Iyenaga Toyokichi, "Japan's Annexation of Korea," *Journal of Race Development* 3, no. 2 (October 1912): 201–223. On Blakeslee, see Brian Masaru Hayashi, "From Race to Nation: The Institute of Pacific Relations, Asia Americans, and George Blakeslee, from 1908 to 1929," *Japanese Journal of American Studies* 3 (2012): 51–71.

27. Ladd, "A Year of 'Benevolent Assimilation,'" *Journal of Race Development* 4, no. 3 (January 1914): 377; Takahira Kogorō to Ladd, May 14, 1908, box 5, folder 1, George Trumbull Ladd Papers, Yale University Archives, New Haven, CT. William McKinley, quoted in Kramer, *Blood of Government*, 110.

28. Kawakami, *American-Japanese Relations: An Inside View of Japan's Policies and Purposes* (New York: Fleming H. Revell Company, 1912), 143–281.

29. Cemil Aydin, "Taraknath Das: Pan-Asian Solidarity as a 'Realist' Grand Strategy, 1917–1918," in *Pan-Asianism: A Documentary History*, ed. Sven Saaler and Christopher W. A. Szpilman (Lanham, MD: Rowman & Littlefield, 2011), 1: 305–310.

30. Taraknath Das, *Is Japan a Menace to Asia?* (Shanghai: The author, 1917), 31, 34, 51; *Annual Report on Reforms and Progress in Chosen (Korea) (1914–1915)* (Keijo: Government General of Chosen, 1916), 155–156.

31. "Japanese Persecution in Korea," *Missionary Review of the World* 35, no. 3 (March 1912): 163; "The Persecution in Korea," *Chicago Continent*, June 13, 1912, 814, 842–843; "Japan's Clash with Korean Missions," *Literary Digest* 44, no. 11 (March 16, 1912): 536–537. Many of the missionaries' private letters can be found at the Presbyterian Historical Society, Philadelphia. See RG 140, box 16, folders 9–11, PHS-KM. For the Japanese colonial government's coverage of the Korean Conspiracy Case trial, see "Yun Ch'i-ho tŭng ŭi kongp'an'gi," *Maeil Sinbo*, May 10, 1912, 3; "Yun Ch'i-ho tŭng ŭi sanggo," *Maeil Sinbo*, March 23, 1913, 2.

32. Chang Sŏk-hŭng, "Ilje ŭi singminji ŏllon jŏngch'aek kwa ch'ongdokpu kigwanji 'maeil sinbo' ŭi sŏnggyŏk," *Han'guk tongnip undongsa yŏn'gu*, no. 6 (December 1992): 409–456.

33. "Miil kukche ŭi changnae," 1.

34. On the Korean Conspiracy Case, see Yun Kyŏng-no, *105-in sakŏn kwa sinminhoe yŏn'gu* (Seoul: Ilchisa, 1990); Alexis Dudden, *Japan's Colonization of Korea: Discourse and Power* (Honolulu: University of Hawai'i Press, 2005), 121–29; Jimin Kim, "Representing the Invisible: The American Perceptions of Colonial Korea (1910–1945)" (PhD diss., Columbia University, New York, 2011), 90–100; Yeon-seung Lee, "Between Nationalism and Internationalism: Yun Ch'i-ho and the YMCA in Colonial Korea" (PhD diss., Boston University School of Theology, 2011), 347–358.

35. Chung-shin Park, *Protestantism and Politics in Korea* (Seattle: University of Washington Press, 2003), 30–36.

36. Underwood to Arthur Judson Brown, March 25, 1912, in *Ŏndŏudŭ Charyojip*, ed. Ok Sŏng-dŭk and Yi Man-yŏl (Seoul: Yonsei University Press, 2009), 4: 440–452.

37. Brown to Chinda Sutemi, May 31, 1912, reprinted as "X." in the document titled "Correspondence of the Presbyterian Board of Foreign Missions with the Japanese Embassy in Washington," 29, WHTP, series 6, reel 444.

38. March 11, 1893, *YCHI*, 3: 43–44; Yun to Young J. Allen, March 16, 1893, *YCHS*, 70–72.

39. Candler to Yun, December 2, 1906, December 4, 1906, February 5, 1907, all in box 17, folder 3, YCHP. Yun to Candler, April 16, 1907, *YCHS*, 158–161.

40. Jang Wook Huh, "The Student's Hand: Industrial Education and Racialized Labor in Early Korean Protestantism," *Journal of Korean Studies* 25, no. 2 (October 2020): 364–365.

41. Candler to Yun, February 5, 1907; "Personal Mention," *Christian Advocate* 85, no. 32 (August 11, 1910): 1134.

42. "Yun Ch'i-ho ssi rŭl hwanyŏngham," *Sinhan Minbo*, February 2, 1910, 1; "Provisional Program for Laymen's Conference," *Dallas Morning News*, February 6, 1910, 22; "The Laymen's Meeting Closes in Memphis," *Jonesboro Evening Sun*, February 10, 1910, 1; "Laymen's Missionary Movement Meetings," *New Orleans Daily Picayune*, February 14, 1910, 4; "Methodist Laymen in Convention at Dallas," *Galveston Daily News*, February 20, 1910, 3; "Life Sketch of Distinguished Korean," *Nashville Tennessean*, February 20, 1910, A1; "Japan Appreciates Help of Americans," *Fort Worth Star-Telegram*, March 4, 1910, 5; "In Honor of Prince Yun," *Muskogee Times-Democrat*, March 8, 1910, 1; "Korean Prince Visits State," *Montgomery Advertiser*, March 22, 1910, 7; "Dr. Yun Pays High Tribute to His Georgia Alma Mater," *Atlanta Constitution*, April 3, 1910, C8.

43. Brian Stanley, *The World Missionary Conference, Edinburgh 1910* (Grand Rapids, MI: William. B. Eerdmans Publishing, 2009), 118–121.

44. Augustus Bacon to Warren Akin Candler, May 25, 1912, box 10, folder 5, WCP.

45. "Denies Torture in Korea," *Washington Post*, June 8, 1912, 4; "Hope to Save Baron Yun," *Washington Post*, June 15, 1912, 6.

46. "The Korean Situation: Representatives of Mission Boards in Washington, July 29, 1912," RG 140, box 16, folder 10, PHS-KM; "Seek Aid for Koreans," *Washington Post*, July 30, 1912, 12.

47. Alexis Dudden, *Japan's Colonization*, 125. The list of attendees is available in "Minutes of Confidential Conference on the Situation in Korea," October 11, 1912, box 1, folder 4, Korean Conspiracy Case Papers, Burke Library Archives, Union Theological Seminary, New York.

48. On Brown and Foster at The Hague in 1907, see Benjamin Allen Coates, *Legalist Empire: International Law and American Foreign Relations in the Early Twentieth Century* (New York: Oxford University Press, 2016), 86–106.

49. Roosevelt to Eliot, April 4, 1904, in *LTR*, 4: 767–770; Eliot, *Some Roads Towards the Peace: A Report to the Trustees of the Carnegie Endowment on Observations Made in China and Japan in 1912* (Washington, DC: Carnegie Endowment for International Peace, 1913), 46.

50. Brown, *Report on a Second Visit to China, Japan, and Korea 1909* (New York: Board of Foreign Missions of the Presbyterian Church in the U.S.A., 1909), 64, 70, 75–76. See also Brown, "The New Japan," *Journal of Race Development* 3, no. 1 (July 1912): 82–94; Brown, "The Japanese in Korea," *Outlook* 96 (November 12, 1910): 591–595.

51. Brown, *The Korean Conspiracy Case* (Northfield, MA: Northfield Press, 1912), 24, 27.

52. Ibid., 24–25.

53. The MECS was represented by another bishop of the church, W. R. Lambuth, who also personally knew Yun from his student days.

54. Mark K. Bauman, *Warren Akin Candler: The Conservative as Idealist* (Metuchen, NJ: Scarecrow Press, 1981); Morris L. Davis, *The Methodist Unification: Christianity and the Politics of Race in the Jim Crow Era* (New York: New York University Press, 2008).

55. Candler continued to pressure the Japanese embassy through Representative William Sulzer. See Chinda Sutemi to Sulzer, August 1, 1912, box 10, folder 8, WCP. On the MECS's attitude toward Yun's incarceration after the sentencing, see C. F. Reid, *Yun Chi Ho, the Korean Patriot and Christian Educator* (Nashville, TN: Publication House of the Methodist Episcopal Church, South, 1914), available in John R. Mott Papers, box 101, folder: Yun Chi Ho, Yale Divinity Library, New Haven, CT.

56. "Prince Yun at Tuskegee," *Montgomery Advertiser*, March 24, 1910, 7.

57. Yun to Candler, October 22, 1895; January 23, 1896, *YCHS*, 115–117, 122–126. On Yun's cabinet appointments, see *KS*, May 10, 1895, art. 6; May 20, 1895, art. 2. It is possible that Yun first learned about Washington due to the popularity of the "Atlanta Compromise" speech, which the American delivered on September 18, 1895.

58. *KS*, December 1, 1905, art. 5.

59. "Report of the Anglo-Korean School—Song Do," *Korea Mission Field* 4, no. 11 (November 1908): 166–168; T. H. Yun, "A Plea for Industrial Training," 185–188. Yun also served as the principal of the Taesŏng School, established by the anti-colonial group Shinminhoe, and this school was forced to close after the Conspiracy Case.

60. May 6, 1906, *YCHI*, 6: 227–229; Yi T'ae-hun, "1900 nyŏndae chŏnban 'taehanjeguk pip'anseryŏk' ŭi tongyang kwa chŏngch'ijŏk kyŏljipkwajŏng," *Yŏksa wa sirhak* 73 (November 2020): 289–292.

61. Kumamoto Shigekichi, "Puk'an chibang e issŏsŏ ŭi kidokkyo hakkyo shich'al pongmyŏng," December 5, 1908, no. 1, TM, Vol. 8.

62. Robert E. Park, "Tuskegee International Conference on the Negro," *Journal of Race Development* 3 (July 1912): 117–120. On the importation of Booker T. Washington's industrial education to Africa, see Louis Harlan, "Booker T. Washington and the White Man's Burden," *American Historical Review* 71, no. 2 (January 1966): 441–467; Sven Beckert, "From Tuskegee to Togo: The Problem of Freedom in the Empire of Cotton," *Journal of American History* 92, no. 2 (September 2005): 498–526.

63. Bureau of Education, *The Chosen Educational Ordinance and Various Attendant Regulations* (Keijo, Korea: Government General of Chosen, 1912), 1.

64. David Fort Godshalk, *Veiled Visions: The 1906 Atlanta Race Riot and the Reshaping of American Race Relations* (Chapel Hill: University of North Carolina Press, 2005), 187–207; Robert J. Norrell, *Up from Slavery: The Life of Booker T. Washington* (Cambridge, MA: Belknap Press of Harvard University Press, 2009), 340–345.

65. Washington to Masaoka Naochi, December 5, 1912, quoted in Marc Gallicchio, *The African American Encounter with Japan and China: Black Internationalism in Asia, 1895–1945* (Chapel

Hill: University of North Carolina Press, 2000), 14; "An Address before the National Negro Business League," August 8, 1915, *BTWP*, 13: 348.

66. Government-General of Chosen, *Annual Report on Reforms and Progress in Chosen (Korea)* (1914–1915) (Keijō, 1916), 47; Ladd, "Japan in the Orient. Part One: Korea," *Journal of Race Development* 6 (October 1915): 141; "Ponsajang ul pangmunhan Yun Ch'i-ho ssi," *Maeil Sinbo*, March 14, 1915, 3.

67. January 17, 1919, January 18, 1919, January 28, 1919, *YCHI*, 7: 236–237, 242. When he was questioned by the colonial government, Yun claimed that he had not been approached by the organizers of the independence movement, and he only mentioned that a student had approached him on March 1st to join the movement. See "Yun Ch'i-ho shinmunjosŏ," July 10, 1919, HTUC, Vol. 11. On Yun's work with the YMCA, see Lee, "Between Nationalism and Internationalism," 359–365.

68. Baldwin, "The March First Movement," 14–77.

69. Yun Ch'i-ho, "Senjin no tame ni kanashimu," *Keijō Nippō*, March 7, 1919 (morning edition), 3; Yun Ch'i-ho, "Chosŏnin ŭl wihayŏ pigŭk," *Maeil Sinbo*, March 8, 1919, 2; March 2, 1919, *YCHI*, 7: 261–262.

70. March 8 and March 10, 1919, *YCHI*, 7: 266–267. On the distribution of the flyer denouncing Yun in Seoul, see "Nam Wi shinmunjosŏ," March 14, 1919, HTUC, Vol. 14. One Korean missionary for the Japanese Congregational Church named Yu Sŏk-u later testified at the Seoul district court that he himself had been dissuaded from joining the uprising after reading Yun's statement published in the *Keijō Nippō*. See "Yu Sŏk-u shinmunjosŏ," Seoul district court, June 7, 1919, HTUC, Vol. 17.

71. For the use of "treacherous" to describe Yun, see "Miju hawai tongp'o nŭn ie pansŏng hasio," *Sinhan Minbo*, April 29, 1919, 3. See also "Tongnip ssaum ŭi sosik," *Sinhan Minbo*, April 10, 1919, 2.

72. July 31, 1919, *YCHI*, 7: 352; "Sin Hŭng-u Kim Dŭk-su rangssi ŭi t'aedo," *Sinhan Minbo*, July 1, 1919, 3.

73. January 27, 1920, *YCHI*, 8: 15. Yun is quoting from "An Address on Abraham Lincoln before the Republican Club of New York City," February 12, 1909, *BTWP*, 10: 33–39.

74. July 31, 1919; August 11, 1919; September 1, 1919, *YCHI*, 7: 353, 359, 370–371.

75. Kim Kiu Sik, "Hon. Mr. Yun Tchi Ho," *Korea Mission Field* 6 (August 1910): 197–199. Kim Kiu Sik is an alternative spelling of Kim Kyu-shik (who usually romanized his name in English as Kim Kiusic). On Kim's mission to Paris, see Baldwin, "March First Movement," 143–148.

76. "Mr. T. H. Yun's New Policy," *Freedom and Peace with Korea under Japan?* 1 (March 1919): 10. This publication would change its name to the *Korea Review*.

77. "Minjok chagyŏl chuŭi e taehayŏ," *Sinhan Minbo*, January 23, 1919, 1; "Hŭgindŭl do p'aerisŭ esŏ hwaltong," *Sinhan Minbo*, June 26, 1919, 1. On Trotter's mission to Paris, see Kerri K. Greenidge, *Black Radical: The Life and Times of William Monroe Trotter* (New York: Liverlight, 2020), 264–269.

78. John Milton Cooper Jr., "'An Irony of Fate': Woodrow Wilson's Pre–World War I Diplomacy," *Diplomatic History* 3, no. 4 (October 1979): 425–438; Link, *Woodrow Wilson and the Progressive Era*, 81–106.

79. Manela, *Wilsonian Moment*, 4, 10.

80. An Address to a Joint Session of Congress, January 8, 1918, *PWW*, 45: 536–537. Emphasis added.

81. Charles E. Neu, *Colonel House: A Biography of Woodrow Wilson's Silent Partner* (New York: Oxford University Press, 2015), 368–369.

82. On Lippmann and the Inquiry, see Ronald Steel, *Walter Lippmann and the American Century* (Boston: Little, Brown, 1980), 128–140. On Lippmann and the Inquiry memorandum's influence on the drafting of the Fourteen Points, see Trygve Throntveit, "The Fable of the Fourteen Points: Woodrow Wilson and National Self-Determination," *Diplomatic History* 35, no. 3 (June 2011): 461–470. The Inquiry memorandum is available as A Memorandum by Sidney Edward Mezes, David Hunter Miller, and Walter Lippmann, December 22, 1917, *PWW*, 45: 459–474.

83. The Lippmann-Cobb report is available as "Three Telegrams from Edward Mandell House," October 29, 1918, *PWW*, 51: 497.

84. Ibid.

85. Ibid.

86. For the list of nine experts on colonial issues, see Lawrence E. Gelfand, *The Inquiry: American Preparations for Peace, 1917–1919* (New Haven, CT: Yale University Press, 1963), 63–65. Blakeslee was in charge of the Pacific islands, political scientist Stanley Hornbeck China, and political scientist W. W. McLaren Japan.

87. Wilson to House, October 30, 1918, *PWW*, 51: 511; Manela, *Wilsonian Moment*, 40–41; Throntveit, "The Fable of the Fourteen Points," 469. See A Memorandum by Sidney Edward Mezes, David Hunter Miller, and Walter Lippmann, *PWW*, 45: 464.

88. Arthur S. Link, *The Higher Realism of Woodrow Wilson and Other Essays* (Nashville, TN: Vanderbilt University Press, 1971), 72–87; Betty Unterberger, "The United States and National Self-Determination: A Wilsonian Perspective," *Presidential Studies Quarterly* 26, no. 4 (Fall 1996): 292; Thomas J. Knock, *To End All Wars: Woodrow Wilson and the Quest for a New World Order* (New York: Oxford University Press, 1992), vii–viii, 43–55, 143–146.

89. Arno Mayer, *Wilson vs. Lenin: Political Origins of the New Diplomacy, 1917–1918* (Cleveland, OH: World, 1964 [1959]), 329–367; William Appleman Williams, *The Tragedy of American Diplomacy* (New York: W. W. Norton, 1972 [1959]), 90–107; N. Gordon Levin, *Woodrow Wilson and World Politics: America's Response to War and Revolution* (New York: Oxford University Press, 1968), 247–251.

90. "An Address to a Joint Session of Congress," February 11, 1918, *PWW*, 46: 321.

91. Mayer, *Wilson vs. Lenin*, 329–267.

92. Link, *The Higher Realism of Woodrow Wilson*, 77–78; Unterberger, "The United States and National Self-Determination," 929–932; Unterberger, "Woodrow Wilson and the Russian Revolution," in *Woodrow Wilson and a Revolutionary World, 1913–1921*, ed. Arthur Link (Chapel Hill: University of North Carolina Press, 1982), 49; John Milton Cooper, *Woodrow Wilson: A Biography* (New York: Alfred A. Knopf, 2009), 240–241, 417.

93. Kramer, *Blood of Government*, 344. The following year Wilson published this speech as part of his book *Constitutional Government in the United States* (1908). For this passage on self-government, see Wilson, *Constitutional Government in the United States*, *PWW*, 18: 104.

94. Lloyd E. Ambrosius, "World War I and the Paradox of Wilsonianism," *Journal of the Gilded Age and Progressive Era* 17, no. 1 (January 2018): 9.

95. Kramer, *Blood of Government*, 352.

96. *Government of the Philippines: Hearings before the Committee on the Philippines, United States Senate, Part 5*, 63rd Cong., 3rd sess. (Washington, DC: US Government Printing Office, 1915), 366; "Roosevelt Flouts League of Nations," *Washington Post*, August 4, 1918, 3, 15; Lloyd Gardner, *Safe for Democracy: The Anglo-American Response to Revolution, 1913–1923* (New York: Oxford University Press, 1987), 45–63; Lars Schoultz, *In Their Own Best Interest: A History of the U.S. Effort to Improve Latin Americans* (Cambridge, MA: Harvard University Press, 2018), 56–63; Teresa Elisabeth Homans Davis, "America for Humanity: Law, Liberalism and Empire in the South Atlantic (1870–1939)" (PhD diss., Princeton University, 2018), 210–215.

97. On the Jones Act, see Kramer, *Blood of Government*, 355, 362–363. For changes in the Philippine policy under Democrats, see Colin D. Moore, *American Imperialism and the State, 1893–1921* (Cambridge: Cambridge University Press, 2017), 231–260.

98. Maximo Manguiat Kalaw, *A Guide on the Philippine Question* (Washington, DC, 1919), 27–31. Harrison, quoted in ibid., 29.

99. Bernardita Reyes Churchill, "The Philippines Independence Missions to the United States (1919–1934)" (PhD diss., Australian National University, Canberra, 1981), 20–58.

100. "P'illip'in tongnim munje e taehayŏ," *Sinhan Minbo*, April 22, 1919, 1.

101. "Attitude of Japan Regarding Korea," *Atlanta Constitution*, April 16, 1919, 2; "Japan to Fight for Race Issue," *Washington Herald*, April 20, 1919, 16.

102. March 10, 1919; March 31, 1919; September 23, 1920, *YCHI*, 7: 267–268, 280, 8: 140.

103. Reo Matsuzaki, *Statebuilding by Imposition: Resistance and Control in Colonial Taiwan and the Philippines* (Ithaca, NY: Cornell University Press, 2019).

104. *Report of the Governor General of the Philippine Islands to the Secretary of the War 1919* (Washington, DC: Government Printing Press, 1920), 25; Yoshihiro Chiba, "The 1919 and

1935 Rice Crises in the Philippines: The Rice Market and Starvation in American Colonial Times," *Philippine Studies* 58, no. 4 (December 2010): 534–539; Alfred McCoy, *Policing America's Empire: The United States, the Philippines, and the Rise of the Surveillance State* (Madison: University of Wisconsin Press, 2009), 262–263.

105. "Egypt and Korea," *New York Times*, March 20, 1919, 12; Frank Polk to Roland Morris, April 14, 1919, 895.00/595, *FRUS 1919*, 2: 462; March 27, 1919, *YCHI*, 7: 278.

106. Kim, *Quest for Statehood*, 46–65; David K. Yoo, *Contentious Spirits: Religion in Korean American History, 1903–1945* (Stanford, CA: Stanford University Press, 2010), 99–101; Heather J. Sharkey, *American Evangelicals in Egypt: Missionary Encounters in an Age of Empire* (Princeton, NJ: Princeton University Press, 2008), 48–95.

107. June 22, 1919, *YCHI*, 7: 329.

108. William M. Tuttle Jr., *Race Riot: Chicago in the Red Summer of 1919* (New York: Atheneum, 1970); Adriane Lentz-Smith, *Freedom Struggles: African Americans and World War I* (Cambridge, MA: Harvard University Press, 2009), 194–199.

109. Arthur Judson Brown, *The Mastery of the Far East: The Story of Korea's Transformation and Japan's Rise to Supremacy in the Orient* (New York: Charles Scribner's Sons, 1919), 372, 342–343, 584.

110. Kim, *Quest for Statehood*, 62–63.

111. William Haven and Sidney Gulick, *The Korean Situation: Authentic Accounts of Recent Events by Eye Witnesses* (New York: Commission on Relations with the Orient, 1919), 6.

112. Sidney Gulick, "Religious Liberty during the Meiji Era," *Japan Evangelist* 19, no. 9 (September 1912): 438.

113. MacMurray to Lansing, March 8, 1919, 895.00/587; Morris to Lansing, March 21, 1919, 895.00/586, DS-IAK, reel 2.

114. Frederick Smith, "Japan Papers' View on U.S. Given Airing," *San Francisco Chronicle*, September 7, 1919, F5. In response to the violence of the Red Summer, the FCCCA established the Commission on Negro Churches and Race Relations, which held its first meeting in 1921. See RG 18, box 57, folder 3, PHS.

115. Naoko Shimazu, *Japan, Race and Equality: The Racial Equality Proposal of 1919* (London: Routledge, 1998), 30–31, 68–88, 138–143; Atkinson, *Burden of White Supremacy*, 166–172.

116. "Views and Reviews," *New York Age*, March 29, 1919, 4; "Views and Reviews," *New York Age*, May 24, 1919, 4. On Johnson, see Kearney, 57–62.

117. Yuichiro Onishi, *Transpacific Antiracism: Afro-Asian Solidarity in the 20th-Century Black America, Japan, and Okinawa* (New York: NYU Press, 2013), 39.

118. "The Looking Glass," *Crisis* 19, no. 1 (November 1919): 343–344. Original text is Y. Soga, "The Korean Question and the Negro Question," *Nippu Jiji*, August 25, 1919, 8 (English section).

119. "Ilbon shinmun kwa miguk sŏn'gyosa, hanin kwa miju hŭgin ŭl pigyo," *Sinhan Minbo*, September 9, 1919, 3. September 22, 1919, *YCHI*, 7: 382. For a representative coverage of the Red Summer in Korea, see "Karyonhan hŭgin ŭi unmyong," *Maeil Sinbo*, September 11, 1919, 3.

120. "Miin ŭi hŭgin taehaksal," *Maeil Sinbo*, December 15, 1919, 3. See also "Tol! Chŏngŭi indo ch'anmi ŭi kuk, kwisŏng ch'uch'u ŭi miguk," *Maeil Sinbo*, December 18, 1919, 3.

121. Michael D. Robinson, *Cultural Nationalism in Colonial Korea, 1920–1925* (Seattle: University of Washington Press, 1988); Eiji Oguma, *The Boundaries of "the Japanese,"* Vol. 2: *Korea, Taiwan and the Ainu, 1868–1945*, trans. Leonie R. Stickland (Victoria: Trans Pacific Press, 2017), 216–285.

122. Sin Chu-baek, "Ilje ŭi saeroun singminji chibae bangsik kwa chaejo ilbonin mit 'chach'i' seryŏk ŭi taeŭng (1919–22)," *Yŏksa wa hyŏnsil* 39 (2001): 35–68; Kim Tong-myŏng, "Singminji sidae ŭi chibang chach'i—pu(hyŏbŭi)hoe ŭi chŏngch'ijŏk chŏn'gae," *Hanil gwan'gyesa yŏn'gu* 17 (2002): 161–197.

123. Erik Esselstrom, *Crossing Empire's Edge: Foreign Ministry Police and Japanese Expansionism in Northeast Asia* (Honolulu: University of Hawai'i Press, 2008), 74–75.

Chapter 4

1. Kawakami to Gulick, June 25, 1919, reprinted in *Japanese Immigration: Hearings before the Committee on Immigration and Naturalization, House of Representatives, Sixty-Sixth Congress, Second Session, July 12, 13 and 14, 1920* (Washington, DC: Government Printing Office, 1921), 1: 16. Hereafter *Japanese Immigration Hearings* (1920).

2. V. S. McClatchy, "Korea's Play for Independence Is Direct Result of the War and Principles It Disseminated," *Sacramento Bee*, April 5, 1919, 1, 9. This was later republished as part of McClatchy's political pamphlet, *The Germany of Asia* (Sacramento, CA: Sacramento Bee, 1920), 15-19.

3. "Taehan tongnip sŏnŏnsŏ," *Sinhan Minbo*, April 5, 1919, 1.

4. McClatchy, *Germany of Asia*, 43.

5. John Higham, *Strangers in the Land: Patterns of American Nativism, 1860-1925* (New Brunswick, NJ: Rutgers University Press, 1988 [1955]), 316-324; Roger Daniels, *The Politics of Prejudice: The Anti-Japanese Movement in California* (Berkeley: University of California Press, 1977 [1962]), 92-105; Mae Ngai, *Impossible Subjects: Illegal Aliens and the Making of Modern America* (Princeton, NJ: Princeton University Press, 2004), 21-55.

6. Gordon H. Chang, "Asian Immigrants and American Foreign Relations," in *Pacific Passage: The Study of American-East Asian Relations on the Eve of the Twenty-First Century*, ed. Warren I. Cohen (New York: Columbia University Press, 1996), 103-118; Donna Gabaccia, *Foreign Relations: American Immigration in Global Perspective* (Princeton, NJ: Princeton University Press, 2012), esp. 22-23, 124-125; Paul Kramer, "The Geopolitics of Mobility: Immigration Policy and American Global Power in the Long Twentieth Century," *American Historical Review* 123, no. 2 (April 2018): 393-438.

7. Marilyn Lake and Henry Reynolds, *Drawing the Global Colour Line: White Men's Countries and the International Challenge of Racial Equality* (Cambridge: Cambridge University Press, 2008), 284-309; Kornel S. Chang, *Pacific Connections: The Making of the U.S.-Canadian Borderlands* (Berkeley: University of California Press, 2012), 89-116; David C. Atkinson, *The Burden of White Supremacy: Containing Asian Migration in the British Empire and the United States* (Chapel Hill: University of North Carolina Press, 2016), 192-219.

8. McClatchy invoked Canada, Australia, and New Zealand's immigration policies in *Percentage Plans for Restriction of Immigration: Hearings before the Committee on Immigration and Naturalization, House of Representatives* (Washington, DC: US Government Printing Office, 1919), 3: 242, 340.

9. *Japanese Immigration and Colonization: Skeleton Brief by Mr. V. S. McClatchy, Representative of the Japanese Exclusion League of California, on "Japanese Immigration and Colonization," Filed with the Secretary of the State*, 67th Cong., 1st Sess., Senate Document no. 55 (Washington, DC: US Government Printing Office, 1921), 122.

10. On the "Yellow Peril," see Daniels, *Politics of Prejudice*, 65-78; Erika Lee, "The 'Yellow Peril' and Asian Exclusion in the Americas," *Pacific Historical Review* 76, no. 4 (November 2007): 537-562.

11. *House Report No. 350* (House Committee Report on the Immigration Act of 1924), 68th Cong., 1st Sess., submitted March 24, 1924, 9.

12. Higham, *Strangers in the Land*, 300-330; Ngai, *Impossible Subjects*, 37-50.

13. Eiichiro Azuma, *Between Two Empires: Race, History, and Transnationalism in Japanese America* (New York: Oxford University Press, 2005); Richard S. Kim, *The Quest for Sovereignty: Korean Immigration Nationalism and U.S. Sovereignty, 1905-1945* (New York: Oxford University Press, 2011).

14. On James McClatchy, see Tamara Venit-Shelton, *A Squatter's Republic: Land and the Politics of Monopoly in California, 1850-1900* (Berkeley: University of California Press, 2013), 37-98.

15. On C. K. McClatchy and the anti-Japanese movements, see Cecilia Tsu, *Garden of the World: Asian Immigrants and the Making of Agriculture in California's Santa Clara Valley* (New York: Oxford University Press, 2013), 112.

16. V. S. McClatchy was mostly occupied with land reclamation before the war. See his letters to Hiram Johnson, part II, box 22, folder McClatchy, Valentine Stuart, 1857-1938, HJP.

17. McClatchy's economic argument can be found in *Germany of Asia*, 22, 25, 41, 43. His Hawaiianization argument can be found in ibid., 27–28, 44–45. His complaints about Japanese birth rates can be found in ibid., 22, 26, 29–30, 32–34. On V. S. McClatchy and anti-Japanese movements, see Daniels, *Politics of Prejudice*, 91–99; Tsu, *Garden of the World*, 123–127. Michael Joseph Meloy, "The Long Road to Manzanar: Politics, Land, and Race in the Japanese Exclusion Movement, 1900–1942" (PhD diss., University of California, Davis, 2004), 154–200.

18. "McClatchy in the Sacramento Bee Writes on the Japanese Question Says Dillingham Bill More Dangerous than Gulick's," *Organized Labor*, September 13, 1919, 8.

19. Rowell to Meyer Lissner, June 10, 1919, box 24, folder Rowell, C. H. #9, 1919, MLP.

20. Rowell, "California and the Japanese Problem," *New Republic* 24, no. 302 (September 15, 1920): 64–65; Rowell to Lissner, January 27, 1920, box 24, folder Rowell, C. H. #9, 1919, MLP; Rowell to Gotō Shinpei, November 29, 1919, box 4, folder 1919, Aug-Dec, CHRP.

21. McClatchy, *Germany of Asia*, 6, 14–15.

22. Ibid., 3, 15–19. McClatchy's *Sacramento Bee* article was also published as "Korean Uprising an Unarmed Revolution," *San Francisco Examiner*, April 6, 1919, 1, 4.

23. "Taehan tongnip sŏnŏnsŏ," *Sinhan Minbo*, April 5, 1919, 1, and April 8, 1919, 1.

24. "Han'guk i pulgŭn chumŏk ŭro hyŏngmyŏng han kŏsŭl mokkyŏnhan cha ŭi mal," *Sinhan Minbo*, April 8, 1919, 2; "Maekk'ŭllaelch'wi ssi ga moktohan pulgŭn chumŏk ŭro irŏnan han'guk hyŏngmyŏng ŭi chinsang (2)," *Sinhan Minbo*, April 10, 1919, 3; "Maekk'ŭllaelch'wi ssi ga moktohan pulgŭn chumŏk ŭro irŏnan han'guk hyŏngmyŏng ŭi chinsang (3)," *Sinhan Minbo*, April 12, 1919, 3.

25. Syngman Rhee to V. S. McClatchy, June 11, 1919, *SMRCE*, 1: 115. On the First Korean Congress and the Korean Commission in Washington, DC, see Kim, *Quest for Statehood*, 46–90.

26. McClatchy to Rhee, June 30, 1919, and December 13, 1919, *SMRCE*, 2: 238–239, 287. McClatchy also corresponded with Kim Kyu-sik, the lone Korean anti-colonial activist who made it to Paris during the peace conference in 1919. See David Fields, *Foreign Friends: Syngman Rhee, American Exceptionalism, and the Division of Korea* (Lexington: University Press of Kentucky, 2019), 80.

27. McClatchy, *Germany of Asia*, 16–17, quoted in *Congressional Record—Senate*, 66th Cong., 1st Sess., September 19, 1919, 5606–5607.

28. McClatchy to William E. Mason, December 11, 1919, *SMRCE*, 4: 588–589.

29. "Korea's Cause Lost, Says Sacramentan," *San Francisco Chronicle*, April 3, 1919, 11; McClatchy, *Germany of Asia*, 18.

30. McClatchy, "Indisputable Facts and Figures," *Grizzly Bear* 26, no. 2 (December 1919): 1. This was also published in McClatchy, *Germany of Asia*, 43.

31. E. Kosterlitzky, Report on the Anti-Asiatic League for June 3–8, 1920, 2. Old German Files 1909–1921, Case: Japanese Activities (389267), BOICF, reel 847.

32. *Japanese Immigration Hearings* (1920), 3: 1037–1038.

33. Elwood Mead, "The Japanese Land Problem of California," *Annals of the American Academy of Political and Social Science* 93 (January 1921): 54.

34. *Congressional Record—Senate*, 66th Cong., 1st Sess., October 1, 1919, 6172; Kim, *Quest for Statehood*, 64.

35. On Phelan, see Daniels, *Politics of Prejudice*, 21, 81–83; Lon Kurashige, *Two Faces of Exclusion: The Untold History of Anti-Asian Racism in the United States* (Chapel Hill: University of North Carolina Press, 2016), 95, 111.

36. Johnson to C. K. McClatchy, March 22, 1919; Johnson to C. K. McClatchy, April 7, 1919, part III, box 2, reel 11, HJP.

37. *Congressional Record—Senate*, 66th Cong., 1st Sess., June 2, 1919, 505.

38. *Congressional Record—Senate*, 66th Cong., 1st Sess., July 17, 1919, 2734–2735. On Borah's isolationist internationalism, see Christopher McKnight Nichols, *Promise and Peril: America at the Dawn of a Global Age* (Cambridge, MA: Harvard University Press, 2011), 229–272.

39. *Congressional Record—Senate*, 66th Cong., 1st Sess., October 13, 1919, 6810. On Norris and Borah's mentioning of Korea, see Fields, *Foreign Friends*, 90–95.

40. *Congressional Record—Senate*, 66th Cong., 1st Sess., November 18, 1919, 8727–8728.

41. "Taehanmin'guk ŭi tongnip ŭl wŏnjo, indo chŏngŭi e tangdanghan p'illaen sangŭiwŏn," *Sinhan Minbo*, October 2, 1919, 1; "U.S. Senate Resolution for Korea," *Korea Review* 1, no. 8 (October 1919), 13. The KNA closely followed the Senate debate over the Treaty of Paris, especially the parts that mentioned Korea. See, for example, "Miguk sangŭiwŏn ŭi t'oron, ilbon ŭi han'guk e taehan chŏngch'aek ŭl kongbak," *Sinhan Minbo*, July 29, 1919, 4.

42. Y. Sōga, "Anti-Japanese Senator and the Korean Question," *Nippu Jiji*, October 7, 1919, 8. Sōga's familiarity with the exclusionists' deployment of the news of Japanese violence in Korea is evident in his newspaper clippings. See box 155, folder 2, YIP.

43. *Korea and Shantung versus the White Peril/The Anti-Japanese Agitation in California* (Keijō, Korea: Seoul Press, 1920), 26; "Colonel Irish Speaks," *Nichibei Shinbum*, June 26, 1920, 5. On John P. Irish, see Kurashige, *Two Faces of Exclusion*, 117, 119–120.

44. On Gulick, see Sandra C. Taylor, *Advocate of Understanding: Sidney Gulick and the Search for Peace with Japan* (Kent, OH: Kent State University Press, 1984), 78–127; Kurashige, *Two Faces of Exclusion*, 102–104, 114–115; David Hollinger, *Protestants Abroad: How Missionaries Tried to Change the World but Changed America* (Princeton, NJ: Princeton University Press, 2017), 139–143.

45. *Percentage Plans for Restriction of Immigration*, 1: 5–26.

46. Robert Newton Lynch to Sidney Gulick, July 25, 1919, box 18, file 1919 July; Wallace R. Farrington to Gulick, June 2, 1919, box 18, folder 1919 June, GFP.

47. Gulick to V. S. McClatchy, June 27, 1919, box 18, folder 1919 June, GFP; William Haven and Sidney Gulick, *The Korean Situation: Authentic Accounts of Recent Events by Eye Witnesses* (New York: Commission on Relations with the Orient of the Federal Council of the Churches of Christ in America, 1919).

48. *Percentage Plans for Restriction of Immigration*, 8; Gulick, "Recent Events in Korea and Their Effect on American Opinion," box 18, folder 1919 Apr., GFP.

49. "Sŏllyanghan yesugyododŭliyo! ijenŭn onyuhan irin ŭl ŏtchi saenggak hanŭnga?," *Sinhan Minbo*, August 7, 1919, 2; "Sangŭiwon pil ssi ga gulick ŭl kongbak," *Sinhan Minbo*, August 19, 1919, 1.

50. *Japanese Immigration Hearings* (1920), 1: 243.

51. McClatchy to Gulick, August 25, 1919, box 18, folder August 1919, GFP.

52. Tasuku Harada, ed., *The Japanese Problem in California: Answers (by Representative Americans) to Questionnaire* (San Francisco: printed for private circulation, 1922), 22, 41, 58, 65, 67, 83.

53. "Chinese Labour in Japan," *Japan Chronicle* (weekly edition), January 16, 1919, 79; "Racial Discrimination," *Japan Chronicle* (weekly edition), February 27, 1919, 299–300. McClatchy mentions that he encountered the story in the *Japan Chronicle* in *Percentage Plans for Restriction of Immigration*, 263–264.

54. *Percentage Plans for Restriction of Immigration*, 1: 36, 264.

55. *Illegal Entry of Aliens: Hearing before the Committee on Immigration United States Senate, Sixty-sixth Congress, First Session Pursuant to S. Res. 176* (Washington, DC: US Government Printing Office, 1919), 41.

56. Keizo Yamawaki, "Foreign Workers in Japan: A Historical Perspective," in *Japan and Global Migration: Foreign Workers and the Advent of a Multicultural Society*, ed. Mike Douglass and Glenda S. Roberts (London and New York: Routledge, 2000), 38–51; Michael Weiner, *Race and Migration in Imperial Japan* (London and New York: Routledge, 1994), 52–54; Ken C. Kawashima, *The Proletarian Gamble: Korean Workers in Interwar Japan* (Durham, NC: Duke University Press, 2009), 28–40.

57. An English translation of the Imperial Ordinance No. 352 is available as "Japanese Law of 1899, Placing Restrictions on the Residence of Foreign Laborers in the Interior of Japan," *American Journal of International Law* 1, no. 4 (October 1907): 414–415. The best explanation of the ordinance can be found in Saburo Yamada, *Legal Status of Aliens in Japan* (Tokyo: Japan Council of the Institute of Pacific Relations, 1931), 11–12; Eric C. Han, "The Nationality Law and Entry Restrictions of 1899: Constructing Japanese Identity between China and the West," *Japan Forum* 30, no. 4 (December 2018): 531–538.

58. Yamada, *Legal Status of Aliens in Japan*, 12; Yamawaki, "Foreign Workers in Japan," 44–46; Kawashima, *Proletarian Gamble*, 39.

59. On the creation of the American national immigration regulation system during this period, see Erika Lee, *At America's Gates: Chinese Immigration during the Exclusion Era, 1882–1943* (Chapel Hill: University of North Carolina Press, 2003), 47–74.

60. Secretary of State to Japanese Ambassador, July 16, 1913, *FRUS 1913*, 2: 642. On the deportation incident, see Chargé d'Affaires to Secretary of State, October 12, 1907, *FRUS 1907*, 2: 769–770.

61. David Starr Jordan to V. S. McClatchy, July 11, 1919, box 72, folder McClatchy, V. S. 1919–1935, DSJP.

62. John Dewey and Alice Chipman Dewey, *Letters from China and Japan* (New York: E. P. Dutton & Company, 1920), 52, 123, 75. On Dewey's time in Japan, see John Thares Davidann, *Cultural Diplomacy in U.S.-Japanese Relations, 1919–1941* (New York: Palgrave Macmillan, 2007), 46–50. On their time in China, see Gordon H. Chang, *Fateful Ties: A History of America's Preoccupation with China* (Cambridge, MA: Harvard University Press, 2015), 124–131.

63. *Percentage Plans for Restriction of Immigration*, 1: 178; *Japanese Immigration Hearings* (1920), 2: 637.

64. William I. Traeger, "Jap Question to the People," *Grizzly Bear* 26, no. 6 (April 1920): 24; George J. Burns, "Japan a Diplomatic Bluffer," *Grizzly Bear* 27, no. 1 (May 1920): 1; McClatchy's 1920 testimony in front of the House committee was published as *Our New Racial Problem* (Sacramento, CA: Sacramento Bee, 1920), box 1, folder 8, SRRR.

65. J. M. Inman, "The Time Has Arrived to Eliminate the Japs as California Landholders," *Grizzly Bear* 27, no. 2 (June 1920): 4.

66. "Japanese Law Relating to Foreigners' Right of Ownership in Land," *American Journal of International Law* 5, no. 3 (July 1911): 175–177; *California and the Oriental: Japanese, Chinese, and Hindus, Report of State Board of Control of California to Gov. Wm. D. Stephens* (Sacramento: California State Printing Office, 1920), 68–69, 72.

67. *Amendments to Constitution and Proposed Statutes with Arguments Respecting the Same, to Be Submitted to the Electors of the State of California at the General Election on Tuesday, November 2, 1920*, 5. https://repository.uchastings.edu/ca_ballot_props/150/.

68. Elwood Mead, "New Agrarian Policies in Australia and California," in *Must We Fight Japan?*, ed. Walter Pitkin (New York: The Century Co., 1921), 474; "Address by Mr. Lothrop Stoddard," *Boston City Club Bulletin* 15, no. 6 (March 1, 1921): 166.

69. T. Iyenaga, "Is Japan Hostile to Foreigners?," *Current History* 15, no. 2 (November 1, 1921): 214–217.

70. Kiichi Kanzaki, "Is the Japanese Menace in America a Reality?," *Annals of the American Academy of Political and Social Science* 93 (January 1921): 88–89. George Shima, the "Potato King," similarly argued that the Japanese immigration issue should be treated as a "purely local matter," "independently of Japanese policy in the Far East." See Shima, *A Farmer's View of the Question* (1920), available in carton 29, folder 20, JDPP.

71. Kawakami, "Japan versus Germany," *Outlook* 108 (September 16, 1914): 128–129; "What Can Japan Do for China?," *Independent* 82 (May 17, 1915): 280–281; "Shall America Prepare against Japan?," *North American Review* 203 (May 1916): 675–689; "Japan and the United States," *Atlantic Monthly* 119 (May 1917): 671–681.

72. Montaville Flowers, *The Japanese Conquest of American Opinion* (New York: George H. Doran Co., 1917), 119–127.

73. Kawakami to Rowell, July 9, 1919, box 18, folder Kawakami, Kiyoshi K., CHRP. On Gotō's tour, see "Baron Goto on U.S. Tour," *Washington Post*, March 18, 1919, 6; "Attitude of Japan Regarding Korea," *Atlanta Constitution*, April 16, 1919, 1–2.

74. Kawakami, "China and the Shantung Question," *Japan* 8, no. 12 (September 1919): 21; "Japan's Acts in China," *North American Review* 210, no. 768 (November 1919): 634.

75. Kawakami, "What Japan Has Done in Korea," *Japan* 9, no. 2 (November 1919): 20–23, 42.

76. Kawakami to Sidney Gulick, June 25, 1919, reprinted in *Japanese Immigration Hearings* (1920), 1: 16. Gulick's reply, dated July 1913, reprinted in Kawakami, *Senator Phelan, Doctor Gulick, and I* (San Francisco: Bureau of Literary Service, 1920), 8–9, JUSPC. On the Kawakami letter, see Taylor, *Advocate of Understanding*, 138–141.

77. *Japanese Immigration Hearings* (1920), 2: 602.

78. Edw. P. Morse, Weekly Intelligence Bulletin of San Francisco District, October 16, 1920, 4, Old German Files, 1909–1921, Case: Japanese Matters (311343), BOICF, reel 731. The three pamphlets were *Facts in the Case: A Statement upon the Report of the State Board of Control* (San Francisco: Japanese Association of America, 1920); John P. Irish, *The Anti-Japanese Pogrom: Facts versus the Falsehoods of Senator Phelan and Others* (self-pub., 1920); *Waving the Yellow Flag in California* (n.p.: Dearborn Independent, n.d.).

79. A. A. Hopkins and E. Kosterlitzky, Weekly Report on Los Angeles District, November 1, 1920, 1, Bureau Section Files, 1909–1921, Case: Japanese Affairs (202600-5), BOICF, reel 919.

80. "Regarding Land Laws in Japan—Kawakami Asserts Foreigners Have Free Hand," *Sacramento Bee*, October 21, 1920; "Use of Land Permitted Foreigners in Japan—Mr. Kawakami Further Explains," *Sacramento Bee*, November 1, 1920, reprinted in *Alien Land Laws and Alien Rights*, House of Representatives Document no. 89, 67th Cong., 1st Sess. (Washington, DC: US Government Printing Office, 1921), 10–13. McClatchy's responses are printed in ibid., 11–14.

81. Yuji Ichioka, *The Issei: The World of the First Generation Japanese Immigrants, 1885–1924* (New York: Free Press, 1988), 209; Eiichiro Azuma, "Dancing with the Rising Sun: Strategic Alliance between Japanese Immigrants and Their 'Home' Government," in *The Transnational Politics of Asian Americans*, ed. Christian Collet and Pei-te Lien (Philadelphia: Temple University Press, 2009), 30–31.

82. Kuno to David P. Barrows, October 30, 1916, carton 2, folder 1916, YKP. Yoshi S. Kuno, "Life in Japan," *Journal of Race Development* 6, no. 2 (October 1915): 192–202.

83. Kuno to Barrows, October 30, 1916, YKP. Gordon H. Chang, "Yamato Ichihashi: A Biographical Essay," in *Morning Glory, Evening Shadow: Yamato Ichihashi and His Internment Writings, 1942–1945*, ed. Gordon H. Chang (Stanford, CA: Stanford University Press, 1997), 23–39, 45.

84. Kuno's articles were published as *The Japanese Situation in California* (Oakland, CA: Tribune Publishing Co., 1920), in box 21, folder 7, SRRR. They were originally published as "Survey of the Japanese Question," from October 25 to October 30, 1920.

85. Kuno, *The Japanese Situation in California*, 6. Originally published as Kuno, "A Survey of the Japanese Situation," first installment, *Oakland Tribune*, October 25, 1920, 1.

86. "Japanese Deny Threat Charged by Prof. Kuno," *Oakland Tribune*, October 23, 1920, 3; Irish to editors of the *Oakland Tribune*, October 24, 1920, box 1, folder 9, John P. Irish Papers, Special Collections, Stanford University.

87. "Japanese War on Countrymen at University Because of His Defense of the United States," *San Francisco Chronicle*, October 23, 1920; "Prof. Kuno at U.C. Accuses His Own Race," *Los Angeles Examiner*, October 23, 1920, carton 6, folder News Clippings, YKP.

88. "Admits Japanese Maintain Tokyo Government Here," *Sacramento Bee*, October 29, 1920; "Japanese Exclude yet They Protest Exclusion Here," *Sacramento Bee*, October 28, 1920, carton 6, folder News Clippings, YKP.

89. McClatchy to Jordan, December 2, 1920, box 72, folder McClatchy, V. S. 1919–1935, DSJP.

90. Kuno to McClatchy, November 3, 1920, carton 2, folder 1920, YKP.

91. Ishibashi Tanzan, "Before Demanding the Abolition of Racial Discrimination," in *Sources of Japanese Tradition*, 2nd ed., eds Wm. Theodore de Bary, Carol Gluck, and Arthur E. Tiedemann (New York: Columbia University Press, 2005), 2: 568–569. On Ishibashi, see Eiji Oguma, *The Boundaries of "the Japanese,"* Vol. 2: *Korea, Taiwan and the Ainu, 1868–1945*, trans. Leonie R. Stickland (Victoria: Trans Pacific Press, 2017), 233–240. On Japanese expansionists' advocacy of settler colonialism, see Eiichiro Azuma, *In Search of Our Frontier: Japanese America and Settler Colonialism in the Construction of Japan's Borderless Empire* (Oakland: University of California Press, 2019).

92. Ichioka, *Issei*, 173–175.

93. Kell F. Mitchell Jr., "Diplomacy and Prejudice: The Morris-Shidehara Negotiations, 1920–1921," *Pacific Historical Review* 39, no. 1 (February 1970): 85–104.

94. McClatchy to Hiram Johnson, April 25, 1921; McClatchy to Charles Evans Hughes, May 5, 1921, enclosed in McClatchy to Johnson, May 6, 1921, part III, box 57, folder McClatchy, Valentine Stuart, February 1917–December 1924, HJP.

95. *Japanese Immigration and Colonization*, 3, 64–68.

96. Akiya Iriye, *After Imperialism: The Search for a New Order in the Far East, 1921–1931* (Cambridge, MA: Harvard University Press, 1965), 13–22; Sadao Asada, *From Mahan to Pearl Harbor: The Imperial Japanese Navy and the United States* (Annapolis MD: Naval Institute Press, 2006), 69–101; Frederick Dickinson, *World War I and the Triumph of a New Japan, 1919–1930* (Cambridge: Cambridge University Press, 2013), 64–66, 107–113.

97. *Papers Relating to Pacific and Far Eastern Affairs Prepared for the Use of the American Delegation to the Conference on the Limitation of Armament, Washington, 1921–1922* (Washington, DC: US Government Printing Office, 1922).

98. *Takao Ozawa v. United States*, 260 U.S. 178 (1922). See Ichioka, *Issei*, 219–226; Ian F. Haney Lopez, *White by Law: The Legal Construction of Race* (New York: New York University Press, 1996), 56–61.

99. *Webb v. O'Brien*, 263 U.S. 313 (1923). See *Documentary History of Law Cases Affecting Japanese in the United States, 1916–1924* (San Francisco: Consulate-General of Japan, San Francisco, 1925), 2: 130, 295.

100. Alfred J. Hillier, "Albert Johnson, Congressman," *Pacific Northwest Quarterly* 36, no. 3 (July 1945): 193–211.

101. The primary targets of this legislation were southern and eastern Europeans and Jews. Higham, *Strangers in the Land*, 308–311. Japan was not included in the 1921 quota law because section 2(a) of the statute declared it did not apply to "aliens from countries immigration from which is regulated in accordance with treaties or agreements relating solely to immigration."

102. McClatchy to Thomas N. Swale, August 22, 1923, attached to McClatchy to Phelan, August 23, 1923, box 45, folder 23, JDPP.

103. *House Report No. 350*, 9.

104. Memorandum by the Secretary of State of a Conversation with the Japanese Ambassador, March 27, 1924, *FRUS 1924*, 2: 337.

105. *Japanese Immigration Legislation: Hearings before the Committee on Immigration United States Senate*, 68th Cong., 1st Sess., on S. 2576 (Washington, DC: US Government Printing Office, 1924), 30–32.

106. *Japanese Immigration Legislation*, 111, 121.

107. *Congressional Record—Senate*, 68th Cong., 1st Sess., April 2, 1924, 5415. The amendment was introduced to the Senate on March 27, 1924, two weeks after the Senate Committee hearings. Hughes wrote the House Committee that Japan would be entitled to an annual immigration quota of 246 without the provision excluding "aliens ineligible to citizenship." Hughes to Albert Johnson, February 8, 1924, *FRUS 1924*, 1: 217.

108. "Johnson's End Seen by Press," *Los Angeles Times*, April 4, 1924, 5.

109. *Congressional Record—Senate*, 68th Cong., 1st Sess., April 2, 1924, 5410, 5415.

110. *Congressional Record—Senate*, 68th Cong., 1st Sess., April 7, 1924, 5747.

111. *Congressional Record—Senate*, 68th Cong., 1st Sess., April 8, 1924, 5805.

112. Report of the Secretary's Trip to Washington, January 20–22, 1924, folder: "Johnson, James Weldon, March–December 1923," Box I:C66 Reel 3, Part I: Administrative File, Special Correspondence, 1910–1939, Papers of the NAACP, Library of Congress.

113. Kurashige, *Two Faces of Exclusion*, 137; Micki McElya, *Clinging to Mammy: The Faithful Slave in Twentieth-Century* (Cambridge, MA: Harvard University Press, 2007), 197–201.

114. Phelan on S. S. Majestic, April 29, 1924, carton 29, folder 24, 1/1924–4/1924, JDPP.

115. Ibid.

116. *Congressional Record*, 68th Cong., 1st Sess., April 12, 1924, 6208–6209.

117. *Congressional Record*, 68th Cong., 1st Sess., April 14, 1924, 6304–6305.

118. Ibid., 6305.

119. Daniels, *Politics of Prejudice*, 100–103; Ngai, *Impossible Subjects*, 48–49.

120. "Congress and the Gentlemen's Agreement," attached to McClatchy to Phelan, April 21, 1924, box 46, folder 1, JDPP.

121. Memorandum by Hughes of a Conversation with Hanihara, May 1, 1924, *FRUS 1924*, 2: 388.

122. Jesse Tarbert, *When Good Government Meant Big Government: The Quest to Extend Federal Power, 1913–1933* (New York: Columbia University Press, 2022), 132–135.
123. Memorandum by the Secretary of State of a Conversation with the Japanese Ambassador, May 23, 1924, *FRUS 1924*, 2: 393–395; Kurashige, *Two Faces of Exclusion*, 137–138.
124. Donald R. McCoy, *Calvin Coolidge: The Quiet President* (New York: Macmillan, 1967), 230–231. Coolidge quoted in Secretary of State to US Ambassador to Japan, May 26, 1924, *FRUS 1924*, 2: 396.
125. Izumi Hirobe, *Japanese Pride, American Prejudice: Modifying the Exclusion Clause of the 1924 Immigration Act* (Stanford, CA: Stanford University Press, 2002), 21–51. Nancy Stalker, "Suicide, Boycotts and Embracing Tagore: The Japanese Popular Response to the 1924 US Immigration Exclusion Law," *Japanese Studies* 26, no. 2 (2006): 153–170.
126. Manako Ogawa, "'Hull-House' in Downtown Tokyo: The Transplantation of a Settlement House from the United States into Japan and the North American Missionary Women, 1919–1945," *Journal of World History* 15, no. 3 (September 2004): 377.
127. Joshua Hammer, *Yokohama Burning: The Deadly 1923 Earthquake and Fire that Helped Forge the Path to World War II* (New York: Free Press, 2006), 220–228.
128. Oguma, *Boundaries of the Japanese*, 237.
129. "Message from Japan to America," *Japan Times and Mail*, October 1, 1924, 6, 8, box 30, folder 284, SRRR.
130. Kawashima, *Proletarian Gamble*, 36, 40.
131. Yamawaki, "Foreign Workers in Japan," 43–47; Hasegawa Kenji, "The Massacre of Koreans in Yokohama in the Aftermath of the Great Kanto Earthquake of 1923," *Monumenta Nipponica* 75, no. 1 (2020): 91–122; Jiaying Shen, "A Great Convergence: The Mass Killing of Chinese in the 1923 Kantō Massacre," *Japanese Studies* 40, no. 3 (2020): 231–248.
132. Kawakami, "Japanese Policy towards Alien Immigration," *Current History* 20, no. 3 (June 1924): 472–474.
133. Kawakami, "Japan's Ordeal through Earthquake and Fire," *Current History* 19, no. 1 (October 1923): 139.
134. "Current History Chronicles," *Current History* 19, no. 4 (January 1924): n.p. (advertisement section); "An Sun-nam ssi nŭn irin ŭi muri rŭl pyŏnbak," *Sinhan Minbo*, November 29, 1923, 1.
135. Hyun Chŏl, "Tongyangin paechŏk ae daehayŏ," *Sinhan Minbo*, May 8, 1924, 4. For other examples of Korean Americans' argument that the Johnson-Reed Act was not just an act against Japanese immigrants, see "Hwangin paech'ŏgan ŭn 7 wŏl 1 il put'ŏ shilshihae," *Sinhan Minbo*, May 15, 1924, 1; "7 wŏl 1 il ihu tongyangin ipkuk chagyŏk," *Sinhan Minbo*, May 29, 1924, 1. Korean immigration to the United States largely stopped after 1905, when Japan made Korea its protectorate, with the exception of students, exiles, and picture brides.
136. *America and Japan: Their Treatment of Foreigners and Resulting Conditions* (San Francisco: California Joint Immigration Committee, 1925).
137. Sidney Gulick, *Adventuring in Brotherhood among Orientals in America* (New York: American Missionary Association, 1925), 14–15, box 1, folder 8, SRRR.

Chapter 5

1. November 1; November 2, 1929, *YCHI*, 9: 244; Conrado Benitez, "Position of the Philippines in the Pacific Comity," *Pacific Affairs* 3, no. 1 (January 1930): 70–91.
2. *Address Given by Mr. James Weldon Johnson on the Institute of Pacific Relations, November 27, 1929*, 5, box 10, folder: IPR-230, JWJ&GNJP. On Johnson's trip to Japan, see Etsuko Taketani, *The Black Pacific Narrative: Geographic Imaginings of Race and Empire Between the World Wars* (Hanover, NH: Dartmouth College Press, 2014), 32–57.
3. Marc Gallicchio, *The African American Encounter with Japan and China: Black Internationalism in Asia, 1895–1945* (Chapel Hill: University of North Carolina Press, 2000), 49.
4. James Weldon Johnson, *Along This Way: The Autobiography of James Weldon Johnson* (New York: Viking Press, 1933), 417.
5. October 15, 1931, *YCHI*, 9: 403.

6. By the time the first IPR conference took place in Hawai'i, the islands had already served as home for several Pan-Pacific conferences. Under the auspices of the Pan-Pacific Union, which was established during the war, the postwar years saw the meeting of the Pan-Pacific Science Congress (1920), the Pan-Pacific Educational Conference (1921), the Pan-Pacific Press Conference (1921), and the Pan-Pacific Commercial Conference (1921). Beginning in 1928, the Pan-Pacific Union began holding Pan-Pacific Women's Conferences. See Hooper, *Elusive Destiny*, 84–111; Tomoko Akami, "From the Center to the Periphery: Hawai'i and the Pacific Community," in *Hawai'i at the Crossroads of the U.S. and Japan before the Pacific War*, ed. Jon Thares Davidann (Honolulu: University of Hawai'i Press, 2008), 13–41; Fiona Paisley, *Glamour in the Pacific: Cultural Internationalism and Race Politics in the Women's Pan-Pacific* (Honolulu: University Press of Hawai'i, 2009).

7. As John Thares Davidann has argued, one of the defining characteristics of the IPR was the institution's belief that "if they could bring objective facts to the forefront, they could promote mutual understanding and the tensions would subside." See Davidann, " 'Colossal Illusions': The Institute of Pacific Relations in U.S.-Japanese Relations, 1919–1938," in Davidann, *Hawai'i at the Crossroads*, 42–67.

8. On the rise of quantitative social science during the 1920s, see Dorothy Ross, *The Origins of American Social Science* (Cambridge: Cambridge University Press, 1991), 434.

9. Daniel T. Rodgers, *Atlantic Crossings: Social Politics in a Progressive Age* (Cambridge, MA: Belknap Press of Harvard University Press, 1998), 318–366.

10. On postwar neo-Malthusianism's effect on Japan's relationship with the rest of the world, see Alison Bashford, *Global Population: History, Geopolitics, and Life on Earth* (New York: Columbia University Press, 2014), 107–132; Greg Cushman, *Guano and the Opening of the Pacific World: A Global Ecological History* (Cambridge: Cambridge University Press, 2014), 205–242; Aiko Takeuchi-Demirci, *Contraceptive Diplomacy: Reproductive Politics and Imperial Ambitions in the United States and Japan* (Stanford, CA: Stanford University Press, 2018), 20–27; Sidney Xu Lu, *The Making of Japanese Settler Colonialism: Malthusianism and Trans-Pacific Migration, 1868–1961* (New York: Cambridge University Press, 2019).

11. Jeremy Adelman, "Introduction: Social Science and Empire—A Durable Tension," in *Empire and the Social Sciences: Global Histories of Knowledge*, ed. Jeremy Adelman (London: Bloomsbury Academic, 2019), 3, 5–6.

12. Akira Iriye, *Cultural Internationalism and World Order* (Baltimore: Johns Hopkins University Press, 1997), 79.

13. "Tentative Statement Concerning a Proposed Pan-Pacific Conference on a Christian Program for the Pacific Area," box 5, folder 9; Davis to Frank Atherton, October 4, 1923; Charles Loomis to J. Merle Davis, December 10, 1923, both in box 5, folder 10, SRRR. On Davis's role in the organizing stages of the IPR, see Tomoko Akami, *Internationalizing the Pacific: The United States, Japan and the Institute of Pacific Relations in War and Peace, 1919–1945* (London: Routledge, 2002), 50–55; Nobuo Katagiri, "Hawai'i, IPR, and the Japanese Immigration Problem: A Focus on the First and Second IPR Conferences of 1925 and 1927," in Davidann, *Hawai'i at the Crossroads*, 96–110.

14. Akami, *Internationalizing the Pacific*, 40–50; Henry Yu, *Thinking Orientals: Migration, Contact, and Exoticism in Modern America* (New York: Oxford University Press, 2001), 20–22; Sarah M. Griffith, *The Fight for Asian American Civil Rights: Liberal Protestant Activism, 1900–1950* (Urbana: University of Illinois Press, 2018), 39.

15. Robert E. Park, "A Race Relations Survey," 196–197, box 23, folder 13, SRRR. On Park and the mask metaphor, see Yu, *Thinking Orientals*, 66–68.

16. *Tentative Findings of the Survey of Race Relations* (Stanford, CA: Survey of Race Relations, 1925), 18–19.

17. Ibid., 18.

18. Eliot G. Mears to Lyman Wilbur, August 18, 1925, box 12, folder 1, SRRR; Yu, *Thinking Orientals*, 73–74.

19. Akami, *Internationalizing the Pacific*, 51–52.

20. *Institute of Pacific Relations, Honolulu Session, June 30–July 14, 1925, History, Organization, Proceedings, Discussions and Addresses* (Honolulu: Institute of Pacific Relations, 1925), 23–24.

21. Alva W. Taylor, "Pursuing Peace in the Pacific," *Federal Council Bulletin* 8, no. 5 (September–October 1925): 26.

22. Paul Scharrenberg, box 34, folder 86, SRRR. Scharrenberg served as the main liaison between the IPR and the CJIC. McClatchy to members of the CJIC, August 5, 1925, box 46, folder McClatchy, Valentine Stewart 1924–1926; McClatchy to members of the CJIC, June 7, 1927, box 46, folder McClatchy, Valentine Stewart 1927–1930, JDPP.

23. Jerome Greene to E. C. Carter, September 12, 1928, box 115, folder McClatchy, V. S., IPRR; On McClatchy's hostility toward the IPR in the 1930s, see Lon Kurashige, *Two Faces of Exclusion: The Untold History of Anti-Asian Racism in the United States* (Chapel Hill: University of North Carolina Press, 2016), 166–169.

24. Rowell, "American Sentiment on Problems of the Pacific," in *Institute of Pacific Relations, Honolulu Session* (Honolulu: Institute of Pacific Relations, 1925), 106.

25. Rowell, "Americanization in Hawaii: Sugar Plantation Interference," *Fresno Republican*, June 27, 1920, carton 2, folder 1920 Jan–July, CHRP. On the Oahu strike, see Masayo Duus, *The Japanese Conspiracy: The Oahu Sugar Strike of 1920* (Berkeley: University of California Press, 1999); Moon-Ho Jung, *Menace to Empire: Anticolonial Solidarities and the Transpacific Origins of the US Security State* (Oakland: University of California Press, 2022), 166–186.

26. Rowell, "East of the East, West of the West," *Survey* 54, no. 11 (September 1, 1925): 547. "Crossroads of the Pacific" was a phrase often deployed by Honolulu's business elites in the 1910s and the 1920s. On Frank Atherton, see Hooper, *Elusive Destiny*, 114–122. Eight Koreans, including Yun's daughter Helen, attended the first IPR conference even though they had not been invited.

27. Rowell, "The Cancer of Ignorance," *Survey* 55, no. 3 (November 1, 1925): 159.

28. Roderick D. McKenzie, *Oriental Exclusion: The Effect of American Immigration Laws, Regulations, and Judicial Decisions upon the Chinese and Japanese on the American Pacific Coast* (Chicago: University of Chicago Press, 1927); Eliot G. Mears, *Resident Orientals on the American Pacific Coast: Their Legal and Economic Status* (Chicago: University of Chicago Press, 1928). Park, upon retirement from the University of Chicago, taught a semester at Yenching University in 1932. On Blakeslee and the IPR, see Brian Masaru Hayashi, "From Race to Nation: The Institute of Pacific Relations, Asian Americans, and George Blakeslee, from 1908 to 1929," *Japanese Journal of American Studies* 23 (2012): 51–71.

29. *The Study of International Affairs in the Pacific Area: A Review of Nine Years' Work in the International Research Program of the Institute of Pacific Relations* (New York: Institute of Pacific Relations, 1936), 5.

30. Lothrop Stoddard, *The Rising Tide of Color: The Threat against White World-Supremacy* (New York: Charles Scribner's Sons, 1920), 8–9.

31. E. A. Ross, *Standing Room Only?* (New York: The Century Co., 1927), v, 270–272, 325, 339.

32. J. Merle Davis to Ray Lyman Wilbur, "Some Observations on Japan," May 26, 1926, in *Notes from a Pacific Circuit: Report Letters of J. Merle Davis, M.A. General Secretary, to President Ray Lyman Wilbur, Chairman, Pacific Council, Institute of Pacific Relations* (Honolulu: Institute of Pacific Relations, 1927), 11.

33. Takeuchi-Demirci, *Contraceptive Diplomacy*, 40–54.

34. Davis, "Some Observations on Japan," 11–12.

35. Ibid., 11–12.

36. Jeffrey Lesser, *Immigration, Ethnicity, and National Identity in Brazil, 1808 to the Present* (New York: Cambridge University Press, 2013), 151–168; Eiichiro Azuma, *In Search of Our Frontier: Japanese America and Settler Colonialism in the Construction of Japan's Borderless Empire* (Oakland: University of California Press, 2019), 135–149; Lu, *Making of Japanese Settler Colonialism*, 186–197.

37. Sawayanagi Masatarō, "Japanese Pacific Relations," *Mid-Pacific Magazine* 30, no. 4 (October 1925): 350; Sawayanagi Masatarō, "The General Features of Pacific Relations as Viewed by Japan," *Institute of Pacific Relations News Bulletin* (August 1927): 26. On Sawayanagi, see "Romaji Possible Thinks Educator," *Nippu Jiji*, June 20, 1922, 8; "Pacific and International Gatherings," *Nippu Jiji*, May 21, 1923, 8.

38. "Problems of the Pacific," *Seamen's Journal* 41, no. 9 (September 1, 1927), 267–269, carton 2, folder IPR, Paul Scharrenberg Papers, Bancroft Library, University of California, Berkeley.

39. Rowell to McClatchy, February 10, 1927, box 6, folder 1927, January–April, CHRP. On Rowell's support to give Japan its immigration quota, see Izumi Hirobe, *Japanese Pride, American Prejudice: Modifying the Exclusion Clause of the 1924 Immigration Act* (Palo Alto, CA: Stanford University Press, 2001), 152–153.

40. Park, "Our Racial Frontier," *Survey Graphic* 56, no. 3 (May 1926): 193.

41. McKenzie, *Oriental Exclusion*, 181–182.

42. Carl Alsberg, *Land Utilization Investigations and Their Bearing on International Relations* (Honolulu: Institute of Pacific Relations, 1933), 15, 20, 28.

43. E. F. Penrose, *Food Supply and Raw Materials in Japan* (Chicago: University of Chicago Press, 1930). On Penrose, see *Japan and World Depression: Then and Now: Essays in Memory of E. F. Penrose*, ed. Ronald Dore and Radha Sinha (New York: St. Martin's Press, 1987).

44. "Opinion Divided on Food Problem," *Nippu Jiji*, July 23, 1927, 1; "Japan Soul Involved in Food Conquest," *Nichibei Shinbun*, December 4, 1929, 1. On Nasu's land utilization survey, see Yung-chen Chiang, *Social Engineering and the Social Sciences in China* (Cambridge: Cambridge University Press, 2001), 91–92.

45. Nasu Shiroshi, *The Problem of Population and Food Supply in Japan* (Honolulu: Institute of Pacific Relations, 1927), 24–26.

46. Nasu Shiroshi, *Land Utilization in Japan* (Tokyo: Japan Council, Institute of Pacific Relations, 1929), 81.

47. Ibid., 83.

48. Ibid., 240.

49. Ibid., 230. On Malthus and British colonization, see Alison Bashford and Joyce Chaplin, *The New Worlds of Thomas Robert Malthus: Rereading the Principle of Population* (Princeton, NJ: Princeton University Press, 2016), 201–236.

50. "In the Magazines," *Pacific Affairs* 3, no. 4 (April 1930): 431. On transpacific organizations affiliated with the Comintern during this time, see Josephine Fowler, *Japanese and Chinese Immigrant Activists: Organizing in American and International Communist Movements, 1919– 1933* (New Brunswick, NJ: Rutgers University Press, 2007), 74–119.

51. Louise Young, *Japan's Total Empire: Manchuria and the Culture of Wartime Imperialism* (Berkeley and Los Angeles: University of California Press, 1998), 3–52.

52. Shuhsi Hsu, "The Manchurian Question," in *Problems of the Pacific, 1929: Proceedings of the Kyoto Conference of the Institute of Pacific Relations*, ed. J. B. Condliffe (Chicago: University of Chicago Press, 1930), 466.

53. Matsuoka Yōsuke, *An Address on Manchuria: Its Past and Present, and Reply to Prof. Shuhsi-Hsu's Criticisms and Observations* (Kyoto, Japan: Institute of Pacific Relations, 1929), 17, 25.

54. October 29, 1929, *YCHI*, 9: 243. On Yun's anti-communism, see December 1, 1921, August 3, 1923, September 6, 1924, *YCHI*, 8: 306, 495. The Korean Group's papers are available in box 113, folder Korean Group, IPRR.

55. *Problems of the Pacific, 1929*, 195. For Korean enthusiasm for Yun's speech, see "Chosŏnin manju iju nŭn tansunhi saeng ŭl wihan noryŏk," *Dong-A Ilbo*, November 8, 1929, 3.

56. Frederick R. Dickinson, *World War I and the Triumph of a New Japan, 1919–1930* (Cambridge: Cambridge University Press, 2013), 167–190; Sadao Asada, *From Mahan to Pearl Harbor: The Imperial Japanese Navy and the United States* (Annapolis, MD: Naval Institute Press, 2006), 126–157.

57. Chester Rowell to Myrtle Rowell, September 21, 1931, box 7, folder 1931, January– September, CHRP; Danny Orbach, *Curse on This Country: The Rebellious Army of Imperial Japan* (Ithaca, NY: Cornell University Press, 2017), 210–220.

58. Yi Jun-shik, "Manbosan sagŏn kwa chunggugin ŭi chosŏn inshik," *Han'guksa yŏn'guhoe* 156 (March 2012): 237–270; Ch'oe Pyŏng-to, "Manbosan sagŏn chik'u hwagyo paech'ŏk sagŏn e taehan ilche ŭi taeŭng," *Han'guksa yŏn'guhoe* 156 (March 2012): 297–329.

59. Sandra Wilson, *The Manchurian Crisis and Japanese Society, 1931–33* (London: Routledge, 2003), 19–20.

60. Rustin Gates, "Meiji Diplomacy in the Early 1930s: Uchida Kōsai, Manchuria, and Post-Withdrawal Foreign Policy," in *Tumultuous Decade: Empire, Society, and Diplomacy in 1930s Japan*, ed. Masato Kimura and Tosh Minohara (Toronto: University of Toronto Press, 2013), 189–214.

61. Andrew Gordon, *Labor and Imperial Democracy in Prewar Japan* (Berkeley and Los Angeles: University of California Press, 1992), 268–269.
62. *Document A: Present Condition of China: With Reference to Circumstances Affecting International Relations and the Good Understanding between Nations upon Which Peace Depends* (Tokyo: Gaimushō, 1932), 74–76, Hoover Institution Library & Archives, Stanford University.
63. *Appeal by the Chinese Government—Report of the Commission on Enquiry* (Geneva: League of Nations, 1932), 122–123, 138–139. Hereafter *Lytton Commission Report.*
64. Ian Nish, *Japan's Struggle with Internationalism: Japan, China, and the League of Nations* (New York: K. Paul International, 1993), 61–62. Of the seven advisers the Lytton Commission depended on to create its report, at least four of them were affiliated with the IPR. In addition to C. Walter Young, there were George Blakeslee, Étienne Dennery, and Ben Dorfman.
65. *Problems of the Pacific, 1929,* 441.
66. Randall E. Stross, *The Stubborn Earth: American Agriculturalists on Chinese Soil, 1898–1937* (Berkeley and Los Angeles: University of California Press, 1989), 161–187.
67. Franklin Ho, *Population Movement to the North Eastern Frontier in China* (Shanghai: China Institute of Pacific Relations, 1931), 15. On Ho and the IPR, see Chiang, *Social Engineering and the Social Sciences in China,* 87–102.
68. C. Walter Young, "Economic Factors in Manchurian Diplomacy," *Annals of the American Academy of Political and Social Science* 152 (November 1930): 297–302.
69. Hoon K. Lee, "Korean Migrants in Manchuria," *Geographical Review* 22, no. 2 (April 1932): 196, quoted by C. Walter Young, "Korean Problems in Manchuria as Factor in the Sino-Japanese Dispute," Special Study No. 9, in *Supplementary Documents to the Report of the Commission of Inquiry* (Geneva: League of Nations, 1932), 260, Hoover Institution Library & Archives, Stanford University.
70. *Lytton Commission Report,* 60.
71. Bang Gi-jung, "Ilcheha Yi Hun-gu ŭi nong'ŏp'ron gwa kyŏngje jarip sasang," *Yŏksa munje yŏn'gu* 1 (December 1996): 120–125.
72. Kristen Hoganson, *The Heartland: An American History* (New York: Penguin, 2019), 178–195.
73. "Yang Yi ssi chungguk sŏ ch'wijik," *Sinhan Minbo,* November 13, 1930, 1.
74. Hoon K. Lee, *Land Utilization and Rural Economy in Korea* (Chicago: University of Chicago Press, 1936), 161, 273.
75. Sandra Wilson, "The 'New Paradise': Japanese Emigration to Manchuria in the 1930s and 1940s," *International History Review* 17, no. 2 (May 1995): 259–260; Lu, *Making of Japanese Settler Colonialism,* 222–229.
76. Henry Stimson to Nelson T. Johnson, October 8, 1932, *FRUS 1932,* 4: 293.
77. Dorothy Borg, *The United States and the Far Eastern Crisis of 1933–1938: From the Manchurian Incident through the Initial Stages of the Undeclared Sino-Japanese War* (Cambridge, MA: Harvard University Press, 1964), 16–21; Michael E. Chapman, "Fidgeting over Foreign Policy: Henry L. Stimson and the Shenyang Incident, 1931," *Diplomatic History* 37, no. 4 (September 2013): 727–748; Gordon H. Chang, *Fateful Ties: A History of America's Preoccupation with China* (Cambridge, MA: Harvard University Press, 2015), 138–143.
78. Thomas W. Burkman, "The Geneva Spirit," in *Nitobe Inazo: Japan's Bridge across the Pacific,* ed. John F. Howes (Boulder, CO: Westview Press, 1995), 187–201; Lydia N. Yu-Jose, *Japan View the Philippines, 1900–1941* (Manila: Ateneo de Manila University Press, 1992), 30–34; Alexis Dudden, "Nitobe Inazo and the Diffusion of a Knowledgeable Empire," in *Empire and the Social Sciences,* ed. Jeremy Adelman (London: Bloomsbury Academic, 2019), 111–122.
79. Nitobe, *Japan: Some Phases of Her Problems and Development* (London: Ernest Benn Limited, 1931), 271, 279.
80. Burkman, "The Geneva Spirit," 205.
81. "Dr. Nitobe Arrives; Pleads for Japan," *New York Times,* May 7, 1932, 4. On Nitobe's North American tour see George Oshiro, "The End, 1929–1933," in Howes, *Nitobe Inazo,* 261–268.
82. Louis Stark, "Manchuria Splits Politics Institute," *New York Times,* August 23, 1932, 8.
83. "The Place of Japan in the Family of Nations," *Rafu Shinpō,* December 21, 1932, 8.
84. "Dr. Nitobe Tells of Japan's Major Issues," *Rafu Shinpō,* March 2, 1933, 6.
85. Eiichiro Azuma, *In Search of Our Frontier,* 153–182.

86. David John Lu, *Agony of Choice: Matsuoka Yōsuke and the Rise and Fall of the Japanese Empire, 1880–1946* (Lanham, MD: Lexington Books, 2002).

87. "Matsuoka Holds Packed House of 5000 Japanese as He Floods Auditorium with Irony, Humor and Oratory," *Shin Sekai*, April 12, 1933, English Section 1; "Matsuoka Meets Ex-President; Both Keep Mum," *Rafu Shimpo*, April 12, 1933, English Section 1.

88. Bruno Lasker and W. H. Holland, *Problems of the Pacific: Economic Control and Conflict. Proceedings of the Fifth Conference of the Institute of Pacific Relations, Banff, Canada, 14–26 August, 1933* (Chicago: University of Chicago Press, 1934).

89. Oshiro, "The End, 1929–1933," 271–272.

90. Akami, *Internationalizing the Pacific*, 200–239.

91. John Merle Davis, *An Autobiography* (Tokyo: Kyo Bun Kwan, 1959), 120. On Davis's resignation, see Akami, *Internationalizing the Pacific*, 128–130.

92. As often noted, a younger generation of American IPR researchers would play important roles in the US government during World War II. Owen Lattimore would direct the Pacific bureau of the Office of War Information (OWI), while John K. Fairbank would work in the Office of Strategic Services (OSS) before working in the Far Eastern section of the OWI headed by George E. Taylor. See Paul F. Hooper, "The Institute of Pacific Relations and the Origins of Asian and Pacific Studies," *Pacific Affairs* 61, no. 1 (Spring 1988): 98–121; Robert P. Newman, *Owen Lattimore and the "Loss" of China* (Berkeley: University of California Press, 1992); Dayna Barnes, "Think Tanks and a New Order in East Asia: The Council of Foreign Relations and the Institute of Pacific Relations during World War II," *Journal of American-East Asian Relations* 22, no. 2 (2015): 89–119.

Chapter 6

1. Kaneko, "Roosevelt on Japan," *Asia* 32, no. 9 (November 1932): 539.

2. Root to Stimson, November 20, 1931, quoted in Christopher Thorne, *The Limits of Foreign Policy: The West, the League and the Far Eastern Crisis of 1931–1933* (London: Hamilton, 1972), 195; George Blakeslee, "The Japanese Monroe Doctrine," *Foreign Affairs* 11, no. 4 (July 1933): 671–681. For earlier critiques, see Stanley Hornbeck, *Contemporary Politics in the Far East* (New York: D. Appleton and Co., 1916), 344–359; Carl Walter Young, *Japan's Special Position in Manchuria* (Baltimore: Johns Hopkins University Press, 1931), 327–371.

3. Louis A. Pérez Jr., *Cuba: Between Reform and Revolution* (New York: Oxford University Press, 1988), 189–209; Lars Schoultz, *Beneath the United States: A History of U.S. Foreign Policy toward Latin America* (Cambridge, MA: Harvard University Press, 1998), 253–315.

4. Nicholas Roosevelt, "Laying Down the White Man's Burden," *Foreign Affairs* 13, no. 4 (July 1935): 680–686.

5. On Theodore Roosevelt Jr., see Geoffrey Alan Cabat, "The Governorship of Theodore Roosevelt Jr. in Puerto Rico, 1929–1931: A Window of Progressivism" (PhD diss., New York University, 1989).

6. Theodore Roosevelt Jr., *Thirty-first Annual Report of the Governor of Porto Rico* (Washington, DC: US Government Printing Office, 1932); "Talk Col. Roosevelt in '32," *New York Times*, March 25, 1931, 16.

7. "Teddy to Pat to Charlie," *Outlook and Independent* (November 11, 1931), 326; "Roosevelt Tactics Win the Filipinos," *New York Times*, June 13, 1932, 4; *Annual Report of the Governor General of the Philippine Islands 1932* (Washington, DC: US Government Printing Office, 1934).

8. 119 House Republicans supported H.R. 7233 (the Hare bill), and 14 Senate Republicans supported S. 3377 (the Hawes-Cutting bill). See, respectively, https://www.govtrack.us/congress/votes/72-1/h29 and https://www.govtrack.us/congress/votes/72-1/s99.

9. Rick Baldoz, *The Third Asiatic Invasion: Empire and Migration in Filipino America, 1898–1946* (New York: New York University Press, 2011), 156–181.

10. Ibid., 179; Thomas Pepinsky, "Trade Competition and American Decolonization," *World Politics* 67, no. 3 (2015): 387–422.

11. Anti-Imperialist League, Minutes of Anti-Imperialist Conference, February 21, 1932, 3, box 8, folder 17, JFP.

12. "Veto of a Bill Providing for the Independence of the Philippine Islands," January 13, 1933, in *Public Papers of the Presidents of the United States, Herbert Hoover: Containing the Public Messages, Speeches, and Statements of the President, January 1, 1932 to March 3, 1933* (Washington, DC: US Government Printing Office, 1977), 935.

13. *Resolution of Philippine Legislature Declining to Accept the Act of Congress Providing for Philippines Independence,* 73rd Cong., 2nd Sess. (Washington, DC: US Government Printing Press, 1934).

14. Baldoz, *Third Asiatic Invasion,* 179–180; Christopher Capozzola, *Bound by War: How the United States and the Philippines Built America's First Pacific Century* (New York: Basic Books, 2020), 121–122.

15. Edward S. Miller, *War Plan Orange: The U.S. Strategy to Defeat Japan, 1897–1945* (Annapolis, MD: Naval Institute Press, 1991), 168.

16. John C. Walter, "Congressman Carl Vinson and Franklin D. Roosevelt: Naval Preparedness and the Coming of World War II, 1932–40," *Georgia Historical Quarterly* 64, no. 3 (Fall 1980): 294–305.

17. Wayne S. Cole, *Senator Gerald P. Nye and American Foreign Relations* (Minneapolis: University of Minnesota Press, 1962); Susie J. Pak, *Gentlemen Bankers: The World of JP Morgan* (Cambridge, MA: Harvard University Press, 2013), 208–211; Richard Drake, *Charles Austin Beard: The Return of the Master Historian of American Imperialism* (Ithaca, NY: Cornell University, 2018), 73–95.

18. April Merleaux, *Sugar and Civilization: American Empire and the Cultural Politics of Sweetness* (Chapel Hill: University of North Carolina Press, 2015), 174–201.

19. Franklin Roosevelt, Honolulu, Hawaii—Radio Address (speech file 717), July 28, 1934, box 18, Master Speech File, 1898–1945, FDRPLM.

20. Theodore Roosevelt to James Wilson, February 3, 1903, *LTR,* 3: 416.

21. Merleaux, *Sugar and Civilization,* 191–193; Roger Bell, *Last among Equals: Hawaiian Statehood and American Politics,* (Honolulu: University of Hawai'i Press, 1984), 63–64.

22. Bell, *Last among Equals,* 65.

23. Shelley Sang-Hee Lee and Rick Baldoz, "'A Fascinating Interracial Experiment Station': Remapping the Orient-Occident Divide in Hawai'i," *American Studies* 49, no. 3/4 (Fall/Winter 2008): 87–109; Dean Itsuji Saranillio, *Unsustainable Empire: Alternative Histories of Hawai'i Statehood* (Durham, NC: Duke University Press, 2018), 81–85.

24. "Round-the-World Notes," 3, series D, folder Round-the-World Notes, n.d., Edward Alsworth Ross Papers, 1866–1951 (Madison: Wisconsin Historical Society, 1985), reel 33.

25. CJIC circular no. 432, "Would Admit 100,000 Ineligible Asiatics: A Feature of Hawaiian Statehood," December 9, 1935, box 13, folder A 16.209, Japanese American Evacuation and Resettlement Records, Bancroft Library, University of California, Berkeley.

26. Joint Committee on Hawaii, *Statehood for Hawaii: Hearings before the Joint Committee on Hawaii, Congress of the United States,* 75th Cong., 2nd Sess. (Washington, DC: US Government Printing Office, 1938), 105–106; Samuel Gompers and Herman Gutstadt, *Meat vs. Rice: American Manhood against Asiatic Coolieism, Which Shall Survive?* (Washington, DC: American Federation of Labor, 1901).

27. *Statehood for Hawaii: Hearings,* 244, 293, 383, 440, 477.

28. Ibid., 13.

29. "Wilson Praises Japanese in Statehood Plea," *Nippu Jiji,* October 12, 1937, 2; *Statehood for Hawaii: Hearings,* 43, 51; "Wilson Praises Japanese in Statehood Plea," *Nippu Jiji,* October 12, 1937, 2.

30. U.S. Congress, Joint Committee on Hawaii, *Statehood for Hawaii: Letter from the Chairman of the Joint Committee Transmitting Pursuant to S. Cong. Res. 18,* 75th *Cong.,* 3rd *Sess.* (Washington, DC: US Government Printing Office, 1938), 95.

31. *Statehood for Hawaii: Hearings,* 70, 113, 200, 293, 322.

32. Greg Robinson, *By Order of the President: FDR and the Internment of Japanese Americans* (Cambridge, MA: Harvard University Press, 2001), 56.

33. Franklin D. Roosevelt, Outerlink Bridge Dedication—"Quarantine" (speech file 1093), October 5, 1937, box 35, Master Speech File, 1898–1945, FDRPLM.

34. On the Neutrality Acts, see Brooke L. Blower, "From Isolationism to Neutrality: A New Framework for Understanding American Political Culture, 1919–1941," *Diplomatic History* 38, no. 2 (April 2014): 345–376; Justus D. Doenecke and John E. Wilz, *From Isolation to War: 1931–1941* (New York: John Wiley & Sons, 2015), 80–96.

35. Alan Brinkley, *The End of Reform: New Deal Liberalism in Depression and War* (New York: Vintage, 1995); William E. Leuchtenberg, *The Supreme Court Reborn: The Constitutional Revolution in the Age of Roosevelt* (New York: Oxford University Press, 1995), 180–212.

36. Chester Rowell, "Cynics and Mr. Roosevelt," *San Francisco Chronicle*, October 14, 1937, 8.

37. Elizabeth Borgwardt, *A New Deal for the World: America's Vision for Human Rights* (Cambridge, MA: Harvard University Press, 2005), 14–45; Dorothy Borg, "Notes on Roosevelt's 'Quarantine' Speech," *Political Science Quarterly* 72, no. 3 (September 1957), 405–433.

38. James F. Cook, *Carl Vinson: Patriarch of the Armed Forces* (Macon, GA: Mercer University Press, 2004), 129–138.

39. To Pass H.R. 9218, a Bill Relating to the Composition of U.S. Navy," May 3, 1938, https://www.govtrack.us/congress/votes/75-3/s148. On Borah, see Christopher McKnight Nichols, *Promise and Peril: America at the Dawn of a Global Age* (Cambridge, MA: Harvard University Press, 2011), 285–319.

40. Robert Dallek, *Franklin D. Roosevelt and American Foreign Policy, 1932–1945*, 2nd ed. (New York: Oxford University Press, 1995), 149–155. On American public opinion regarding the *Panay* incident, see Ernest R. May, "U.S. Press Coverage of Japan, 1931–1941," in *Pearl Harbor as History: Japanese-American Relations, 1931–1941*, ed. Dorothy Borg and Shumpei Okamoto (New York: Columbia University Press, 1973), 523–525.

41. *Congressional Record*, 75th Cong., 3rd Sess., February 1, 1938, 1326. On Johnson, see Richard Coke Lower, *A Bloc of One: The Political Career of Hiram W. Johnson* (Stanford, CA: Stanford University Press, 1993), 288–297. On 1937 as the end of genuine economic reform, see Brinkley, *End of Reform*.

42. Warren I. Cohen, *America's Response to China: A History of Sino-American Relations* (New York: Columbia University Press, 2019), 89–114.

43. Arthur Waldron, "Introduction," in John Van Antwerp MacMurray, *How the Peace Was Lost: The 1935 Memorandum: Developments Affecting American Policy in the Far East*, ed. Arthur Waldron (Stanford, CA: Hoover Institution Press, 1991), 2–4.

44. "Roosevelt Weighs Orient Policy," *New York Times*, July 16, 1937, 1.

45. MacMurray, *How the Peace Was Lost*, 129. George F. Kennan cites this passage in *American Diplomacy* (Chicago: University of Chicago Press, 1951), 55.

46. MacMurray, *How the Peace Was Lost*, 62.

47. Mira Wilkins, "The Role of U.S. Business," in Borg and Okamoto, eds., *Pearl Harbor as History*, 341–370.

48. Mrs. Theodore Roosevelt Jr., "Escape from Shanghai," *Saturday Evening Post* 210, no. 18 (October 1937): 55–56, 59, 62, 64.

49. "Col. Roosevelt Plans Drive for Youth in China," *New York Herald Tribune*, July 7, 1938, 8A. On "Bowl of Rice" events, see Karen J. Leong and Judy Tzu-Chun Wu, "Filling the Rice Bowls of China: Staging Humanitarian Relief during the Sino-Japanese War," in *Chinese Americans and the Politics of Race and Culture*, ed. Sucheng Chan and Madeline Y. Hsu (Philadelphia: Temple University Press, 2008), 132–152.

50. Gordon H. Chang, *Fateful Ties: A History of America's Preoccupation with China* (Cambridge, MA: Harvard University Press, 2015), 146–150, 164–165; T. Christopher Jespersen, *American Images of China, 1931–1949* (Stanford, CA: Stanford University Press, 1996), 11–44; Hollinger, *Protestants Abroad*, 24–46.

51. "War in China," *March of Time* newsreel, September 10, 1937.

52. Henry Luce selected Chiang Kai-shek and his wife, Mei-ling Soong, as *Time* magazine's 1937's People of the Year.

53. Mei-ling Soong, "What China Has Faced," in General Chiang Kai-shek, *An Account of the Fortnight in Sian When the Fate of China Hung in the Balance* (Garden City, NY: Doubleday, Doran, 1937), 58, 61.

54. Du Bois, "Man Power," March 7, 1937, reproduced in *W. E. B. Du Bois on Asia: Crossing the World Color Line*, eds. Bill V. Mullen and Cathryn Watson (Jackson: University Press of Mississippi, 2005), 76.

55. Du Bois, "A Forum of Fact and Opinion," October 23, 1937, quoted in Yuichiro Onishi, *Transpacific Antiracism: Afro-Asian Solidarity in 20th-Century Black America, Japan, and Okinawa* (New York: New York University Press, 2013), 89–90; Etsuko Taketani, *The Black Pacific Narrative: Geographic Imaginings of Race and Empire between the World Wars* (Hanover, NH: Dartmouth College Press, 2014), 170–171.

56. Du Bois, "Forum of Fact and Opinion," *Pittsburgh Courier*, February 13, 1937, 7, 18.

57. Ibid., 7.

58. Marc Gallicchio, *The African American Encounter with Japan and China: Black Internationalism in Asia, 1895–1945* (Chapel Hill: University of North Carolina Press, 2000), 95–101; Keisha N. Blain, "'For the Rights of Dark People in Every Part of the World: Pearl Sherrod, Black Internationalist Feminism, and Afro-Asian Politics during the 1930s," *Souls* 17, nos. 1–2 (June 2015): 90–112; Gerald Horne, *Facing the Rising Sun: African Americans, Japan, and the Rise of Afro-Asian Solidarity* (New York: New York University Press, 2018), 57–75.

59. *Is Japan the Champion of the Colored Races?* (New York: Workers Library Publishers, 1938).

60. "Harlem Storekeepers Join Boycott against Japanese Made Goods," *New York Age*, January 29, 1938, 2.

61. "Paul Robeson Aiding China against Japan," *Chicago Defender*, November 27, 1937, 24; Greg Robinson, "Internationalism and Justice: Paul Robeson, Asia, and Asian Americans," in *AfroAsian Encounters: Culture, History, Politics*, ed. Heike Raphael-Hernandez and Shannon Steen (New York: New York University Press, 2006), 260–276.

62. Draft of Speech by Langston Hughes at the Second International Writers Congress, Paris, July 16, 1937, Box 479, Folder 11924, Langston Hughes Papers, Beinecke Rare Book and Manuscript Library, Yale University Library, New Haven, CT. On Hughes in Japan, see Taketani, *Black Pacific Narrative*, 116–147.

63. George Padmore, "Hitler, Mussolini and Africa," *The Crisis* 44, no. 9 (September 1937): 262–263, 274.

64. Takashi Yoshida, *The Making of the "Rape of Nanking": History and Memory in Japan, China, and the United States* (New York: Oxford University Press, 2006), 37–42.

65. *Life* magazine, quoted in Chang, *Fateful Ties*, 159.

66. "Stop Helping Japan—Stimson," *Washington Post*, October 7, 1937, 1, 7; Philip J. Jaffe, "The United States Continues to Arm Japan," *Amerasia* 3, no. 5 (July 1939): 210–214; Elizabeth Boody Schumpeter, "The Problem of Sanctions in the Far East," *Pacific Affairs* 12, no. 3 (September 1939): 252–262.

67. Andrew Johnstone, *Against Immediate Evil: American Internationalists and the Four Freedoms on the Eve of World War* (Ithaca, NY: Cornell University Press, 2014), 17–35. The use of the term "rape" is in *America's Share in Japan's War Guilt* (New York: American Committee for Non-Participation in Japanese Aggression, 1938), 33.

68. *Neutrality, Peace Legislation, and Our Foreign Policy: Hearings before the Committee on Foreign Relations, United States Senate, April 5, 1939* (Washington, DC: US Government Printing Office, 1939), 548–559.

69. Ibid., 554. On Crow, see Chang, *Fateful Ties*, 154–156.

70. "Cotton Trade Pact Sought by Mission," *Rafu Shimpō*, January 8, 1937, 6; "American Cotton Industry Mission Arrives in Japan," *Nippu Jiji*, January 8, 1937, 2.

71. Kurt Bloch, "American Cotton in the Far East," *Far Eastern Survey* 9, no. 20 (October 9, 1940): 231–237; Greg Robinson, "L'évolution de l'économie cotonnière de la Nouvelle-Orléans entre 1890 et le milieu du XXe siècle: Le rôle du Japon," in *La Nouvelle-Orléans, 1718–2018: Regards sur trois siècles d'histoire partagée*, ed. Dominique Barjot and Denis Vialou (Paris: Maisonneuve & Larose, 2019), 435–449.

72. "Cotton Subsidy Plan May Aid Japan," *Atlanta Journal Constitution*, July 30, 1939, 2A.

73. Hull to Eugene Dooman (chargé d'affaires in Japan), July 1, 1939, *FRUS 1939*, 4: 214.

74. W. H. M. [Walter H. Mallory], "Economic Warfare with Japan or a New Treaty?," *Foreign Affairs* 18, no. 2 (January 1940): 366.

75. Dallek, *Franklin D. Roosevelt and American Foreign Policy*, 194–196; Lawrence S. Kaplan, *The Conversion of Senator Arthur H. Vandenberg: From Isolation to International Engagement* (Lexington: University Press of Kentucky, 2015), 61–66.
76. "Reaction to Cancellation of Trade Pact Reflects Wide Divergence of Opinion," *Shin Sekai Asahi Shinbun*, July 29, 1939, English section, 1; "Abrogation of U.S.-Nippon Pact Worries Japanese in Territory," *Nichibei Shinbun*, October 9, 1939, 1.
77. "Severing the Shackles," *Shin Sekai Asahi Shinbun*, February 26, 1940, English section, 1.
78. Kiyoshi Kawakami, "Anti-Japanism in U.S. Laid to Unreasoning Chronic Psychosis," *Shin Sekai Asahi Shinbun*, February 12, 1940, English section, 1.
79. Interview with Clarke H. Kawakami and Yuri Morris, May 22, 1968, Japanese American Research Project Interviews, sound recording, reel 10, Bancroft Library, University of California, Berkeley.
80. Kawakami, "Mussolini Bans Arms Reduction," *New York Times*, April 22, 1937, 6; Kawakami, *Japan in China, Her Motives and Aims* (London: John Murray, 1938).
81. "Japan Policy Clarified on Three Points," *Hawaii Hochi*, February 10, 1940, English section, 1, 3; "Tokyo Press Unfavorable to Hull's Views," *Shin Sekai Asahi Shinbun*, April 20, 1940, English section, 1; "Nippon to Insist U.S. Recognize 'Monroe Doctrine for Asia,'" *Rafu Shimpō*, July 11, 1940, 10.
82. "Uncle Fujii Speaks," *Kashu Mainichi Shinbun*, October 31, 1938, 5; "Uncle Fujii Speaks," *Kashu Mainichi Shinbun*, April 23, 1940, 5. On Fujii, see Yuji Ichioka, *Issei: The World of the First Generation Japanese Immigrants, 1885–1924* (New York: Free Press, 1988), 39, 190.
83. Yuji Ichioka, "The Meaning of Loyalty: The Case of Kazumaro Buddy Uno," *Amerasia Journal* 23, no. 3 (Winter 1997–1998): 45–71.
84. "Japan's Policies and the California Nisei," attached to V. S. McClatchy to E. C. Carter, February 3, 1938, Box 17, Folder: "McClatchy, V. S.," IPRR.
85. Melissa Paa Redwood, "Exile under Exclusion: Ayako Ishigaki and the Unstable Politics of Gender, Anti-Militarism, and Radical Free Speech between the U.S. and Japan, 1926–1996" (PhD diss., Yale University, forthcoming), chapter 2.
86. John Kitahara, "Views and Reviews," *Dōhō*, June 10, 1938, 6; John Kitahara, "Views and Reviews," *Dōhō*, July 1, 1939, 4; David K. Yoo, *Growing Up Nisei: Race, Generation, and Culture among Japanese Americans of California, 1924–49* (Urbana: University Illinois Press, 2000), 71, 75, 87; Lon Kurashige, *Japanese American Celebration and Conflict: A History of Ethnic Identity and Festival, 1934–1990* (Berkeley: University of California Press, 2002), 53–59.
87. "U.S. Urged to Accept Doctrine," *Nichibei Shinbun*, October 21, 1940, 1; "Japanese Monroe Doctrine Seen as Boon to Trade of United States by W. R. Castle," *Nippu Jiji*, October 9, 1940, 3.
88. W. R. Castle, "A Monroe Doctrine for Japan," *Atlantic Monthly* 166, no. 4 (October 1940): 445–452.
89. Sumner Welles, *The United States and World Crisis* (New York: New York University School of Law, 1941), 8–9.
90. Alan McPherson, "Herbert Hoover, Occupation Withdrawal, and the Good Neighbor Policy," *Presidential Studies Quarterly* 44, no. 4 (December 2014): 623–639.
91. Sumner Welles to Cordell Hull, September 18, 1933, *FRUS 1933*, 5: 446–448.
92. Jeremy A. Yellen, *The Greater East Asia Co-Prosperity Sphere: When Total Empire Met Total War* (Ithaca, NY: Cornell University Press, 2019), 26–45; Michael A. Barnhart, *Japan Prepares for Total War: The Search for Economic Security, 1919–1941* (Ithaca, NY: Cornell University Press, 1987), 153, 165–66.
93. Joyce C. Lebra, ed., *Japan's Greater East Asia Co-Prosperity Sphere in World War II* (Kuala Lumpur, Malaysia: Oxford University Press, 1975).
94. Timothy Brook, *Great State: China and the World* (New York: Harper, 2019), 347–371.
95. Charlotte Brooks, *American Exodus: Second-Generation Chinese Americans in China, 1901–1949* (Oakland: University of California Press, 2019), 168–172.
96. Leo T. S. Ching, *Becoming Japanese: Colonial Taiwan and the Politics of Identity Formation* (Berkeley: University of California Press, 2001); Mark Caprio, *Japanese Assimilation Policies in Colonial Korea, 1910–1945* (Seattle: University of Washington Press, 2009).

97. February 11, 1932, February 22, 1932, March 23, 1934, *YCHI*, 10: 14, 16, 234. On Japan's suppression of radicalism during this period, see Max M. Ward, *Thought Crime: Ideology and State Power in Interwar Japan* (Durham, NC: Duke University Press, 2019).

98. Yun Ch'i-ho visited An in jail and hospital several times. See July 15, 1932, March 24, 1935, and February 7, 1938, *YCHI*, 10: 48, 415, 11: 16. On his refusal to join the Privy Council, see February 23, 1938, *YCHI*, 11: 20.

99. August 16, 1938, *YCHI*, 11: 87; "Minami ch'ongdok i Yun Ch'i-ho ong e ponaen sŏhan," *Samch'ŏlli* 10, no. 12 (December 1, 1938): 14–15; "Paeyŏng ponghwa nop'i tŭlgo nodo kat'ŭn shiwi haengjin," *Chosun Ilbo*, July 23, 1939, 3 (Morning Edition); "Ch'waong Yun Ch'i-ho ssi Ito urŏ ch'angssi," *Maeil Sinbo*, June 18, 1940, 2.

100. Grant K. Goodman, "Pio Duran and Philippine Japanophilism," *The Historian* 32, no. 2 (February 1970): 228–242; Goodman, "The Philippine Society of Japan," *Monumenta Nipponica* 22, no. 1/2 (1967): 131–146; Lydia N. Yu-Jose, *Japan View the Philippines, 1900–1941* (Manila: Ateneo de Manila University Press, 1992), 141–154; Capozzola, *Bound by War*, 132–133.

101. "The Philippines: Moral Criticism," *Time* 32, no. 9 (August 29, 1938): 12; Yellen, *Greater East Asia Co-Prosperity Sphere*, 111.

102. Federal Bureau of Investigation (FBI) Files on Doho Newspaper, box 21, folders 1–6, JFP; Hua Hsu, *A Floating Chinaman: Fantasy and Failure across the Pacific* (Cambridge, MA: Harvard University Press, 2016), 200–210.

103. "Kiyoshi K. Kawakami," Washington, DC, file no. 65–86, FBI Files, box 39, YIP; Hayashi, *Asian American Spies*, 81–82.

104. Stanley High, "Alien Poison," *Saturday Evening Post*, August 31, 1940, 9–11, 75–77. For Kawakami's response, see pamphlet titled "Alien Poison," box 154, folder 1, JARPC. On the Smith Act, see Julia Rose Kraut, *Threat of Dissent: A History of Ideological Exclusion and Deportation in the United States* (Cambridge, MA: Harvard University Press, 2020), 107–110.

105. After his arrest on December 8, 1941, Kawakami was detained for several weeks at Immigration Center at Gloucester City, New Jersey, until he appeared before the Enemy Alien Hearing Board at Fort Howard, Maryland, on January 10. On February 11, Kawakami was released on parole by the order of US Attorney General Francis Biddle. See Kiyoshi Kawakami to Willard and Yuri Kawakami, February 19, 1942; Felix Morley to Francis Biddle, December 22, 1941, Box 154, folder 1, JARPC.

106. Kawakami to Matsuoka, March 19, 1919, box 39, folder 1, YIP; Kawakami, *Manchoukuo: A Child of Conflict* (New York: Macmillan, 1933), 1–2.

107. Kawakami, "Yosuke Matsuoka: Japan's Undiplomatic Foreign Minister," *Washington Post*, August 11, 1940, 27; Kawakami, "Tokyo Is Held Duped [*sic*] into Alliance That Aids Germany and Its Expense," *New York Times*, October 1, 1940, 5. On Matsuoka's decision, see Yellen, *Greater East Asia Co-Prosperity Sphere*, 26–42.

108. Janis Mimura, *Planning for Empire: Reform Bureaucrats and the Japanese Wartime State* (Ithaca, NY: Cornell University Press, 2011).

109. "Count Kaneko's Condition Still Serious," *Nichibei Shinbun*, March 6, 1940, 1.

110. Waldo H. Heinrichs, *American Ambassador Joseph C. Grew and the Development of the United States Diplomatic Tradition* (New York: Oxford University Press, 1966), 154, 188–190.

111. Grew to Roosevelt, December 14, 1940, box 43, folder Japan January–September 1941, The President's Secretary's File (PSF), 1933–1945, FDRPLM.

112. Stephen Wertheim, *Tomorrow, The World: The Birth of U.S. Global Supremacy* (Cambridge, MA: Belknap Press of Harvard University Press, 2020), 62–79.

113. Irvine H. Anderson Jr., "The 1941 *De Facto* Embargo on Oil to Japan: A Bureaucratic Reflex," *Pacific Historical Review* 44, no. 2 (May 1975): 201–231; Waldo H. Heinrichs, *Threshold of War: Franklin D. Roosevelt and American Entry into World War II* (New York: Oxford University Press, 1990), 118–145.

114. Earl S. Pomeroy, *Pacific Outpost: American Strategy in Guam and Micronesia* (Stanford, CA: Stanford University Press. 1951), 144–146.

115. Lloyd Gardner, "The Role of the Commerce and Treasury Departments," in Borg and Okamoto eds., *Pearl Harbor as History*, 281–282.

116. R. Douglas Jr. to Jay C. Hormel, December 4, 1940, in *In Danger Undaunted: The Anti-Interventionist Movement of 1940–1941 as Revealed in the Papers of the America First Committee*, ed. Justus D. Doenecke (Stanford, CA: Hoover Institution Press, 1990), 95; Lower, *Bloc of One*, 331.

117. "Nobody Knows the Trouble We're In, July 24, 1941" and "New York AFC Executive Committee, New York Chapter Bulletin, August 2, 1941," in *In Danger Undaunted*, 364–365, 77.

118. Frank D. McCann, *The Brazilian-American Alliance, 1937–1945* (Princeton, NJ: Princeton University Press, 1973), 213–239.

119. Frank Costigliola, "Freedom from Fear," in *The Four Freedoms: Franklin D. Roosevelt and the Evolution of an American Idea*, ed. Jeffrey A. Engel (New York: Oxford University Press, 2016), 165–192.

120. Hubert Kay, "Boss Isolationist: Burton K. Wheeler," *Life* 10, no. 20 (May 19, 1941): 110–112, 114, 117–119.

121. Joseph Driscoll, "President Says Dodd Told Him Senator Expected Hitler Rule of Europe," *New York Herald Tribune*, February 1, 1941, 1A.

122. Bert Andrews, "Welles Asserts Japanese Expansion Is Peril to U.S. Interests in Pacific," *New York Herald Tribune*, July 25, 1941, 1A.

123. "Nobody Knows the Trouble We're In," 365. On US import of rubber from Southeast Asia, see Anne L. Foster, *Projections of Power: The United States and Europe in Colonial Southeast Asia, 1919–1941* (Durham, NC: Duke University Press, 2010), 119–121, 135–141. On synthetic rubber, see Daniel Immerwahr, *How to Hide an Empire: A History of the Greater United States* (New York: Farrar, Straus & Giroux, 2019), 262–277.

124. "Danger in Orient Seen by Wheeler," *New York Times*, August 28, 1941, 3. Castle, quoted in Alfred L. Castle, "William R. Castle and Opposition to U.S. Involvement in an Asian War, 1939–1941," *Pacific Historical Review* 54, no. 3 (August 1985): 345.

125. John L. Spivak, "'America First' Exposed," *New Masses*, 40, no. 14 (September 30, 1941): 10–14.

126. Eri Hotta, *Japan 1941: Countdown to Infamy* (New York: Vintage, 2013), 261–268.

127. William Castle Jr., "Why War with Japan?," *New York Herald Tribune*, December 7, 1941, A9.

128. Beth Bailey, "The Attacks of December 7/8," in *Beyond Pearl Harbor: A Pacific History*, ed. Beth Bailey and David Farber (Lawrence: University Press of Kansas, 2019), 9–18.

129. "Mr. Castle's Letter Delayed," *New York Herald Tribune*, December 14, 1941, A7. The letter is dated December 8.

Epilogue

1. "Yŏngguk ŭl t'ado hara! paeyŏng tongjihoe t'ansaeng," *Dong-A Ilbo*, July 13, 1939, 3; August 22, 1941, *YCHI*, 11: 406.

2. December 9, 1941, *YCHI*, 11: 409; "Taedonga chŏnjaeng kwa pando ŭi mujang," *Samch'ŏlli* 14, no. 1 (January 1, 1941): 20.

3. "Taedonga chŏnjaeng kwa pando ŭi mujang," 20.

4. December 26, 1941, *YCHI*, 11: 11: 410.

5. David Levering Lewis, *W. E. B. Du Bois, 1919–1963: The Fight for Equality and the American Century* (New York: Henry Holt, 2000), 419; FBI report on W. E. B. Du Bois, New York City, May 1, 1942, 1, FBI file 100-99729.

6. W. E. B. Du Bois, "A Chronicle of Race Relations," *Phylon* 2, no. 2 (2nd Quarter 1941): 181–183. In his autobiography, *Dusk of Dawn* (1940), Du Bois said that it was "only years after" 1924 that he learned about the connection between the defeat of the Dyer Anti-Lynching bill and the passage Japanese exclusion. It is probable that he learned about it from reading Rodman W. Paul, *The Abrogation of the Gentlemen's Agreement. Being the Harvard Phi Beta Kappa Prize Essay for 1936* (Cambridge, MA: The Society, 1936). See Du Bois to Harvard University Press, November 30, 1939, WEBDBP; Du Bois, *Dusk of Dawn: An Essay toward an Autobiography of a Race Concept* (New York: Harcourt, Brace and Company, 1940), 270.

7. On Yun Ch'i-ho's place in the Korean historiography, see Mark Caprio, "Loyal Patriot? Traitorous Collaborator? The Yun Ch'i-ho Diaries and the Question of National Loyalty,"

Journal of Colonialism and Colonial History 7, no. 3 (2006): n.p. On the influence of Du Bois on writings about the US empire, see Ryan Irwin, "Mapping Race: Historicizing the History of the Color-Line," *History Compass* 8, no. 9 (September 2010): 984–999.

8. On the erasure of the Philippines from FDR's "Day of Infamy" speech, see Daniel Immerwahr, *How to Hide an Empire: A History of the Greater United States* (New York: Farrar, Straus & Giroux, 2019), 3–7.

9. *Summary of Past Policy and of More Immediate Events, in Relation to the Pacific Area* (Washington, DC: US Government Printing Office, 1941), 1.

10. Ibid., 2. On FDR and Japanese Americans, see Greg Robinson, *By Order of the President: FDR and the Internment of Japanese Americans* (Cambridge, MA: Harvard University Press, 2001).

11. John W. Dower, *War without Mercy: Race and Power in the Pacific War* (New York: Pantheon, 1986).

12. On African American support for Japan during World War II, see Reginal Kearney, *African American Views of the Japanese: Solidarity or Sedition?* (Albany: State University of New York Press, 1998), 92–127; Marc Gallichio, *The African American Encounter with Japan and China: Black Internationalism in Asia, 1895–1945* (Chapel Hill: University of North Carolina Press, 2000), 123–138; Gerald Horne, *Facing the Rising Sun: African Americans, Japan, and the Rise of Afro-Asian Solidarity* (New York: New York University Press, 2018), 41–111. On the "Double V" campaign, see Kimberley L. Phillips, *War! What Is It Good For?: Black Freedom Struggles and the U.S. Military* (Chapel Hill: University of North Carolina Press, 2012), 20–64.

13. Richard S. Kim, *The Quest for Statehood: Korean Immigrant Nationalism and U.S. Sovereignty, 1905–1945* (New York: Oxford University Press, 2011), 132–157; Anne Soon Choi, "Unity for What? Unity for Whom?: The United Korean Committee of North America, 1941–1945," in *From the Land of Hibiscus: Koreans in Hawai'i, 1903–1950*, ed. Yŏngho Ch'oe (Honolulu: University of Hawai'i Press, 2007), 220–254. On Koreans who fought for the Japanese empire, see Takashi Fujitani, *Race for Empire: Koreans as Japanese and Japanese as Americans during World War II* (Berkeley: University of California Press, 2013), 35–77; Brandon Palmer, *Fighting for the Enemy: Koreans in Japan's War, 1937–1945* (Seattle: University of Washington Press, 2013).

14. Christopher Capozzola, *Bound by War: How the United States and the Philippines Built America's First Pacific Century* (New York: Basic Books, 2020), 151–190; Fujitani, *Race for Empire*, 78–121.

15. Thomas A. Guglielmo, *Divisions: A New History of Racism and Resistance in America's World War II Military* (New York: Oxford University Press, 2021).

16. Robert Dallek, *Franklin D. Roosevelt and American Foreign Policy, 1932–1945*, 2nd ed. (New York: Oxford University Press, 1995), 420; Warren Kimball, *Forged in War: Roosevelt, Churchill, and the Second World War* (New York: William Morrow, 1997), 201–205. Hull, quoted in John Lewis Gaddis, *The United States and the Origins of the Cold War, 1941–1947* (New York: Columbia University Press, 1972), 26.

17. Du Bois, *Color and Democracy: Colonies and Peace* (New York: Harcourt, 1945), 6–7, 58–59. On the racial equality proposal at the Dumbarton Conference, see Paul Gordon Lauren, *Power and Prejudice: The Politics and Diplomacy of Racial Discrimination* (New York: Taylor & Francis, 1988), 147–158; Gallichio, *African American Encounter with Japan and China*, 184–189.

18. "Chronicle of Race Relations," *Phylon* 1, no. 2 (2nd Quarter 1940): 179; idem., *Phylon* 3, no. 2 (2nd Quarter 1942): 211; idem., *Phylon* 4, no. 1 (1st Quarter 1943); 74; idem., *Phylon* 4, no. 2 (2nd Quarter 1943): 167.

19. Karen Leong, "Foreign Policy, National Identity, and Citizenship: The Roosevelt White House and the Expediency of Repeal," *Journal of American Ethnic History* 22, no. 4 (Summer 2003): 3–30; Madeline Y. Hsu, *The Good Immigrants: How the Yellow Peril Became the Model Minority* (Princeton, NJ: Princeton University Press, 2015), 81–103. On Soong's tour, see Karen Leong, *The China Mystique: Pearl S. Buck, Anna May Wong, Mayling Soong, and the Transformation of American Orientalism* (Berkeley: University of California Press, 2005), 131–154.

20. Fred Riggs, *Pressures on Congress: A Study of the Repeal of Chinese Exclusion* (New York, King's Crown Press, 1950), 83–88.

21. Robert A. Kinney, report on Yun Ch'i-ho, April 8, 1944, RG 165, Records of the Military Intelligence Division (MID, G-2), Regional File 1922–44, entry 77, box 2262, folder 5590-Korea, Who's Who, location 390/32/33/04, National Archives, College Park, MD.

22. OSS report on Yun Ch'i-ho, June 23, 1945, HTUC, 28: 84–85.

23. "Counter Intelligence Corps (CIC) Area Study: Korea, August 1945," p. 23, RG 554, USAFIK: XXIV Corps, G-2 Historical Section, 1945–1948, entry 1256(A1), box 51, location 290/51/19–23/3-5/E.1256(A1), National Archives, College Park, MD.

24. "Fortnightly Intelligence Report, No. 3 (1945): Japan," February 1st–15th, 1945, RG 208, Records of the Office of War Information, 1926–1951, Records of the Regional Analysis Division, Informational File on Asia, 1942–1946, entry 370, box 404, National Archives, College Park, MD.

25. G-2 Periodic Report, 9/8–10/31/45, p. 4, RG 554, USAFIK XXIV Corps, G-2, Historical Section, 1945–1948, box 45, location 290/51/19-23/3–5/E.1256(A1)/box 45, National Archives, College Park, MD.

26. "Old Man's Ruminations (I)," October 15, 1945, in YCHS, 262–263. This document did not become available until 1980, when Yun's oldest son, Yun Yong-sun (1896–1988), donated it to Kuksa P'yŏnch'an Wiwŏnhoe (National Institute of Korean History).

27. Ngũgĩ wa Thiong'o, Decolonising the Mind: The Politics of Language in African Literature (London: J. Currey, 1986).

28. Du Bois, Color and Democracy, 108–109.

29. Carol Anderson, Eyes off the Prize: The United Nations and the African American Struggle for Human Rights, 1944–1955 (Cambridge: Cambridge University Press, 2003), 56–61.

30. Du Bois, "Africa Today" (1948), quoted in Bill Mullen, W. E. B. Du Bois: Revolutionary across the Color Line (London: Pluto Press, 2016), 126.

31. MacArthur to Joint Chief of Staff, December 16, 1945, FRUS 1945, 6: 1145–1146; United States Delegation Minutes, First Formal Session, Conference of Foreign Ministers, Spiridonovka, Moscow, December 16, 1945; Memorandum by the United States Delegation at the Moscow Conference of Foreign Ministers, December 17, 1945, FRUS 1945, 2: 618–621, 641–643.

32. Historian Monica Kim aptly names the actions of the US military government in postcolonial South Korea as "Civilizing Mission, Improvised." See Monica Kim, The Interrogation Rooms of the Korean War: The Untold History (Princeton, NJ: Princeton University Press, 2019), 48–56.

33. On the roots of postwar modernization and development in the colonial experiences of the United States, see David Ekbladh, The Great American Mission: Modernization and the Construction of an American World Order (Princeton, NJ: Princeton University Press, 2009).

34. Douglas MacArthur, quoted in John W. Dower, Embracing Defeat: Japan in the Wake of World War II (New York: W. W. Norton, 1999), 550.

35. For the most insightful analysis of this irony, see Simeon Man, Soldiering through Empire: Race and the Making of the Decolonizing Pacific (Oakland: University of California Press, 2018).

36. For the best analysis of how Cold War imperatives changed US immigration policies toward Asia, see Jane Hong, Opening the Gates to Asia: A Transpacific History of How America Repealed Asian Exclusion (Chapel Hill: University of North Carolina Press, 2019). For classic works on how Cold War imperatives changed US domestic policy toward African Americans, see Mary L. Dudziak, Cold War Civil Rights: Race and the Image of American Democracy (Princeton, NJ: Princeton University Press, 2000); Thomas Borstelmann, The Cold War and the Color Line: American Race Relations in the Global Arena (Cambridge, MA: Harvard University Press, 2001).

BIBLIOGRAPHY

Archives Consulted

UNITED STATES

Bancroft Library, University of California, Berkeley, Berkeley, CA
    California Joint Immigration Committee Press Release and Documents
    Japanese American Research Project Interviews
    Hiram Johnson Papers
    Yoshi Saburo Kuno Papers
    Panama-Pacific International Exposition Records
    James D. Phelan Papers
    Chester H. Rowell Papers
    Paul Scharrenberg Papers
Beinecke Rare Book and Manuscript Library, Yale University, New Haven, CT
    Langston Hughes Papers
    James Weldon Johnson and Grace Nail Johnson Papers
Burke Library Archives, Union Theological Seminary, New York, NY
    Korean Conspiracy Case Papers
Charles E. Young Research Library, University of California, Los Angeles, Los Angeles, CA
    Josephine Fowler Papers
    Yuji Ichioka Papers
    Japanese American Research Project Collection
    Karl Yoneda Papers
Division of Rare and Manuscript Collections, Cornell University, Ithaca, NY
    Willard Dickerman Strait Papers
Franklin D. Roosevelt Presidential Library and Museum, Hyde Park, NY.
    Franklin D. Roosevelt, Master Speech File, 1898–1945
    President's Secretary's File (PSF), 1933–1945
Green Library, Special Collections, Stanford University, Stanford, CA
    John P. Irish Papers
    David Starr Jordan Papers
    Meyer Lissner Papers
    E. A. Ross Papers
Hoover Institution on War, Revolution and Peace Archives, Stanford, CA
    Hoji Shinbun Digital Collection
    Japanese in the United States Pamphlet Collection
    David Starr Jordan Papers
    Kanzaki Kiichi Papers

Survey of Race Relations Records
Houghton Library, Harvard University, Cambridge, MA
        Gulick Family Papers
Howard Gotlieb Archival Research Center, Boston University, Boston, MA
        Guardian of Boston / William Monroe Trotter Collection
Manuscript Division, Library Congress, Washington, DC
        George Kennan Papers
        Philander Knox Papers
        Papers of the NAACP
        Theodore Roosevelt Papers
        William Howard Taft Papers
Manuscripts and Archives Division, New York Public Library, New York, NY
        Horace Newton Allen Papers
Presbyterian Historical Society, Philadelphia, PA
        Federal Council of the Churches of Christ in America Records (RG 18)
        United Presbyterian Church in the U.S.A. Commission on Ecumenical Mission and
            Relations. Secretaries Files: Korea Mission, 1903–1972 (RG 140)
Rare Book & Manuscript Library, Columbia University, New York, NY
        Institute of Pacific Relations Records
Special Collections and University Archives, University of Massachusetts Amherst Libraries,
    Amherst, MA
        W. E. B. Du Bois Papers
Stuart A. Rose Manuscript, Archives, and Rare Book Library, Emory University, Atlanta, GA
        Warren A. Candler Papers
        Philip J. Jaffe Papers
        Yun Ch'i-ho Papers
US National Archives, College Park, MD
        Records of the Department of State (RG59)
            Despatches from United States Ministers to Korea, 1883–1905, M-134
            *Records of the Department of State Relating to Internal Affairs of Korea (Chosun) 1910–
                1929,* M-426
        Records of the Federal Bureau of Investigation (RG65)
            *Investigative Case Files of the Bureau of Investigation, 1908–1922, Old German Files
                1909–1921,* M-1085
        Records of the Immigration and Naturalization Service (RG85)
            Subject correspondence, 1906–132
        Records of the War Department General and Special Staffs (RG165)
            Records of the Military Intelligence Division (MID, G-2), Regional File 1922–1944
        Records of the Office of War Information (RG 208)
            Records of the Regional Analysis Division, Informational File on Asia, 1942–1946
        Records of General Headquarters, Far East Command, Supreme Commander Allied
            Powers, and United Nations Command (RG 554)
            USAFIK XXIV Corps, G-2, Historical Section, 1945–1948
Wisconsin Historical Society, Madison, WI
        Richard T. Ely Papers
        Edward Alsworth Ross Papers
Yale Divinity School Library, New Haven, CT
        Arthur Judson Brown Papers
        John R. Mott Papers
Yale University Archives, New Haven, CT
        George Trumbull Ladd Papers
        Francis G. Newlands Papers

SOUTH KOREA

Kungnip Chung'ang Tosŏgwan (National Library of Korea)
  Taehanmin'guk Shinmun Ak'aibŭ (Archive of Korean Newspapers)
Kuksa P'yŏnch'an Wiwŏnhoe (National Institute of Korean History)
  Chuhan Ilbon Kongsagwan kirok (Records of the Japanese Legation in Korea)
  Hanminjok tongnip undongsa charyojip (Documents of the Korean Independence
    Movement)
  Kojong Sillok (Veritable Royal Records of Emperor Kojong)
  Tongambu munsŏ (Records of the Resident General of Korea)

Letters, Articles, and Diaries in Edited Volumes

Aptheker, Herbert, ed. *Writings by W. E. B. Du Bois in Non-Periodical Literature*. Millwood,
  NY: Kraus-Thomson, 1982.
Doenecke, Justus D., ed. *In Danger Undaunted: The Anti-Interventionist Movement of 1940–1941
  as Revealed in the Papers of the America First Committee*. Stanford, CA: Hoover Institution
  Press, 1990.
Doenecke, Justus D., ed. *The Diplomacy of Frustration: The Manchurian Crisis of 1931–1933 as
  Revealed in the Papers of Stanley K. Hornbeck*. Stanford, CA: Hoover Institution Press, 1981.
Harlan, Louis R., ed. *Booker T. Washington Papers*. Urbana: University of Illinois Press, 1972–1984.
Kuksa P'yŏnch'an Wiwŏnhoe, ed. *Yun Ch'i-ho Ilgi* (Yun Ch'i-ho's Diary). Seoul: Kuksa P'yŏnch'an
  Wiwŏnhoe, 1973–1989.
Kuksa P'yŏnch'an Wiwŏnhoe, ed. *Yun Ch'i-ho Ilgi Sŏhanjip* (Letters of Yun Ch'i-ho). Seoul: Kuksa
  P'yŏnch'an Wiwŏnhoe, 1980.
Lew, Young Ick, ed. *The Syngman Rhee Correspondence in English, 1904–1948*. Seoul: Institute for
  Modern Korean Studies, Yonsei University, 2009.
Link, Arthur S., ed. *Papers of Woodrow Wilson*. Princeton, NJ: Princeton University Press,
  1966–1993.
Morrison, Elting E., ed. *Letters of Theodore Roosevelt*. Cambridge, MA: Harvard University Press,
  1951–1954.
Mullen, Bill V., and Cathryn Watson, eds. *W. E. B. Du Bois on Asia: Crossing the World Color Line*.
  Jackson: University Press of Mississippi, 2005.
Ok Sŏng-dŭk and Yi Man-yŏl, eds. *Ŏndŏudŭ Charyojip* (Underwood Papers). Seoul: Yonsei
  University Press, 2009.

Government Documents

*Administration of Immigration Laws: Hearings before the Committee on Immigration and
  Naturalization, House of Representatives, 66th Cong., 2nd Sess.* Washington, DC: Government
  Printing Office, 1920.
Alien Land Laws and Alien Rights, House of Representatives Document no. 89, 67th Cong., 1st Sess.
  Washington, DC: Government Printing Office, 1921.
Annual Report of the Governor General of the Philippine Islands 1932. Washington, DC: Government
  Printing Press, 1934.
Congressional Record. Washington DC: US Government Printing Office, 1873–.
*Document A: Present Condition of China: With Reference to Circumstances Affecting International
  Relations and the Good Understanding between Nations upon Which Peace Depends*.
  Tokyo: Gaimushō, 1932.
Government-General of Chosen. *Annual Report on Reforms and Progress in Chosen (Korea)*. Keijo
  (Seoul): Government-General of Chosen, 1911–1923.
*Government of the Philippines: Hearings before the Committee on the Philippines, United States Senate,
  Part 5, 63rd Cong., 3rd Sess.* Washington, DC: Government Printing Office, 1915.

His Imperial Japanese Majesty's Residency General. *Annual Report on Reforms and Progress in Korea.* Seoul: Resident General of Korea, 1907–1910.

Illegal Entry of Aliens: Hearing before the Committee on Immigration United States Senate, 66th Cong. 1st sess. Pursuant to S. Res. 176. Washington, DC: Government Printing Office, 1919.

"Japanese Immigration": Hearings before the Committee on Immigration and Naturalization, House of Representatives, 66th Cong., 2nd Sess. Washington, DC: Government Printing Office, 1921.

Japanese Immigration and Colonization: Skeleton Brief by Mr. V. S. McClatchy, Representative of the Japanese Exclusion League of California, on "Japanese Immigration and Colonization," Filed with the Secretary of the State, 67th Cong., 1st Sess. Senate Document no. 55. Washington, DC: Government Printing Office, 1921.

Japanese Immigration Legislation: Hearings before the Committee on Immigration United States Senate, 68th Cong., 1st Sess., on S. 2576. Washington, DC: Government Printing Office, 1924.

Japanese in the City of San Francisco, Cal, Senate Document no. 147, 59th Cong, 2nd Sess. Washington, DC: Government Printing Office, 1907.

Labor Problems in Hawaii, Committee on Immigration and Naturalization, House of Representatives. Washington, DC: Government Printing Office, 1921.

Neutrality, Peace Legislation, and Our Foreign Policy: Hearings before the Committee on Foreign Relations, United States Senate, April 5, 1939. Washington, DC: US Government Printing Office, 1939.

Papers Relating to the Foreign Relations of the United States. Washington, DC: US Government Printing Office.

"Percentage Plans for Restriction of Immigration," Hearings before the Committee on Immigration and Naturalization, House of Representatives, 66th Cong., 1st Sess. Washington, DC: Government Printing Office, 1919.

Philippines Independence: Hearings before the Committee on the Philippines, United States Senate, and the Committee on Insular Affairs, House of Representatives, Held Jointly. Washington, DC: Government Printing Office, 1919.

Report of the Honorable Roland S. Morris on Japanese Immigration and Alleged Discriminatory Legislation against Japanese Residents in the United States. Washington, DC: Government Printing Press, 1921.

Resolution of Philippine Legislature Declining to Accept the Act of Congress Providing for Philippines Independence, 73rd Cong., 2nd Sess. Washington, DC: US Government Printing Press, 1934.

Restriction of Immigration: Hearings before the Committee on Immigration and Naturalization, House of Representatives, 63rd Cong., 2nd Sess. on H. R. 6060. Washington, DC: Government Printing Press, 1913.

Statehood for Hawaii: Hearings before the Joint Committee on Hawaii, Congress of the United States, 75th Cong., 2nd Sess. Washington, DC: US Government Printing Office, 1938.

Thirty-first Annual Report of the Governor of Porto Rico. Washington, DC: Government Printing Press, 1932.

League of Nations Documents

Appeal by the Chinese Government—Report of the Commission on Enquiry. Geneva: League of Nations, 1932.

Young, C. Walter. "Korean Problems in Manchuria as Factor in the Sino-Japanese Dispute." Special Study No. 9, *Supplementary Documents to the Report of the Commission of Inquiry.* Geneva: League of Nations, 1932.

Newspapers

UNITED STATES

Atlanta Constitution

Chicago Daily Tribune
Chicago Defender
Dōhō (Los Angeles)
Fresno Republican
Hawaii Hōchi (Honolulu)
Honolulu-Star Bulletin
Kashū Mainichi Shinbun (Los Angeles)
Los Angeles Examiner
Los Angeles Times
New York Age
New York Herald Tribune
New York Times
Nichibei Shinbun (San Francisco)
Nippu Jiji (Honolulu)
Oakland Tribune
Organized Labor (San Francisco)
Pittsburgh Courier
Rafu Shinpō (Los Angeles)
Sacramento Bee
San Francisco Call
San Francisco Chronicle
San Francisco Examiner
Shin Sekai (San Francisco)
Shin Sekai Ashashi Shinbun (San Francisco)
Sinhan Minbo (San Francisco)
Washington Post

JAPAN

Japan Chronicle (Kobe)
Japan Times & Mail (Tokyo)

SOUTH KOREA

Dong-A Ilbo (Seoul)
Keijō Nippō (Seoul)
Maeil Sinbo (Seoul)
Seoul Press

Periodicals

UNITED STATES

American Journal of International Law
Annals of the American Academy of Political and Social Science
Asia
Atlantic Monthly
Boston City Club Bulletin
California Outlook
Christian Advocate
Collier's
Crisis
Current History
Federal Council Bulletin
Foreign Affairs

Geographical Review
Grizzly Bear
Harper's Weekly
Independent
Japan
Journal of Race Development
Literary Digest
Missionary Review of the World
Nation
New Masses
New Republic
North American Review
Outlook
Pacific Affairs
Pacific Monthly
Time
World To-Day

JAPAN

Japan Evangelist

SOUTH KOREA

Korea Mission Field
Korea Review
Samch'ŏlli

Selected Secondary Sources

Adelman, Jeremy, ed. *Empire and the Social Sciences: Global Histories of Knowledge.* London: Bloomsbury Academic, 2019.

Akami, Tomoko. *Internationalizing the Pacific: The United States, Japan, and the Institute of Pacific Relations in War and Peace, 1919–45.* London: Routledge, 2003.

Atkinson, David C. *The Burden of White Supremacy: Containing Asian Migration in the British Empire and the United States.* Chapel Hill: University of North Carolina Press, 2017.

Aune, Stefan. "Indian Fighters in the Philippines: Imperial Culture and Military Violence in the Philippine-American War." *Pacific Historical Review* 90, no. 4 (Fall 2021): 419–447.

Auslin, Michael R. *Negotiating with Imperialism: The Unequal Treaties and the Culture of Japanese Diplomacy.* Cambridge, MA: Harvard University Press, 2006.

Asada, Sadao. *From Mahan to Pearl Harbor: The Imperial Japanese Navy and the United States.* Annapolis, MD: Naval Institute Press, 2006.

Aydin, Cemil. *The Politics of Anti-Westernism in Asia: Visions of World Order in Pan-Islamism and Pan-Asian Thought.* New York: Columbia University Press, 2007.

Azuma, Eiichiro. *Between Two Empires: Race, History, and Transnationalism in Japanese America.* New York: Oxford University Press, 2005.

Azuma, Eiichiro. "Dancing with the Rising Sun: Strategic Alliance between Japanese Immigrants and Their 'Home' Government." In *The Transnational Politics of Asian Americans,* edited by Christian Collet and Pei-te Lien, 25–37. Philadelphia: Temple University Press, 2009.

Azuma, Eiichiro. *In Search of Our Frontier: Japanese America and Settler Colonialism in the Construction of Japan's Borderless Empire.* Oakland: University of California Press, 2019.

Baldoz, Rick. *The Third Asiatic Invasion: Empire and Migration in Filipino America, 1898–1946.* New York: New York University Press, 2011.

Baldwin, Frank. "The March First Movement: Korean Challenge and Japanese Response." PhD diss., Columbia University, 1969.

Bang, Gi-jung, "Ilcheha Yi Hun-gu ŭi Nong'ŏp'ron kwa Kyŏngje charip sasang." *Yŏksamunjeyŏn'gu* 1 (December 1996): 113–162.

Bashford, Alison. *Global Population: History, Geopolitics, and Life on Earth*. New York: Columbia University Press, 2014.

Beale, Howard K. *Theodore Roosevelt and the Rise of America to World Power*. Baltimore: Johns Hopkins University Press. 1956.

Bederman, Gail. *Manliness & Civilization: A Cultural History of Gender and Race in the United States, 1880–1917*. Chicago: University of Chicago Press, 1995.

Beisner, Robert L. *Twelve against Empire; the Anti-Imperialists, 1898–1900*. New York: McGraw-Hill, 1968.

Bell, Duncan. *Dreamworlds of Race: Empire and the Utopian Destiny of Anglo-America*. Princeton, NJ: Princeton University Press, 2020.

Bell, Roger. *Last among Equals: Hawaiian Statehood and American Politics*. Honolulu: University of Hawai'i Press, 1984.

Bender, Thomas. *A Nation among Nations: America's Place in World History*. New York: Hill and Wang, 2006.

Benton-Cohen, Katherine. *Inventing the Immigration Problem: The Dillingham Commission and Its Legacy*. Cambridge, MA: Harvard University Press, 2019.

Bönker, Dirk. *Militarism in a Global Age: Naval Ambitions in Germany and the United States before World War I*. Ithaca, NY: Cornell University Press, 2012.

Borg, Dorothy. *The United States and the Far Eastern Crisis of 1933–1938 from the Manchurian Incident through the Initial Stage of the Undeclared Sino-Japanese War*. Cambridge, MA: Harvard University Press, 1964.

Borg, Dorothy, and Shumpei Okamoto, eds. *Pearl Harbor as History: Japanese-American Relations, 1931–1941*. New York: Columbia University Press, 1973.

Borstelmann, Thomas. *The Cold War and the Color Line: American Race Relations in the Global Arena*. Cambridge, MA: Harvard University Press, 2001.

Borstelmann, Thomas. *Just Like Us: The American Struggle to Understand Foreigners*. New York: Columbia University Press, 2020.

Brooks, Charlotte. *American Exodus: Second-Generation Chinese Americans in China, 1901–1949*. Oakland: University of California Press, 2019.

Burbank, Jane, and Frederik Cooper. *Empires in World History: Power and the Politics of Difference*. Princeton, NJ: Princeton University Press, 2010.

Capozzola, Christopher. *Bound by War: How the United States and the Philippines Built America's First Pacific Century*. New York: Basic Books, 2020.

Caprio, Mark. *Japanese Assimilation Policies in Colonial Korea, 1910–1945*. Seattle: University of Washington Press, 2009.

Caprio, Mark. "Loyal Patriot? Traitorous Collaborator? The Yun Ch'iho Diaries and the Question of National Loyalty." *Journal of Colonialism and Colonial History* 7, no. 3 (2006): n.p.

Chan, Sucheng, ed. *Entry Denied: Exclusion and the Chinese Community in America, 1882–1943*. Philadelphia: Temple University Press, 1991.

Chan, Sucheng, and Madeline Y. Hsu, eds. *Chinese Americans and the Politics of Race and Culture*. Philadelphia: Temple University Press, 2008.

Chang, Gordon H. "Asian Immigrants and American Foreign Relations." In *Pacific Passage: The Study of American–East Asian Relations on the Eve of the Twenty-First Century*, edited by Warren I. Cohen, 103–118. New York: Columbia University Press, 1996.

Chang, Gordon H. *Fateful Ties: A History of America's Preoccupation with China*. Cambridge, MA: Harvard University Press, 2015.

Chang, Gordon H., ed. *Morning Glory, Evening Shadow: Yamato Ichihashi and His Internment Writings, 1942–1945*. Stanford, CA: Stanford University Press, 1997.

Chang, Kornel. *Pacific Connections: The Making of the US-Canadian Borderlands*. Berkeley: University of California Press, 2012.

Chiang, Yung-chen. *Social Engineering and the Social Sciences in China.* Cambridge: Cambridge University Press, 2001.

Ch'oe Pyŏng-to. "Manbosan sagŏn chik'u hwagyo paech'ŏk sagŏn e taehan ilche ŭi taeŭng." *Han'guksa yŏn'guhoe* 156 (March 2012): 297–329.

Chŏn, Bok-hee. "19 segi mal chinbojŏk chishigin ŭi injongjuŭijŏk t'ŭksŏng: tongnipshinmun kwa yun ch'i-ho ilg rŭl chungshim ŭro." *Han'guk chŏngch'i hakhoe po* 29, no. 1 (October 1995): 125–145.

Choy, Catherine Ceniza. *Empire of Care: Nursing and Migration in Filipino American History.* Durham, NC: Duke University Press, 2003.

Coates, Benjamin Allen. *Legalist Empire: International Law and American Foreign Relations in the Early Twentieth Century.* New York: Oxford University Press, 2016.

Cooper, John Milton. *The Warrior and the Priest: Woodrow Wilson and Theodore Roosevelt.* Cambridge, MA: Belknap Press of Harvard University Press, 1983.

Cooper, John Milton. *Woodrow Wilson: A Biography.* New York: Alfred A. Knopf, 2009.

Cullinane, Michael Patrick. *Liberty and American Anti-Imperialism, 1898–1909.* New York: Palgrave Macmillan, 2012.

Cumings, Bruce. *Dominion from Sea to Sea: Pacific Ascendancy and American Power.* New Haven, CT: Yale University Press, 2009.

Cushman, Gregory T. *Guano and the Opening of the Pacific World: A Global Ecological History.* Cambridge: Cambridge University Press, 2013.

Daniels, Roger. *The Politics of Prejudice: The Anti-Japanese Movement in California and the Struggle for Japanese Exclusion.* Berkeley: University of California Press, 1977.

Davidann, Jon Thares. *Cultural Diplomacy in U.S.-Japanese Relations, 1919–1941.* New York: Palgrave Macmillan, 2007.

Davidann, Jon Thares, ed. *Hawai'i at the Crossroads of the U.S. and Japan before the Pacific War.* Honolulu: University of Hawai'i Press, 2008.

Davis, Teresa Elisabeth Homans. "America for Humanity: Law, Liberalism and Empire in the South Atlantic (1870–1939)." PhD diss., Princeton University, 2018.

De Ceuster, Koen. "From Modernization to Collaboration: The Dilemma of Korean Cultural Nationalism: The Case of Yun Ch'i-ho (1865–1945)." PhD diss., Katholieke Universiteit Leuven, 1994.

Dennett, Tyler. *Roosevelt and the Russo-Japanese War; a Critical Study of American Policy in Eastern Asia in 1902–5, Based Primarily upon the Private Papers of Theodore Roosevelt.* Garden City, NY: Doubleday, Page & Company, 1925.

Dickinson, Frederick R. *War and National Reinvention: Japan in the Great War, 1914–1919.* Cambridge: Cambridge University Press, 1999.

Dickinson, Frederick R. *World War I and the Triumph of a New Japan, 1919–1930.* Cambridge: Cambridge University Press, 2013.

Dirlik, Arif. *Anarchism in the Chinese Revolution.* Berkeley: University of California Press, 1991.

Dower, John W. *War without Mercy: Race and Power in the Pacific War.* New York: Pantheon, 1986.

Dudden, Alexis. *Japan's Colonization of Korea: Discourse and Power.* Honolulu: University of Hawai'i Press, 2005.

Dudziak, Mary L. *Cold War Civil Rights Race and the Image of American Democracy.* Princeton, NJ: Princeton University Press, 2000.

Duus, Masayo. *The Japanese Conspiracy: The Oahu Sugar Strike of 1920.* Berkeley: University of California Press, 1999.

Duus, Peter. *The Abacus and the Sword: The Japanese Penetration of Korea, 1895–1910.* Berkeley: University of California Press, 1998.

Fields, David. *Foreign Friends: Syngman Rhee, American Exceptionalism, and the Division of Korea.* Lexington: University Press of Kentucky, 2019.

Foster, Anne L. *Projections of Power: The United States and Europe in Colonial Southeast Asia, 1919–1941.* Durham, NC: Duke University Press, 2010.

Fowler, Josephine. *Japanese and Chinese Immigrant Activists: Organizing in American and International Communist Movements, 1919–1933.* New Brunswick, NJ: Rutgers University Press, 2007.

Fujitani, Takashi. *Race for Empire: Koreans as Japanese and Japanese as Americans during World War II.* Berkeley and Los Angeles: University of California Press, 2011.

Gabaccia, Donna R. *Foreign Relations: American Immigration in Global Perspective.* Princeton, NJ: Princeton University Press, 2012.

Gallicchio, Marc. *The African American Encounter with Japan and China: Black Internationalism in Asia, 1895–1945.* Chapel Hill: University of North Carolina Press, 2000.

Geiger, Andrea. *Subverting Exclusion: Transpacific Encounters with Race, Caste, and Borders, 1885–1928.* New Haven, CT: Yale University Press, 2011.

Gerstle, Gary. *American Crucible: Race and Nation in the Twentieth Century.* Princeton, NJ: Princeton University Press, c2001.

Gillette, Howard. "The Military Occupation of Cuba, 1899–1902: Workshop for American Progressivism." *American Quarterly* 25, no. 4 (October 1973): 410–425.

Godshalk, David Fort. *Veiled Visions: The 1906 Atlanta Race Riot and the Reshaping of American Race Relations.* Chapel Hill: University of North Carolina Press, 2005.

Gordon, Andrew. *Labor and Imperial Democracy in Prewar Japan.* Berkeley: University of California Press, 2001.

Griffith, Sarah M. *The Fight for Asian American Civil Rights: Liberal Protestant Activism, 1900–1950.* Urbana: University of Illinois Press, 2018.

Guglielmo, Thomas A. *White on Arrival: Italians, Race, Color, and Power in Chicago, 1890–1945.* New York: Oxford University Press, 2003.

Ha, Yong-Chool, ed. *International Impact of Colonial Rule in Korea, 1910–1945.* Seattle: University of Washington Press, 2019.

Han, Eric C. "The Nationality Law and Entry Restrictions of 1899: Constructing Japanese Identity between China and the West." *Japan Forum,* 30, no. 4 (December 2018): 531–538.

Harlan, Louis. "Booker T. Washington and the White Man's Burden." *American Historical Review* 71, no. 2 (January 1966): 441–467.

Harrington, Fred Harvey. *God, Mammon, and the Japanese; Dr. Horace N. Allen and Korean-American Relations, 1884–1905.* Madison: University of Wisconsin Press, 1944.

Hayashi, Brian Masaru. "From Race to Nation: The Institute of Pacific Relations, Asia Americans, and George Blakeslee, from 1908 to 1929." *Japanese Journal of American Studies* 3 (2012): 51–71.

Heinrichs, Waldo H. *American Ambassador Joseph C. Grew and the Development of the United States Diplomatic Tradition.* New York: Oxford University Press, 1966.

Heinrichs, Waldo H. *Threshold of War: Franklin D. Roosevelt and American Entry into World War II.* New York: Oxford University Press, 1990.

Henning, Joseph M. *Outposts of Civilization: Race, Religion, and the Formative Years of American-Japanese Relations.* New York: New York University Press, 2000.

Higham, John. *Strangers in the Land: Patterns of American Nativism, 1860–1925.* New Brunswick, NJ: Rutgers University Press, 1955.

Hirobe, Izumi. *Japanese Pride, American Prejudice: Modifying the Exclusion Clause of the 1924 Immigration Act.* Stanford, CA: Stanford University Press, 2001.

Hofstadter, Richard. *The Age of Reform: From Bryan to F.D.R.* New York: Vintage Books, 1955.

Hoganson, Kristin L. *Fighting for American Manhood: How Gender Politics Provoked the Spanish-American and Philippine-American Wars.* New Haven, CT: Yale University Press, 1998.

Hoganson, Kristin L. *The Heartland: An American History.* New York: Penguin, 2019.

Hollinger, David A. *Protestants Abroad: How Missionaries Tried to Change the World but Changed America.* Princeton, NJ: Princeton University Press, 2017.

Hong, Jane. *Opening the Gates to Asia: A Transpacific History of How America Repealed Asian Exclusion.* Chapel Hill: University of North Carolina Press, 2019.

Hopkins, A. G. *American Empire: A Global History.* Princeton, NJ: Princeton University Press, 2017.

Horne, Gerald. *Facing the Rising Sun: African Americans, Japan, and the Rise of Afro-Asian Solidarity.* New York: New York University Press, 2018.

Horne, Gerald. "Race from Power: U.S. Foreign Policy and the General Crisis of 'White Supremacy.'" *Diplomatic History* 23, no. 3 (Summer 1999): 437–461.

Hotta, Eri. *Pan-Asianism and Japan's War, 1931–1945.* New York: Palgrave Macmillan, 2007.

Hsu, Madeline Y. *The Good Immigrants: How the Yellow Peril Became the Model Minority.* Princeton, NJ: Princeton University Press, 2015.

Hunt, Michael H. *Frontier Defense and the Open Door: Manchuria in Chinese-American Relations, 1895–1911.* New Haven, CT: Yale University Press, 1973.

Ichioka, Yuji. *Issei: The World of the First Generation Japanese Immigrants, 1885–1924.* New York: Free Press, 1988.

Immerwahr, Daniel. *How to Hide an Empire: A History of the Greater United States.* New York: Farrar, Straus & Giroux, 2019.

Iriye, Akira. *After Imperialism: The Search for a New Order in the Far East, 1921–1931.* Cambridge, MA: Harvard University Press, 1965.

Iriye, Akira. *Cultural Internationalism and World Order.* Baltimore: Johns Hopkins University Press, 1997.

Iriye, Akira. *Pacific Estrangement: Japanese and American Expansion, 1897–1911.* Cambridge, MA: Harvard University Press, 1972.

Israel, Jerry. *Progressivism and the Open Door: America and China, 1905–1921.* Pittsburgh: University of Pittsburgh Press, 1971.

Jacobson, Matthew Frye. *Barbarian Virtues: The United States Encounters Foreign Peoples at Home and Abroad, 1876–1917.* New York: Hill and Wang, 2000.

Jung, Moon-Ho. *Menace to Empire: Anticolonial Solidarities and the Transpacific Origins of the US Security State.* Oakland: University of California Press, 2022.

Kawashima, Ken C. *The Proletarian Gamble: Korean Workers in Interwar Japan.* Durham, NC: Duke University Press, 2009.

Kearney, Reginald. *African American Views of the Japanese: Solidarity or Sedition?* Albany: State University of New York Press, 1998.

Keevak, Michael. *Becoming Yellow: A Short History of Racial Thinking.* Princeton, NJ: Princeton University Press, 2011.

Kim, Hyung-chan. *Letters in Exile: The Life and Times of Yun Ch'i-ho.* Oxford: Oxford Historical Shrine Society, 1980.

Kim, Kwi-ok. "1905 nyŏn mekshik'o imin hanin nodongja yŏn'gu—hawai imin kwa pigyohamyŏnsŏ." *Chaeoe hanin yŏn'gu* 5 (1995): 162–195.

Kim, Monica, *The Interrogation Rooms of the Korean War: The Untold History.* Princeton, NJ: Princeton University Press, 2019.

Kim, Richard S. *The Quest for Statehood: Korean Immigrant Nationalism and U.S. Sovereignty, 1905–1945.* New York: Oxford University Press, 2011.

Kim, Seung-young. *American Diplomacy and Strategy toward Korea and Northeast Asia, 1882–1950 and After: Perception of Polarity and US Commitment to a Periphery.* New York: Palgrave Macmillan, 2009.

Kim, Tong-myŏng. "Singminji sidae ŭi chibang chach'i—pu(hyŏbŭi)hoe ŭi chŏngch'ijŏk chŏn'gae." *Hanil kwan'gyesa yŏn'gu* 17 (2002): 161–197.

Knock, Thomas J. *To End All Wars: Woodrow Wilson and the Quest for a New World Order.* Princeton, NJ: Princeton University Press, 1995.

Ko, Chŏng-hyu. "T'aep'yŏngyang munje yŏn'guhoe chosŏn chihoe wa chosŏn sajŏng yŏn'guhoe." *Yŏksa wa Hyŏnsil* 6 (December 1991): 282–326.

Kramer, Paul A. *The Blood of Government: Race, Empire, the United States, & the Philippines.* Chapel Hill: University of North Carolina Press, 2006.

Kramer, Paul A. "The Geopolitics of Mobility: Immigration Policy and American Global Power in the Long Twentieth Century." *American Historical Review* 123, no. 2 (April 2018): 393–438.

Kramer, Paul A. "Imperial Openings: Civilization, Exemption, and the Geopolitics of Mobility in the History of Chinese Exclusion, 1868–1910." *Journal of the Gilded Age and Progressive Era* 14 (2015): 336–337.

Kramer, Paul A. "Power and Connection: Imperial Histories of the United States in the World." *American Historical Review* 116, no. 5 (December 2011): 1348–1391.

Kurashige, Lon. *Two Faces of Exclusion: The Untold History of Anti-Asian Racism in the United States.* Chapel Hill: University of North Carolina Press, 2006.

Kwŏn, Tae-ŏk. "1904–1910 nyŏn ilche ŭi han'guk ch'imnyak kusang kwa shijŏnggaesŏn." *Han'guksaron* 31 (1994): 213–260.

Laderman, Charlie. *Sharing the Burden: The Armenian Question, Humanitarian Intervention, and Anglo-American Visions of Global Order.* New York: Oxford University Press, 2019.

LaFeber, Walter. *The Clash: U.S.-Japanese Relations through History.* New York: W. W. Norton, 1997.

Lake, Marilyn. *Progressive New World: How Settler Colonialism and Transpacific Exchange Shaped American Reform.* Cambridge, MA: Harvard University Press, 2019.

Lake, Marilyn, and Henry Reynolds. *Drawing the Global Colour Line: White Men's Countries and the International Challenge of Racial Equality.* Cambridge: Cambridge University Press, 2008.

Lee, Erika. *At America's Gates: Chinese Immigration during the Exclusion Era, 1882–1943.* Chapel Hill: University of North Carolina Press, 2003.

Lee, Erika. "The 'Yellow Peril' and Asian Exclusion in the Americas." *Pacific Historical Review* 76, no. 4 (November 2007): 550–553.

Lee, Erika. "The 'Yellow Peril' in the United States and Peru." in *Transnational Crossroads: Remapping the Americas and the Pacific,* edited by Camilla Fojas and Rudy P. Guevera Jr., 315–358. Lincoln: University of Nebraska Press, 2012.

Lee, Erika, and Judy Yung. *Angel Island: Immigrant Gateway to America.* New York: Oxford University Press, 2010.

Lee, Shelley Sang-Hee. *Claiming the Oriental Gateway: Prewar Seattle and Japanese America.* Philadelphia: Temple University Press, 2011.

Leong, Karen J. *The China Mystique: Pearl S. Buck, Anna May Wong, Mayling Soong, and the Transformation of American Orientalism.* Berkeley: University of California Press, 2005.

Lesser, Jeffrey. *Immigration, Ethnicity, and National Identity in Brazil, 1808 to the Present.* New York: Cambridge University Press, 2013.

Lesser, Jeffrey. *Negotiating National Identity: Immigrants, Minorities, and the Struggle for Ethnicity in Brazil.* Durham, NC: Duke University Press, 1999.

Leuchtenburg, William. "Progressivism and Imperialism: The Progressive Movement and American Foreign Policy, 1898–1916." *Mississippi Valley Historical Review* 39 (December 1952): 483–504.

Levin, N. Gordon. *Woodrow Wilson and World Politics; America's Response to War and Revolution.* New York: Oxford University Press, 1968.

Lewis, David Levering. *W. E. B. Du Bois, 1919–1963: The Fight for Equality and the American Century.* New York: Henry Holt, 2000.

Lew-Williams, Beth. "'Chinamen' and 'Delinquent Girls': Intimacy, Exclusion, and a Search for California's Color Line." *Journal of American History* 104, no. 3 (December 2017): 632–655.

Lew-Williams, Beth. *The Chinese Must Go: Violence, Exclusion, and the Making of the Alien in America.* Cambridge, MA: Harvard University Press, 2018.

Link, Arthur S. *Woodrow Wilson and the Progressive Era, 1910–1917.* New York: Harper, 1954.

Lopez, Ian F. Haney. *White by Law: The Legal Construction of Race.* New York: New York University Press, 1996.

Lu, Sidney Xu. *The Making of Japanese Settler Colonialism: Malthusianism and Trans-Pacific Migration, 1868–1961.* New York: Cambridge University Press, 2019.

Lui, Mary Ting Yi. *The Chinatown Trunk Mystery: Murder, Miscegenation, and Other Dangerous Encounters in Turn-of-the-Century New York City.* Princeton, NJ: Princeton University Press, 2005.

Lye, Colleen. *America's Asia: Racial Form and American Literature, 1893–1945*. Princeton, NJ: Princeton University Press, 2005.

Man, Simeon. *Soldiering through Empire: Race and the Making of the Decolonizing Pacific*. Oakland: University of California Press, 2018.

Manela, Erez. *The Wilsonian Moment: Self-Determination and the International Origins of Anticolonial Nationalism*. New York: Oxford University Press, 2007.

Matsuzaki, Reo. *Statebuilding by Imposition: Resistance and Control in Colonial Taiwan and the Philippines*. Ithaca, NY: Cornell University Press, 2019.

May, Glenn Anthony. *Social Engineering in the Philippines: The Aims, Execution, and Impact of American Colonial Policy, 1900–1913*. Westport, CT: Greenwood Press, 1980.

McCoy, Alfred. *Policing America's Empire: The United States, the Philippines, and the Rise of the Surveillance State*. Madison: University of Wisconsin Press, 2009.

McKee, Delber L. *Chinese Exclusion versus the Open Door Policy, 1900–1906: Clashes over China Policy in the Roosevelt Era*. Detroit: Wayne State University Press, 1977.

Milne, David. *Worldmaking: The Art and Science of American Diplomacy*. New York: Farrar, Straus & Giroux, 2015.

Moon, Yumi. *Populist Collaborators: The Ilchinhoe and the Japanese Colonization of Korea, 1896–1910*. Ithaca, NY: Cornell University Press, 2013.

Mowry, George E. *The California Progressives*. Berkeley: University of California Press, 1951.

Neu, Charles E. *An Uncertain Friendship: Theodore Roosevelt and Japan, 1906–1909*. Cambridge, MA: Harvard University Press, 1967.

Ngai, Mae M. *Impossible Subjects: Illegal Aliens and the Making of Modern America*. Princeton, NJ: Princeton University Press, 2004.

Nichols, Christopher McKnight. *Promise and Peril: America at the Dawn of a Global Age*. Cambridge, MA: Harvard University Press, 2011.

Norrell, Robert J. *Up from Slavery: The Life of Booker T. Washington*. Cambridge, MA: Belknap Press of Harvard University Press, 2009.

Oguma, Eiji. *The Boundaries of "the Japanese,"* Vol. 2: *Korea, Taiwan and the Ainu, 1868–1945*, translated by Leonie R. Stickland. Victoria: Trans Pacific Press, 2017.

Olin, Spencer C. *California's Prodigal Sons; Hiram Johnson and the Progressives, 1911–1917*. Berkeley: University of California Press, 1968.

Onishi, Yuichiro. *Transpacific Antiracism: Afro-Asian Solidarity in Twentieth-Century Black America, Japan, and Okinawa*. New York: New York University Press, 2013.

Orbach, Danny. *Curse on This Country: The Rebellious Army of Imperial Japan*. Ithaca, NY: Cornell University Press, 2017.

Park, Albert L. *Building a Heaven on Earth: Religion, Activism, and Protest in Japanese Occupied Korea*. Honolulu: University of Hawai'i Press, 2015.

Patterson, Wayne. *The Ilse: First-Generation Korean Immigrants in Hawai'i, 1903–1973*. Honolulu: University of Hawai'i Press, 2000.

Patterson, Wayne. *The Korean Frontier in America: Immigration to Hawaii, 1896–1910*. Honolulu: University of Hawai'i Press, 1988.

Pérez, Louis A. *Cuba under the Platt Amendment, 1902–1934*. Pittsburgh: University of Pittsburgh Press, 1986.

Preston, Andrew. *Sword of the Spirit, Shield of Faith: Religion in American War and Diplomacy*. New York: Alfred A. Knopf, 2012.

Rafael, Vicente L. *White Love and Other Events in Filipino History*. Durham, NC: Duke University Press, 2000.

Robinson, Greg. *By Order of the President: FDR and the Internment of Japanese Americans*. Cambridge, MA: Harvard University Press, 2001.

Robinson, Greg. "Internationalism and Justice: Paul Robeson, Asia, and Asian Americans." In *AfroAsian Encounters: Culture, History, Politics*, edited by Heike Raphael-Hernandez and Shannon Steen, 260–276. New York: New York University Press, 2006.

Robinson, Greg. *A Tragedy of Democracy: Japanese Confinement in North America*. New York: Columbia University Press, 2009.

Rodgers, Daniel T. *Atlantic Crossings: Social Politics in a Progressive Age*. Cambridge, MA: Belknap Press of Harvard University Press, 1998.

Rosenberg, Emily S. *Financial Missionaries to the World: The Politics and Culture of Dollar Diplomacy, 1900–1930*. Cambridge, MA: Harvard University Press, 1999.

Ross, Dorothy. *The Origins of American Social Science*. Cambridge: Cambridge University Press, 1991.

Saaler, Sven, and J. Victor Koschmann, eds. *Pan-Asianism in Modern Japanese History Colonialism, Regionalism and Borders*. New York: Routledge, 2007.

Saranillio, Dean Itsuji. *Unsustainable Empire: Alternative Histories of Hawai'i Statehood*. Durham, NC: Duke University Press, 2018.

Schmid, Andre. *Korea between Empires, 1895–1919*. New York: Columbia University Press, 2002.

Schoultz, Lars. *In Their Own Best Interest: A History of the U.S. Effort to Improve Latin Americans*. Cambridge, MA: Harvard University Press, 2020.

Shah, Nayan. *Contagious Divides: Epidemics and Race in San Francisco's Chinatown*. Berkeley: University of California Press, 2001.

Shimazu, Naoko. *Japan, Race and Equality: The Racial Equality Proposal of 1919*. London: Routledge, 1998.

Shin, Gi-Wook, and Michael Edson Robinson, eds. *Colonial Modernity in Korea*. Cambridge, MA: Harvard University Press, 2000.

Shin, K. Ian. "Making 'Chinese' Art: Knowledge and Authority in the Transpacific Progressive Era." PhD diss., Columbia University, 2016.

Sin, Chu-baek. "Ilje ŭi saeroun singminji chibaebangsik kwa chaejoilbonin mit 'chach'i' seryŏk ŭi taeŭng (1919–22)." *Yŏksa wa hyŏnsil* 39 (2001): 35–68.

Sin, Yong-ha. *Kabo kaehyŏk kwa Tongnip Hyŏphoe undong ŭi sahoesa*. Seoul: Sŏul Taehakkyo Ch'ulp'anbu, 2002.

Slate, Nico. *Colored Cosmopolitanism: The Shared Struggle for Freedom in the United States and India*. Cambridge, MA: Harvard University Press, 2012.

Sohi, Seema. *Echoes of Mutiny: Race, Surveillance, and Indian Anticolonialism in North America*. New York: Oxford University Press, 2014.

Steinbock-Pratt, Sarah. *Educating the Empire: American Teachers and Contested Colonization in the Philippines*. Cambridge: Cambridge University Press, 2019.

Stephanson, Anders. *Manifest Destiny: American Expansionism and the Empire of Right*. New York: Hill and Wang, 1995.

Taketani, Etsuko, *The Black Pacific Narrative: Geographic Imaginings of Race and Empire Between the World Wars*. Hanover, NH: Dartmouth College Press, 2014.

Takeuchi-Demirci, Aiko. *Contraceptive Diplomacy: Reproductive Politics and Imperial Ambitions in the United States and Japan*. Stanford, CA: Stanford University Press, 2018.

Tarbert, Jesse. *When Good Government Meant Big Government: The Quest to Extend Federal Power, 1913–1933*. New York: Columbia University Press, 2022.

Thompson, John M. *Great Power Rising: Theodore Roosevelt and the Politics of U.S. Foreign Policy*. New York: Oxford University Press, 2019.

Thorne, Christopher. *The Limits of Foreign Policy: The West, the League and the Far Eastern Crisis of 1931–1933*. London: Hamilton, 1972.

Tsu, Cecilia M. *Garden of the World: Asian Immigrants and the Making of Agriculture in California's Santa Clara Valley*. New York: Oxford University Press, 2013.

Tyrrell, Ian R. *Reforming the World: The Creation of America's Moral Empire*. Princeton, NJ: Princeton University Press, 2010.

Uchida, Jun. *Brokers of Empire: Japanese Settler Colonialism in Korea, 1876–1945*. Cambridge, MA: Harvard University Press, 2011.

Urban, Andrew. "Yun Ch'i-ho's Alienation by Way of Inclusion: A Korean International Student and Christian Reform in the 'New' South, 1888–1893." *Journal of Asian American Studies* 17 (October 2014): 305–336.

Vitalis, Robert. *White World Order, Black Power Politics: The Birth of American International Relations.* Ithaca, NY: Cornell University Press, 2015.

Wang, Guanhua. *In Search of Justice: The 1905–1906 Chinese Anti-American Boycott.* Cambridge, MA: Harvard University Press, 2001.

Ward, Max M. *Thought Crime: Ideology and State Power in Interwar Japan.* Durham, NC: Duke University Press, 2019.

Wertheim, Stephen. *Tomorrow, The World: The Birth of U.S. Global Supremacy.* Cambridge, MA: Belknap Press of Harvard University Press, 2020.

Williams, William Appleman. *The Tragedy of American Diplomacy.* Cleveland: World Pub. Co., 1959.

Woods, Colleen. "Seditious Crimes and Rebellious Conspiracies: Anti-Communism and US Empire in the Philippines." *Journal of Contemporary History* 53, no. 1 (January 2018): 61–88.

Yellen, Jeremy A. *The Greater East Asia Co-Prosperity Sphere: When Total Empire Met Total War.* Ithaca, NY: Cornell University Press, 2019.

Yi, Jun-shik. "Manbosan sagŏn kwa chunggugin ŭi chosŏn inshik." *Han'guksa yŏn'guhoe* 156 (March 2012): 237–270.

Yi, Tae-jin. *Ilbon ŭi Han'guk pyŏnghap kangje yŏn'gu: choyak kangje wa chŏhang ŭi yŏksa.* Kyŏnggi-do P'aju-si: Chisik Sanŏpsa, 2016.

Yoo, David K. *Contentious Spirits: Religion in Korean American History, 1903–1945.* Stanford, CA: Stanford University Press, 2010.

Young, Louise. *Japan's Total Empire: Manchuria and the Culture of Wartime Imperialism.* Berkeley: University of California Press, 1998.

Yu, Henry. *Thinking Orientals: Migration, Contact, and Exoticism in Modern America.* New York: Oxford University Press, 2001.

Yu, Yŏng-ik, *Kabo kyŏngjang yŏn'gu.* Seoul: Ilchogak, 1990.

Yu-Jose, Lydia N. *Japan View the Philippines, 1900–1941.* Manila: Ateneo de Manila University Press, 1992.

Yun, Kyŏng-no. *105-in sakŏn kwa sinminhoe yŏn'gu.* Seoul: Ilchisa, 1990.

Zimmerman, Andrew. *Alabama in Africa: Booker T. Washington, the German Empire, and the Globalization of the New South.* Princeton, NJ: Princeton University Press, 2010.

INDEX